D0143974

# HITLER, GERMANS, AND THE "JEWISH QUESTION"

# HITLER, GERMANS AND THE "JEWISH QUESTION"

Sarah Gordon

PRINCETON UNIVERSITY PRESS

Library of Congress Cataloging in Publication Data will be found on
the last printed page of this book

ISBN 0-691-05412-6
      0-691-10162-0 (LPE)

This book has been composed in Linotron Times Roman
Clothbound editions of Princeton University Press books are printed on
acid-free paper, and binding materials are chosen for strength and
durability. Paperbacks, although satisfactory for personal collections,
are not usually suitable for library rebinding

Printed in the United States of America by Princeton University Press
Princeton, New Jersey

Second printing, with corrections, 1984

The author gratefully acknowledges permission to quote from
the following sources: Geoffrey Pridham, *Hitler's Rise to
Power: The Nazi Movement in Bavaria, 1923-1933* (New York:
Harper and Row, 1973), p. 244; Michael Balfour and Julian
Frisby, *Helmuth von Moltke: A Leader Against Hitler* (London
and Basingstoke: Macmillan), pp. 83, 84, 85, 86; and Seymour
Martin Lipset, *Political Man: The Social Bases of Politics*
(Baltimore: Johns Hopkins Univ. Press, 1981, expanded and
updated edition), p. 139. Special thanks also go to Professor
Peter Merkl for permission to interpret data sheets on early Nazi
party members. Apologies to Walter Laquer for misspelling his name
throughout the text.

TO MY BELOVED HUSBAND

Donald

# Contents

CONTENTS

# List of Tables

# Abbreviations

ARCHIVES AND PRIMARY SOURCES

BA    Bundesarchiv, Koblenz
DB    *Deutschland-Berichte* der SOPADE (Social Democratic Party in Exile) and Primary Sources
GR    *Germany Reports*, English translation (condensed) of *Deutschland-Berichte*
HA    Hoover Institution, Stanford University
HSD    Hauptstaatsarchiv Düsseldorf
LBI    Leo Baeck Institute, New York City
NA    National Archives, Washington, D.C.
PGA    Preussisches Geheimes Staatsarchiv, West Berlin
SD    Stadtarchiv Düsseldorf
SK    Staatsarchiv Koblenz
YIVO    YIVO Institute, New York City

POLITICAL PARTIES

DDP    Deutsche Demokratische Partei (German Democratic party)
DNVP    Deutschnationale Volkspartei (German National People's party)
DVP    Deutsche Volkspartei (German People's party)
KPD    Kommunistische Partei Deutschlands (Communist party of Germany)
NSDAP    Nationalsozialistische Deutsche Arbeiterpartei (National Socialist German Workers' party)
SPD    Sozialdemokratische Partei Deutschlands (Social Democratic party of Germany)
WP    Wirtschaftspartei (Economic party)

# Acknowledgments

I wish to thank several individuals and institutions for their assistance in the preparation of this book. Professor William S. Allen of the State University of New York at Buffalo provided unflagging encouragement and invaluable guidance for the dissertation from which the book originated. Professors Leo Loubere, John Milligan, and Norman Solkoff of the same institution provided many useful comments. Special thanks go to Professors Richard Hamilton, Jeremy Noakes, and Peter Merkl for reading the manuscript with great care and sharing their excellent insights. Professor Merkl was also extremely generous in providing copies of his unpublished data on anti-Semites in the early Nazi party. Professors Franklin Littell, Henry Feingold, and Henry Turner, Jr. gave moral support by inviting me to speak on my research results at the National Conference of Christians and Jews (Seattle, 1978), the ZACHOR Faculty Seminar on the Holocaust (March, 1979), and the Yale Scholars' Conference on "Knowledge" (November, 1982), respectively.

Particular gratitude is also extended to Herr Ziegahn of the Hauptstaatsarchiv Düsseldorf for his location of appropriate Gestapo files and to the very helpful staffs of the Bundesarchiv, Staatsarchiv Koblenz, Hauptstaatsarchiv Düsseldorf, Stadtarchiv Düsseldorf, and Institut für Zeitgeschichte. The Gestapo records at the Preussisches Geheimes Staatsarchiv (West Berlin) have been in the editing process for many years and were not available in time for inclusion in this book; however, thanks are extended to the archivists for their assistance. In the United States, Sybil Milton at the Leo Baeck Institute, Robert Wolfe at the National Archives, Agnes Peterson at the Hoover Institution (Stanford), and the staff of the YIVO Institute provided intelligent and efficient service.

Financial support for research was, as always, a great asset, and I wish to thank the Graduate School of the State University of New York at Buffalo, the Council for European Studies, and the Richard M. Weaver Fellowship of the Institute for Intercollegiate Studies for their generous assistance.

Special thanks go to my editors, Alice Calaprice and Miriam Brokaw, and personal gratitude is extended to my family and friends, whose love and cheer relieved the sadness of dealing with so gruesome a topic.

*April 5, 1983*

# HITLER, GERMANS, AND THE "JEWISH QUESTION"

"It was not the first time in recorded history that the expulsion and the extermination of the Jews were but the most spectacular demonstration and terrifying example of inhumanity, presaging the collapse of governments and the decay of states and nations in which human values are disregarded."
Ernst Hamburger, "Jews, Democracy and Weimar Germany," in the Leo Baeck Institute *Memorial Lecture Number 16* (1973), p. 27.

# Introduction

The background and German reactions to one of the most incredible political phenomena of our century, the deliberate murder of millions of European Jews, are the subjects of this book. The study attempts to answer a number of interrelated questions about German-Jewish relations between 1870 and 1945, especially under Hitler. What were the characteristics of Jews in Germany and how important was anti-Semitism before Hitler came to power? What role did anti-Semitism play in the rise of the Nazi party and Hitler's electoral success? What did Hitler think about Jews and how did he fit this into his theories about the world? What was Hitler's role as instigator of persecution and extermination? What did Germans know and think about persecution and extermination, and how did their knowledge and attitudes change over time? Who was most likely to oppose the persecution of the Jews? What were the churches' attitudes? Where did pockets of opposition exist? And what role did the military and bureaucrats play in the exterminations?

Jews in Germany between 1870 and 1933 did not suffer from a lack of hope for their future. In chapter 1 I shall outline some of the characteristics of German Jews of this period, which indicate that Jews were gradually attaining status equal to that of Germans. This would be even more apparent if we compared their socioeconomic characteristics to those of Jews in other European countries and in North America, but that is beyond the scope of this study. There were, to be sure, pockets of virulent anti-Semitism in Germany between 1870 and 1933—particularly intellectual and social anti-Semitism—but some Germans did sympathize with Jews and attempted to insure their fair treatment.

The great watershed in German-Jewish relations was World War I and the attendant beginnings of the Weimar Republic. Accusations of Jewish treachery poisoned the atmosphere of postwar Germany and left a residue of ill will that made Hitler's rise

3

to power a great deal easier. Hitler's paranoid anti-Semitism and bigotry were extreme even among Nazis, but he managed to entice a large number of less radical anti-Semites into the Nazi party along with the smaller number of hard-core anti-Semites who shared his extraordinary racial hatred. Surprisingly, the importance of anti-Semitism for the electorate at large is still an unsettled issue; however, I shall discuss the appeal of anti-Semitism for both Nazis and the general electorate in chapter 2.

Hitler developed a racial or ethnic theory to explain all of human history, and in this theory anti-Semitism played a central role, as is discussed in chapter 3. Hitler believed that Jews should be ostracized and persecuted by all nations in which they lived in order to prevent their attaining world domination over other races. After his rise to power he introduced his racial policies in a haphazard manner, yet they served specific identifiable political functions both within and outside of the Nazi party. Anti-Semitic propaganda likewise served specific political functions that are clarified when we study Nazi press directives. In chapters 4 and 5 I shall explore the functions of anti-Semitism, propaganda, and Hitler's responsibility for persecution and extermination.

General public reactions to racial persecution have only recently been explored; in chapter 6 I shall discuss shifts in attitudes during separate phases of persecution and the extent of public knowledge of deportations and exterminations. Because general reports on public opinion give us neither a detailed picture of the chronological development of support for or opposition to racial persecution, nor a significant amount of information on types of opponents, in chapter 7 we shall supplement them by examining data from Gestapo files on opponents of anti-Semitism in a major part of the Rhineland, the Government District Düsseldorf.[1] Fortunately, the Gestapo files for this district contain information on an adequate number of such opponents, and an analysis of these previously untapped sources provides an accurate profile of the types of Germans who were most likely to sympathize with Jews and to aid them in the face of Nazi terror.

Much has been written on the apathetic response of the churches to Nazi persecution and extermination of Jews, and in chapter 8

I shall attempt to determine whether Protestants or Catholics were more likely to oppose anti-Semitism, and whether the socioeconomic characteristics of Protestants and Catholics were significantly different.

Some readers may be surprised to learn that some Nazis aided Jews, had sexual relations with them, and were critics of Jewish persecution. In chapter 9 I shall determine which Nazis were likely to sympathize with Jews, and I shall compare their socioeconomic characteristics to those of non-Nazi opponents of anti-Semitism. Pockets of opposition among conservatives, military leaders, bureaucrats (civil servants), socialists, and the press will also be examined.

Because German opposition to racial persecution is a highly sensitive topic, an important caveat must be observed. The purpose of studying German opponents of anti-Semitism, especially during the Nazi period, is not to write a "revisionist" apologia to exonerate any guilty Germans from the murder of Jews. The Germans who aided Jews and criticized persecution, often at considerable personal risk, were only a small percentage of all Germans. It would be as ridiculous to consider all Germans blameless because a small number aided Jews as to claim that all Germans were guilty because a minority participated in exterminations. Aiders of Jews are of course to be commended for their courage, but to generalize from their behavior would be totally unwarranted. Most Germans were apathetic to the persecution of Jews, and no study, past or future, can ever change that fact.

Apathy has many causes, and we shall never know the precise reasons for apathy during the Nazi reign of terror. Was it due to simple hatred of Jews among large numbers of Germans? Was it fear of reprisals? Was it preoccupation with recovery from the Great Depression and the hardships of World War II? Or was it a lack of courage? Any or all of these factors may have been at play, but available sources do not answer these questions.

I should point out that the term "opposition" is used here in its broadest sense, in order to include not only Germans who aided Jews but also Germans who publicly disapproved of persecution. The major reason for using this broad definition is that it allows

5

us to study public attitudes toward Nazi persecution in addition to analyzing the types of Germans who aided or sympathized with Jews. Distinctions between types of opposition, that is, public disapproval of anti-Semitism, verbal condemnation of persecution, and overt acts to aid Jews, should be clear in any given context.

This book covers a number of difficult and disturbing topics, yet objective analysis requires the suspension of one's natural horror and wrath. It would be simple to dismiss all Germans as bloodthirsty satans, but that is the easy way out of a very complex problem. If we are ever to understand the extermination of European Jewry, we must study it within the complex milieu of German, as well as Jewish, history.

Readers who are pressed for time or dislike numbers may wish to utilize the summaries in chapters 1 and 7.

# The Setting

"The Jew, no matter how he strove to assimilate, remained identifiable in Germany as he did in the rest of Europe and in America; and his difference marked him off and down."
Eugene Davidson, *The Making of Adolf Hitler*, p. 39.

## JEWS IN GERMANY, 1870–1933: A SOCIOECONOMIC PROFILE

Until the nineteenth century Jews subsisted in Germany at the pleasure of kings, lords, princes, barons, and lesser nobilities. German-Jewish communities were subjected to pogroms, extraordinary taxes, limitations on land ownership, bans on intermarriage with Gentiles, special residential and sumptuary laws, and a host of other restrictions that were common in Europe before the French Revolution. With the victory of Napoleon, Jews were granted new freedoms in southwestern Germany; however, these were truncated during the reactionary 1830s and 1840s.

During the revolution of 1848 Jews and liberal Christians alike advocated Jewish emancipation. Although the revolution failed and therefore did not realize its goals, German liberals retained their commitment to equality for all citizens in an evenhanded legal state. Many German and Jewish liberals believed that Jews could never become true citizens of the state until they abandoned their distinctive customs, and that their legal equality was a prerequisite to this end. Their aspirations were fulfilled by the legal emancipation of 1869, which was extended to all of Germany under the German Constitution of 1871. This was a milestone in German-Jewish relations, marking the start of sixty-four years of at least nominal equality.

Before one can understand the status of Jews in German society during these years, one must have a general picture of their numbers, occupational distribution, rates of religious conversion, intermarriage, and political behavior; thus I will provide a very cursory discussion of these factors for the years 1870–1933.[1] Without this information one can understand neither the Jews' vulnerability to anti-Semitism nor the specific stereotypes of anti-Semites.

The reader may be surprised to learn that Jews were never a large percentage of the total German population; at no time did they exceed 1.09 percent of the population during the years 1871 to 1933, and their percentage declined steadily from 1880 to 1933. By 1933 roughly 500,000 Jews lived in Germany.[2] However, the percentage of foreign Jews increased considerably during these years, from 14 percent (76,387) of all Jews in 1910 to 20 percent (98,747) in 1933.[3] This increase of foreign Jews did not swell the ranks of the Jewish community relative to other Germans, however, since the rate of natural increase among Jews was extremely low compared to that of the German population.[4] Mohrmann and Rudel-Adler indicate that approximately 150,000 to 160,000 foreign Jews were in Germany by 1920 and that about 47,000 of these had left by 1922.[5] However, this period was one of enormous flux. If 90,000 foreign Jews were in Germany in 1914, and 30,000 entered as conscript labor during the war, plus another 100,000 immigrated in postwar years, the total number could have reached 220,000, of whom 100,000 subsequently left Germany for other lands.[6] Actions of the Prussian government to stem immigration included arrest, incarceration in holding camps, and deportation; some government officials adopted neutral stances and others advocated expulsion.[7]

Jews were more visible than their numbers might indicate because they were concentrated in large cities (those with 100,000 or more inhabitants). In 1910, 55 percent of Prussian Jewry lived in large cities, compared to slightly less than 25 percent of the Prussian population who made their homes there.[8] This urban concentration was most marked in the case of Berlin, where almost one-third of all Jews lived by 1933.[9] An additional 20 percent were located in Frankfurt am Main, Breslau, Hamburg, Cologne, Leipzig, Munich, Essen, Dresden, and Dortmund.[10] Within large cities Jews were frequently concentrated in specific districts rather than evenly distributed among the population.[11] A higher percentage of foreign-born Jews resided in large cities than did German Jews; in 1933, 88 percent of the foreign-born Jews lived in large cities, while only 66 percent of the German Jews resided there.[12]

Both foreign and German Jews were highly mobile. Although 71 percent of all Jews lived in large cities in 1933, less than 38 percent were born there, whereas over 62 percent were born somewhere other than inside their census city. It should be particularly noted that the average of 62 percent was not due to wide differences from city to city in the percentages of Jews who were born outside of their census city. These ranged from 57 to 72 percent in all large cities except Hamburg (49 percent) and Krefeld (52 percent). For example, in large cities with 4,000 or more Jews, the following percentages of Jews were born elsewhere: 66–72 percent in Dresden, Düsseldorf, Essen, and Hannover; and 59–62 percent in Berlin, Breslau, Cologne, Dortmund, Frankfurt am Main, Leipzig, Mannheim, Münich, Nuremberg, and Stuttgart.[13] This is quite astonishing, since it means that a majority of both foreign and German Jews were recent migrants to their areas of residence, with all that this implies: the necessity to find new homes, to start new businesses or find new jobs, to enroll children in new schools, and to form new friendships. This was of course most difficult for foreign Jews, but it also meant that German Jews faced similar difficulties because they were in an extreme state of migrational flux. As mentioned above, almost two-thirds of their number lived in large cities where migration was the norm.

These statistics on immigration and internal mobility call into question the extremely widespread assumption that the majority of German-Jewish families had resided for generations in a given city and that they therefore had close and long-standing local affiliations and associations. At best, this "assimilated old-timer" image might apply to a minority of German Jews. Immigration of foreign Jews and the high level of mobility among both foreign

9

and German Jews thus fostered the anti-Semites' stereotype of the Jews as an alien and rootless people.

Foreign Jews faced particularly difficult problems; they were highly visible because of their distinctive black clothing, side-locks, yarmulkas, Yiddish speech, Orthodox religious customs, and support for Zionism.[14] In addition, they tended to live in self-contained areas of large cities to a greater extent than German Jews.[15] Not only did these characteristics distinguish newly immigrated Eastern Jews from non-Jews, but they also occasioned substantial disdain among German Jews.[16] Some Jewish leaders demanded that further immigration be stopped because it increased latent anti-Semitism,[17] and many German Jews considered the newly arrived Jews as foreigners who did not give their first loyalty to Germany, as they themselves did.[18] This dislike of Eastern Jews manifested itself in attempts to deny them voting rights in religious organizations that represented Jews in every locality.[19] To complicate the situation even more, there were conflicts between the various nationalities of the Jewish immigrants.[20]

It is now apparent that severe divisions within the Jewish community itself were caused by the immigration of so many Eastern Jews during the war and postwar years.[21] Many of these Jews had been subjected to pogroms in their own countries, particularly in Poland and Russia. The Central Association of German Citizens of Jewish Faith (Centralverein), the major representative of German Jewry, did try to help these individuals, particularly in obtaining transit visas through Germany to other lands; however, the presence of the Eastern Jews created substantial economic and political problems for the Jewish community and caused much fear and resentment among both non-Jews and German Jews who were in various states of assimilation and national identification.[22]

Though Jews were a small and declining minority, they had specific occupational characteristics that distinguished them from the population at large. They were overrepresented in business, commerce, and public and private service; they were underrepresented in agriculture, industry, and domestic service. These characteristics were already evident in the Middle Ages and appeared in the census data as early as 1843.[23] In 1933 business and commerce occupied 61 percent of all Jews in the labor force, as compared to 18 percent of all working Germans; and whereas 22 percent of Jews were employed in industry, 40 percent of Germans were similarly employed. Most striking, however, was the fact that only 2 percent of Jews were engaged in agriculture, in contrast to 29 percent among their German counterparts; this was true for both German and immigrant Jews.[24] Immigrant Jews tended to enter the industrial labor market more than did German Jews, and this reflected their weaker financial position and lesser assimilation.[25] In Prussia, where three-fourths of the Jews lived, by 1925 the percentage of Jewish executives in commerce and trade was over eight times that of non-Jews, and in industry it was over two times higher. These characteristics also held true at middle levels of management.[26] Some cities, particularly Berlin, Frankfurt am Main, Cologne, and Breslau, had even higher percentages of Jews in high and middle-level positions.[27]

Within the fields of business and commerce, Jews were very active in the retail and wholesale trade. For example, between 1928 and 1932 Jews represented 25 percent of all individuals employed in retail businesses and handled 25 percent of total sales, although they comprised only 0.74 percent of the labor force.[28] This high percentage of Jewish retailers was not evenly distributed among all retail trades, but it was concentrated in certain areas such as textiles and clothing, the grain trade, and in warehouses and department stores.[29] Jews were also very active as wholesale traders in specific industries; for example, they owned 41 percent of iron and scrap iron firms and 57 percent of other metal businesses.[30]

In addition to being active as middlemen, Jews were prominent in private banking under both Jewish and non-Jewish ownership or control.[31] They were especially visible in private banking in Berlin, which in 1923 had 150 private (versus state) Jewish banks, as opposed to only 11 private non-Jewish banks.[32] It should be noted, however, that the percentage of private banks under Jewish control was declining. Whereas private Jewish banks represented 23 percent of all banks in 1923, this number had dropped to 18 percent by 1930.[33] Still, the influence of Jews in banking is not completely illustrated by these figures. In 1930, 43 percent of the leading positions in private Jewish banks were occupied by Jews, which is not surprising.[34] What is interesting, however, is that Jews also occupied 5.8 percent of the leading positions in non-Jewish banks.[35] This represented almost eight times the percentage of Jews in the labor force.[36] In 1913, fifteen prominent Jews held 211 seats on boards of directors of banks, and by 1928 this number had risen to 718.[37]

Jews were also influential in joint-stock corporations, the stock market, the insurance industry, and legal and economic consulting firms.[38] Before the First World War, for example, Jews occupied 13 percent of the directorships of joint-stock corporations and 24 percent of the supervisory positions within these corporations.[39] Even by 1932, when anti-Semitism was supposed to have reached a new high, Jews represented almost 3 percent of the German Economic Council, which advised the government during the depression.[40] Jews were very active in the stock market, particularly in Berlin, where in 1928 they comprised 80 percent of the leading members of the stock exchange.[41] By 1933, when the Nazis began eliminating Jews from prominent positions, 85 percent of the brokers on the Berlin Stock Exchange were dismissed because of their "race."[42]

If one considers all of the branches of the economy, it is clear that Jews were significantly overrepresented as "independents," that is, a larger percentage of Jews than non-Jews was self-employed. This reflected not only self-employment of Jews in business and commerce, but also their very considerable numbers in free professions. They were also more highly represented as white-collar workers than the German population as a whole, and correspondingly underrepresented as blue-collar workers and domestic servants.[43] These occupational characteristics were true for both German and immigrant Jews. There was, however, only a small percentage of immigrant Jews in leading positions; they were more likely than German Jews to secure positions as blue-collar workers and comprised 36 percent of all Jews engaged in blue-collar work, although they represented only 23 percent of the Jewish labor force.[44]

During the years 1873 to 1929, between 1 and 3 percent of civil servants were Jewish.[45] They could be found at all levels of civil service during the Weimar years, especially in states where the SPD was influential.[46] Even though, as already mentioned, Jews represented only 0.74 percent of the labor force, in Prussia during 1904 they comprised 27 percent of all lawyers, 10 percent of all apprenticed lawyers, 5 percent of court clerks, 4 percent of magistrates, and up to 30 percent of all higher ranks of the judiciary.[47] Clearly, then, Jews were overrepresented as civil servants and as high-level white-collar workers, especially within the judicial system. Strauss indicates that between 1933 and 1939, 17,375 lawyers, junior barristers, and civil servants were dismissed because they were Jewish.[48]

German universities admitted Jews on an equal footing as early as 1790,[49] and Jews were overrepresented among university professors and students between 1870 and 1933. For example, in 1909–1910, although Jews represented less than 1 percent of the German population, almost 12 percent of the instructors at German universities were Jewish, and an additional 7 percent were Jewish converts to Christianity, so that almost 19 percent of the instructors in Germany were of Jewish origin. At higher academic levels, their overrepresentation was smaller but nonetheless highly significant. Among full professors, 3 percent were Jewish, and an additional 4 percent were converts. Thus German society permitted a rich and hitherto unique flowering of Jewish academia.[50] Ringer interprets these figures as indicating that there was evidence of discrimination against Jews at the higher academic levels. However, he also points out that these figures are open to the interpretation that Jews were not excluded from the academic world and that they fared quite well even in Wilhelminian Germany— in fact, they probably were even better off between 1918 and 1933 than earlier. Jews also represented an extremely high number of university students; for example, in 1905–1906 Jewish students comprised 25 percent of the law and medical students and 34 percent of the graduate students in philosophy.[51] The percentage of Jewish doctors was also quite high, especially in large cities, where they sometimes were a majority.[52]

As has become evident now, Jews were in general more highly educated than non-Jews, and this education began early. For example, in Berlin around 1890, 25 percent of all children attending grammar school were Jewish, even though Jews represented only 4 percent of the Berlin population,[53] and between 1905 and 1931 ten of the thirty-two Germans who received Nobel prizes for contributions to science were Jews.[54] Because of their success at attaining high levels of scholarship, Jews were extremely overrepresented among the leading and middle positions in commerce, banking, joint-stock companies, the stock market, the civil service, and the free professions.

Jews were also highly active in the theater, the arts, film, and journalism. For example, in 1931, 50 percent of the 234 theater directors in Germany were Jewish, and in Berlin the number was 80 percent; 75 percent of the plays produced in 1930 were written by Jews; the leading theater critics were Jewish; and a large number of prominent actresses and actors were Jewish.[55] The prominence of Jews in architecture and within the entire gamut of "Weimar culture" has been widely recognized, and they were very influential as editors and journalists for leading newspapers such as the *Berliner Tageblatt, Vossiche Zeitung*, and *Frankfurter Zeitung*. Even in 1881 Jews comprised 9 percent of all journalists, and this percentage increased very substantially by 1933.[56] Thus Jews were also overrepresented in cultural fields, where public exposure was by nature great. Unfortunately, many of them tended to use their works as vehicles to oppose or criticize prevalent German values.[57] This offended a great number of non-Jews and Jews alike, and the anti-Semites attacked such works as being "un-German" and "alien."

The high level of scholarship and entrepreneurial skill of Jews brought them average incomes that were higher than those of non-Jews. This in itself gave the Jewish minority considerable visibility. High incomes were partially a product of the small number of extremely wealthy Jews, but they also reflected the large percentage of Jews at middle-income levels. Although no thorough comparison of incomes for Jews and non-Jews has been made, several sources attest to the higher income of Jews. For example,

14

a large number of Jews made up the first electoral class, that is, the wealthier voters.[58] Jews also paid higher taxes than their percentage in the population would have warranted. For example, in 1905 Jews comprised nearly 5 percent of the total Berlin population, yet they represented over 14 percent of all residents liable for an income tax of more than 21 marks (or all citizens having an income of at least 1,500 marks a year). This 14 percent of the taxpayers paid 31 percent of income taxes collected. Of the nearly thirty thousand Jews gainfully employed in Berlin, few earned less than 1,500 marks a year.[59] If one examines the average taxes paid by members of different religious denominations, the high income of Jews is likewise indicated. Average taxes paid in Berlin for the year 1905 were as follows: Jews, 357 marks; Protestants, 133 marks; Catholics, 111 marks; and nondenominationals, 270 marks.[60] It is very likely that many of the nondenominational taxpayers had previously been members of the Jewish community, but had subsequently left, which would account for the higher income of those who listed themselves as nondenominational. By 1929 it was estimated that the per capita income of Jews in Berlin was twice that of other Berlin residents.[61] There was, however, a significant minority of poorer Eastern European immigrants who were a source of concern for the entire Jewish community because they constituted the majority of Jews who received social welfare from Jewish agencies.

In twenty-nine other Prussian cities Jews paid between three and nine times the taxes of non-Jews;[62] higher taxes were also paid in non-Prussian cities.[63] For Germany as a whole, Jews paid an average of nearly 4 percent of the income tax, or over four times their percentage in the population.[64] There are other indirect indications of high income among Jews. Bennathan points out the high levels of consumption in rich Jewish residential areas and the large number of domestic servants in the two most important Jewish areas of Berlin during the 1920s.[65] Later indications of the high income of Jews were the large emigration taxes successfully extracted by the Nazis from Jews between 1933 and 1939. According to Walter Funk, the Nazi minister of economics, taxes paid by emigrant Jews from 1933 to 1939 amounted to approximately 3.5 billion marks. Another 7 billion marks were directly confiscated, and an additional one billion marks were paid to "cover" damage during *Kristallnacht*, the Nazi-directed pogrom of 1938.[66]

By examining the occupational distribution and income of Jews from 1870 to 1933, one gains the impression that Jews were more successful in their careers and income than were non-Jews.[67] It would, however, be a misconception to assume that Jews had a stranglehold on the German economy. Jews were never the powerful "captains of industry" who produced the bulk of Germany's manufactured goods; rather, their roles were predominately those of middlemen, financiers, and members of the free professions and cultural fields. Nevertheless, it is clear that Jews had an occupational and income distribution different enough from that of other Germans to serve as a base upon which gross exaggerations and stereotypes could be built.

Foremost among other characteristics of German Jews that set them apart from non-Jews was their religion. From the Middle Ages to the present, an antagonism based upon doctrinal differences has existed between Christians and Jews, and this antagonism was as strong in Germany as elsewhere. At the same time, a tradition of religious toleration among both Christians and Jews made coexistence possible. In Germany between 1870 and 1933, religious freedom was guaranteed by law and even extended to controversial customs such as ritual slaughter of animals. Conversion from Judaism to Christianity and vice versa was also permitted, and these years saw a significant number of conversions—primarily from Judaism to Christianity but also from Christianity to Judaism. These took place mostly to facilitate intermarriage, although both Christian and Jewish religious leaders opposed intermarriage. There was a feeling that converts were more influenced by expediency than by genuine religious devotion. This was particularly true with respect to Jewish converts because conversion was often used as a method of reducing the stigma of being Jewish. Those Jews who did convert rather than simply leave the Jewish community chose Protestantism in the majority of cases.[68] About 10 percent of Germany's Jews left

Judaism between 1800 and 1933.[69] Between 1881 and 1933 there were 19,469 adult conversions from Judaism to Protestantism.[70] A small number of Jews joined the Catholic religion, and a larger number simply severed all formal religious affiliations.

A more significant source of loss for the Jewish community was brought about through intermarriage. In 1875 intermarriage between members of different religions was legalized. From 1901 to 1905, 15 percent of all Jews married non-Jews; from 1926 to 1932, 36 percent married non-Jews; and by 1933, 44 percent of all Jews married non-Jews.[71] Since these figures are based on religion given at the time of marriage, they do not include those individuals who converted in order to marry, which would make the percentage of those intermarrying even higher. The advent of Hitler significantly reduced intermarriage in 1934, and another big decline occurred in 1936 after the Nuremberg Laws virtually eliminated intermarriage.

Noticeable attrition also befell the Jewish community because only a small percentage of children issuing from intermarriages were reared in the Jewish faith. Estimates of the percentage of children from mixed marriages who entered Judaism vary between 11 and 25 percent.[72] These estimates would probably be even lower if all illegitimate children were included, as most of the illegitimate children stemming from liaisons of Jews and non-Jews were fathered by Jewish males.[73] In such cases it appears reasonable to assume that non-Jewish mothers were pressured into raising their illegitimate children in the Christian faith.

Conversion, intermarriage, and loss of children through mixed marriages were seen as significant problems by German Jews because their rate of natural increase did not compensate for this attrition. Only the influx of Eastern European Jews partially offset Jewish assimilation into the non-Jewish majority. Despite concern among Jewish leaders over these numerical losses, the process of assimilation accelerated. According to some Jewish scholars, this process gradually would have eliminated Jews as a minority group had it continued.[74]

The gradual assimilation of Jews into the non-Jewish population was not confined to economic integration, intermarriage, and the

17

other factors discussed above. Jews participated quite actively with non-Jews in the political life of Germany. They had been entitled to vote in national elections since 1848, when the first national elections were held.[75] Between 1893 and 1914, four hundred Jews were active in national politics and another fifteen hundred were active in local politics.[76] Between 1867 and 1916, there were fifty-two Jewish delegates out of a total of approximately three thousand delegates in the German parliament, the Reichstag;[77] this represented 1.73 percent of all delegates, which was almost twice the average percentage of Jews in the population during these years.[78] If one includes Jewish delegates who served more than one term, Jews represented an average of 2.2 percent of all delegates.[79] Two historians specializing in the political orientation of Jews have pointed out the tendency of Jews to participate actively in left-wing political parties, and some consideration should be given to this phenomenon.[80] It undoubtedly gave credence to right-wing expressions of anti-Semitism even if it was not the cause for it. Table 1.1 represents the distribution of both Jewish and non-Jewish Reichstag delegates in selected political parties during the years 1867 to 1916. It shows that Jewish Reichstag delegates had roughly the same party affiliations as non-Jewish delegates between 1867 and 1878; that is, both groups were predominately affiliated with the Right. Between 1878 and 1892, only 11 percent of the Jewish Reichstag delegates came from parties of the Right. This represented an enormous drop from 75 percent between 1867 and 1878. There was a corresponding increase in the percentage of Jewish delegates from parties of the Middle and Left. It was during these years that parties of the Middle obtained their greatest support from all Reichstag delegates, but notably from Jewish delegates. This was also the first period in which Jewish delegates were affiliated with the Social Democratic party (SPD) in substantial percentages. Over one-third of the Jewish delegates were members of the SPD. However, the highest percentage of Jewish delegates (72 percent) were in the SPD during the years 1893–1916. A considerable shift to the Left also took place among non-Jewish delegates, but this was clearly less significant than that among Jewish delegates. Whereas 75

18

TABLE 1.1 Percentage Distribution of Jews and Non-Jews in Selected
Parties of the Reichstag, 1867–1916

|  | Non-Jews in Reichstag | Jews in Reichstag | Party Affiliations of Jewish Populace |
|---|---|---|---|
|  | | 1867–1878 | |
| Right | 80 | 75 | 78 |
| Middle | 17 | 23 | 20 |
| Left | 3 | 2 | 2 |
| N | 1,055 | 48 | |
|  | | 1879–1892 | |
| Right | 63 | 11 | 26 |
| Middle | 29 | 52 | 67 |
| Left | 8 | 37 | 8 |
| N | 989 | 27 | |
|  | | 1893–1916 | |
| Right | 54 | 16 | 21 |
| Middle | 19 | 12 | 61 |
| Left | 28 | 72 | 19 |
| N | 1,152 | 50 | |

SOURCES: Non-Jews in the Reichstag calculated from the total number of
delegates in the selected political parties as listed in Koppel Pinson, *Modern
Germany: Its History and Civilization*, 272–273, minus Jewish delegates
listed by Ernst Hamburger, *Juden im öffentlichen Leben Deutschlands*,
251–253. Jewish party affiliations are estimates from Jacob Toury, *Die
politischen Orientierungen der Juden in Deutschland von Jena bis Weimar*,
275. Some percentages do not equal 100 because the Zentrum (Center
party) was excluded and these are rough estimates. For the percentages of
SPD votes cast by Jews before World War I, see also Hamburger, 147,
and Hans-Helmuth Knütter, *Die Juden und die deutsche Linke in der
Weimarer Republik*, 98. For political parties that were included, see note
in table 1.2.

percent of the Jewish delegates belonged to conservative parties
between 1867 and 1878, almost the same percentage belonged to
the Socialist party from 1893 to 1916. This represented the most
dramatic political shift among Jewish delegates for all the years
covered in this study. Between 1879 and 1916, there was a corresponding decline in the percentage who supported parties of the

Middle, from 29 to 19 percent among non-Jewish delegates, and from 52 to 12 percent among Jewish delegates. The SPD thus gained the most from these significant losses in the Middle, although there was also a slight increase in the percentage of Jewish delegates coming from the Right.

To summarize these findings, we can say that parties of the Right showed very significant percentage losses between 1867 and 1916 and that these losses were much more extreme among Jewish delegates. Parties of the Middle had temporary increases in their percentage of delegates among both Jews and non-Jews between 1879 and 1892; however, these were followed by declines from 1893 to 1916—declines which were extremely large among Jewish delegates. Finally, the percentage of all delegates who were affiliated with the SPD increased significantly between 1867 and 1916; this trend was most pronounced among Jewish delegates.

One may wish to ask how well the Jewish Reichstag delegates reflected the political attitudes of the Jewish population as estimated by Jacob Toury (see table 1.1). A brief look at the party preferences of Jews indicates some similarities and differences. During the years 1867 to 1878, Jewish Reichstag delegates mirrored the estimated political affiliations of the Jewish population very accurately. Between 1879 and 1892 this was not the case; the Jewish population demonstrated much stronger support for the Right and Middle, with correspondingly less support for the Left, than did Jewish Reichstag delegates. By the years 1893–1916 it is even clearer that Jews in the Reichstag had party affiliations that were dissimilar to those of the Jewish population. A low level of support for parties of the Right among both groups is not surprising, as this was evident in earlier years. However, it is surprising that only 12 percent of the Jewish delegates came from parties of the Middle, whereas 61 percent of the Jewish population are estimated to have supported these parties. Even more striking is the low (19 percent) support for the SPD among the Jewish population; this contrasts very sharply with the 72 percent of the Jewish delegates who represented the SPD. In summary, it is clear that the party affiliations of Jewish Reichstag delegates did not reflect the estimated voting habits of the more moderate Jewish population, among whom support for parties of the Middle was the outstanding characteristic between 1879 and 1916.[81]

Jewish Reichstag delegates were also more left-oriented than other Jewish politicians and Jewish delegates in the Prussian parliament, the Landtag. Table 1.2 represents the party affiliations of these groups. It is clear from this table that the same movement from Right to Left that occurred among Jewish Reichstag delegates

TABLE 1.2
Percentage Distribution of Party Affiliations among Jewish Reichstag and Landtag Delegates and Other Politically Active Jews, 1867–1916

| | Jewish Landtag Delegates | Jewish Reichstag Delegates | Other Jews Active in Politics |
|---|---|---|---|
| | 1867–1878 | | |
| Right | 66 | 75 | 22 |
| Middle | 34 | 23 | 47 |
| Left | 0 | 2 | 31 |
| | 1879–1892 | | |
| Right | 55 | 11 | 36 |
| Middle | 41 | 52 | 44 |
| Left | 5 | 37 | 20 |
| | 1893–1916 | | |
| Right | 29 | 16 | 11 |
| Middle | 44 | 12 | 49 |
| Left | 27 | 72 | 40 |

SOURCES: Jewish Landtag delegates are given by Jacob Toury, *Die politischen Orientierungen*, 351–354. See also Ernst Hamburger, *Juden im öffentlichen Leben*, 393. Jewish Reichstag delegates are given by Hamburger, pp. 251–253. Numbers of Jews active in politics outside of the Reichstag and Landtag were determined by subtracting Reichstag and Landtag delegates from the total number of Jews active in politics. These figures can be found in Toury, 197, 235 (note 20), 245.

NOTE: Parties included in tables 1.1 and 1.2 were the following:
Right—Conservatives, Free Conservatives, National Liberals; Middle—Progressives, *Freisinnige Sezession*; Left—Social Democrats. Note, however, that a small number of delegates from the South German People's party are included in estimates among parties of the Middle in table 1.2, but not table 1.1. Reelected delegates are included only if they were represented in more than one set of years.

also had an impact upon Jewish Landtag delegates and other Jewish politicians. Yet Jewish Landtag delegates were consistently affiliated with the Right in larger percentages than Jewish Reichstag delegates and other Jewish politicians. (This was also true of non-Jewish Landtag delegates.) In contrast, with the exception of the period 1867–1878, Jewish Reichstag delegates were affiliated with the SPD in percentages that were greater than those for Jewish Landtag delegates and for all other Jews who were active in politics. Thus, Jewish Reichstag delegates were not only more left-oriented than the Jewish population, but also more left-wing than any other group of Jewish politicians. By referring to table 1.2 one can compare the party affiliations of all Jewish politicians outside of the Landtag and Reichstag with the Jewish population as a whole. Again, it is obvious that the Jewish population was far more moderate than were Jews elected to office, presumably by significant numbers of non-Jews.

It is important to examine differences in political orientation both between non-Jews and Jews, and among Jews, because these differences gave rise to problems at that time as well as during later years. The identification of Jews first with the Middle's opposition and later with socialist opposition to Bismarck's Germany had very unfortunate consequences. The stereotype of Jews as opponents of the government was in great measure based upon the political activities of a select group of Reichstag delegates and other Jewish politicians who gained national prominence and visibility, but who unfortunately were far more radical than the general Jewish population whom they were assumed, in the main, to represent. This was a problem of considerable concern to the conservative and moderate Jewish leadership in prewar years; it became an even greater problem during World War I, the subsequent "socialist revolution," and the Weimar Republic because anti-Semites labeled all Jews as socialists and revolutionaries.

It was undeniably true that several highly vocal Jewish politicians and intellectuals had socialist inclinations in the years immediately before and after World War I, and many Zionists were also Communists;[82] however, it is uncertain that the majority of the Jewish population supported socialism.[83] This created the paradoxical situation in which the moderate Jewish majority was stereotyped as socialist, internationalist, and revolutionary. There has been a tendency to circumvent or simply ignore the significant role of Jewish intellectuals in the SPD and Communist party (KPD) and thereby seriously neglect one of the genuine and objective reasons for increased anti-Semitism during and after World War I. Many Germans erroneously assumed that prominent Jewish intellectuals represented the political attitudes of the majority of German Jews, and it was this popular misconception that was politically most dangerous to Jews as a minority.

Support for the SPD among Jewish politicians and intellectuals was not simply a Nazi myth. After 1881 a larger percentage of Jewish Reichstag delegates always came from the SPD more than from any other political party.[84] Between 1890 and 1914, 67 percent (thirty-nine out of fifty-eight) of all Jewish Reichstag delegates were in the SPD.[85] After 1890 Jews constituted an average of 10 percent of all SPD delegates but less than 1 percent of the German population.[86] Jewish political leaders such as Eduard Bernstein and Rosa Luxemburg were very active and highly visible speakers for various branches of the SPD, and they represented only a tiny fraction of the prominent Jewish theorists and propagandists for the party. Of the four hundred Jews who were active in national politics between 1867 and 1914, 31 percent were employed as editors, writers, journalists, or propagandists for SPD organizations, publishers, or newspapers.[87] The affiliation of Jewish intellectuals with socialist publications was clearly not negligible.

In addition, there were very close ties between Jewish self-defense organizations and the SPD, primarily involving transfers of money from Jewish organizations to SPD propaganda offices.[88] This was true from around 1914 through the Weimar Republic and even up to 1940, when socialist leaders appealed to Jewish groups to support their underground press.[89] The prominence of Jews in the revolution and early Weimar Republic is indisputable, and this was a very serious contributing cause for increased anti-Semitism in postwar years.[90]

With the exception of secret donations by Jewish organizations,

23

close affiliations between Jewish intellectuals and the SPD were public knowledge. As mentioned, the total percentage of Jewish affiliation with the SPD was small; but the visibility of the SPD contacts of a minority of Jews, even those who had left Judaism or were dissenters, contributed very significantly to the socialist stereotype that was associated with German Jews from around 1900 to 1933. It is bitterly ironic that the SPD leadership were well aware of the hesitance of most Jews to support socialism, and indeed this reticence created a certain tension between the SPD and Jewish leaders.[91] Yet it was only with the overall collapse of the parties of the Middle in 1932 that the SPD succeeded in securing a majority of Jewish voters.[92] It is clear, then, that the stereotype of Jews as socialists and communists was an exaggerated yet nevertheless important one, because it led many Germans to distrust the Jewish minority as a whole and to brand Jews as enemies of the German nation.

## ANTI-SEMITISM, 1870–1933

Given the universal propensity of "insiders" to reject "outsiders," it is of some interest to discover the general intellectual and political response of Germans to Jewish emancipation. Current secondary literature is almost unanimous in maintaining that Jewish emancipation was soon held in disdain by German intellectuals, students, and significant numbers of the middle classes. A rise in "respectable" anti-Semitism is frequently cited as a symptom of the decline of German liberalism after 1880. The list of nineteenth- and twentieth-century Germans whom historians have considered to be anti-Semites (in sharply varying degrees) includes Karl Marx, Julius Langbehn, Paul de Lagarde, Heinrich von Treitschke, Oswald Spengler, Moeller van den Bruck, Friedrich Nietzsche, Constantin Franz, Rudolf Meyer, Paul Blötticher, Wilhelm Marr, Ernst Heinrici, Eugen Düring, Adolf Stoecker, Paul Foerster, Otto Boeckel, Theodor Fritsch, Hermann Ahlwardt, Heinrich Class, Wilhelm Raab, Oswald Zimmerman, Gustav Freytag, Otto von Glagau, Arthur Dinter, Anton Drexler, and Richard Wagner.

One school of thought, the *völkisch* school, is considered of paramount importance in the popularization of anti-Semitism. George Mosse has examined the *völkisch* ideology in some detail.[93] He believes that it included many disparate elements such as antibourgeois values, nature worship, romantic and cultural nationalism, paganism, mysticism, historicism, hatred of "modernism," and reverence for medieval values. Most of all, however, he believes the *völkisch* ideology was typified by anti-Semitism. *Völkisch* anti-Semites perpetuated stereotypes of Jews as rootless, soulless, materialistic, aggressive, ugly, weak, dishonest, unassimilable, shallow, loud, urban, internationalist, liberal, conspiratorial, evil, godless, competitive, abstract, insincere, cosmopolitan, sneaky, shrewd, lazy, usurious, opportunistic, and most important, alien.[94] Many of these stereotypes were traditional staples of anti-Semites in all European countries from the Middle Ages onward. There were, however, some new elements in anti-Jewish propaganda that were potentially more destructive: accusations of Jewish predominance in finance capitalism, socialism, communism, and internationalism.

Some *völkisch* thinkers simply updated older anti-Semitic arguments or elaborated upon the mythical "Jewish world conspiracy" that appealed to a fairly naive readership.[95] Other anti-Semites, however, used potentially more powerful arguments that were designed to make anti-Semitism acceptable to more sophisticated readers. The latter arguments included four "isms": Social Darwinism, nationalism, imperialism, and Social Conservatism. Some historians believe that a new virulence was incorporated into anti-Semitic arguments after 1870 because of the impetus it received from these four "isms".[96]

Social Darwinists postulated inherent racial differences between humans that could not be altered by assimilation.[97] They simultaneously glorified natural selection in which "inferior" species were eliminated by their "superiors." They also deified the "struggle for life" and "survival of the fittest" as creative forces that ensured progress throughout nature. Social Darwinists correspondingly justified anti-Semitism by arguing that Jews were racial inferiors whose assimilation could never eradicate their inherent

25

inferiority. They considered it the duty of good Germans to maintain racial purity either by excluding Jews from Germany or restricting their "baleful" influence by strict immigration quotas and laws against intermarriage.

Some historians consider nationalism and imperialism as important as Social Darwinism in fostering virulent anti-Semitism after 1870.[98] Both "isms" popularized a "we" versus "they" dichotomy that promoted anti-Semitism, where "we" meant Germans and "they" meant Jews. Though Social Darwinism was not a necessary component of nationalism or imperialism because these "isms" did not define aliens as immutable racial inferiors, it was frequently used to buttress anti-Semitic arguments for national homogeneity.

The same was true of Social Conservatism, which espoused a return to the "good old days" before Jews had ostensibly corrupted German values.[99] Social Conservatives were a motley collection of individuals who had no consistent response toward Jews. Some were indifferent to the "Jewish question" and some were moderate anti-Semites, but rabid anti-Semitism was not typical of these thinkers. Their major complaint against Jews was their prominent role in the spread of alien "modern" versus "medieval" institutions. They regarded Jews as undesirable harbingers of change but did not consider them subhuman, as did rabid anti-Semites.

Several historians have traced the heritage of intellectual anti-Semitism, yet they have seldom counterposed this heritage with competing intellectual influences.[100] It should be pointed out that *völkisch* thinkers were not the only intellectuals in Germany, nor were the majority of them leading intellectuals. There were other prominent spokesmen for the German intellectual tradition who did not sympathize with anti-Semitism, among them G.W.F. Hegel, G. E. Lessing, Friedrich von Schelling, Johann Goethe, Theodor Mommsen, Wilhelm von Humboldt, Johann Droysen, Rudolf Virchow, Friedrich Engels, Thomas Mann, and Max Weber.[101]

Richard Hamilton raises several important issues regarding the spread of "cultural" anti-Semitism. He points out that some Jews were Wagner enthusiasts.[102] Because of the high level of literacy required, it is probable that some of the more "serious" anti-Semitic works would have been read by the urban upper and upper-middle classes rather than the less literate rural lower-middle class that is supposed to have voted disproportionately for Hitler.[103] Much of the "trashy anti-Semitic literature" was given away and therefore may have been discarded as junk mail is today.[104] Also, it is possible that the relatively small coterie of hard-core anti-Semites bought every new anti-Semitic work so that there was overlapping readership. Because of the free distribution and possible overlapping of readership, one cannot assume that there was an anti-Semite for every printed anti-Semitic work.

Hamilton correctly points out that "cultural" factors are given a central place by many historians in explaining the rise of Hitler without showing sufficient justification for this. He states: "If the culture was one and all-pervasive, it is necessary to explain why the Protestant countryside was moved to the National Socialists and why the Catholic countryside, by comparison, remained with the Center Party."[105] In short, cultural explanations that include anti-Semitism as a central reason for Hitler's electoral success are inadequate as explanatory tools because of their nebulous formulation and because counterexamples from the works of famous scholars and writers indicate that cultural influences were diverse; for example, Treitschke wrote an anti-Semitic tract, but Mommsen wrote a countering statement. Thus Germany's cultural heritage was not uniformly anti-Semitic.

Moreover, a deep commitment to a legal and constitutional state was shared by late-nineteenth-century liberals and conservatives. Both groups rejected all attempts to nullify the legal equality of Jews; not a single law was passed between 1869 and 1933 to rescind the new freedoms granted during the foundation of Germany.[106] Of course, in practice there were many instances of job discrimination, social snobbery, and other types of hostility toward Jews; these were common in all Western countries at the time. Nevertheless, legal emancipation was accepted as part and parcel of the new state despite pressure from rabid anti-Semites to reimpose legal restrictions on Jews.

Not only liberals and conservatives but also many Catholics

and Protestants were opposed to anti-Semitic legislation on ideological or intellectual grounds. Catholics were seldom philo-Semitic because age-old religious conflicts lingered on; however, they shared minority status with Jews and were loathe to condone religious discrimination against them. This was obviously a rational pragmatic stance, but in addition it was an expression of the humanitarianism embodied in Christian ethics. In 1891 Catholics and Protestants joined to form a Christian defense league, the Association for Defense Against Anti-Semitism, which "campaigned against the antisemitic parties in elections and published pamphlets and a weekly newspaper refuting antisemitic lies and half-truths and publicising the crimes and disreputable character of the antisemites."[107] This organization functioned until November 1933 except for the war years, and, according to Richard Levy, it was quite active and at least partially effective in stemming the spread of anti-Semitism. By 1893 it had thirteen thousand members, predominately non-Jewish, and it gained some membership thereafter.[108] Its newspaper sold better than did the major anti-Semitic newspaper, although not better than the anti-Semitic press as a whole.[109] Even though it included members of all political parties, it gradually came to represent primarily the left-liberals. It would be informative for comparative purposes to know which other Western countries could boast of a similar Christian organization to defend Jews so consistently against anti-Semitic attacks.

Some socialist theorists, for humanitarian reasons and because they believed religious conflicts were secondary to class struggle, opposed renewed restrictions on Jews. From their viewpoint the "Jewish question" was an irrelevant issue used by rabid anti-Semites to obscure more significant problems brought on by the capitalist system.

These indications that intellectual anti-Semitism had definite limits within liberal, conservative, religious, and socialist circles do not prove that anti-Semitism was insignificant from 1870 to 1933. They are cited only to illustrate the need to examine the sources of anti-Semitism within the context of other intellectual trends.

Because intellectual and social anti-Semitism are difficult to measure, historians have written more extensively on political anti-Semitism. The implicit assumption is that if either social or intellectual anti-Semitism had been virulent, this would have been reflected in electoral support for anti-Semitic parties. Accordingly, historians have examined the sources of support for and opposition to anti-Semitism in political parties to determine whether or not it was influential.

*Political Parties*

Several important books on political anti-Semitism in Imperial Germany have been written. For the Weimar years, Donald Niewyk's recent book, *The Jews in Weimar Germany* and the essays in Werner Mosse's *Entscheidungsjahr 1932* are very informative.[110] What follows here is a cursory summary of the general trends in political anti-Semitism as discussed in these books. Table 1.3 summarizes the electoral success and failure of anti-Semitic parties and parties that adopted anti-Semitic platforms,[111] as well as parties that rejected political anti-Semitism as a drawing card between 1870 and 1933.[112] It is clear from this table that parties whose primary appeal was anti-Semitism never drew a large percentage of total votes.[113] Only in the elections of 1930 and later years did the Nazis succeed in obtaining strong support, and, as will be discussed later, the causative role of anti-Semitism in this success is by no means clear.

The political organizations that promoted anti-Semitism before 1928 were by and large small splinter parties and independent groups that had checkered political histories. At times their prospects appeared bright and auspicious. Between 1879 and 1886 Pastor Adolf Stöcker organized a temporarily influential Christian-Social party in Berlin. He advocated a decrease in Jewish employment in the civil service, suspension of Jewish immigration, restoration of a special census for Jews, and strengthening of the Christian-German spirit against "pernicious" Jewish influence. These were fairly typical demands of anti-Semites before World War I.[114] Stöcker and other moderates believed Jews could be assimilated into German life and culture if and when they aban-

29

TABLE 1.3 Percentage of Valid Votes Cast, Selected Political Parties, 1870–1933

| | AS | C | Total | FC | NL | Total | CT | PR | SPD | Total |
|---|---|---|---|---|---|---|---|---|---|---|
| 1871 | | 13 | 13 | 15 | 28 | 43 | 18 | 9 | 3 | 30 |
| 1874 | | 7 | 7 | 8 | 29 | 37 | 27 | 9 | 7 | 43 |
| 1877 | | 10 | 10 | 8 | 27 | 35 | 24 | 11 | 9 | 44 |
| 1878 | | 13 | 13 | 14 | 23 | 37 | 23 | 10 | 8 | 41 |
| 1881 | | 16 | 16 | 7 | 14 | 21 | 22 | 22 | 6 | 50 |
| 1884 | | 15 | 15 | 7 | 17 | 24 | 22 | 19 | 9 | 50 |
| 1887 | .2 | 15 | 17 | 10 | 22 | 32 | 20 | 14 | 10 | 44 |
| 1890 | .7 | 12 | 19 | 7 | 16 | 23 | 18 | 18 | 20 | 56 |
| 1893 | 3 | 14 | 17 | 6 | 13 | 19 | 19 | 14 | 23 | 56 |
| 1898 | 4 | 11 | 15 | 4 | 13 | 17 | 19 | 11 | 27 | 57 |
| 1903 | 3 | 10 | 13 | 4 | 14 | 18 | 20 | 9 | 32 | 61 |
| 1907 | 2 | 9 | 11 | 4 | 15 | 19 | 19 | 11 | 29 | 59 |
| 1912 | 1 | 9 | 10 | 3 | 14 | 17 | 16 | 12 | 35 | 63 |

|  | NS | DN | Total | DD | DV | W | Total | CT | SPD | USPD, KPD | Total |
|---|---|---|---|---|---|---|---|---|---|---|---|
| 1919 |  | 10 | 10 | 19 | 4 | 1 | 24 | 20 | 38 | 8 | 66 |
| 1920 |  | 15 | 15 | 8 | 14 | 1 | 23 | 14 | 22 | 20 | 56 |
| 1924[a] | 7 | 20 | 27 | 6 | 9 | 2 | 17 | 13 | 21 | 13 | 47 |
| 1924[b] | 3 | 21 | 24 | 6 | 10 | 3 | 19 | 14 | 26 | 9 | 49 |
| 1928 | 3 | 14 | 17 | 5 | 9 | 5 | 19 | 12 | 30 | 11 | 53 |
| 1930 | 18 | 7 | 25 | 4 | 5 | 4 | 13 | 12 | 25 | 13 | 50 |
| 1932[c] | 37 | 6 | 43 | 1 | 1 |  | 2 | 13 | 22 | 15 | 50 |
| 1932[d] | 33 | 9 | 42 | 1 | 2 |  | 3 | 12 | 20 | 17 | 49 |
| 1933[e] | 44 | 8 | 52 | 1 | 1 |  | 2 | 12 | 18 | 12 | 42 |
| 1933[f] | 92 |  | 92 |  |  |  |  |  |  |  |  |

SOURCE: Calculated from Koppel Pinson, *Modern Germany*, 572–575.

NOTES: Parties are arranged from left to right in decreasing order of anti-Semitism in three clusters, to which totals refer. When no percentages are given, the party did not run.

AS-Anti-Semites; C-Conservative party; FC-Free Conservatives; NL-National Liberals; CT-Center party; PR-Progressives; SPD-Socialists; NS-National Socialists; DN-German National People's party; DD-German Democratic party; DV-German People's party and State party after 1930; W-Economic party; USPD-Independent Socialists; KPD-Communist party.

[a] May, 1924.
[b] December, 1924.
[c] July, 1932.
[d] November, 1932.
[e] March, 1933.
[f] November, 1933.

doned their exclusively Jewish religion and customs. Stöcker himself sat in the Reichstag as a conservative delegate from 1881 to 1908, although his anti-Semitic following was largest primarily in the years 1879 to 1886. His program received considerable attention at the time, but it was an electoral failure.[115]

In opposition to Stöcker's assimilationist program, several radicals formed organizations that advocated the total exclusion of Jews from Germany. These included Paul Förster's German People's League, the German Anti-Semitic League, Max Liebermann von Sonnenberg's German Social Anti-Semitic party, and Otto Boeckel's Anti-Semitic People's party. None of these parties was a notable success. Their maximum number of votes was 284,250 in 1898,[116] and their largest number of Reichstag delegates was 16 out of 397 in 1907.[117] Between 1887 and 1912 anti-Semitic deputies represented only 2 percent of all Reichstag delegates, including all who were reelected,[118] and by 1914 the anti-Semitic parties were practically defunct and their press was in ruins.[119] After World War I additional small anti-Semitic parties arose with racist programs, but once again their electoral strength was less than 5 percent of all valid votes.[120] These small *völkisch* groups eventually either allied with and were absorbed by the Nazis or gradually faded into insignificance. The track record of anti-Semitic parties was very poor even from their own point of view. The anti-Semites could nevertheless take delight from the incorporation of some of their goals into programs of other organizations such as the German Farmer's League, German National League of Commercial Employees, League of German Students, Pan-German League, *Stahlhelm*, and other small, generally right-wing groups.

The occasional moderation and "middle-class" respectability of anti-Semitic parties resulted from sporadic alliances with the Conservative parties, the National Liberals after 1890, and the DNVP during the Weimar Republic.[121] A resolution to "combat the manifold upsurging and decomposing Jewish influence in our national life"[122] was first formally adopted by Conservatives in the Tivoli Program against considerable opposition in the party before the 1893 elections. It may have contributed to their slight increase in votes at that time; however, for the most part a continuous decline in the Conservative party's electoral support occurred irrespective of its inclusion or exclusion of anti-Semitism in party programs. Conservatives attempted to stave off political decline by adopting anti-Jewish rhetoric even though they severed formal ties with anti-Semitic parties after 1896. According to Richard Levy and others, they preferred to ally with the Farmers' League, which was also anti-Semitic but which shared more similar economic goals than those of the "pure" anti-Semites. Anti-Semitism was used by Conservatives in areas where it appeared to draw votes, and some historians consider this a matter of opportunism rather than dyed-in-the-wool racism.[123] The "insincerity" of the Conservative party's commitment to anti-Semitism was a great disappointment to rabid racists. The Free Conservatives, or Reichspartei, were apparently less anti-Semitic than was the Conservative party, especially after 1900.[124]

According to George Mosse and Lewis Hertzman, during and after World War I the Conservative party's successor, namely, the DNVP, employed anti-Semitism as a standard campaign and propaganda tool. They consider the DNVP to have been the one political party that rivaled the Nazis in its anti-Semitism during the Weimar Republic. P. B. Wiener, however, believes that the DNVP was basically silent on the "Jewish question."[125] If Mosse and Hertzman are correct, the DNVP's losses during the Reichstag election of 1930 made it clear that anti-Semitism could not save the party from electoral defeat. The DNVP gained no more political advantage from anti-Semitism than had the Conservatives before World War I.

During its "liberal" years between 1870 and 1890 the National Liberal party was strongly opposed to anti-Semitism.[126] It was headed by prominent Jewish delegates, Eduard Lasker and Ludwig Bamberger. During the "nationalist" years between 1890 and 1918, however, the party was more reticent about taking a stance on issues that dealt specifically with the "Jewish question." This was partially as a response to earlier charges of philo-Semitism and partially a reflection of changing sentiment within the party itself. In some elections the National Liberal party cooperated with anti-Semites, especially after the liberal secession, which left the party in the hands of mild and moderate anti-Semites.[127] By 1914 it had lost its former "liberal" image as the "party of the Jews" and was considered a potential ally by leaders of anti-Semitic parties. After the dissolution of the National Liberal party in 1918, some former members joined the moderately anti-Semitic DNVP; others joined the less anti-Semitic parties of the Middle.

In Imperial Germany the parties of the Middle included the Fortschrittspartei, Freisinnige Partei, Freisinnige Volkspartei, Freisinnige Vereinigung, and Fortschrittliche Volkspartei, all of which eventually united to form one Progressive party. These liberals and left-liberals specifically condemned anti-Semitism and refused to use it as a campaign issue.[128] In an effort to defeat the SPD during the elections of 1907, left-liberals supported four anti-Semites out of 35 non-SPD candidates in runoff elections; however, this was atypical.[129] Generally they were sympathetic toward Jews, publicly rejected anti-Semitism, defended Jews in Reichstag debates, and were very active leaders in the Association for Defense Against Anti-Semitism.[130]

After the First World War the new parties of the Middle continued their moderate stance. The German Democratic party was more vocal than other Middle parties in openly opposing the use of anti-Semitism as a campaign issue before 1930, although there was an undertone of anti-Semitism within the party; after 1930 the party split on the "Jewish question."[131] The successor to the German Democratic party, the German State party, was similarly divided on anti-Semitism. Some members fought to prevent anti-Semitism from entering party programs while others pushed for its inclusion. The anti-Semitic wing triumphed by 1930, with the result that many prominent Jews left the German State party as they had earlier left the Democratic party, and the State party's votes approached the vanishing point.

The German People's party was less eager to protect Jews than was the German Democratic or State party. Although it did not publicly employ anti-Semitic arguments, the party approved anti-Semitic platforms in 1919 and 1931.[132] Early in the Weimar Republic it was willing to support a right-wing Jewish organization, the Association of German National Jews under the leadership of Max Naumann, a Berlin lawyer and former captain in the Bavarian army. However, this affiliation cooled in later Weimar years.[133] After the moderate party leader Gustav Stresemann's death in 1929, anti-Semitism made significant advances among the party leaders, but the party's votes nevertheless declined.

In summary, for most of the years between 1870 and 1930 the parties of the Middle were publicly opposed to or neutral toward anti-Semitism. They cooperated with anti-Semites only occasionally to defeat what they considered greater evils from the Right or Left. This tolerance toward Jews was also evident during Weimar years before the Great Depression. Only between 1930 and 1933 did they loosen or sever ties with Jews to prevent defection of anti-Semitic party members and potential voters. Nevertheless, the futility of abandoning their traditional moderation was clearly demonstrated by severe electoral losses in 1932, when parties of the Middle virtually collapsed, as had the DNVP in 1930. Thus anti-Semitism as a separate and distinct issue does not appear to have produced significant electoral victories for either the traditional Right or the Middle during the Great Depression and attendant crises.

The Zentrum (Center party) represented Catholics from all socioeconomic groups. Guenter Lewy believes that Catholics were by and large anti-Semitic because the official church policy included traditional religious, but not racial, anti-Semitism.[134] Richard Levy agrees that there was moderate anti-Semitism among Catholic leaders, but implies that before World War I it was far less significant than Lewy indicates.[135]

Considerable antagonism existed between Catholic and Jewish Reichstag delegates in the 1870s during Bismarck's attack against the Catholic church (the *Kulturkampf*) because Eduard Lasker, a prominent Jewish Reichstag delegate, supported the anti-Catholic May Laws; however, Richard Levy and others indicate that future relations between Jews and the Zentrum were amicable.[136] Leading Catholics such as Ludwig Windthorst, a very prominent Zentrum leader, were not anti-Semitic, although Werner Jochmann believes some Center party delegates used anti-Semitism in elec-

35

tion campaigns.[137] Windthorst opposed an anti-Semitic petition in 1880 and Richard Levy believes his followers by and large continued his policies;[138] however, Marjorie Lamberti feels that they only tolerated Jews and did not regard them as equals.[139] Jewish leaders entertained formal alliances with the Zentrum because its policies were designed to protect religious minorities, but this was doomed to failure. Jews would have been a minority within a minority party that was itself seeking parity.

During the Weimar Republic the Zentrum was either neutral toward or opposed to anti-Semitism emanating from *völkisch* and Nazi parties.[140] Zentrum leaders emphasized the incompatibility of racial theories and Catholicism, urging their followers to avoid all connection with the Nazis because of fundamental ideological differences.[141] Zentrum leaders denounced ritual-murder charges against Jews and sporadic outbreaks of anti-Semitism in the Catholic publication *Germania*, even though this periodical had occasionally chastised Jews in Wilhelminian years.[142] The Zentrum ran a Jewish candidate for the Reichstag in Berlin during the election of September 1930 and, in general, defended Jewish rights against anti-Semites even after 1930.[143] Unfortunately, the archives of the Zentrum and the protocols of its parliamentary delegation were destroyed during World War II, but by the use of extant documents one historian has concluded that the Zentrum did not become more anti-Semitic during Weimar years.[144] It is interesting that a publication that was affiliated with the *Reichsbanner*, a large socialist paramilitary organization, considered the Catholic church to be the only real power in Germany that opposed anti-Semitism after 1932.[145] Whether or not this was true, it does indicate that the Catholic church was not considered strongly anti-Semitic even by ideologically incompatible groups.

One of the problems in evaluating the importance of anti-Semitism in the Zentrum is that the church appears to have perpetuated ambiguity. Jews were still regarded as misguided religious antagonists, yet they were defended against virulent racial anti-Semites who wanted to strip them of their humanity. Thus the Catholic church tolerated moderate religiously based anti-Semitism, but rejected Nazi racial doctrines as neo-barbarianism.[146]

Given this ambiguity on the "Jewish question," it is nearly impossible to determine what, if anything, a vote for the Zentrum meant to average Catholics vis-à-vis Jews. Before November 1932 the Zentrum did not openly cooperate with anti-Semites; afterward it did. Nevertheless, its percentage of votes remained nearly the same. The Zentrum lost only 0.2 percent of the total votes between November 8, 1932 and March 5, 1933.[147] It is not obvious from these figures that anti-Semitism was an issue of decisive importance among Catholic voters.

Between 1870 and 1933 the parties representing the socialist Left, as distinct from the left-liberals in the Middle, were the SPD (Social Democratic party), the USPD (Independent Social Democratic party), and the KPD (Communist party). Some differences of interpretation on the "Jewish question" existed both within and between these parties. In part this arose from divergent interpretations of Marx's *Zur Judenfrage*. According to Massing, this publication could be interpreted as an anti-Semitic treatise outside of the "philosophical milieu" for which it was written. Massing states that "the Jews of *Zur Judenfrage* appeared as a parasitic, clannish, asocial and alien group, held together by a reactionary religion."[148] Edmund Silberner also believes that Marx's attacks on Jewish capitalism promoted anti-Semitism, particularly before World War I.[149] There is considerable discussion of this issue in the pertinent literature; however, some historians consider socialist leaders to have been neutral toward or directly opposed to anti-Semitism by 1890.[150] A very specific reason for the SPD's attack on anti-Semitism, for example, was that the Christian Socials tried to use anti-Semitism to attract working-class votes; hence the SPD had a tradition of antagonism toward the "socialism of fools" (anti-Semitism) from 1878 onward. Anti-Semitism was traditionally associated with the political Right, so socialists in Germany and elsewhere opposed it as a vestige of medievalism.

During Wilhelminian years, Engels attacked anti-Semitism as a remnant of feudal reaction, while other prominent socialist leaders, such as Karl Kautsky and August Bebel, advocated assimilation of German Jews.[151] The SPD specifically rejected anti-

37

Semitism in 1893, and most party leaders appear to have favored a neutral public stance on the "Jewish question."[152] Socialist leaders were indubitably still antagonistic toward Jewish capitalism, but no more so than toward non-Jewish capitalism.[153] For socialists the primary issue was never race or religion, but class conflict.[154] Thus both before and after the First World War, leaders of the SPD concerned themselves with the "Jewish question" only insofar as it bore upon the conflict between the "proletariat" and its opponents. It would be mistaken, however, to assume that there were no pockets of anti-Semitism even among SPD leaders, particularly since they associated Jews with capitalism and occasionally let anti-Semitic remarks slip into their propaganda.[155] The SPD leaders also rejected the defense of specifically Jewish religious issues and were far from philo-Semitic. In 1908 the Central Association of German Citizens of Jewish Faith (CV) was of the opinion that the SPD would oppose attempts to curtail Jewish rights, "But when it is a question of the threatened religious interests of the Jews, the Social Democrats in view of their principles cannot speak out for them, and the Social Democrats also will not ignore the fact that they may hope for a rich harvest wherever antisemitism has ploughed the soil."[156] This conclusion was reached presumably because of the anticapitalist propaganda of the anti-Semites. The overall assessment has been confirmed by Leuschen-Seppel's study of the SPD and the "Jewish question" in Wilhelminian years. Although the SPD opposed attempts to curtail Jewish religious freedoms and rights as guaranteed by the constitution, it made Jews the butt of many jokes, political cartoons, caricatures, and so on, especially in its cultural and anticapitalist publications. According to Leuschen-Seppel, these expressions of anti-Semitism fostered exactly the type of hostility toward Jews that the SPD's leaders attempted to combat in their purely political propaganda. In any case, the SPD appears to have been ambivalent and inconsistent in its attitudes toward Jews.[157]

Because small anti-Semitic parties never directly threatened the "proletariat," they did not command a great deal of attention in the prewar socialist press. Yet it became increasingly necessary for the SPD to defend itself against charges by radical anti-Sem-

ites. Because of the SPD's open acceptance of Jewish party theo-
reticians, journalists, and propagandists, it came under heavier
and harsher attack. In anti-Semitic literature the SPD replaced the
National Liberal party as the "party of the Jews," and this presented critical problems for the SPD during and after World War
I.

Jewish socialists were prominent among those who questioned
Germany's war aims.[158] This became increasingly obvious after
the SPD split over the annexationist issue (whether Germany should
annex foreign territory) and when many Jewish socialists joined
the Spartacists and the Independent Social Democratic party.[159]
The participation of Jews in socialist revolutionary activities during 1918-1919 presented grave difficulties not only for the majority of German Jews who supported neither the revolution nor
socialism but also for the "evolutionary" versus "revolutionary"
SPD. Despite its comparative moderation from 1918 to 1933, the
SPD was accused, along with the USPD and KPD, of unpatriotic
behavior, Jewish bolshevism, internationalism, and the fall of the
monarchy. In the face of these stigmas, it is indeed remarkable
that the SPD retained high levels of support from its constituents
during the Weimar Republic.

The SPD continued to defend Jews against attacks by anti-
Semites and even attempted to aid Eastern European Jews who
passed through Germany after World War I. Party leaders did not
favor permanent immigration of Eastern Jews, but they did ally
with agencies that assisted transients. This of course precipitated
new charges of philo-Semitism, but the SPD nevertheless retained
its close relations with Jews in the party and Jewish defense
organizations outside of the party.[160]

The general policy of the SPD during most of the Weimar years
was to oppose anti-Semitism without making this opposition a
central ideological or political issue. According to Niewyk's recent analysis, the SPD leadership did include small numbers of
covert anti-Semites and it even consciously decreased the number
of Jewish SPD candidates in a few elections; however, its formal
program and almost all of its publications on the "Jewish question" either specifically condemned anti-Semitism or treated it as

39

a nonissue.[161] There are some problems in interpreting Niewyk's findings, however. He relies heavily upon socialist publications written by Jewish socialists or distributed to the SPD by Jewish defense organizations.[162] As he indicates, this hinders a thorough evaluation of anti-Semitism among the non-Jewish SPD leadership. However, the fact that the SPD distributed these writings implies that SPD leaders were not strongly anti-Semitic.

If one considers Leuschen-Seppel's conclusions regarding the spread of anti-Semitism by the SPD through jokes, caricatures, cartoons, and narratives before World War I, one is led to wonder whether these types of publications continued in Weimar years. If they did, they again would have confused the average worker because on the one hand he would have heard political propaganda denouncing anti-Semitism as a remnant of feudal reaction, and on the other hand he would have perceived Jews as usurious financiers and capitalists who were milking the workers. More research needs to be done to determine exactly what the average worker might have absorbed from SPD propaganda.

The USPD had a short-lived existence (1916–1922), but during its brief life it does not appear to have been anti-Semitic.[163] Many prominent USPD leaders were Jewish, and in some of the postwar people's councils over 30 percent of their delegates were Jews.[164] By mid-1919 and in Scheidemann's cabinet about 14 percent of the USPD delegates were Jewish.[165] This represented a significant drop in percentage, but not in absolute numbers. It is not clear whether the percentage decrease occurred because Jewish delegates were disillusioned with the USPD or because the USPD's non-Jewish leaders were anti-Semitic. In any case, the ratio of Jews was still quite high given their small percentage in the German population.

The KPD also had many prominent Jewish leaders, yet it resorted to anti-Semitism in the immediate postwar years and during the depression.[166] At both times this appears to have been an attempt to attract workers who resented the influence of Jews, especially Jewish intellectuals, in the SPD. The KPD also used anti-Semitism to placate nationalist sentiment and to compete with the NSDAP after 1928. Although the immediate postwar anti-

Semitic tactics did not seriously damage the SPD, significant losses to the KPD occurred during the depression. It is not clear whether anti-Semitism precipitated these losses, but it cannot be peremptorily dismissed as a contributing cause. Defections to the KPD were significant, and if anti-Semitism were one cause, this may in part explain the relative timidity of the SPD in combatting anti-Semitic propaganda after 1930.

In the face of charges of philo-Semitism by Nazis on the Right and the KPD on the Left, the SPD could undoubtedly have intensified its already considerable political problems by mounting a strong and well-publicized attack on anti-Semitism after 1930. Yet its relative quiescence on the "Jewish question" between 1930 and 1933 can be said to have been a necessary response to political reality rather than an abandonment of its traditional opposition to anti-Semitism. If this argument is used to explain the behavior of the SPD, it should also be extended to the parties of the Middle that faced similar charges of philo-Semitism from the NSDAP and KPD. If one compares party reactions to this crossfire from Right and Left, however, it is clear that even the SPD's silence was more favorable to Jews than the Middle parties' feeble attempts to stave off disaster by adopting anti-Semitism.

## SUMMARY AND INTERPRETATIONS

Between 1870 and 1933 Jews represented less than one percent of the German population, yet they were more visible than their numbers would indicate. They were sometimes distinctive in physical appearance and attire, practiced different religious customs, and were concentrated in urban areas. These characteristics were most pronounced among Eastern European Jews, who represented approximately a fifth of the Jewish population in 1933. Eastern European Jews retained their native customs and dress to a greater extent than did German Jews and generally lived in exclusively Jewish sections of large cities.

Both Eastern and German Jews concentrated heavily in commercial occupations and in the free professions, primarily because of their traditional exclusion from landowning. Prominence of

41

Jews in commercial and financial fields had both favorable and unfavorable consequences. The economic boom in Germany during the late nineteenth and twentieth centuries created new opportunities for individuals engaged in commerce and finance. Given their occupational distribution, Jews quite naturally prospered during these years, and this prosperity was reflected in their comparatively high per capita income. However, Jews also faced unfavorable consequences of economic growth because increased competition undoubtedly aggravated tensions between them and other Germans. Yet despite these and other tensions Jews found employment at approximately the same rate as other Germans and maintained satisfactory business relations with non-Jews in more fields and occupations than, for example, before 1870.

A large number of Jews attempted to integrate with the German majority by rejecting their own Jewish religion and distinctive customs. Many German Jews underwent religious conversion or simply abandoned both orthodox and reformed Judaism, in part out of sincere conviction and in part to facilitate relations with non-Jews. A large number also intermarried with non-Jews and baptized children issuing from these marriages. Adult conversion, intermarriage, and baptism of children resulted in significant numerical losses to the Jewish community. This was starkly clear to Jewish leaders because the rate of natural increase among German-born Jews was not sufficient to maintain their percentage in the German population. This decline was partially offset by the large influx of Eastern European Jews; however, this immigration created considerable difficulties for the partially or fully assimilated German Jews, who feared that their presence would stir up hostility against all Jews and who resented the economic burden of supporting large numbers of immigrants.

Jews were not only engaged in the social and economic life of Germany but they also participated actively in politics, frequently as prominent leaders. The majority affiliated first with the Right (1867–1878) and then the Middle (1879–1930). According to Toury's estimates, it was only after 1930 that the majority of the Jewish electorate switched from the Middle to the SPD on the Left. Nevertheless, the elected Jewish Reichstag delegates were far more left-wing than the Jewish voters, as estimated by Toury; they were also more left-wing than non-Jewish Reichstag delegates, the Jewish delegates to the Prussian diet (Landtag), and other Jews active in politics. This led anti-Semites and others to assume that their attitudes were representative of all Jews and to stereotype Jews as left-wing radicals. The prominence of Jews in the SPD, the German revolution of 1918–1919, and the Weimar Republic—especially in states controlled by the SPD—further contributed to the popular image of Jews as left-wing radicals. The frequent attacks on traditional values by Jewish dissidents also encouraged to the Germans' perception of the Jews as an alien people who were not truly committed to Germany's welfare.

From this brief discussion it is clear that Jews were able to overcome many traditional economic, political, religious, and social obstacles to their assimilation during the years 1870–1933. The extensiveness of their self-integration is, however, a matter of interpretation. One viewpoint is offered by Eva Reichmann in *Hostages of Civilization*.[167] She maintains that objective differences between Germans and Jews were traditionally a contributing cause of anti-Semitism because they fostered group tensions. According to Reichmann these group tensions were based upon real versus imaginary conflicts; that is, they were the product of concrete personal rather than abstract or intellectual anti-Semitism.[168] She develops the thesis that objective differences that fostered group tensions diminished after 1870 so that they were virtually insignificant contributing causes of anti-Semitism during the Weimar Republic. Thus she interprets assimilation as extensive and successful between 1870 and 1933.[169]

If one accepts Reichmann's contention that objective differences were necessary causes of anti-Semitism, then it is important to determine whether these were as insignificant by 1933 as she maintains. This presents an interesting problem of interpretation that has not been fully explored by other writers. After examining Jewish occupational distribution, religious conversions, rates of intermarriage, and political behavior, one can conclude that by 1933 there were still highly significant objective differences be-

43

tween German Jews, Eastern European Jews, and German non-Jews, most particularly in occupations, income, and political affiliations. It is difficult to reject these differences out of hand as nonexistent or unimportant, and they probably continued to contribute to anti-Semitism because they fostered group tensions, to use Reichmann's terminology.

We must be aware that recognition of objective differences does not necessitate either the acceptance or rejection of Reichmann's theory that Jews were a scapegoat for the aggressions of Germans. It merely illustrates that whatever the causes of anti-Semitism might have been, they could have been exacerbated by objective differences between Germans and Jews both before and during the Weimar Republic. The differences between Germans and partly assimilated German Jews were not nearly so extreme as those between Germans and Eastern European Jews. Ironically, however, there were enough objective differences between German and Eastern European Jews to generate considerable antagonism that overrode religious identifications even within the Jewish minority.[170]

One can argue that only the continuation of significant objective differences is consistent with the adoption of anti-Semitism by otherwise educated and rational individuals. This is presumably what Peter Pulzer means when he refers to the "grain of truth" that made anti-Semitic propaganda believable. According to Pulzer,

> The "big lie," that propaganda technique about which Hitler was so disarmingly frank, would have the most minimal appeal if it were pure invention, if it were a fabrication from beginning to end. To succeed it needs to be a half-truth, difficult to refute without elaborate logical argument and a vast apparatus of evidence.[171]

The charateristics of Jews as outlined above are consistent with Pulzer's interpretation, though it should be noted that some historians would reject his interpretation completely.[172]

However, to point out objective differences between Germans and Jews is not to imply that Jews somehow "caused" anti-Semitism and their own annihilation. This is, of course, patent nonsense, because it assumes that objective differences between Jews and non-Jews were not only necessary, but also *sufficient* causes of anti-Semitism. Even a cursory comparison demonstrates that there were (and are) many objective differences between Jews and non-Jews in France, Britain, and the United States, yet these did not (and do not) lead to radical or genocidal anti-Semitic policies. Logically, the mere existence of objective differences between Jews and non-Jews is not a sufficient cause of anti-Semitism, and non-Nazi historians have unanimously rejected claims to the contrary. In general, historians have also deemphasized the differences between Germans and Jews as a necessary cause of anti-Semitism because these do not in themselves explain the types and extensiveness of anti-Semitism in any given situation. Instead, historians have studied the causes of anti-Semitism by examining the subjective attitudes of Germans, which may or may not have been related to objective differences between them and Jews.

Between 1870 and 1933 several intellectual forces favored anti-Semitism. These included *völkisch* ideology, Social Darwinism, nationalism, imperialism, and Social Conservatism. At the same time, however, strong intellectual influences mitigated against anti-Semitism. These included the German liberal tradition, conservative opposition to rowdy anti-Semitism, Catholic humanitarianism, and socialist indifference to purely racial issues.

As we have seen, between 1870 and 1933 there were a number of small political parties whose primary offering was anti-Semitism; however, none of these parties obtained strong electoral support. Other parties, notably the Conservatives, some Middle parties, and the KPD, also occasionally campaigned on anti-Semitic platforms. It may be argued that these parties would not have secured even the slight political support they did attain without capitalizing on anti-Semitism, yet there are strong indications that levels of support for these parties did not rise and fall directly or obviously with their anti-Semitic rhetoric. In no case did these parties secure monumental electoral victories as a result of anti-Semitic propaganda.

According to some historians, intellectuals in Germany became anti-Semitic during the 1870s and 1880s and continued to be so

45

during Wilhelminian and Weimar years.[173] Youth groups and students are especially accused of adopting *völkisch* anti-Semitism.[174] Moreover, many historians believe that the level of social anti-Semitism increased during the years 1870–1914 and rose even higher during the Weimar Republic.[175] Historians do not claim that direct personal attacks on Jews increased before Nazi rowdies became active, but rather that "intellectual anti-Semitism" became an acceptable social value.[176] Still, other historians emphasize the slightness of social discrimination in Germany and the prevailing attitude that anti-Semitism was only of importance in "backward" countries like Poland and Russia.[177]

Davidson, Kren, and Rappoport claim that mainly latent anti-Semitism existed in Germany before 1914, as compared to the rampant and violent anti-Semitism in Russia and in Eastern European countries.[178] Davidson recalls the announcements of the German army to Jews in Eastern Europe and Russia during World War I, in which the Germans portrayed themselves as liberators, and notes that these announcements could not have been made by really anti-Semitic countries such as Russia and its territories—Poland, the Ukraine, Latvia, Lithuania, and Estonia.[179] Kren and Rappoport state:

> Indeed, during the nineteenth century and for several years after World War I, Jews received better treatment in Germany than in Russia, Poland, the Habsburg Empire and its succession states, Scandinavia, and even France, where the Dreyfus affair made Jews targets for substantial abuse. In brief, anti-Semitism is a European tradition. It was never confined to Germany, nor was it more intense in Germany than elsewhere. Yet complete destruction of the Jews was never made a state policy, let alone attempted on a broad scale, anywhere except in Germany. Consequently, although historical anti-Semitism was clearly relevant to the Holocaust, it cannot be accepted as its primary cause.[180]

As for the Weimar years, Davidson says of Germany:

> Intellectually and politically, it was an open society with a high degree of religious toleration where political anti-Semi-

tism had faded away to nothing. Einstein, Ballin, the Zweigs, Rathenau, and hundreds of thousands of their coreligionists, who were mainly middle-class, merchants, doctors, dentists, lawyers, with few big landowners or indigent proletarians among them, were very likely more at home there than they would have been anywhere else in Europe, with the possible exception of Britain.[181]

Also, Leo Baeck's biographer claims:

> The United States and the rest of the western world were not free of the virus that affected Germany. Anti-Semitism was prevalent. The restrictions under which German Jews had lived in the 1920s were little different from those Jews faced in the United States and England. They could not buy property in certain locations. Many hotels and resorts refused to admit them. Schools like Harvard University made no secret of their quota systems. Advancement in many careers was denied Jews. Violence often erupted. Anti-Semitism existed at all levels, in the country club and at the corner bar. Intellectuals like Toynbee in England wrote histories of civilization that dismissed the Jews as insignificant. In the United States during the early 1920s the Ku Klux Klan, which opposed blacks and Catholics as well as Jews, gained control of the Democratic Party in some states and exerted a powerful influence on the party in others.[182]

In Germany some Jews even supported Hitler despite his anti-Semitism, apparently thinking it was only a way to stir up the "masses." Hans Joachim Schoeps headed the German Vanguard, the German-Jewish followers of Hitler.[183] Max Naumann, the head of the Association of German National Jews, ardently solicited support from the Nazi party after Hitler had come to power, pointing out the national loyalty of his members and their service to the German nation.[184] Gerhart Hauptmann, a Nobel Prize recipient for literature, even voted for Hitler.[185] Many Jews were quite comfortable living in Germany despite latent anti-Semitism, whether intellectual or social. Eastern European and *nouveauriche* Jews might have been looked down upon by Germans, but their habits were considered extremely embarrassing by German Jews as well.[186]

Clearly, many Jews did not perceive anti-Semitism as the dire threat it became. According to George Salzberger, a rabbi in Frankfurt am Main and field rabbi in World War I, "There were indications, yes. But not an expressed anti-Semitism. One could lead a normal life until 1933 when Hitler came to power, then everything changed. None of us could guess what his coming to power meant. Not even the greatest pessimist."[187]

In the years after World War II, scholars in various disciplines have sought the roots of anti-Semitism in the uniquely distorted "German mind" or "German character." Unfortunately, these studies have led nowhere. Even though Jews had distinctive socioeconomic characteristics, they had advanced in many occupations, in income, through intermarriage, and in political life from 1870 to 1933. It is clear that Germany was in many ways a good place for Jews to live during these years. Had the German population been uniquely rabid in its hatred of Jews, it is inconceivable that Jews could have fared so well, especially compared to Jews in other nations. Therefore, the attributions of anti-Semitism to a uniquely distorted "German mind" or "German character" are largely irrelevant, whether based on psychology, sociology, intellectual history, or demonology.

If we hypothesize that prejudice is endemic to all human societies, how does this help us to explain why the Jews of Germany and Europe were slaughtered? The answer is: prejudice can explain the slaughter only to a limited extent. No matter how much or how little anti-Semitism existed in Germany, systematic extermination, as opposed to sporadic pogroms, could be carried out only by an extremely powerful government, and probably could have succeeded only under the cover of wartime conditions. It was only the advent of Hitler and his radical anti-Semitic followers and their subsequent centralization of power that made the extermination of European Jewry possible. Before the war public opinion toward Jews was to some extent taken into consideration in Nazi policies; by World War II concentration of power by Hitler and Himmler made it possible for them to ignore public opinion.

Yet the process of organized exclusion and murder required co-operation by huge sections of the military and bureaucracy, as well as acquiescence among the German people, whether or not they approved of Nazi persecution and extermination. Therefore, it is important for us to ask some questions about German attitudes toward Jews and the role of anti-Semitism in Hitler's rise to power, subjects to which we shall now turn.

# Who Supported Hitler?

"By 1932 the NSDAP had become a unique phenomenon in German electoral politics, a catch-all party of protest whose constituents, while concentrated primarily in a socially diverse middle class, were united above all by a vehement rejection of an increasingly threatening present."
Thomas Childers, "The Social Bases of the National Socialist Vote," p. 31.

Although anti-Semitism appears to have been of relatively limited importance for non-Nazi parties, it is a commonplace assumption that the Nazi party secured considerable support *because* of its anti-Semitism. To test the validity of this assumption, we should ask several questions. First, what was the nature of anti-Semitism in early Weimar years? Second, what was the putative role of anti-Semitism as a drawing card among Nazi party members? Third, how successful was Nazi anti-Semitic propaganda with the electorate? And fourth, was anti-Semitism the primary motivation of Germans who voted for Hitler after 1928?[1]

To be sure, these questions are closely related to the overriding question, "Who supported Hitler, and for what reasons?" The answers to this more general question are extremely complex and cast historians into frequent disagreement. Therefore, I shall focus on anti-Semitism as a separate and distinct source of Nazi appeal. If anti-Semitism were central to Nazi magnetism, or conversely, if it were not, this fact has implications for the subsequent re-actions of Germans to Nazi persecution of Jews.

## ANTI-SEMITISM IN THE EARLY WEIMAR YEARS

When we ask our first question, What was the nature of anti-Semitism in early Weimar years? we should first reiterate that many historians believe the failure of political anti-Semitism between 1870 and 1914 did not preclude the spread of intellectual and social anti-Semitism, especially among the middle classes.[2] They think that these types of anti-Semitism were already significant by World War I and that they became much more intense during the Weimar Republic, again despite the political failure of *völkisch* parties and the NSDAP before 1930.[3]

Several reasons are frequently given for the intensification of anti-Semitism in Weimar years. During World War I about half of the Jewish Reichstag delegates refused to vote for war credits. Jews were also accused of shirking their military duties by failure to enlist in numbers proportionate to their percentage in the population. A special study was undertaken to clarify this issue; however, the government did not release the results of this study during World War I. An anti-Semitic general leaked the results to Alfred Roth, who published them in 1919 using the pseudonym Otto Armin. In an attempt to demonstrate that actual Jewish front-line service and casualties were proportionately much lower than those of non-Jews, he juxtaposed very detailed figures that had been gathered by Jewish leaders during 1916—and were later collected by the army—against comparable statistics for non-Jews. It is unclear that these figures were accurate, but Armin's book portrayed Jews as unpatriotic and cowardly.[4] This became a popularly accepted "truth" about Jews.

Anti-Semitic suspicions were later reinforced by the disproportionate number of Jews who were visibly active in the new government that capitulated to the Allies at the end of World War I. Because the basic futility of Germany's military situation was never clearly communicated to the German public, the "stab-in-the-back" theory of Jewish betrayal appeared credible at the time.[5] Thus Jews, as well as communists, Free Masons, and Jesuits, were suspected of playing an important role in Germany's defeat

51

and surrender. The foremost example of hostility toward Jews was the murder of Walter Rathenau, who was accused of ruining Germany's war economy, and who was disliked for his "treasonous" advocacy of a friendship treaty with Russia, the Treaty of Rapallo.[6]

Suspicions of Jewish treachery were further promoted by the disporportionate percentage of Jews among leading German and foreign revolutionaries during the German Revolution of 1918–1919.[7] Spartacists, the USPD, the KPD, and the revolutionary councils had extremely high percentages of Jews in their memberships, even though the majority of Germany's Jews were not revolutionary. According to Merkl, a vast wave of rabid and virulent Jew-hatred, or *Judenkoller*, affected many future Nazis because of their contempt for "Jewish revolutionaries."[8] Jews were suspected of importing and implanting alien bolshevism on German soil. Even though Jews had always been considered, in varying degrees, "alien" even by their supporters, the activity of Jews as leaders in the revolution lent a practical dimension to what had previously been a more abstract concept.

After the revolution, Jews were very active in the early Weimar government at federal, state, and local levels.[9] Later, during the years of the republic, they became influential primarily in areas that were controlled by the SPD, especially Prussia. The early prominence of Jews thus fostered the public identification of Jews with the new and unpopular Weimar "system"; they were thought to have been overly influential in the adoption of new, foreign, and unwanted democratic institutions.

As indicated above, between 1918 and 1922 about 100,000 Eastern European Jews immigrated to Germany. Of these, many were transients who eventually settled outside of Germany, but the specter of enormous increases in the number of Jews from Poland and Russia was frightful to many Germans and even to a great number of German Jews.[10] The arrival of these immigrants, who were not only foreign but also Jewish, accentuated postwar anti-Semitism.

Still another source of anti-Semitism was the popular belief that Jews had been highly active as war profiteers between 1914 and

1918, and that they had promoted or gained from postwar inflation by questionable activities as financiers and middlemen.[11] Anti-Semites eagerly compiled statistics on Jewish criminal activity, both real and bogus, to buttress their arguments. A more general cause of increased anti-Semitism was the very strong and unfortunate propensity of dissident Jews to attack national institutions and customs in both socialist and nonsocialist publications.[12]

Since we are dealing with belief systems rather than with quantifiable data, we cannot be certain why these various suppositions activated racist sentiments among some Germans. Still, because of the many factors contributing to anti-Semitism between 1914 and 1924, this decade was probably the most seminal and potentially destructive breeding period for rabid political anti-Semites in German history. There is some empirical evidence to support the hypothesis that the war and immediate postwar years bred a new type of anti-Semite who was more dangerous than any prewar racist.[13] The paramount example, of course, was Hitler himself. Whatever his conscious or subconscious attitudes toward Jews may have been before 1914, it is abundantly clear that these came to fruition only after his disappointment at Germany's defeat in the war and (simultaneously) with the unrest that occurred during and after the revolution. It was during the years 1920 to 1924 that Hitler integrated into his consistent, barbaric world view the Jews' ostensible responsibility for the war, Germany's defeat, and the revolution.[14]

## ANTI-SEMITISM IN THE EARLY NAZI PARTY

One would naturally predict that the enthusiastic racists who shared Hitler's rabid anti-Semitism would have joined the NSDAP quite early, given Hitler's strongly anti-Semitic early rhetoric (1920–1924). Yet surprisingly few of the top Nazi leaders were virulent anti-Semites before 1925. None of the more prominent men in the Nazi party joined it primarily because of anti-Semitism. This was true of Joseph Goebbels, head of the Propaganda Ministry; Heinrich Himmler, leader of the SS; Hermann Goering, the second man under Hitler; Hans Frank, governor of Poland; the Strasser brothers, early party organizers; Baldur Schirach, leader of the Hitler Youth; Albert Speer, Hitler's architect and minister of armaments; Gottfried Feder, an early party ideologist; and Adolf Eichmann, the SS officer who arranged the transport of millions of European Jews to their deaths. The major Nazi leaders of later importance who were rabid anti-Semites in the early 1920s were Hitler himself; Julius Streicher, who published the anti-Semitic *Der Stürmer*; and Alfred Rosenberg, Nazi ideologist and later head of the East Ministry for occupied territories. Anti-Semitism became a fundamental issue of practical importance among other top Nazi leaders only during the later 1920s and subsequent years. Hermann Rauschning concluded that "To the great majority of the Nazi clique of leaders the whole racial doctrine is 'Adolf's buntcum' (sic)."[15] In short, many Nazi leaders simply accepted anti-Semitism as part of the baggage of Nazism—in the bargain for other things.[16]

One may legitimately speculate that this may also have been true of the average party member and voter. According to some historians and some Nazis, acceptance of national-socialist ideology was never uniform, nor did the Nazis intend it to be so.[17] This was perceived quite clearly by German socialists who underestimated the danger of anti-Semitism because they thought that only a few racist leaders really believed what they said about the Jews.[18] Jews were certainly not alone in their conviction that Hitler's rise to power was not synonymous with their own destruction.

Given the horrendous mistreatment and later destruction of Jews between 1933 and 1945, these indications of great diversity in the intensity of anti-Semitic prejudice among party leaders appear paradoxical. If NSDAP leaders were indeed divided in their attitudes toward Jews, we should pose our second question: How did anti-Semitism appeal to early Nazis in the rank and file? In order to determine the degree of anti-Semitism among early party members, we can examine Peter Merkl's intriguing analysis of 581 early Nazis whose biographies were solicited by Theodore Abel in 1932. The FBI later seized about 100 of the original 681 records and they now appear lost; however, the remaining 581 cases are very informative.[19] Merkl's book is a tour de force of considerable interest to scholars and general readers because it provides insight into many of the characteristics and attitudes of Nazi "pioneers"—those who were active until 1934, before the bandwagon effect and the coerced membership. It is especially noteworthy because it contains excellent data on causes, types, and degrees of anti-Semitism within the Nazi party.

According to Merkl's study there were six types of anti-Semites and one group that demonstrated no prejudice. In order to highlight differences between groups on the basis of degrees of anti-Semitism and to obtain larger numbers for comparative purposes, I shall condense these groups into four categories: mild, moderate, and paranoid anti-Semites, and a "no evidence" category. The term "paranoid" is used despite objections from several readers of the manuscript version of this book simply because this is Merkl's word of choice and it is used throughout his book. The categories "mild," "moderate," and "paranoid" anti-Semites are used for two reasons. First, mild and paranoid anti-Semites were quite different, so they must be treated separately. Second, moderate anti-Semites were more similar to each other than to either mild or paranoid anti-Semites. Moderate anti-Semites include Merkl's "choleric" and "anecdotal" anti-Semites who were confirmed bigots, but who did not threaten "countermeasures" against Jews. The "no evidence" category must be treated separately because they showed no signs of prejudice and, according to Merkl, were probably not anti-Semitic.[20]

Table 2.1 shows the percentages of anti-Semites and the "no evidence" category as they were classified by Merkl and as they will be classified in this analysis.[21] When examining this table several facts become clear. Those demonstrating no evidence of prejudice comprised a third of Merkl's sample. If these individuals were, as Merkl suspects, not genuine anti-Semites, or even if they were similar in outlook to mild anti-Semites, early Nazi party members who were fairly uninterested in the "Jewish question" comprised 48 percent, or nearly half of Merkl's sample. However, a large 29 percent of the early Nazi party members underwent sudden and virulent (choleric) Jew-hatred in the face of war,

TABLE 2.1 Classification of Early Nazi Anti-Semites

| | Merkl's Classification | | | New Classification | |
|---|---|---|---|---|---|
| | Number | Percentage | | Number | Percentage |
| No evidence | 146 | 33.3 | No evidence | 146 | 100.0 |
| Mild verbal projections, party clichés | 63 | 14.3 | Mild | 63 | 21.4 |
| Judenkoller from cultural shock, 1918 | 84 | 19.1 | Moderate | | |
| Judenkoller from economic or personal crises | 38 | 8.6 | Moderate | 174 | 59.2 |
| Anecdotal episodes | 43 | 9.8 | Moderate | | |
| Anecdotal episodes with sex angle | 9 | 2.0 | Moderate | | |
| Paranoid; threats of "countermeasures" | 57 | 12.9 | Paranoid | 57 | 19.4 100.0 |

NOTE: *Judenkoller* refers to sudden adoption of virulent anti-Semitism.

defeat, and revolution. This indicates that real or fallacious suppositions regarding Jewish activities during these years were a powerful catalyst in the formation of anti-Semitism. Paranoids who advocated "countermeasures" against Jews comprised nearly one-fifth of all anti-Semites, but according to Merkl they were quite vague about the specifics of these measures, generally favoring quotas in professions or a halt to immigration.[22] The majority, or nearly 60 percent of all anti-Semites, were moderates, that is, confirmed but nonaggressive bigots.

56

As indicated earlier, rabid anti-Semitism was not the norm for party leaders in the early 1920s, and it does not appear to have been the norm even for pre-1933 recruits. According to Merkl, however, paranoid anti-Semites later progressed most quickly and to the highest levels of the NSDAP, just as the rabid anti-Semites Hitler, Streicher, and later Goebbels and Himmler set the pace for anti-Semitic measures in the Third Reich.[23]

It may be of some interest to determine how specific groups (age, sex, and residential, religious, occupational, or educational groups) differed from one another in degrees of anti-Semitism. For this purpose it is necessary to regroup and interpret much of Merkl's original data on anti-Semites. This allows us to discover significant differences between anti-Semites and the "no evidence" category according to their respective socioeconomic characteristics. We concern ourselves here only with significant differences, namely, those that would not be attributable merely to chance.[24] Because this was not a random sample, these results are indicative rather than definitive and are of value primarily to isolate extreme and unusual results.

From Merkl's data it is possible to create prototypes of early Nazis who were overrepresented or underrepresented among anti-Semites, as presented in table 2.2.[25] When we compare the total sample of anti-Semites to the "no evidence" category in table 2.2, we find that Nazis aged 17–38 were underrepresented among anti-Semites, while Nazis aged 49 and over were overrepresented.[26] This is in accord with Merkl's conclusion that older Nazis displayed more anti-Semitic prejudice than did younger Nazis.[27] This difference is most important in the cases of moderate and paranoid anti-Semites. Nazis over age 48, and to a lesser extent those aged 39–48, were overrepresented among moderate anti-Semites, i.e., the category that comprised around 60 percent of all anti-Semites.[28] Nazis aged 49–55 were not only overrepresented among moderate anti-Semites, but also they were the only age group that was overrepresented among paranoid anti-Semites. In general we can conclude that older Nazis were the most prejudiced of the "pioneers."

Additional support for this conclusion is found by comparing

TABLE 2.2 A. Socioeconomic Groups Overrepresented among Early Nazi Anti-Semites

| | Total Sample | Mild | Moderate | Paranoid |
|---|---|---|---|---|
| Age | 49+ | 56+, 17–31[a] | 49+, 39–48[a] | 49–55 |
| Sex | F[b] | M or F | F[b] | M or F |
| Residence | Urban | Urban | Urban | Urban |
| Religion | P[b] | Pr | C or Pr | P[a] |
| Religious area of residence | None | None | P[b] | M |
| Occupation | WCW, BP[a], MCS[b] | WCW | WCW, MCS, BP[a] | WCW, BP |
| Father's occupation | MCS | MSC | None | MCS |
| Education | Sec., Univ.[a] | Univ. | Sec. | Univ., Sec.[b] |

B. Socioeconomic Groups Underrepresented among Early Nazi Anti-Semites

| | Total Sample | Mild | Moderate | Paranoid |
|---|---|---|---|---|
| Age | 17–31, 32–38[a] | 49–55, 32–48[b] | 17–31, 32–38 | 17–31[a] |
| Sex | M[b] | M or F | M[b] | M or F |
| Residence | R, MS | R, MS | R, MS | R |
| Religion | C[b] | C | C or Pr | C[a] |
| Religious area of residence | C[b] | None | None | C |
| Occupation | FR, BCW | FR[a], BCW[b] | FR, BCW | FR, BCW |
| Father's occupation | Fr | B/WCW, A[b] | None | Fr |
| Education | P | P[a] | P | P |

[a] Slight overrepresentation (probability between .13 and .17)
[b] Very slight overrepresentation (probability between .18 and .22)
NOTE: M-male, F-female, Pr-Protestant, C-Catholic, M-mixed, WCW-white-collar worker, BP-business-professional, FR-farmer, A-artisan, MCS-military-civil servant, Sec.-secondary, P-primary, Univ.-university, R-rural, MS-middle-sized, B/WCW-blue- or white-collar worker.

the age distribution of anti-Semites to that of all Nazi party members in 1933.[29] Anti-Semites in Merkl's sample (table 2.3) had a significantly lower percentage of 17 to 31-year-olds and a significantly higher percentage of individuals aged 56 and over than was true for the Nazi party as a whole.

What sense can we make of our comparisons of age and anti-Semitism within the Merkl sample? We know that the majority

TABLE 2.3 Age Distribution of the NSDAP and Anti-Semites in Merkl's Sample, 1933 (*in percentages*)

| Age Anti-Semites | Age NSDAP | NSDAP | Anti-Semites | Prob.[a] |
|---|---|---|---|---|
| 17–31 | 18–30 | 42.7 | 31.0 | −4.03 |
| 32–38 | 31–40 | 27.2 | 25.5 | |
| 39–48 | 41–50 | 17.2 | 23.4 | .005 |
| 49–55 | 50–60 | 9.3 | 10.0 | |
| 56+ | 60+ | 3.6 | 10.0 | 5.85 |

SOURCES: Numbers of anti-Semites in each age group are in appendix B, table B.1. Age distribution of the NSDAP is calculated from Peter Merkl, *Political Violence under the Swastika*, 15.

[a] Probabilities are computed using test statistic A (see appendix A).

of those who were overrepresented among anti-Semites were 49 and older. We shall assume that most of these individuals were between 49 and 69 because those over 69 were unlikely to have been a large percentage of the age group "56 and over." We shall also assume that most individuals form their political outlook in their twenties. On these assumptions, we shall hypothesize that the majority of the age groups that were overrepresented among anti-Semites formed their political views between 1884 and 1914. What significance do these dates have?

In the earlier discussion of political anti-Semitism (see chapter 1) we found that although some historians disagree on the question of whether political anti-Semitism succeeded or failed during these years, they all believe that intellectual and social anti-Semitism became more pronounced before 1914.[30] Overrepresentation of individuals aged 49 and over among anti-Semites in Merkl's sample lends indirect support for this belief. It is ironic that 49 to 55-year-olds, who composed the age group that was overrepresented as paranoid anti-Semites, formed their political views between 1898 and 1914. These years are generally considered fairly free of political anti-Semitism even by those who think it was strong in prewar years. Nevertheless, the results from Merkl's data support the theory that intellectual and social anti-Semitism gained firm ground during the Wilhelminian period, at least among those anti-Semites who joined the Nazi party by 1934.

59

Extreme differences in degrees of anti-Semitism among males and females are not apparent. Comparing the sample of anti-Semites to the "no evidence" category, the only significant difference is a slight tendency for women to be overrepresented among moderate anti-Semites and in the total sample; since this category included 60 percent of all anti-Semites, this result may reflect greater anti-Semitism among women.[31]

Anti-Semites with all levels of prejudice tended to be urban residents rather than residents of small or medium-sized areas.[32] Lower levels of anti-Semitism among rural or small-town residents and residents of middle-sized towns is an important finding pointed out by Merkl.[33] It is of additional interest to note the preponderance of urban residents among more serious (moderate and paranoid) anti-Semites. Many historians believe the typical Nazi voter resided in rural or middle-sized areas.[34] This certainly may have been true of voters; however, if residents from rural and middle-sized areas supported the NSDAP in disproportionate numbers compared to urban dwellers, they do not appear to have done so specifically *because* of anti-Semitism. The small percentage of anti-Semites from rural and middle-sized areas in Merkl's sample indicates that they joined the Nazi party primarily for other reasons. Heberle's study of Schleswig-Holstein does illustrate the presence of anti-Semitism in rural areas; however, it also demonstrates the highly efficient Nazi campaign among farmers that was directed toward their more concrete economic and political aspirations.[35] There was a great deal of hostility toward Jewish cattle traders in rural areas, both before and after Hitler's appointment as chancellor, but this alone did not lead to wholesale acceptance of anti-Semitism in rural areas. Likewise, although there were pockets of anti-Semitism in middle-sized cities, Jews were well assimilated in local economic life, frequently in respected professions, so that non-Nazi attacks on Jews were rare; general levels of anti-Semitism were lower than in large cities where Jews, particularly Eastern Jews, were more numerous, less assimilated, and less respected. For example, Berlin, which had the largest percentage of Jews of any German city, contained almost half of the paranoid anti-Semites in Merkl's sample.[36] Familiarity or propinquity apparently bred contempt.

Protestants had a slight tendency to be overrepresented among anti-Semites in the total sample. They were also slightly more likely than Catholics to be either mild or paranoid anti-Semites, whereas Protestants and Catholics were equally likely to be moderate anti-Semites. The slight tendency of Protestants to adopt mild or paranoid anti-Semitism is indirectly supported by the later bifurcation of the Protestant clergy into two groups, one (Confessing church) that disagreed with Hitler's racial policies and one (German Christians) that supported them. This tendency of Protestants to adopt paranoid attitudes toward Jews may account for the disproportionate drawing power of Nazis in these areas.[37] It may also have been due to the fact that Jews lived predominately in Protestant rather than Catholic areas, and that this resulted in more competition and anti-Semitism. Most Jews lived in Prussia, where 64 percent of the population was Protestant. In Berlin, which contained the highest percentage of both Jews and paranoid anti-Semites, 71 percent of the population was Protestant;[38] yet because only 17 percent of the early Nazis indicated a religious preference, these findings should be considered merely indicative.[39]

When we compare anti-Semites to the Nazis in the "no evidence" category by occupation, we find that white-collar workers were overrepresented in the total sample and within each category of anti-Semites;[40] that is, white-collar workers were the most extremely anti-Semitic occupational group. Business-professionals were next in order of anti-Semitic prejudice, as they were significantly overrepresented among paranoids and slightly overrepresented among moderate anti-Semites. In contrast, military-civil servants were overrepresented among moderate but not among paranoid anti-Semites.

The attitudes of blue-collar workers and farmers were strikingly different from those of white-collar workers, business-professionals, or military-civil servants. Blue-collar workers and farmers were significantly underrepresented in the total sample, among moderate and paranoid anti-Semites, and to a limited extent among mild anti-Semites. These results lend support to the generally accepted theory that the middle classes were more anti-Semitic than the lower classes.[41] It should be noted, however, that the small sample of blue-collar workers makes any strong conclusion impossible.

Another indication of "class" differences is the occupation of the fathers of anti-Semites. Anti-Semites had a significantly higher percentage of fathers who were military-civil servants than did the Nazis in the "no evidence" category.[42] It should be noted that Nazis whose fathers were military-civil servants were significantly overrepresented among both mild and paranoid anti-Semites. Nazis whose fathers were farmers were significantly underrepresented among paranoids as well as in the total sample.[43] Nazis with blue-collar or white-collar fathers were underrepresented among mild anti-Semites, but not in the total sample. Having middle-class fathers obviously did not predispose early Nazis to become anti-Semites, except that Nazis whose fathers were military-civil servants were more likely than others to be paranoid anti-Semites.

On the other hand, it is clear that highly educated Nazis, who should probably be classified as "middle class," were more anti-Semitic than less-educated Nazis. Compared to the "no evidence" category, Nazis with secondary or university education were overrepresented among anti-Semites.[44] More particularly, Nazis with primary education were underrepresented among all three categories of anti-Semites. Early Nazis with secondary education were overrepresented among moderate anti-Semites, the category that included nearly 60 percent of all the anti-Semites in Merkl's sample. They also had a slight tendency to be overrepresented among paranoid anti-Semites. Nazis with university education were overrepresented among both mild and paranoid anti-Semites, which demonstrates a "split" in their attitudes toward Jews. This lends support to the theory that although the middle classes adopted intellectual anti-Semitism more readily than did Germans with only primary education, they also contained a minority who were more sympathetic toward Jews than were Germans with secondary education.

Thus it appears that the widely held theory that middle classes were more anti-Semitic than other classes is supported by Merkl's data on anti-Semitism among early Nazis with middle-class occupations, military-civil servant fathers, and "middle-class" educational levels. At least during the early years of the party (before 1934), Nazis in middle-class occupations (military-civil servants, business-professionals, and particularly white-collar workers) were more likely to be overrepresented among anti-Semites than were Nazis with blue-collar occupations. Although farmers are also normally classified as middle class, they were underrepresented among anti-Semites. In addition, children of farmers who joined the early NSDAP were also underrepresented, so the theory of middle-class anti-Semitism holds only for three occupational groups.

One should not, moreover, conclude from these results that the middle classes as a whole can be stereotyped as anti-Semites. To highlight this, we should examine the distribution of middle and lower classes according to levels of anti-Semitism,[45] as shown in table 2.4. Several observations can be made about this comparison. First, it is clear that 74 percent of the middle-class Nazis and 58 percent of the lower-class Nazis demonstrated some degree of anti-Semitism. Second, the chief sources of this overall difference were the higher percentage of the lower class giving no evidence of prejudice and the high percentage of the middle class who were moderate (but not paranoid) anti-Semites. And third, within *both* the middle class and lower class there was a broad spectrum of attitudes toward Jews. Therefore, neither class can be simplistically stereotyped as rabid anti-Semites, particularly because 39 percent of the middle class and 57 percent of the lower

TABLE 2.4 Distribution of Middle and Lower Classes by Levels of Anti-Semitism (*in percentages*)

|  | No evidence | Mild | Moderate | Paranoid | Total |
|---|---|---|---|---|---|
| Middle class | 26 | 13 | 46 | 15 | 100 |
| Lower class | 42 | 15 | 31 | 12 | 100 |

class showed no evidence of anti-Semitism or were mild anti-Semites. These results justify only the conclusion that the middle class as a whole had higher percentages of anti-Semites, particularly moderate anti-Semites (confirmed bigots, but not rabid Jew-haters of Hitler's ilk) than had the lower class.

The same caution should be applied to any other group that was overrepresented among anti-Semites in Merkl's sample, for example urban residents, or Nazis with secondary or university education. These groups were overrepresented among anti-Semites when compared to the "no evidence" category, but this does not mean the groups as a whole were anti-Semitic. For example, of the 243 urban residents in Merkl's sample, 65, or 27 percent, showed no evidence of prejudice even though urban residents were overrepresented when compared to the "no evidence" category.[46] Overrepresentation only indicates that some groups (age, residential, religious, occupational, etc.) had a significantly larger percentage of anti-Semites than the "no evidence" category and that this cannot be attributed to chance.[47] This should not lead one to stereotype middle classes, or Protestants, or urban residents, or university graduates, or any other group as uniformly anti-Semitic.

It should also be pointed out that lower levels of anti-Semitism among a particular age, sex, religious, occupational, or educational group do not necessarily imply "moral superiority." For example, the lower class had far fewer professional or occupational contacts with Jews, as well as less direct economic competition with them, and these conditions may have reduced their concern about the "Jewish problem."[48] In contrast, a large percentage of Jews had middle-class occupations in which business contacts and competition may have antagonized normal relations, particularly during economic crises between 1918 and 1924 and after 1929.[49] Middle-class anti-Semitism may have had less to do with genuine hatred of Jews per se (which is the mark of a genuine anti-Semite) than with middle-class resentment of *all* competitors during periods of economic crises. Unfortunately, extreme overrepresentation of Jews in middle-class occupations made them a visible target for middle-class special interest groups that wanted to eliminate competition. And of course, the desire for "quotas" in given occupations or educational institutions was hardly unique to middle-class Germans. The establishment of occupational "quotas" does not necessarily imply genocidal intentions, no matter how disagreeable it is to true believers in equal opportunities. Thus one cannot assume that anti-Semitism among middle classes who resented economic competition from Jews was synonymous with their desire to build gas ovens to annihilate Jews.

There is a wealth of other interesting information on early Nazis and anti-Semitism in Merkl's book. We shall consider only a fraction of it here. Merkl and other historians have pointed out the large number of *völkisch* anti-Semites who joined the NSDAP during the early 1920s.[50] Although the Nazi party only had a membership of 108,717 in 1928, an in-gathering of the most prejudiced anti-Semites was in the party and frequently came from *völkisch* homes or schools.[51] Adult experiences that shaped the prejudice of anti-Semites included their reactions to war, revolution, and the new Weimar leaders. Anti-Semites as a whole tended to blame the old regime and its leadership for the war and defeat, but choleric and paranoid anti-Semites blamed Jews.[52] On the other hand, anti-Semites as a whole blamed Jews for the revolution.[53] More particularly, cholerics and paranoids felt that the revolution played an important part in their formative experiences.[54] As indicated earlier, 29 percent of the anti-Semites underwent a sudden outbreak of *Judenkoller* from cultural shock in 1918–1919.[55] And in Merkl's sources, 30 percent of the early Nazis viewed the Weimar Republic as a state run by Jews.[56]

Given that *völkisch* backgrounds and *Judenkoller* predisposed anti-Semites to join the Nazi party, what did anti-Semites expect the NSDAP to do regarding the "Jewish question?"[57] If we look at the anti-Semites as a group, they apparently did *not* envision freeing Europe of Jews, but instead hoped for German imperialist resurgence, socioeconomic recovery, and individual payoffs for themselves.[58] Ironically, it was the imperialists rather than the anti-Semites who dreamed of freeing Europe of Jews and Marxists.[59] There might be several reasons for this anomaly. The imperialists may have associated national resurgence with attacks

65

on Poland and Russia, both of which they considered dominated by Jews and Marxists. Those who wanted individual payoffs may have considered confiscation of Jewish property the easiest route to their own personal gain. And those who wanted social and economic recovery may have accepted the Nazi propaganda that ascribed Germany's social and economic problems almost entirely to Jews. Merkl himself offers what he describes as a farfetched theory to explain the fact that paranoids did not envision freeing Europe of Jews, namely "that the persecution and genocide was not part of the old fighters' expectations in 1934 and that it was in fact closely linked to the imperialist drive to the East."[60] The theory may be farfetched, but that does not necessarily make it erroneous. At a later point we shall consider this question in relation to expectations of Nazi voters.

That severe measures against Jews were not anticipated does not mean that anti-Semitism was unimportant to early Nazis. Although only 13 percent of Merkl's sample threatened counter-measures against Jews, 40 percent were still moderate anti-Semites. Thus 53 percent of Merkl's sample expressed a dislike of Jews. Another 14 percent were only mild verbal anti-Semites, and 33 percent showed no prejudice.[61] We conclude, therefore, that approximately half of the sample were genuinely hostile toward Jews and approximately half were not. This diversity of anti-Semitic prejudice and the expectations of anti-Semites in 1934 are consistent with the assertions of other historians that party members had no uniform attitude toward Jews and no clear conception or anticipation of the severe persecution and genocide that followed. Moreover, with the possible exception of paranoids, it is not clear from Merkl's study that other anti-Semites joined the party primarily *because* of anti-Semitism. After all, very few individuals in any society would join a political party for only one reason. All political parties offer a host of issues in their party platforms specifically to lure new members. The Nazi party was expert at this technique, offering something for everyone even when its promises were clearly contradictory. One need not conclude that because there were anti-Semites in the Nazi party, party members had joined with a preconceived determination to attack Jews on a personal and regular basis.

## NAZI ANTI-SEMITIC PROPAGANDA AFTER 1927

There are conflicting views on levels of anti-Semitism in Germany after the postwar surge of hostility toward Jews. Anti-Semitism was apparently strong among the DNVP, Farmers' League, Bavarian People's party, *völkisch* groups, counterrevolutionaries, civil servants, the army, and even some liberals who opposed "Jewish self-segregation."[62] For example, Jews could sue for slander, as they did against Streicher; however, courts generally imposed lenient sentences in such cases.[63] Nevertheless, few personal attacks on Jews or Jewish property were launched by non-Nazi Germans during Weimar years.[64] In some areas there was clearly popular opposition to Nazi anti-Jewish activities.[65] In general, historians describe the years from 1924 to 1929 as a period with little overt anti-Semitism.[66]

Given the absence of overt anti-Semitism outside of the Nazi party, how successful was Nazi anti-Semitic propaganda with the electorate? According to Bracher, Nazi anti-Semitic propaganda had three major themes: Jews were the mainstays and beneficiaries of exploitive capitalism; Jews were the major proponents of Marxian socialism and internationalism; and Jews were engaged in a worldwide conspiracy against national and "Aryan" racial interests.[67] To support these charges, Nazis relied upon historical sentiments of religious anti-Semitism among the peasantry;[68] among city dwellers they used attacks on Jewish capitalism;[69] and among conservatives they appealed to nationalist sentiments.[70] Mainly, however, the adjective "Jewish" was tacked onto supposed evils that were attacked by the Nazis. Of course, this had enormous tactical advantages.[71]

The NSDAP was not the only party that appealed to anti-Semitism. Some writers believe that the DNVP vied with the Nazis in economic anti-Semitism, and the Bavarian People's party and others sometimes used anti-Semitic propaganda.[72] Even so, the Nazis were more consistent in their anti-Semitic themes because

67

they had a brand of anti-Semitism for every class and for every cause; it was the common denominator that united contradictory Nazi promises.

Although Nazi election posters were strongly anti-Semitic, anti-Semitism was seldom used as a propaganda technique in and of itself; it was generally tied to other issues.[73] For example, among propaganda pamphlets used by the NSDAP in 1928, anti-Semitism was not a major theme,[74] and, according to several historians, there was little anti-Semitic propaganda before the critical election of 1930.[75] Hackett searched archives for a representative sample of 1930 election propaganda and found that anti-Semitism was not a major campaign theme even at this time.[76] Using word frequency as a test among twenty-eight campaign leaflets, he found the results given in table 2.5.[77] Jews were mentioned much less than half as often as the word-group average (forty-seven times). There were, however, posters that tied Jews to socialists, Weimar leaders, Versailles, the Young Plan, unemployment, corruption, and profiteering.[78]

Hackett also claimed that Hitler's speeches for 1930 did not deal with the "Jewish question," especially if the audience was comprised of upper-middle classes.[79] In October 1930 Hitler even proclaimed that he had nothing against "decent" Jews and discountenanced violent anti-Semitism.[80] He particularly avoided any discussion of future measures against Jews.[81] His speech before major industrialists in Düsseldorf during 1932 also omitted anti-Semitic references.[82] Jews were hardly mentioned in Hitler's ma-

TABLE 2.5 Word Frequency of Campaign Leaflets, 1930 Election

| People | 83 | Jews | 37 |
|---|---|---|---|
| German | 75 | Lies | 37 |
| SPD | 74 | Taxes | 35 |
| Civil servants | 56 | Hitler | 35 |
| Workers | 50 | Germany | 31 |
| Young Plan | 49 | Unemployment | 27 |
| Center party, | | Parties | 25 |
| Bavarian People's | | | |
| party | 45 | | |

jor speeches from January 1932 to January 1933.[83] According to Domarus, the compiler of his early speeches, Hitler never directly announced his intentions for Jews before 1939; the same view is shared by another compiler, Baynes.[84]

Apparently, even though anti-Semitic propaganda attracted bigots to the early Nazi party, it did not have strong drawing power among the electorate; consequently, Hitler toned down his anti-Semitism to win votes after 1928.[85] The view of the years between 1930 and 1932 as fairly low in Nazi anti-Semitic propaganda is shared by several other historians.[86] There are, however, historians who believe that there was an upsurge of anti-Semitic propaganda between 1929 and 1933.[87] Some believe that Goebbels became more bellicose in his anti-Semitic propaganda between 1928 and 1933, particularly because he was trying to capture anti-Semitic elements in the Berlin working class. These apparent discrepancies in historians' interpretations are probably reconcilable. Even though Hitler himself may have toned down his anti-Semitic propaganda, Goebbels and other party leaders may have increased it between 1930 and 1933. Existing sources do not permit a definitive conclusion on this issue.

The best summary of the appeal of anti-Semitic propaganda is made by Pridham in his study of Nazis in Bavaria:

> The party's racialist ideology had a public impact in so far as it related to circumstances. Anti-semitism had received an impetus in Munich after the War, because it became linked with anti-Communism through the experience of the revolutionary left-wing regimes there in 1918–1919. The broad mass of Nazi voters in the early 1930's were not conscious racialists, for they were motivated primarily by political and economic discontent. But in some areas the NSDAP's exploitation of discontent was reinforced by anti-semitic propaganda, depending on whether feeling against the Jews was based on a tradition there or was provoked by economic competition. Much depended on the public's consciousness of the party's racialism. Conscious anti-semites were more likely to be found among Nazi activists than Nazi voters. The possibility of the NSDAP

69

alienating public support by the violence of its anti-semitism was diminished by the tactics of party propagandists, but more generally by the fact that the party's anti-Semitism was at this time largely an abstraction, apart from physical attacks by individual Nazis on Jews. Although they had warnings in the racialist hatred of Nazi speakers, who made threats about the position of the Jews in the future Nazi state, the majority of voters did not seem to realize how seriously the Nazis meant to put their ideas into practice as part of their programme of social as well as political change.[88]

And Needler says: "The point is, I think, that it was not anti-Semitism itself which gained Hitler votes; but anti-Semitism made possible the other features of the Nazi program, those which actually attracted voters."[89] Schoenbaum, in particular, views Nazi success as the product of a universal desire for change.[90]

A number of other historians do not ascribe Hitler's electoral success to anti-Semitism.[91] They especially do not believe that a vote for the NSDAP was a vote to persecute or murder Jews. The apparent reason for this is that a large number of historians think there was no general awareness of Hitler's intentions either among non-Jews or Jews.[92] Earlier we cited Merkl's evidence that anti-Semites in the early NSDAP did not in 1934 expect the elimination of Jews from Europe.[93] This finding is consistent with the belief of many historians that despite open hostility toward Jews in Nazi propaganda, there was no clear conception of Nazi goals among the general public. It is probable that supporters of Nazism hoped the Nazis would deal with Jews in whatever manner the individuals themselves desired. One may speculate that the open-endedness of anti-Semitic propaganda was a deliberate ploy. Any definitive statement of future plans might have alienated either mild, moderate, or paranoid anti-Semites, depending on their degrees of prejudice and the severity of the plans, and only by evasive tactics could Nazis use anti-Semitism as a genuine common denominator.

Regardless of Nazi voters' interpretations of Nazi anti-Semitism and their expectations of future measures against Jews, 37.4 percent of the valid votes in the free election of July 1932 went to the NSDAP.[94] Those Germans who voted for Hitler obviously knew that some measures would be taken against Jews, and in that sense they acquiesced to the possibility of future persecution, even if they were drawn to the Nazi party for other reasons. Anti-Semitism may not have been the major drawing card of the Nazis among the electorate, but neither was it a deterrent to their success.

NAZI VOTERS

This leads up to our fourth question, Who voted for Hitler, and was anti-Semitism their primary motivation? To examine this issue, we should review the sources of Nazi electoral support to determine which Germans appear to have accepted his more general propaganda and promises. Table 2.6 (compiled by Seymour M. Lipset) represents the total vote received by various parties between 1928 and 1933, plus the percentage of 1928 votes retained in the last free election of November, 1932.[95] From the data in this table Lipset concludes that the biggest Nazi electoral gains were at the expense of middle-class parties. They lost approximately 80 percent of their 1928 support by 1932. The DNVP, while suffering very significant losses in 1930 and in July 1932, was able to regain an even higher percentage of total votes in November 1932 than it had in 1930. Between 1928 and November 1932, the DNVP lost 40 percent of its electoral support compared to 80 percent lost by middle-class parties and 8 percent lost by workers' parties. Since the total vote went up between 1928 and 1932, the SPD-KPD vote as a percentage appears to have fallen, but in absolute numbers it actually *increased* by about 600,000 over this period. Yet the total increase in NSDAP votes was 1,277 percent! Increases in support for the KPD and NSDAP are often cited as evidence of the radicalization of politics in the face of economic and political crises between 1930 and 1933; however, it is obvious that this shift was far more beneficial to the Nazis than to the KPD.

According to Lipset, the overall gains and losses of votes between 1928 and 1930 were due primarily to shifts of votes from middle-class parties to the Nazis, and only secondarily to Nazi

71

TABLE 2.6 Percentages of Total Vote Received by Various German Parties, 1928–1933, and Percentage of 1928 Vote Retained in Last Free Election, 1932

| Party | | Percentage of Total | | | | Ratio of 1928 to second 1932 election expressed as a percentage |
|---|---|---|---|---|---|---|
| | | | July | Nov. | | |
| Conservative | 1928 | 1930 | 1932 | 1932 | 1933 | |
| party | | | | | | |
| DNVP | 14.2 | 7.0 | 5.9 | 8.5 | 8.0 | 60 |
| Middle-class parties | | | | | | |
| DVP (Right liberals) | 8.7 | 4.85 | 1.2 | 1.8 | 1.1 | 21 |
| DDP (Left liberals) | 4.8 | 3.45 | 1.0 | 0.95 | 0.8 | 20 |
| Wirtschaftspartei (small business) | 4.5 | 3.9 | 0.4 | 0.3 | 0ᵃ | 7 |
| Others | 9.5 | 10.1 | 2.6 | 2.8 | 0.6 | 29 |
| Total proportion of middle-class vote: | | | | | | 21 |
| Center (Catholic) | 15.4 | 17.6 | 16.7 | 16.2 | 15.0 | 105 |
| Workers' parties | | | | | | |
| SPD (Socialist) | 29.8 | 24.5 | 21.6 | 20.4 | 18.3 | 69 |
| KPD (Communist) | 10.6 | 13.1 | 14.3 | 16.85 | 12.3 | 159 |
| Total proportion of working-class vote: | | | | | | 92 |
| Fascist party | | | | | | |
| NSDAP | 2.6 | 18.3 | 37.3 | 33.1 | 43.9 | 1277 |
| Total proportion of Fascist party vote: | | | | | | 1277 |

SOURCE: Seymour Martin Lipset, *Political Man*, 139; see also Samuel Pratt, "The Social Basis of Nazism and Communism in Urban Germany," 29, 30. The same data are presented and analyzed in Karl Dietrich Bracher, *Die Auflösung der Weimarer Republik*, 86–106.

ᵃ The *Wirtschaftspartei* did not run any candidates in the 1933 election.

gains from the DNVP and new or previous nonvoters.[96] Some scholars have challenged Lipset's conclusions for the 1930 election, claiming that new voters and previous nonvoters accounted for a larger portion of Nazi gains than did voters from middle-class parties.[97] O'Lessker maintains that the DNVP was a large source of gains for the Nazis in 1930. He estimates major sources of Nazi support as follows: 38 percent from the DNVP, 32 percent from new and previous nonvoters, and 23 percent from the non-Catholic middle class.[98] Winkler believes that many previous supporters of middle class parties switched to the DNVP before opting for the Nazis.[99] Weber and Jones also believe Nazi voters came from parties in which they had only short-term affiliations.[100] O'Lessker, Hamilton, and Winkler question Lipset's theory of "extremism of the middle," especially for the 1930 election; on the other hand, they and many others agree that the middle classes gave the NSDAP electoral support in the 1932 elections, although Hamilton would confine this by and large to the upper-middle class.

What were the characteristics of new voters, previous nonvoters, and middle-class voters who supported the NSDAP? New voters were apparently disproportionately young and female. According to one estimate for Nuremberg, 62 percent of new voters were under the age of forty and of these 61 percent were female.[101] Females represented 58 percent of new voters under age 30;[102] thus, new voters were predominately young females.

Hackett reported that previous nonvoters included disproportionate percentages of white-collar workers, domestic servants, and persons with no profession (retirees, pensioners, invalids, etc.).[103] Childers also found correlations between persons with no profession and NSDAP voters, particularly among Protestants.[104] Previous nonvoters were primarily older women and, to a lesser extent, older men.[105] It is possible that since they were older, previous nonvoters may have voted more heavily for traditional parties than for the Nazis, and if this were true, it would mean that the parties of the Right and Middle may actually have lost more of their *regular* voters than existing studies have indicated.[106] This speculation may be sensible because Childers found that persons with no profession voted more heavily for the DNVP than for the NSDAP in every election from 1920 to December 1932, with the sole exception of the July 1932 election in which the correlations between persons with no profession and DNVP and NSDAP votes were almost identical.[107] If this speculation is justified, then disintegration of support for the DNVP among voters *other* than persons with no profession must have been extreme.

It should be noted that in contrast to the persons with no profession, both the self-employed and blue-collar workers were underrepresented among previous nonvoters.[108] If, as indicated above, white-collar workers, domestic servants, and persons with no profession were overrepresented as previous nonvoters, while the self-employed and blue-collar workers were underrepresented, then previous nonvoters were clearly not "sociologically very similar to the active clientele structure of the bourgeois parties which were being swallowed up . . . by the Nazi contagion."[109] Also, as we shall see below, Childers and Hamilton conclude that the overrepresentation of white-collar workers as Nazi voters was very limited (Childers) or almost nonexistent (Hamilton). If this is true, and if O'Lessker is correct in maintaining that in 1930 almost a third of the NSDAP's source of gains came from previous nonvoters,[110] then clearly those persons with no profession who entered the electorate in 1930 were a very important and (in hindsight) powerful group. But since they do not fit into theories of "class" voting, their voting patterns *cannot* be used to support or refute the theory that the NSDAP succeeded because of "extremism of the middle." At best their entry into the electorate indicates the crisis mentality that led even "marginal" (in the labor force) Germans to become politically active.

What does this support by persons with no profession for the DNVP and later also the NSDAP mean in terms of anti-Semitism? Although the DNVP did adopt anti-Semitism in some of its propaganda, anti-Semitism was not its major campaign issue, and the relative loyalty of persons with no profession cannot therefore be directly ascribed to anti-Semitism in the DNVP, though it may have played a secondary role. It is not clear whether the same conclusion could be drawn with respect to the NSDAP. So little is known about the persons with no profession—who were a diverse group with little in common—that their motives may or may not have focused on anti-Semitism. This issue simply cannot be resolved using existing sources.

What of the middle classes? Did they support Hitler disproportionately? If so, which particular occupational groups were likely to do so? As table 2.6 indicates, there was a dramatic decline in electoral support for parties of the so-called Right (DNVP) and Middle (DVP, DDP, WP, etc.) in 1930 and 1932, and many writers have interpreted this to mean that voters who formerly supported these parties either shifted en masse to the NSDAP or first voted for another party and later switched to the NSDAP. Social scientists typically include three socioeconomic groups among the middle classes: independents or self-employed (old middle class), civil servants, and white-collar workers (new middle class). These three groups represented about a third of the labor force in Germany in 1933.[111] As a general rule, the self-employed are assumed to include the upper-middle class and middle class, although the distinctions are often vague or implicit; in contrast, white-collar workers are almost without exception considered to be lower-middle class. A sociologist named Theodore Geiger originally concluded that among these branches of the middle class, white-collar workers, or the lower-middle class, were the most pro-Nazi. He based this conclusion upon nonstatistical inferences and personal insights. Later, Pratt, Heberle, Lipset, Winkler, Weber, Hackett, and others concluded that the lower-middle class tended to vote Nazi.[112] In contrast, in his book *Political Violence under the Swastika*, Merkl suggested that the bases of Nazi party support were far wider than existing sources had indicated.[113] Thomas Childers concluded the same with regard to Nazi voters. His results indicated that there was only a slight relationship between being a white-collar worker and voting for the NSDAP.[114] Yet when Childers wrote his article, he was almost alone in questioning the accepted theory that the lower-middle classes were disproportionately pro-Nazi. More recently, Hamilton has also questioned this theory, and I shall discuss his work later in this chapter in detail because he uses residential rather than strictly occupational criteria to evaluate "class."

Another occupational group, the independents or self-employed, which, to reiterate, includes the upper-middle and middle classes in most studies, has also frequently been described as pro-Nazi. Pratt's correlations between occupation and NSDAP votes were higher among independent businessmen and executives than among white-collar workers and lower-level civil servants.[115] In addition, Winkler found independent businessmen to be Nazi voters.[116] Only Weber reported that in one city, Berlin, self-employed businessmen retained their support for the Brüning coalition rather than vote for the NSDAP.[117] This may in part, however, have been due to the large percentage of Jewish businessmen in Berlin.

The more recent study by Childers confirmed the correlations between being independent or self-employed and voting for the Nazis. His results can and perhaps should be interpreted as showing only a slight relationship when one considers the occupational group as a whole.[118] Only among self-employed Protestants and among both Protestants and Catholics engaged in handicrafts did his results indicate strong relationships.[119] It should also be noted that Childers's correlation between NSDAP votes and relatively poorer independents was strong, whereas better-off independents tended to vote for liberals in July 1932.[120]

Childers found some correlation between civil servants and Nazi votes, as have others. For example, both Pratt and Winkler found a correlation between leading civil servants and NSDAP votes. However, if we examine Childers's data more closely, we see that the correlation between NSDAP votes and civil servants was only slight and was overshadowed by the consistent and higher correlation between civil servants and DNVP votes throughout the entire Weimar period, including the depression elections.[121] Childers pointed out the marginality of civil servants to NSDAP success after 1928, but he did not emphasize how consistently they supported the DNVP.

Childers's interpretations of voting behavior of persons with no profession, white-collar workers, the self-employed, and civil servants present some difficulties. At several points he mentioned

TABLE 2.7 Childers's Correlations between NSDAP and DNVP Votes and Four Occupational Groups, 1930, 1932

| | 1930 | July 1932 | November 1932 |
|---|---|---|---|
| Self-employed (independents) | | | |
| NSDAP | .27 | .31 | .26 |
| DNVP | .19 | .06 | .05 |
| Nonmanual (white-collar workers) | | | |
| NSDAP | .23 | .29 | .25 |
| DNVP | .15 | .22 | .25 |
| Berufslose (persons with no profession) | | | |
| NSDAP | .28 | .34 | .27 |
| DNVP | .32 | .32 | .40 |
| Nonmanual in professional services (civil servants) | | | |
| NSDAP | .21 | .27 | .22 |
| DNVP | .31 | .33 | .35 |

SOURCE: Thomas Childers, "The Social Bases of the National Socialist Vote," 40, 41, tables II.A, II.B, IV, VI.

the relatively low correlation between Nazi voters and white-collar workers both before and during the depression; however, if one examines his correlations between Nazi votes and occupational groups, they do not appear to be very different. They are as presented in table 2.7.[122] First, none of these correlations is strong and each indicates a slight relationship. Second, all of these correlations are fairly close together, so that one cannot speak of extreme differences among these occupational groups, particularly if one ignores the relatively small number of civil servants. For example, if we compare persons with no profession, white-collar workers, and the self-employed, the biggest difference among the correlations in each of the three elections is only five percentage points, and this is a small difference. There is a slightly higher

77

correlation between each of these groups (including civil servants) and the NSDAP from 1930 to July 1932, but one could hardly conclude that any *one* occupational group showed a more dramatic increase in Nazi support than did others. Likewise, they each declined slightly in December 1932, but again this is only a slight decrease. Therefore, looking at these occupational groups as a whole, it is hard to understand why Childers made such a clear distinction between the "marginal" levels of support among civil servants during the depression,[123] the "limited" support among white-collar workers after 1928, and the "intensified and broadened" support among the self-employed in 1930.[124] Also, his regression coefficients for persons with no profession were high for Protestants but near to those for other occupational groups, if one compares his data for *all* persons with no profession.[125] Therefore, his distinctions are not clearly justified by the data he presents. All one can conclude is that each of these occupational groups had a fairly *similar* correlation with NSDAP votes, which was slight in all years but which increased somewhat from 1930 to July 1932 and then declined somewhat in December 1932. I shall discuss the relevance of votes for the NSDAP by the middle class (independents, white-collar workers, and civil servants) to anti-semitism later.[126]

The electoral studies cited above were based on statistical correlations between NSDAP votes and either new voters, previous nonvoters, or occupational groups. However, in a more recent electoral analysis, Hamilton argued convincingly that census occupational categories for 1925 and 1933 cover far too great a range of income and status to be useful indicators of class differences.[127] The categories "self-employed," "civil servants," "white-collar workers," and "blue-collar workers" each included people who were either well off, middling, or poor. Hamilton found that most large cities had an upper-class area, a few upper-middle class areas, mixed areas that included the lower-middle classes and blue-collar workers, and areas that were predominately working class.[128] Therefore, instead of correlating Nazi votes to census occupational data, he examined NSDAP election returns for separate "class" districts in a number of large cities to discover which classes voted for Hitler. Hamilton used electoral returns for cities because he considered class differences to be stronger there than in the countryside.

As a result of his study Hamilton joined Childers and Merkl in questioning the widely accepted theory that the middle classes (particularly the lower-middle classes) in which he included independents, white-collar workers, and lesser civil servants, became pro-Nazi extremists.[129] Instead he found that Hitler's supporters came from all classes, but most disproportionately from the upper and upper-middle classes. After examining party propaganda and platforms and rightist or centrist newspapers, Hamilton concluded that both the conservative and liberal media treated Hitler with qualified acceptance and in some cases enthusiasm.[130] They frequently adopted traditional, nationalist, and anti-Semitic elements of Nazism and tried to outdo Hitler by moving to the right on these issues. The attitude of bourgeois and rightist newspapers indicated "anti-Marxist alarmism, anti-regime attacks, occasional favor shown for the Italian Fascist model, an avuncular attitude towards the National Socialists, and a belief that the party could be tamed."[131] Although he did not conduct a systematic analysis of the content of these newspapers, it is likely that they also were mildly anti-Semitic in their anti-Marxist propaganda, and this may have appealed to some right-wing and upper-class or upper-middle class voters who switched to Hitler, particularly in rural areas.[132]

Even though Hamilton's methodology was different from theirs, Hamilton joined Winkler, O'Lessker, Childers, and Merkl in questioning the predominant theory that the middle classes, particularly the lower-middle class (white-collar workers) adopted Lipset's "extremism of the middle." Rather, Hamilton concluded that the urban lower-middle class had very diverse voting behavior. This was in part due to the working-class origins of many white-collar workers who apparently still lived either in predominately working-class districts or in districts that were heavily mixed with blue-collar workers. Hamilton inferred from this that they did not adopt a "middle-class mentality" but rather continued to support the SPD and KPD, the traditional parties of blue-collar workers. It should be noted that the SPD was not exclusively a blue-collar workers' party, but that, for example, in 1930 the SPD received 25 percent of white-collar votes, 33 percent of civil service votes, and 25 percent of votes from the self-employed.[133] Hamilton ascribed some of this SPD support to urban lower-middle class voters in mixed- or working-class districts.[134]

In the critical mixed districts, which he assumed were approximately equally split between the urban lower-middle class and blue-collar workers, Hamilton speculated that the younger and less secure white-collar workers were most likely to support the SPD and KPD during the depression, while the older employed workers probably comprised the white-collar segment of Hitler's electoral supporters who may have suffered from "status panic."[135] Thus one of Hamilton's major conclusions was that lower-middle class Nazi voters were from working-class backgrounds or were younger insecure white-collar workers, but that the lower-middle class was variegated in its voting behavior and was not predominately pro-Nazi.

Hamilton also found that blue-collar workers had more diverse voting patterns during the depression than previous studies have indicated.[136] Even using traditional estimates based on census occupational data, the absolute numbers of lower-middle class and working-class Nazi voters were nearly identical; therefore Hamilton tried to explain the sources of working-class votes using his residential definition of class. He decided that Hitler's supporters from working-class districts included a significant number of conservative "Tory workers," whose motives were traditionalism, nationalism, respect for authority, and religious attachment.[137] According to Hamilton, they probably grew up in small towns or villages where their parents' and their own "traditionalism" was reinforced by the community. He also speculated that the experience of World War I may have strengthened their nationalism so that they felt betrayed by the socialist revolution and shared no common political beliefs with the majority of SPD or KPD supporters among their blue-collar coworkers. This attitude was certainly present among a number of early Nazis and members of the SA and Hitler Youth, which drew disproportionately from the working class. Hamilton speculated that they may have joined rightist or liberal parties before the depression but then switched to the NSDAP. These findings are consistent with those of Jones, Winkler, and Weber, which indicated that there was a great deal of shifting first to parties of the Right and Middle and only later to the Nazis, as these parties appeared unable to protect either themselves or their constituents during the depression. Anti-Marxism would have been a major motivation of Tory workers who joined other political parties and later switched to the Nazis, yet it is unclear whether there was an anti-Semitic component to their aversion to the SPD to KPD. Historically the SPD had a reputation of being the "party of the Jews," and this image was strengthened during the revolution and Weimar Republic. "Tory workers" might either have been indifferent to this stereotype or they might have come to dislike the SPD because they were already anti-Semites and it was considered too "Jewish." In contrast to the SPD the Nazis had an economic program, organization, and the look of a winner, all of which appealed to "Tory workers," apoliticals, and "bread and butter" voters.[138] Certainly the working class cannot axiomatically be treated as part of an anti-Nazi leftist monolith.

It may be helpful to compare Hamilton's study with others cited above. Hamilton would agree that the upper-middle classes and some groups among the lower-middle classes (however vaguely defined) supported Hitler disproportionately; yet he would maintain that the upper class and "Tory workers" also contributed significantly to Hitler's success. He believes that the urban lower-middle class voted far less heavily for Hitler than has been indicated in practically all relevant secondary literature. Hamilton also suggests that *all* political parties in Weimar Germany were comprised of a variety of socioeconomic groups rather than being the exclusive preserve of any one particular class.[139] This insight is very important because it illustrates the limits of Marxist and "class" frameworks as explanatory tools in evaluating Nazi electoral success.[140] It also helps to explain the ease with which some voters shifted to Hitler, since "class" may not have been their major concern.

If Weimar parties were "multi-class" parties, and if they ad-

81

vocated economic policies that would benefit only some "classes" among their constituents during the depression, they could be outmaneuvered by Hitler, who simply promised everything to everyone and picked up the economically disaffected voters. Only the large old parties with historically loyal followers, the SPD and Center, were immune from this process of attrition. To illustrate, Hamilton points out that when the so-called middle-class parties shifted to the right by adopting fiscal conservatism around 1930, they lost their "Tory workers."[141] However, the biggest problem of these parties was not simply that they lacked a class following; it was that they lacked appeal for many Germans from all classes.

Childers would argue that by 1930 the Nazis had become both a class (middle class) and a religious (Protestant) party.[142] Hamilton certainly concurs that the Nazis had a Protestant base;[143] however, his study and even many of Childers's own statistical results make it appear that the Nazis appealed to certain segments of *all* classes. Childers's correlations showed only a slight relationship, rather than strong support, between the majority of middle-class occupational groups and the NSDAP.

Nevertheless, Merkl, Childers, O'Lessker, and Hamilton would perhaps agree that any typification of the NSDAP as appealing mainly to a lower-middle class constituency is too narrow to encompass historical reality. The Nazi party might better be described as a "catchall" or "hodgepodge" party that increasingly mirrored all socioeconomic groups rather than just the lower-middle class, at least by 1930.

However, for those who still subscribe to the theory that the middle classes supported Hitler disproportionately, some additional discussion might be useful.[144] We know from Merkl's data that the middle classes were overrepresented among anti-Semites in the early NSDAP. Was anti-Semitism the major reason for middle-class support of Hitler? This is a problematic issue that leads to other important questions. First, if anti-Semitism had been a primary concern of large numbers of the middle classes, why did they not give extensive support to political anti-Semitism during the Wilhelminian and early Weimar years when anti-Semitic parties were receiving only 1 to 5 percent of all valid votes? Second, why did they not vote for the NSDAP in large numbers in 1924 and 1928, or even in 1930 when the NSDAP received only 18.3 percent of total votes? If the main attraction of the Nazi party for the middle classes were anti-Semitism, why did they only "erupt" in a pro-Nazi groundswell as late as 1932? And third, since other political parties adopted an anti-Jewish stance during the depression, why did the middle classes support the Nazi party more strongly than, for example, the DNVP? As noted above, the DNVP was also willing to use anti-Semitism to attract voters.[145] To answer these questions one might speculate that anti-Semitism was not of paramount importance to the middle classes, even though Merkl's study shows that the early Nazi party contained many moderate anti-Semites from the middle classes.

During the Weimar years and even before, the middle classes attempted at great length to find a political party that would represent their economic and political aspirations.[146] Yet the middle classes were a congeries of occupational groups that only occasionally shared common political and economic goals: white-collar workers, hair dressers, independent businessmen, civil servants, farmers, professors, secondary school teachers, nurses, and a host of others. Their adoption of the Nazi party came only after a long and bitter struggle to obtain political influence, and this struggle was, of course, made difficult by the fact that the middle classes had disparate and conflicting interests.

In addition, fear of bolshevism was common to many members of the middle classes, and this played a significant role in their electoral support for Hitler.[147] This common enemy was a far more real and menacing threat than the Jews. Even though the Communist party spouted revolutionary rhetoric which it could not carry out, these threats conjured up images of the chaos, murder, and violence that nearly destroyed Germany in 1918–1919.

Middle-class and other voters did not vote for Hitler because he promised to exterminate European Jewry. Neither did they vote for him because he promised to tear up the constitution, impose a police state, destroy trade unions, eradicate rival political parties,

83

or cripple the churches. Even Hitler's *Mein Kampf* did not forecast these events. In any case, how many people had bothered to read *Mein Kampf* in 1930 or 1932?[148] And of those, how many would have interpreted his wildest threats literally rather than as exaggerated political rhetoric? Who could rationally have predicted that he would pursue his goals with ruthless and devastating consistency? After all, consistency is usually the most unexpected and rarest of all political phenomena.[149]

There were, of course, political observers, including some Jews, who predicted disaster. But in 1930 and 1932 they were certainly engaging in wild speculation or had very intimate personal associations with Hitler.[150] No promises or propaganda of Hitler or other Nazi leaders informed the middle classes or other Nazi voters of the barbaric measures that Hitler was about to introduce, with Jews as the foremost, but not the only, target. Anyone over six years old knew that the NSDAP was anti-Semitic, but that hardly differentiated the Nazi party from many other parties after 1928 and at the latest by 1930. Parties of the middle were adopting anti-Semitic platforms, the SPD tried to avoid the "Jewish question," and both the DNVP and KPD increased their anti-Semitic propaganda.[151]

The middle classes could have voted for other parties had they only wished to vent their anti-Semitism. The NSDAP was more anti-Semitic than any other party, and it therefore undoubtedly did win support from those members of the middle (and other) classes who equated Jews with their own economic destruction. But why (to repeat our previous question), if large numbers of the middle classes regarded anti-Semitism as their most important political concern, did Hitler win only 2.6 percent of valid votes in 1928?[152] Why was it only in 1932 that we find seemingly incontrovertible evidence that the middle classes supported Hitler at the polls?[153]

We might hypothesize that the middle classes suffered more in the depression and vented their outrage against Jews primarily for economic reasons, as was suggested earlier.[154] But there are several empirical considerations that weigh against this hypothesis. First, the middle classes did not suffer more than the working classes during the depression. Neither civil servants, white-collar workers, artisans, nor small businessmen suffered as much economic dislocation from the depression as did blue-collar workers.[155] Second, unemployment did not appear to have caused an increase in voting for Hitler among one significant middle-class occupational group, white-collar workers. Although Pratt reported a high positive correlation between white-collar unemployment and Nazi votes in cities, a more recent study of fifty-two German cities with populations of 100,000 or more inhabitants failed to duplicate this result.[156] Neither unemployed white-collar workers nor unemployed blue-collar workers were more likely than their employed counterparts to vote NSDAP. Only farmers with declining incomes had a propensity to vote for the Nazi party.[157] These findings do not support the hypothesis that the middle classes suffered more during the depression, blamed the Jews for their suffering, and joined or voted for the NSDAP because of "economic anti-Semitism."

Even if the depression did not "cause" Nazi success by prompting the middle classes to vote for Hitler because of a combination of economic hardship and anti-Semitism, it did radicalize politics. Given the previous failure of middle-class parties to satisfy the broad spectrum of Germans in middle-class occupations, the depression undoubtedly made them more likely to vote Nazi than they would have been at other times: *they had very few alternatives*. A significant minority voted for the SPD, and others supported the DNVP or splinter parties, but they hardly found a welcome home in the KPD. The NSDAP was thus the only party left that promised (mendaciously) to fulfill their needs. Depending on their occupations, these voters found any or all of the following aspects of the Nazi economic program appealing: end of "interest bondage"; return to "corporate" society; an end to the depression; easier loan policies; increased social status; government support for special interest groups; or higher salaries.

Even if the depression did not hit the middle classes as severely as the lower class, there were many pressing problems in the German economy, let alone in the political system, that were more important to them in a practical sense than was the "Jewish question.'' Insofar as these problems could be ascribed to Jews, of course, they led to sympathy for the Nazis; but only the most paranoid and irrational Jew-haters could have blamed the entire depression and the collapse of the Weimar government on Jews, who represented less than 1 percent of the population in 1933.[158] Even in the early Nazi party, only 15 percent of the middle-class members were paranoids who proposed countermeasures against Jews, ostensibly to "get revenge" for Germany's decline. The other 85 percent were either confirmed bigots, mild anti-Semites, or individuals who showed no evidence of prejudice.[159] It therefore seems improbable that anti-Semitism was the primary motive of the middle classes in voting for Hitler, because large numbers of them voted for him only in 1932, or 1930 at the very earliest. It is more likely that they supported Hitler for other reasons, such as fear of communism; previous failure of middle-class or other parties to represent their political and economic interests; and lack of a viable alternative to the Nazis.

To conclude our discussion of Nazi voters, it is useful to study table 2.8, which contrasts Nazi voters with groups that were overrepresented among anti-Semites in Merkl's sample of early Nazis.[160] With the exception of new voters and previous nonvoters who were disproportionately female, Nazi voters were predomi-

TABLE 2.8 Socioeconomic Characteristics of Nazi Voters and Early Nazi Anti-Semites

|  | Nazi Voters | Anti-Semites |
|---|---|---|
| Age | New young voters & older previous nonvoters | 49 + |
| Sex | Male | Female[a] |
| Residence | Rural, middle-sized towns | Urban |
| Religion | Protestant | Protestant[a] |
| Occupation[b] | Lipset: WCW, BP, MCS Childers: BP, CS Hamilton: UC, BP, CS, Tory BCW | WCW, BP, MCS |

[a] Probabilities are low; results are only indicative.

[b] WCW-white-collar workers; BP-business-professionals; MCS-military-civil servants; CS-civil servants; BCW-blue-collar workers; UC-upperclass.

nately male.[161] They were also disproportionately Protestant and came from small towns or rural areas.[162] They frequently had previous affiliations with centrist or regional parties that had opposed big business and big labor.[163] New voters were young and previous nonvoters were older, as was probably true of voters who switched from other parties to the NSDAP and partially true of early anti-Semites. Females in the early NSDAP were somewhat more likely to be anti-Semites than were males, but males were more likely to vote for the NSDAP if all age groups are considered. Urban residents were more likely to be anti-Semites in the early NSDAP than to be Nazi voters in 1930 and 1932. Protestants were slightly more likely than were Catholics to be anti-Semites in the early party and very likely to be Nazi voters later. Using Lipset's and Merkl's data, white-collar workers especially, but also business-professionals and military-civil servants, were likely to be both Nazi voters and anti-Semites in the early Nazi party. Yet according to Childers and Hamilton, white-collar workers should be excluded from those overrepresented among Nazi voters. Hamilton also added the upper classes and "Tory workers" as Nazi voters.

What do these profiles of Nazi voters tell us about the possible drawing power of anti-Semitism for the NSDAP? Protestants and members of the middle classes were the two groups that were overrepresented among both voters and anti-Semites in the early Nazi party. Can we infer from this that the Protestants and the middle classes voted for the NSDAP primarily *because* of Nazi anti-Semitism? To some extent we would be justified in making this inference because Protestants, white-collar workers, business-professionals, and sons of military-civil servants were overrepresented among paranoid anti-Semites who were drawn to the party mainly because of its anti-Semitism. On the other hand, Protestants, white-collar workers, and sons of military-civil servants were also overrepresented among *mild* anti-Semites. At best we can speculate that a minority of Protestants and the middle classes were paranoid anti-Semites who may have voted for the Nazi party primarily because of its anti-Semitism.

CHAPTER TWO

SUMMARY

During the years 1918–1924 anti-Semitism appears to have been much stronger than during the Wilhelminian period and even more virulent than in the remaining Weimar years. Jews were not the only target of popular wrath—communists were also the object of contempt and fear for many Germans. However, Jews were particularly vulnerable because they were considered to be alien troublemakers. Postwar Germany was the breeding ground for a new type of extreme anti-Semite, of which Hitler himself was the paramount example.

Yet paranoid anti-Semitism of Hitler's type was not typical of early Nazi party members, even though anti-Semitism was an important reason for their joining the party and even though it contained the hard core of Germany's anti-Semites. Only *one-eighth* of Merkl's sample of early party members were paranoid anti-Semites who called for countermeasures against Jews. The paranoids did not usually say what measures they had in mind other than calling for "action," "defense," or boycotts, and their main concern was to mobilize like-minded Germans and take over the country.[164] These measures were vague, but they were still a far cry from confiscation of property, destruction of Jewish synagogues, forced emigration, concentration camps, or genocide. We do know that as of 1934 anti-Semites in the Nazi party did *not* envision the elimination of Jews (and Marxists) from Europe, even though paranoid anti-Semites joined the party primarily because of their anti-Semitism. Moderate anti-Semites (confirmed bigots), mild anti-Semites, and of course the Nazis who demonstrated no evidence of anti-Semitism most probably joined for other reasons. Anti-Semites in the early NSDAP tended to be older, female, resident in large cities, middle class, and Protestant.

Although the early Weimar years were marked by a wave of anti-Semitism—as symbolized, for example, by the assassination of Rathenau—the years between 1924 and 1929 were not a period of overt attacks on Jews. Because of this the Nazis had to temper their propaganda in order to avoid alienating voters. Instead of concentrating on the "Jewish question" per se, they associated

Jews with other evils that they promised to eradicate: finance capitalism, socialism, internationalism, Germany's weakness as a consequence of the Treaty of Versailles, and the depression, with its attendant dislocations. These were some of the primary issues that concerned the electorate.

What about voters? Who were they, and did they vote for the NSDAP primarily because of anti-Semitism? New voters were obviously young, whereas previous nonvoters and those who shifted from other parties to the NSDAP were probably older. The typical Nazi voters were disproportionately male, from rural areas or middle-sized towns, and Protestant.

There is considerable debate about the role of the middle classes as Nazi voters. Lipset's contention that the Nazi party gained many votes because of "extremism of the middle" has been contested by several writers. An examination of their work shows that both the early Nazi party and the Nazi electorate were drawn from all classes and that it was a "catchall" party for those who were disaffected with the other options, rather than simply a product of middle-class support.

Because Protestants and members of the middle classes were overrepresented among both paranoid and mild anti-Semites in the early Nazi party, we can infer that only a minority of Protestants and the middle classes were paranoid anti-Semites who may have voted for the NSDAP mainly because of its anti-Semitism. We speculated that the middle classes may have voted for Hitler not primarily because of anti-Semitism, but because they feared communism, because previous political parties had failed to represent their political and economic interests, and because they lacked a viable alternative to the Nazis.

Many Germans hoped Hitler could pull Germany out of the depression and others thought he was the only man capable of restoring dignity to the nation after its humiliating defeat in World War I and the Treaty of Versailles. Still others counted on his giving precedence, both economically and politically, to their own special interest groups; and some were merely fed up with the Weimar government and wanted a change. In short, there was a myriad of reasons for joining the Nazi party or voting for Hitler.

89

Anti-Semitism was only one and not necessarily the most important one, and it was apparently not a major determinant of Nazi success at the polls. Nevertheless, it did not prevent potential voters from supporting the NSDAP, and Nazi victory meant that Hitler and the radical anti-Semites in the Nazi party, not the German electorate in general, would determine Jewish policy.

# Hitler's Ethnic Theory

"Far from being irrational, the Holocaust can only be
epitomized in terms of excessive rationality, an example of
logical thought slipping the bonds of human feeling."
George Kren and Leon Rappoport, *The Holocaust and the
Crisis of Human Behavior*, p. 9.

## THE BASICS

One cannot understand the dire consequences of Hitler's election and anti-Semitism without examining Hitler's own ideas. Hitler might have been the world's foremost exterminator of human beings (some would argue that this dishonor belongs to Stalin or Mao Tse-Tung), but he did not kill randomly and it is important to understand why he murdered. Therefore, we must answer the extremely critical question, What were Hitler's racial conceptions? The rudiments of Hitler's thought have been analyzed particularly well by Jaeckel and Haffner,[1] and they will be discussed here because of their great significance to the fate of the European Jews. As H. R. Trevor-Roper has said, "That Hitler's mind was vulgar and cruel I readily agree; but vulgarity and cruelty are not incompatible with power and consistency."[2]

To Hitler the Jews were not merely inferior and despicable subhumans, as they were to previous anti-Semites and to his contemporaries; they were the embodiment of an absolute immutable evil, namely, the "Jewish spirit." He believed the "Jewish spirit" took many forms including Judeo-Christianity, democracy, parliamentarianism, liberalism, rationalism, individualism, legalism, bolshevism, humanism, and intellectualism. In short,

91

Hitler conceived of the "Jewish spirit" as an extraordinarily powerful, almost metaphysical force that transcended the mere existence of Jews on earth.[3] He believed that it was responsible for the distinctive characteristics of Western civilization, which Hitler loathed. To his mind Jews were engaged in an international conspiracy to dominate Gentiles that would result in the subjugation of other nations and eventually the entire human race. He believed that the only counterforce against the "Jewish spirit" was a revival of the strong and aggressive "Aryan spirit" that sustained the Germanic invasions of Europe at the end of the Roman Empire, that is, before "Aryans" were corrupted by both Jewish genes and "Jewish" values.

Hitler did not consider the existing German population as pure "Aryan"; instead he thought it contained "Aryan" elements that could be strengthened through careful genetic selection.[4] He began this process with his euthanasia program, the breeding of "Aryan" women, and the extermination of Jews and other "genetic inferiors" during World War II. Hitler suspected that the existing German nation would be at a distinct disadvantage in any future "Aryan"-Jewish struggle because it was not comprised of pure "Aryans." It was partially this fear that prompted his obsession with destroying European Jews himself before further degeneration weakened "Aryans" and undermined their willingness to combat the Jews.

It is important to understand that to Hitler, "Jewishness" was not confined to "racial Jews"; non-Jews who sympathized with "Jewish" inventions (democracy, socialism, internationalism, etc.) were also classified as Jews—not "racial Jews," but "spiritual Jews." This made Hitler's anti-Semitism far more flexible and destructive than the purely racial anti-Semitism of his radical predecessors and contemporary followers; his conceptions served as the pretext for the destruction not only of millions of Jews, but also millions of other Europeans who supported some "ism" on Hitler's list of "Jewish inventions." Hitler did, however, reserve the harshest fate for "racial" Jews and developed a racial theory to justify their persecution and later extermination.

Haffner believes that Hitler used the term "race" in two senses:

first, as a stockbreeder who attempts to improve his animals through selective breeding; second, as a neutral describer of variations within the same species. Haffner maintains that Hitler's stockbreeder sense of race was incompatible with the neutral-describer sense and that this accounts for his development of two separate and in some respects incompatible racial theories.[5] Hitler did use the word "race" in two senses, but it is not clear that this in itself accounts for his two (according to Haffner) separate racial theories. In what way does the neutral-describer sense of the "Jewish race" as opposed to the yellow race, "Slavic race," or brown race somehow necessitate a second, anti-Semitic theory? Simply to state or believe that Jews may be classified as a separate race does not necessitate an anti-Semitic theory; indeed, during the 1920s and 1930s even some rabbis considered the Jews to be a separate race. But whether or not Hitler's use of the term "race" in both the stockbreeder and neutral-describer senses led to his formulating both an ethnic and an anti-Semitic theory, his racial theory should still be examined in some detail.

Haffner summarizes parts of Hitler's historico-political theory as follows:

> Politics is the art of implementing a nation's vital struggle for its earthly existence. Foreign policy is the art of ensuring for a nation the amount and quality of living space it needs at a given time. Domestic policy is the art of procuring for a nation the power necessary for this, in the form of its racial quality and its numbers.
>
> In short, politics is war and the preparation for war, and war is mainly about living space. . . . Secondly, however, wars are about domination and subjection. . . . Thirdly, however, and ultimately, the perpetual warlike struggle between nations is about world domination.
>
> Every being strives for expansion and every nation strives for world domination.[6]

Although Haffner concludes that to Hitler wars were "mainly about living space," he goes on to emphasize Hitler's ideas on domination, subjection, and finally, national struggles for world domination. Since Hitler regarded the Jews as a race and also as a *nation*, which Haffner points out elsewhere,[7] he clearly thought that Jews sought world domination, as did all nations. Haffner describes what he terms Hitler's stockbreeder or ethnic theory as follows:

> The actors of history, in that case, are the nations, history itself consists of their wars, their rivalry for living space and world domination, and so for that struggle they must be perpetually rearmed; not only militarily and ideologically but also biologically, i.e. by raising their racial quality, by the elimination of the weak and by the deliberate selective breeding of their militarily useful characteristics.[8]

Yet in his second briefer summary on the next page, Haffner says: "According to the former (ethnic theory) all history consists of the continuous struggle of nations for living space. Now we are suddenly informed that this is not the whole of history after all."[9] Here Haffner omits the words "and world domination," and includes only "living space," as if the rivalries between nations were *only* about living space. Since, according to Hitler, the Jewish nation did not fight for living space, Haffner apparently believes that Hitler needed a separate anti-Semitic theory to explain rivalries between Jews and other nations. This, however, would be logically necessary only if one omits the words "and world domination." If they are included, as in Haffner's first description of Hitler's ethnic theory, then Jews are clearly part of "history itself" or "all history" because Hitler believed that they sought world domination, as did all nations. Hitler stated that Jews did not seek living space through direct warfare with other nations, but used different methods (internationalism, pacifism, capitalism, communism, etc.); nevertheless, the Jewish goal was identical: world domination. This is clear from Haffner's quotation of Hitler on the Jew:

> His ultimate aim is the de-nationalization, the inter-bastardization of other nations, the lowering of the racial level of the noblest, as well as domination over that racial jumble through

the extermination of the national intelligentsias and their replacement by members of his own nation.[10]

Thus Hitler's theory of anti-Semitism is actually subsumed within his ethnic theory; it is not separate and incompatible.

The integration of Hitler's anti-Semitism into his ethnic theory might be summarized as follows: All history consists of national struggles for living space and world domination. Since Jews are a nation they participate in these national struggles, not for living space, but for world domination (racial supremacy through dominance, subjection, and extermination). Their methods threaten the political, military, economic, cultural, and most importantly, racial strength of other nations among whom they are dispersed. Therefore, all nations should give utmost priority to their defeat in order to prevent Jewish world domination.

If the above synthesis is accepted, we should examine Haffner's interpretation of the reasons why Hitler felt that nations should unite against Jews:

> Why did all nations have to unite against the Jews when surely they had their hands full fighting against each other for living space? Answer: they had to unite just *because* they had to fight for their living space, and *in order that* they might devote themselves undisturbed to their pre-ordained struggle. The Jews were the spoilsports in this pleasant game; with their internationalism and pacifism, their (international) capitalism and their (equally international) communism they were diverting the "Aryan" nations from their main task and their main occupation, and that is why they had to be removed from the world, and not from Germany only.[11]

In this interpretation Haffner speaks of the Jews "diverting" the "Aryan" nations from their main task and their main occupation; however, this is too mild. Hitler was not only concerned about the nations being "diverted" from their main task (struggles for living space and world domination); he was worried that "international Jewry" would succeed in destroying the nations internally. Moreover, according to Hitler they might ". . . push the nations into wars against each other," as Haffner points out.

95

However, Haffner notes in brackets, "but surely this was just what, according to Hitler, the nations were for?"[12] We should indicate here that Hitler's ethnic theory, as summarized by Haffner, did postulate perpetual warfare for living space and world domination as a historical necessity; nevertheless, Hitler's hatred of the Jews was based on his belief that they fomented wars that were *against* the national and racial interests of the countries involved, and that Jews were the only gainers from these "unnatural" wars that resulted from conspiracies of "international Jewry." Implicit in Hitler's thought there were "good wars" (wars to demonstrate the superiority of a race that sought territory for itself and its racial descendants against competing races) and "bad wars" (wars contrived by Jews in which "racial brothers" fought senselessly, while the Jews gained more power and came closer to world domination).[13] In any case, to Hitler Jews were not merely "diverting" other nations, but they were a positive *threat* to both their internal and external security.

Most "Aryan" peoples lived within parts of Europe or had emigrated from there, but maintained their racial characteristics. Jews, however, were densely concentrated within Poland, Russia, and other Eastern European nations and (according to Hitler) also had international affiliations that gave them a supranational world power block. Therefore, when Hitler attacked to the east he was fighting a *racial* war for two reasons: first, to win territory controlled by "racially inferior" "non-Aryans" (Poles, Russians, Slavs, and Jews); and second, to destroy the "parasitic" Jews who formed the primary nexus of an "insidious world conspiracy" against other nations. Thus to Hitler Eastern European Jews were enemies on two grounds: they held territory that Hitler wanted for "Aryan" expansion and they comprised the bulk of the population and headquarters of the supranational "Jewish state."

According to Hitler, the failure of nations to recognize their true interests by waging war against the Jews would result in apocalyptic consequences. As he put it, "If the Jew with his Marxist creed remains victorious over the nations of this world, then his crown will be the wreath on the grave of mankind, then this planet will once more, as millions of years ago, move through the ether devoid of human beings.''[14] This was one of Hitler's most revealing statements, not only (as Haffner points out) because it implies the extermination of non-Jews, but most particularly because it reveals what genuinely *was* Hitler's second theory, which is in no way compatible with either what Haffner calls Hitler's ethnic theory or his anti-Semitic theory. This statement announces to anyone who reads it that Hitler had another, truly astounding theory about Jews—that they were not human beings. If they were to obtain control of all of the world, multiply their race, and exterminate all other races and nations, then they would be the only survivors on earth. But since Hitler described the planet as devoid of human beings after Jewish victory, then clearly he did not here recognize them as a race, whereas he did so in Haffner's interpretation of his anti-Semitic theory; instead he classified them as nonhuman.[15]

This illuminates an exceedingly important dichotomy in Hitler's thought and in his subsequent actions. He labeled Jews alternately as a nation or a race and bacteria or viruses. This dichotomy runs throughout his written works, speeches, and conversations. Even early in World War II when the Madagascar Plan was under consideration,[16] he was willing to grant European Jews (as a separate race) an island on which they would be enslaved to insure their impotence. As this plan was impracticable, he chose extermination to solve the "Jewish problem."

It should be pointed out, however, that to Hitler the extermination of Jews could have been "theoretically justified" on either ground: that they were "racial threats" to other nations or that they were dangerous "parasites." Hitler himself explicitly and more often implicitly justified persecution and extermination of Jews on both grounds. As his *Testament* makes clear, after millions of Jews had been exterminated, he referred to them not as a race, but as "parasites" and "poison," and as an "abscess," "virus," or "contagion," all of which nevertheless shared a "community of the mind."[17] This complete mental transformation from thinking of Jews as a separate race to considering them nonhuman probably took place between March and October of 1941 with the decision to exterminate the Russian Jews.

This second justification, that Jews were nonhuman "parasites," indicates more than anything else that Hitler's destruction of European Jewry was not undertaken just to maintain theoretical or logical consistency, but rather to satisfy his personal aversion, contempt, loathing, fear, and horror when contemplating the Jews either as real beings or, most often, as the distorted mental abstraction of his obsessive and feverish imagination. By adopting this second theory of anti-Semitism, Hitler lost all touch with possible reality. What is genetically human remains genetically human, at least until scientists can alter genes significantly by deliberate manipulation, but this simple fact seemed to escape Hitler. He placed himself in the ludicrous and logically untenable position of predicating his racial policies on impossible biological assumptions (humans are not human), while declaring that his principles were founded on "nature." His theory was logically consistent so long as he merely considered the Jews to be a dangerous nation. Had they been powerful and determined enough to attain world domination, as Hitler thought they would, and had they planned to exterminate all other races or nations, their "preventive" extermination might have been logically justified. That they lacked the power, will, or desire for world domination was the critical reality that Hitler chose to ignore; the calamitous consequences of this deliberate ignorance boggle the mind's comprehension of both human cruelty and the depth of human anguish that it can create.

## HITLER'S RACIAL HIERARCHY

Although Hitler never defined precisely what he meant by the term "Aryan race," by examining his comments on other peoples one can discern certain racial assumptions that clarify his ethnic theory. To Hitler history consisted of national struggles for living space and world domination, and "Whoever wants to live must therefore fight, and whoever does not wish to do battle in this world of eternal struggle does not deserve life."[18] In keeping with his theory that victory in warfare was a measure of a race's superiority, Hitler concluded at the end of World War II that the future belonged to the stronger Eastern nation (Russia).[19] This indicates that he actually believed that a nation must earn its right to life. To Hitler, ''A desperate fight remains for all time a shining example.''[20] He felt that the Austrians should be proud because they had never been dominated by another race.[21] And he said of Japan after its entry into World War II, ''Now we have a partner who has not been defeated in three thousand years.''[22] He also believed it was a law of nature that one should not treat nonequal races as equals and he was bitterly self-recriminating because he had done so in the case of Italy, since ''Life does not forgive weakness.''[23] He also thought that the British had lost the right to world domination because of their racial degeneration, particularly through intermarriage of the aristocracy with Jews.[24] Thus to Hitler the measure of a race's historical worth was its purity, willingness to fight, and, by implication, its success in wars with other races. If a race had not historically proven its worth in warfare, then it did not deserve to live. Any one defeat, however, would not necessarily condemn a race. As he said when Germany was in ruins and his own death was near, ''And should Providence abandon us, in spite of our sacrifices and our resolute steadfastness, it only means that Fate is subjecting us to even greater trials, in order to give us the chance to confirm our right to live.''[25]

Earlier German racists proposed concrete measures to reduce Jewish influence or to drive Jews from Germany. Hitler, however, adopted a more abstract racism that included a continuum of superior-to-inferior races, and he proposed different treatments of conquered races by the ''superior Aryan race.'' These treatments varied in direct proportion to Hitler's evaluation of the historic worth or worthlessness of a particular race. His estimations were logically based on how well or badly they had fared in their struggles with other races (using Hitler's definition of races, which divided Europe itself into an ''Aryan''-to-''non-Aryan'' continuum). Thus England, which he admired for its conquest of the Indian subcontinent with a few thousand troops, was given a privileged place in his hierarchy. France, which had not only been defeated in 1815 and 1870 and was badly mauled from 1914 to 1918, and which had even dared to use Negro troops in World

War I and during the subsequent occupation of parts of Germany, was accorded a less glorious position than was England; half of France was occupied and the other half became a satellite under the collaborationist Vichy government. The Poles, whom he considered to be subhumans who had been conquered by a succession of overlords historically, were to be severely repressed and partially exterminated. Likewise, Slavs and other "races" in the Russian Empire were to be enslaved, starved, and partially exterminated because their historical subjection demonstrated their "slavelike nature" and lack of "racial worth." The Jews were, of course, held in utmost contempt as a race of nomadic "parasites" without even the stamina to acquire a homeland, and they were to be ghettoized, enslaved, and almost completely exterminated.[26]

In his interesting article on German treatment of elites in conquered nations during World War II, Allan Mitchell quite clearly demonstrates that Hitler had a hierarchy of superior-to-inferior nations. In some cases, such as with the French, Hitler could not make up his mind about their racial worth, because "the French were neither subhuman nor Aryan."[27] But in Poland and Russia the elites were exterminated because they were clearly at the bottom of Hitler's list of subhumans. Even the extermination of the Jews was most thoroughly carried out in nations that Hitler considered subhuman.[28] There were, of course, strategic and tactical considerations before and during World War II that may have concealed the racial nature of Hitler's goals, but the Second World War was nevertheless fought to fulfill his ethnic theory. To cite Calleo, one of the few historians who explicitly and unequivocally makes this point, "To observe that race policy was fatally impolitic or seriously intervened with the conduct of the war is to miss the point. Racial policy was the object of the war."[29]

It should be emphasized that top Nazi leaders, including Goebbels and Goering, also viewed World War II as a racial war. For example, in a public meeting Goering exclaimed the following: "This is not the Second World War, this is the Great Racial War."[30] And in an article in *Das Reich* in May 1943, Goebbels wrote: "Our policy may here and there lead to difficult decisions but they are trifling by comparison with the menace. For this war is a racial war.''[31]

The following examples will illustrate that neither Hitler's ethnic theory nor its practical application was directed exclusively against Jews. As early as 1928 Hitler wrote that Germany must pursue a territorial policy with the peoples to the East: ''. . . remove them altogether and make over to its own people the land thereby released.''[32] For Germans he clearly planned future euthanasia on a large scale, because in 1929 he said that ''if a million children were born in a year and 800,000 of the weakest and most 'unworthy' were killed, the end result would be a strengthening of the population.''[33] In March 1939 Hitler envisioned deporting six million Czechs, and in August 1939 he told a field marshal that in Poland ''things would be done of which the German generals would not approve. He did not therefore wish to burden the army with the necessary liquidations but . . . would have them carried out by the SS.''[34] In October 1939 a press directive announced that Poles, Jews, and Gypsies should be treated as equally subhuman.[35] Before the Polish campaign, Hitler said: ''Whatever we can find in the shape of an upper class in Poland is to be liquidated; should anything take its place, it will be placed under guard and done away with at an appropriate time.''[36] At the end of September 1939, Heydrich, an SS officer who was second only to Himmler, claimed that only 3 percent of the Polish upper classes in the occupied territories were still present.[37] The Polish victims included lawyers, doctors, businessmen, teachers, landowners, priests, and government officials.[38] In contrast, the Jews were not killed at this time, but ''terrorized into local provincial ghettos, and then transported out to a few special reserves.''[39] In May 1940 Himmler submitted a document to Hitler about which he noted: ''The Führer directed that only a limited number of copies should be made, that it was not to be reproduced, and that it was to be treated as top secret.''[40] As the ultimate goal of German policy in the East, Himmler

proposed that what had once been Poland with its numerous races (Poles, Ukrainians, White Russians, Jews, Gorals, Lemkes

101

and Kashubs) should be "broken up into the largest possible number of parts and fragments." . . . "in our area" it should be possible "to cause the Ukrainians, the Gorals and the Lemkes to disappear as racial entities. Making allowance for the larger area involved, the same should apply . . . in the case of the Poles."[41]

In January 1941 Himmler confided to Lieutenant General Bach-Zelewski that "the German master plan for the East necessitated the elimination of thirty million Slavs."[42] By the end of June 1941 one million Poles had been driven from their homes,[43] and between 1939 and 1941 the euthanasia program purged between 70,000 and 275,000 "unworthy" sick and mentally ill Germans to "purify" the racial stock of Germany.[44] Altogether, approximately three million non-Jewish Poles and 3,300,000 Russian prisoners of war were exterminated, starved, or worked to death.[45] Even the first gassings were conducted on Russian prisoners of war on September 3, 1941, and late in the war Himmler and Thierack, the justice minister, planned to exterminate prisoners simply because they were ugly![46]

Nazi racism was not confined to anti-Semitism. In August 1941 the SD (*Sicherheitsdienst*, or security service of the SS) complained that Poles did not wear their insignia, as required by law, and that they used park benches, supplanting Aryans.[47] The SD in Erfurt complained in 1942 that Germany was becoming an international state because foreigners were everywhere, and that many citizens doubted the desirability of this for the duration of the war.[48] The SD in Bielefeld was distressed that a German had sexual relations with a Chinese soldier; it claimed that people were excited about this and wanted laws against relations with all foreigners, since the current law only applied to Jews.[49] A leaflet from the (Nazi) People's Union for Germans Abroad warned the German population late in the war not to associate with Polish workers:

> Germans be proud and do not forget what the Polish people have done to you! If someone should tell you that his Pole is decent, answer him, "Today everyone knows a decent Pole

in the same way as everyone used to know a decent Jew!''
. . . The Pole is inferior to every German on your farm or in
your factory . . . never forget that you belong to the master
people![50]

On September 12, 1943, the Propaganda Ministry issued a guide-
line with strong warnings of dangers to the German race because
Polish female workers became pregnant by German men. It continued: ''Every act of sexual intercouse is a defilement of the
German people and an act of treason against them, and each will
be harshly punished by law.''[51] In late 1943 the Informative Service of the Racial-Political Office of the Nazi party condemned
marriages between Germans and foreigners as dangerous because
of the different racial and/or cultural backgrounds of foreign elements.[52]

Yehuda Bauer, whose brilliant analyses have enlightened much
thought on the holocaust, states that: '' 'Aryan' actually had only
the quality of distinguishing it from 'non-Aryan'; the only non-
Aryan was the Jew. Antisemitism was therefore not a result of
Nazi racism, but the obverse was true: racism was a rationalization
of Jew-hatred.''[53] It is, of course, true that Hitler hated Jews more
than any other ''race'' and that ''Jew-hatred was probably the
most consistent central dimension in his chaotic personality.''[54]
Yet it may be an overstatement to claim that the only ''non-
Aryan'' was a Jew, if one considers the cruel treatment meted
out to Poles, Gypsies, Russians, and others because of their supposedly ''non-Aryan'' and subhuman status in Hitler's thought.
Jews and Bolsheviks were virtually synonymous to Hitler, and
Communist party members were executed because they were to
him ''spiritual Jews,'' even if they were not ''racial Jews,'' a
phenomenon that we discussed earlier.[55] Yet Hitler allowed about
three and a half million ordinary Russian prisoners of war to starve
to death and executed many others outright.[56] The epithet ''Jewish
Bolshevik'' was also secondary to that of ''subhuman'' in the
cases of the millions of murdered Poles and other Eastern Europeans.

It is misleading to concentrate *only* on the Jewish experience, not because it was less horrifying than it is portrayed to be, but because such an approach conceals the logical unity and ruthless consistency of Hitler's ethnic theory, which provided the rationale and impetus for both Jewish and other deaths. Not only slightly over five million Jews but also ten million non-Jews were directly killed, and about forty million others died as a direct or indirect result of World War II, and all were killed because of Hitler's attempt to actualize his logical construct.[57] As indicated above, if certain races had failed in historical struggles with other races, their "punishment" or "reward" from the logical arbiter Hitler was in direct proportion to their past successes and failures in the natural evolution of races, as Hitler defined them. Thus the political and territorial structure in conquered nations, the extermination of both Jews and non-Jews, and World War II itself were the product of Hitler's practical application of his ethnic theory.[58]

In World War II Hitler applied his ethnic theory as follows: "Aryans" must prove their historical worth by conquering living space to the East at the expense of inferior races (Poles, Russians, Jews, etc.). To secure this living space against future threats, the defeated inferior races must be enslaved and their leadership exterminated. The Jews pose a double threat: first, they occupy valuable living space; and second, they are part of the "international Jewish conspiracy"; therefore, they are the primary target for extermination.

This is not to say that Hitler had a master plan in the 1920s or 1930s that *concretely* envisioned future extermination. Nevertheless, by mid-July of 1941 and after his initial successes in Russia, this line of thought would appear to have been consistent with his previously developed ethnic theory.[59]

To recognize that the murder of millions of both Jews and non-Jews was a logical extension of Hitler's ethnic theory only explains Hitler's demonism; it does not fully account for his messianism. What the world as a whole considers demonic (the exorcism of the Jewish "racial degenerates" by enslavement, forced labor, starvation, torture, murder, etc.), Hitler regarded as his holy task, his mission of deliverance as a messiah come to save both Europe and the world. To him, since these "racial inferiors" were either nonhuman or subhuman, extermination was a positive good, a glorious cause worthy of all mankind's respect and gratitude. Hitler sincerely believed this, and he was constantly disgusted that other peoples, especially "racial brothers," did not share his messianic vision. For example, he said: "The blood of every single Englishman is too valuable to be shed. Our two people belong together, racially and traditionally—this is and always has been my aim even if our generals can't grasp it."[60] Because of this attitude he was reluctant to invade England. He said: "I do not intend to conquer her, I want to force her to accept my friendship and to drive out the whole Jewish rabble that is agitating against me."[61] His attitude toward the "Jewish rabble" around the "Jew Roosevelt" was similar, although he did not actively seek an alliance with the United States.[62]

What, exactly, did Hitler's messianic vision entail over and above the extermination of Jews, selected non-Jews, and the depredation of other nations? As we saw above, he believed that history itself consisted of the wars between nations for living space and world domination. How did this apply to Hitler's vision for Europe's future? From his *Testament* and other works, we might summarize his goals as follows:

1. The conquest of Europe with simultaneous extermination of Jews and non-Jews who posed a future security threat; enslavement of "subhumans" for future labor;
2. The reorganization of Europe according to the racial worth of each nation, including the creation of satellites and subject states;
3. The establishment of a huge power block including Germany, Austria, and other German-speaking areas in the heart of Europe; this "thousand-year Reich" would be strong enough to withstand all internal and external threats and would therefore provide peace in Europe for centuries to come.

Clearly Hitler had a vision on a grand scale and considered himself to be Europe's last hope for unification and strength. This vision of Europe's future, as his military victories and exterminatory policies demonstrated, had a serious chance of being realized. Yet Hitler himself did not consider his goals utopian. After contemplating the issue of utopianism during the final months of his life, he concluded the following:

> The universalists, the idealists, the Utopians all aim too high. They give promises of an unattainable paradise, and by doing so they deceive mankind. Whatever label they wear, whether they call themselves Christians, Communists, humanitarians, whether they are merely sincere but stupid or wire-pullers and cynics, they are all makers of slaves. I myself have always kept my eye fixed on a paradise which, in the nature of things, lies well within our reach. I mean an improvement in the lot of the German people.[63]

In 1941, before Stalingrad, many Germans might have agreed with Hitler's assessment; there can have been few who still agreed in the summer of 1945.

In any case, the above quotation was propaganda, and, as usual, it was a lie. Hitler was not merely concerned about improving the lot of the German people, even before they "proved themselves unworthy" of becoming the master race in Europe by their defeat in World War II. Instead, Hitler was determined to carry his ethnic theory to its logical conclusion—to attain world domination. He had conquered most of Europe by the fall of 1941, and had he stopped to digest his conquests before his attack on the Russians, he might have defeated them. But would the subsequent unification of Europe under German domination have resulted in an improvement in the lot of the German people and peace in Europe for centuries to come? Not according to his secret handwritten notes:

> The most important point of final victory will be the exclusion of the United States from world politics for all time and the destruction of their Jewish community.
>
> For this purpose Dr. Goebbels will have dictatorial authority as Governor to accomplish the total re-education of the racially mixed and inferior population. Göring will also help in this

respect, above all by mobilizing all those with German blood, at least fifty percent of the inhabitants, so they can be educated militarily and regenerated nationalistically.[64]

In short, Hitler would have sought to defeat the one remaining large power, to exterminate its Jews, and to reeducate its population on racial issues; in the process the German people would again have had to endure the hardships of an even longer war. Had Hitler ruthlessly enslaved the peoples of Russia, how effectively would they have strengthened his agricultural and industrial base? Would not the countries of the entire western hemisphere have let their quarrels fall into abeyance and united to form an even greater base of resources and manpower than Hitler could milk from an enslaved Europe? And would not the preparations for this titanic struggle have taken many years, so that Hitler would have had to rely on a successor of questionable determination to continue the quest for world domination? Only when these questions are asked can one perceive the true utopian in Hitler. His vision of conquering Europe, exterminating Jews and other "inferiors," and establishing a united Europe under German hegemony was nearly realized and was not entirely utopian, although it rested on some questionable assumptions about the behavior of the United States. However, his vision of conquering the world assumed success in the face of far more formidable obstacles and uncertainties; it was utopian because it was founded on imaginary perfections. Hitler's attempt to realize his messianic and utopian visions—to purify Europe and the world of Jews and other "racial inferiors" and to establish "Aryan" world domination—resulted in the most horrendous cataclysm in human history. The Russians alone lost between twenty and thirty million men. But as a group only the Jews were singled out for total extermination. As Yehuda Bauer so cogently states,

> To sum up, there may be no difference between Holocaust and genocide for the victim of either. But there are gradations of evil, unfortunately. Holocaust was the policy of the total, sacral Nazi act of mass murder of all Jews they could lay hands on. Genocide was horrible enough, but it did not entail *total*

murder if only because the subject peoples were needed as slaves. They were, indeed, "subhumans" in Nazi terminology. The Jews were not human at all.[65]

Both World War II and the destruction of European Jewry were consequences of Hitler's determination to make real the visions that a less willful, consistent, and ruthless man would have confined to daydreams. As it happened, he turned millions of lives into a living nightmare.

## DOMESTIC IMPLICATIONS

Domestic policy logically demanded the use of all available means to eliminate those who might work against or ignore the common racial good, because a given race could only prove its "historical superiority" by fighting as a homogeneous whole against its enemies. Brutality was thus logically necessary to both foreign and domestic policy. A major objective of Hitler's social engineering was racial purity. Anti-Semitism led to the gradual impoverishment, deportation, and eventual murder of Jews, but it was also important in other domestic policies, which is not often pointed out. Let us clarify this. When Hitler became chancellor, he immediately launched a campaign to destroy all political parties except the Nazis. This was done not only for the obvious reason that they threatened his political power, but also because democracy and political parties were to him the subtle invention of the "Jewish race" to weaken, and therefore to destroy, other races. Political leaders of the SPD and KPD were more ruthlessly suppressed than were those of other parties not just because they were numerous and influential, but also because they had historically been represented by prominent Jewish politicians and generally had had closer ties to Jews than had other political leaders. They were the symbol of the Jewish "stab-in-the-back," which in many minds had led to Germany's defeat, the "Jewish" revolution of 1918–1919, and the unpopular Weimar democracy. Those who believed in democracy were to Hitler "spiritual Jews" and representatives of an alien race, because they accepted the political system of an inferior race. The same logic applied to the trade unions, which had close political ties to the "Jewish" SPD.

Hitler considered the churches culpable because they accepted the Judeo-Christian heritage, which he despised, and because they relied on spiritual rather than biological criteria of morality. Although the churches were too popular for Hitler to devastate them completely before the war, he had plans to accomplish this after World War II.[66]

The military were reduced to acquiescence in Hitler's decisions, primarily because their loyalties were to the Prussian tradition and to the German state rather than to the racial principles that provided Hitler's justification for expansion, at least before World War II. Under Hitler, anti-Semitic indoctrination was standard fare in the training of all branches of the military. The state bureaucracy was purged because it had many of the "reactionary" loyalties that were common in the army: it dragged its feet in implementing Nazi party directives, concealed Jews in its ranks, and accepted the legal system, which protected Jews. The legal system was likewise purged because judges and lawyers could not be relied upon to activate Hitler's arbitrary and overriding reformulation of the law to conform to his racial principles.

The Nazi party itself, although it did not undergo a purge of the same magnitude as did the Communist party under Stalin, was subjected to a lower-keyed but continuing purge through the Nazi party courts. According to McKale, violations of racial regulations were the most compelling reason for dismissal from the Nazi party.[67]

The entire educational establishment was taken over by Nazi leaders, and race was introduced as a central theme of education to spread Hitler's racial world view among the young. This indoctrination was reinforced in religious and other youth organizations; it was predictably most prevalent in the SS. All forms of media were controlled and instructed not to let a week go by without delivering an anti-Semitic message to the public. Endless streams of racist propaganda inundated the German people, and reports on foreign affairs were couched in anti-Semitic terminology.[68] Private organizations were eliminated or taken over because they were based on nonracial criteria for affiliation and might serve as hotbeds of dissent, not so much against the persecution of Jews, but against the destruction of German institutions and organizations that Hitler in part undertook to purify the "Aryan" race of "evil and alien" Jewish influences.

Thus Hitler's ethnic theory, particularly its anti-Semitic component, underlay many of his major domestic policies. Power accumulation was of course an absolutely necessary and critical part of Hitler's overall design, because he could not (in his closed logical system) purify the race domestically or extend its territory abroad without domestic power and control. Nevertheless, Hitler's piecemeal destruction of all institutions or individuals who seriously constrained his own extension of power should not be taken to mean that he was merely a power-hungry madman. His increasing domestic power over and control of all aspects of German life through party agencies and the police apparatus were logically necessary to insure racial purity and unity; racial homogeneity and unity were in turn essential prerequisites for the final aim of his ethnic theory—to prove the historical superiority of the "Aryan" race by acquiring territory at the expense of "inferior" races, especially the Jews.

## NOTES ON HITLER'S PSYCHOLOGY

Although Hitler can be studied from a Freudian or psychoanalytic point of view,[69] it is also important to examine other possible links between his paranoia and his racial theories. We know that Hitler was deeply affected by the death of his father, and more importantly, that of his mother when he was only 18. Because he was devoted to his mother, her death was a critical personal loss that left him emotionally rootless and genuinely alone in the world. We also know that Hitler was ecstatic at being able to serve for four years as a runner of dispatches in the German army, because his years from 1907 to 1914 had been those of a wandering, purposeless youth who had been rejected at his chosen career as an artist. Even during World War I Hitler was a fanatic who objected to other soldiers' complaints about the hardships of war, since he thought that Germany was worth all sacrifices.

Between 1918 and 1924 Hitler formulated his world view, which was very much influenced by his belief that Germany's defeat and the Weimar Republic were caused by Jews. Whereas he had previously disliked Jews on meeting them in large numbers in Vienna, after World War I he transformed his personal loathing for Jews into "rational anti-Semitism" in which the Jews were seen as conspirators seeking world domination. This transformation was probably motivated in part by a desire to place the blame for his personal sorrows on a convenient scapegoat, but this in itself does not explain his transformation from "emotional" to "rational anti-Semite."

As a result of his experiences during the war, Hitler was psychologically attuned to "resist" his enemies, as are all soldiers; Hitler, however, carried this mindset beyond the wartime situation and continued to "resist" Germany's humiliation, which he attributed to Jews. Kren and Rappoport have developed an extremely important model of resisters that may elucidate our understanding of Hitler's transformation from an "emotional" to a "rational anti-Semite" who could exterminate European Jewry. They postulate a triad of necessary conditions for resistance.

> First, the *probability of success*: how likely is it that resistance will succeed in achieving its purpose? Judgments here require analysis of the relative strength and weakness of both the established authority and the resistance. To be effective, the resistance must be concerned with plausible goals and offer a practical route toward their attainment.[70]

If we examine Hitler's decision to "resist" Jews, we find that he made it within two years of the war, simultaneously with his decision to become a politician. Only by going into politics could he hope to fulfill his goal of eliminating Jewish influence in Germany by "practical" means. Since the established authority was new and weak, he obviously thought he had some probability of success.

> Second, the *intensity of oppression*: how severe is the pain or suffering imposed by the established authority? Those physical and psychological perils of resistance discussed earlier will

111

hardly be risked by rational men unless obedience to the status quo is accompanied by significant awareness of oppression. In situations where oppression is only latent, or else present but not experienced as such by its victims, some form of consciousness-raising is needed before effective resistance can be set in motion.[71]

To Hitler, the Jews had imposed pain and suffering both during and after World War I, and the "Jewish" Weimar Republic negated everything for which he had thought he was fighting. Certainly he felt oppressed by them in a psychological sense and used every Jewish activity to raise his consciousness of their "threatening" nature.

And third, the presence of an *alternative authority system*: to what extent is resistance supported or justified by values and norms contradicting those of the authority system in force?[72]

Hitler formulated his ethnic theory, starting with Jews as an "alien" race, and working toward a reinterpretation of all human history based on racial criteria; in this theory he established a "rational" or ideological basis for contesting the authority of the Weimar Republic and supplanting it with a Führer state. He also had the *will* to "resist," which Kren and Rappoport consider essential for successful resistance.[73]

According to Kren and Rappoport, the decision to become a resister entails euphoria:

The euphoria characterizing serious resistance signals the experience of a new world-view. Once engaged, action against that which has been avoided, feared, and repressed works a sudden and deeply pervasive change on the individual. This is the therapeutic effect that Fanon observed in his discussion of anti-colonial revolts. The release of pent-up energy allows the victim to feel himself suddenly different: healed of the internal conflicts that had troubled him, and relieved of the burden of tension and guilt that had accumulated in consequence of his status as a victim. In more general terms, the resister is one who has "taken arms against a sea of troubles" and ended them even at the cost of his own life.[74]

When Hitler "discovered" the "Jewish world conspiracy," he also experienced the euphoria that Kren and Rappoport describe, and in later years recreated this feeling by stressing how grateful the world would be for his "discovery" and subsequent extermination of the "Jewish pest."

Other comments of Kren and Rappoport are of interest:

Viewed in the broader context of contemporary history, moreover, there can be little doubt that the chief inspiration of all serious resistance movements is not survival but some value system. This may be rooted either in a fully articulated worldview such as Marxism or Catholicism, or it may involve only a simple belief in certain humanitarian norms; but whatever its roots, it must generate ideas powerful enough to overwhelm the desire for personal survival. In this connection, a good deal of relevant evidence suggests that the abstract values inspiring resistance may gradually come to dominate the individual and literally compel dangerous action despite contrary fears or rationalizations.[75]

Again, applying this description to Hitler, it is clear that he was a completely politicized man, for whom ideation definitely took on a life of its own and who assimilated other factors so intensively that living became meaningless unless the logic of his ethnic theory was carried out, despite the risks that this entailed.

Kren and Rappoport describe one form of resistance in which it was a "style of life beginning in childhood,"[76] and again this applies to Hitler, who conducted a campaign of passive resistance against his father's values and plans for him. Also, in discussing Hans Scholl, a student who resisted Hitler's regime in Munich, Kren and Rappoport conclude that ". . . failing all else, if he and his colleagues were killed they could at least have shown to future generations that the German people were not entirely without honor."[77] In his *Testament* Hitler echoed this refrain, but obviously interpreted the "honor" of the German people in diametrically opposed ways. In a further discussion, Kren and Rappoport state that:

> The ideological basis for resistance is very clear in all the cases noted above. It was founded on militant movements for Zionism, socialism, or Communism—movements that had always provided their members with a strong historical sense of struggle and an identification with group goals rather than individual satisfaction.[78]

It was clearly Hitler's conception that he was working for group goals—those of the "Aryan" people—and that he was involved in a historical struggle of unprecedented importance. He even demonstrated mental attitudes that were similar to those of concentration-camp inmates, such as Primo Levi, who stated:

> In history and in life one sometimes seems to glimpse a ferocious law which states: "To he that has, will be given; to he that has not, will be taken away." In the *Lager*, where man is alone and where the struggle for life is reduced to its primordial mechanism, this unjust law is openly in force, is recognized by all.[79]

This passage could have come from Hitler himself; its description of a primordial mechanism, however, would have been applied to *all* human affairs and not confined to a concentration camp or exceptional circumstances.

Kren and Rappoport, in discussing Jewish resisters, state that ". . . the only factor standing against compromise was ideology combined with organization. Ideological considerations set the boundary conditions for survival, the limits beyond which survival lost its meaning."[80] When Hitler finally evolved his ethnic theory, this ideology, which to him explained all of human history, became the prime motivating force that determined the tenor of his movement, his decision to organize for strength, and his personal conviction that he was acting out a world-historical role in which his own personal survival was immaterial.

Among Jewish resisters, Ringelblum, a survivor of the Warsaw uprising, stated:

A paradoxical situation arose. The older generation with half a lifetime behind it, spoke, thought and concerned itself about surviving the war, dreamt about life. The youth—the best, the most beautiful, the finest that the Jewish people possessed—spoke and thought only about an honorable death. They did not think about surviving the war. They did not procure Aryan papers for themselves. They had no dwellings on the other side. Their only concern was to discover the most dignified and honorable death, befitting an ancient people with a history stretching back over several thousand years.[81]

Ironically, Hitler and the most ardent young Nazis were concerned about the dignity of the German people and thought that they were dying an honorable death when they died in the struggle against the "Jewish pest."

In examining these comparisons of the psychology of resisters and Hitler's transformation from an "emotional" to a "rational anti-Semite," it is important to understand that we are here dealing with transitions that are not normally discussed in psychobiographies of Hitler. It is fruitful, however, to realize that the psychological mechanisms at work in Hitler's mind were similar to those of resisters, who based their actions on an alternative world view. The decisions of Jews to resist were clearly based on dire physical danger and real threats. Hitler, on the other hand, "misperceived" the "Jewish threat" because he refused to examine all of the evidence on Jews, but instead facilely incorporated the "Jewish world conspiracy" into an equally facile argument that all human history is based on the competition between races. These "misperceptions," however, were very real to him, as they are to all true paranoids. Yet only the depth of his "ideological resistance" to the supposed danger of Jews explains his ruthless, willful, and obdurate actualization of his ethnic theory by extermination and enslavement.

Hitler's closest historical counterpart is Josef Stalin. The dictionary definition of paranoia is "having systematized delusions of persecution and one's own greatness." Both Stalin and Hitler had delusions of persecution; Stalin saw conspiracies to unseat him everywhere and launched preventive domestic wars against all real and imaginary rivals; Hitler saw conspiracies of world Jewry everywhere and also launched "preventive wars" at home and abroad, but these were against imaginary foes. In this sense he was completely out of touch with reality, whereas Stalin had at least some cause to suspect machinations against him, since the Russian Communist party is and always has been a hotbed of intrigue and jockeying for power. With respect to the other half of the definition, having delusions of one's own greatness, it is not clear that this applies either to Stalin or to Hitler. It is difficult to find evidence of megalomania in Stalin's early life or career, and certainly his later achievement of clawing his way to dictatorship over one of the world's largest nations would have justified his thinking of himself as a "great man" in historical terms. With Hitler we find that during his youth he had a strong sense of mission and a mystical feeling that he was destined by fate to achieve greatness. Since he had the energy, stamina, and cleverness to rise from obscurity to the near-domination of all of Europe, this sense of having greatness within himself was not delusional. And as with Stalin, this accomplishment places him among the "great men" of history. Thus both Hitler and Stalin might be described as egomaniacs rather than megalomaniacs. In both cases, however, their "greatness" should also be measured by the magnitude of human suffering that they foisted upon their own populations, and in Hitler's case, the enormity of destruction that he caused in the rest of Europe, particularly for Jews.

Hitler and Stalin were complete and rigid ideologues for whom the implementation of their beliefs was the center and purpose of their daily lives. Both were without a conscience or mercy in their treatment of "enemies," and both measured a man's worth by his willingness to use brutality to achieve his goals; therefore, Hitler and Stalin feared and respected each other.[82] Both Hitler and Stalin knew that they were engaged in a mortal combat of like minds—two titans fighting with no holds barred for survival, and later in the war, for the domination of Central and Eastern Europe. Stalin proved the stronger opponent in part because he did not deliberately tie one arm behind his back, as did Hitler when he wasted valuable manpower and rolling stock to transport Jews and others to their deaths. Stalin was also stronger because he pursued only one goal at a time—victory in war. Hitler was weaker because he simultaneously sought a victory against Russia and the destruction of Jews and "subhumans," thus wiping out a much-needed labor force and alienating potential allies. This was one of Hitler's fatal errors. When he spoke about the psychology of propaganda, he insisted that one must concentrate on only one enemy, but he did not utilize this insight in the conduct of World War II. Thus Hitler's monomaniacal obsession with his ethnic theory, which was based on psychological and conceptual "misperceptions," contributed significantly to Germany's defeat and to the birth of the colossus to the east that he so much feared.

## SUMMARY

To Hitler the "Jewish spirit" was not confined to racial Jews, but extended to all who approved of "Jewish inventions," and he thought that it was necessary to eradicate Jewry before the nations of the world were destroyed by the "Jewish world conspiracy." Although Haffner believes that Hitler had two theories, an ethnic theory and an anti-Semitic one, his anti-Semitic theory is actually subsumed in his ethnic theory. This can be summarized as follows: All history consists of national struggles for living space and world domination. "Aryans" must prove their historical worth by conquering living space to the East at the expense of inferior races (Poles, Russians, Jews, etc.). To secure this living space against future threats, the defeated inferior races must be enslaved and their leadership exterminated. The Jews pose a double threat: first, they occupy valuable living space; and second, they are part of the "international Jewish conspiracy"; therefore, they are the primary target for extermination.

In actualizing this theory, Hitler was able only to attempt the extension of living space, but he did have plans for world conquest, as his handwritten notes indicate. While we might consider this goal demonic, he thought of it as messianic, an act of salvation for those nations that had been "corrupted" by "Jewish values."

117

As a first step, he attempted to purge Germany of all "Jewish influences," particularly political parties, civil servants, and others who might stand in the way of his attacks on Jews and plans for foreign conquest.

Psychologically, Hitler "misperceived" the "Jewish threat" and was paranoid by common understandings of that term. However, this led him to adopt the frame of mind of a "resister" who calculated his odds of destroying the Jews by political action, perceived an irrational Jewish "threat to Aryans," and formulated a new world view, his ethnic theory, which was designed to eliminate this "threat." Both Hitler and Stalin were in some sense paranoid, but Stalin had at least a firmer grasp of reality. Certainly Hitler's delusions about the Jews hindered him in World War II and contributed to the weakening of Germany relative to the "Jewish Bolsheviks."

Some historians do not believe there was a coherent Nazi ideology. Nevertheless, if human history can ever be ascribed to the realization of ideas, the destruction of European Jewry and World War II may be attributed to Hitler's attempt to actualize his unalterable ethnic theory.

# Persecution, Party Unity, and Hitler's Responsibility

"Do I intend to exterminate whole races? . . . Of Course I do.
. . . Cruelty is impressive."
Adolf Hitler, quoted in Robert Waite, *The Psychopathic God*,
p. 46.

Between 1933 and 1939 the Jews were systematically driven out of German political, religious, economic, social, and intellectual life.[1] For mid-1933 the German census reported approximately 500,000 Jews in Germany, and Herbert Strauss estimated that there had been about 525,000 in January 1933.[2] If we examine the entire period 1933 to 1945, it appears that approximately 300,000 Jews emigrated from Germany.[3] During the years 1940–1944, 134,000 Jews were sent to labor and death camps, and of these only an estimated 5,000 survived. In Germany another 5,000 or so survived by hiding, and about 12,000 others in mixed marriages escaped destruction.[4] An estimated 30,000 Jews emigrated to other European nations but were subsequently caught by the Nazis and sent to the death camps. Thus the final estimate for German Jews killed is approximately 160,000.[5]

Because the Nazis destroyed most of German and European Jewry, we must ask two important and interrelated questions. First, what were the chronological stages of persecution and who instigated persecution from stage to stage? Second, what was the function of anti-Semitism to Hitler, as leader of the NSDAP? Most readers are familiar with the escalation of persecution be-

119

tween 1933 and 1945; however, the major events will be discussed in the context of their functions. In determining responsibility for anti-Semitic policies, it is obviously necessary to know who the main instigators were, and they will therefore be discussed. Although Hitler was a rabid Jew-hater, we cannot assume that he pursued anti-Semitic polices for this reason alone. We wish to determine the political functions of anti-Semitism within the Nazi party. Because the questions of timing, instigation, and party political functions of anti-Semitism are interrelated, they will be discussed as a unit.

Another section will examine Hitler's responsibility for and timing of persecution and extermination. We are interested in both his abstract decision to apply his ethnic theory to the Jews and his concrete orders that this be done. To determine his responsibility and timing, we shall examine a fair number of Hitler's own speeches as well as statements by others regarding his role in the Final Solution.

## FUNCTIONS OF ANTI-SEMITISM INSIDE THE NAZI PARTY

The stages of persecution can be divided into four periods, 1933–1935, 1935–1938, 1938–1941, and post-October 1941. Although Hitler had no detailed plan for persecution until 1933, by April or May of that year he had envisioned all of the measures that would be taken by 1938.[6] During stage 1 (between 1933 and the summer of 1935) there was no systematic approach to the "Jewish question." A party-directed boycott against Jewish businesses, doctors, and lawyers took place for four days in April 1933; however, this was abandoned when it failed to receive domestic or foreign support.[7]

The boycott of 1933 was undertaken for several reasons. Party radicals were engaging in violent attacks on Jews, which threatened Hitler's new image as chancellor and statesman of a legal and orderly state.[8] In order to control the SA (*Sturmabteilung*), his paramilitary organization, he had to channel their attacks through a disciplined boycott that he could call off at will. He also wished to demonstrate Germany's control over German Jews to foreign

Jews who boycotted Germany. In addition, he wished to demonstrate the need for legal measures against Jews, especially to business competitors of Jews whom he hoped to entice into the *Kampfbund des gewerblichen Mittelstand*.[9] The boycott, however, proved unpopular at home and abroad, so that Hitler was forced to terminate it in four days.[10] The boycott appeared to threaten law and order, private property rights, and Germany's international reputation.

The next major campaign against Jews was their exclusion from the civil service between the late spring of 1933 and 1935. A series of legal and pseudo-legal decrees stripped Jews of many civil rights. Restrictions were placed on their employment in the civil service, legal and medical professions, public services, public schools, universities, armed forces, cultural organizations, publishing, and other occupations. In addition, Jewish membership in trade, professional, sports, and labor organizations was severely curtailed. General quotas restricted hiring of Jews and Jewish attendance at universities and public schools. Given the occupational characteristics of the Jewish community, these restrictions took a heavy toll.[11] They were accompanied by a mixed bag of large and small discriminatory acts by the Nazi party at all levels. The years 1933–1935 were especially noteworthy for the commonplace and arbitrary imposition of new extra-legal restrictions by a myriad of party leaders and organizations that were competing to outdo rivals in showing anti-Semitic zeal. Although central direction was rare, political, social, and particularly economic harassment became a normal method of ostracizing Jews. These measures were implemented by Hitler because it had long been assumed by moderate and fanatic party members that Jews would be excluded from any control over the state or German society. This was the very least sop to the party that Hitler could have offered after the failure of the boycott of 1933.

In 1935 Hitler introduced stage 2 of his racial policy with the enactment of the Nuremberg Laws. Under the Nuremberg Laws not only were Jews classified as "state subjects" rather than as "citizens" possessing civil rights, but also they were defined as a separate race whose marriage or sexual contact with "Aryans"

121

was forbidden by law. Illegal sexual relations were called *Rassenschande*, or "race defilement." Although the Nuremberg Laws were welcomed by both Jews and non-Jews as a harbinger of order, their subsequent application through thirteen implementing ordinances demonstrated their true function; they served as a tool to exclude Jews from public life and to isolate them socially.[12] The Nuremberg Laws were not immediately followed by a pogrom because Hitler wished Germany to sponsor the 1936 Olympic games; however, after the Olympics a number of additional occupational, passport, foreign currency, and other restrictions were imposed. Many of these restrictions were pseudo-legal because Hitler opposed "wild" or unorganized pogroms in which he tended to lose central control over participants.

There were several reasons for Hitler's enactment of the Nuremberg Laws. Whatever his ultimate intention, in the early years of the Third Reich he was politic enough to suppress his most hateful impulses. The summer of 1935 witnessed an increasing number of attacks on Jews and Jewish businesses, especially in Berlin.[13] Party radicals who wanted a "second revolution" (after the purge of the SA on June 30, 1934) were discontent with measures taken to date. They were also incensed that some Jews who had emigrated were returning to Germany.[14] Streicher and Goebbels were the chief instigators of unrest in the party, especially through their organs *Der Stürmer* and *Der Angriff*, which incited attacks by party members against Jews.[15] Some party members demanded that every "fourth-Jew" or "eighth-Jew" be considered a full Jew, that all mixed marriages be dissolved, and that some Jews be sterilized.[16] The SS also pressed for uniform legislation to control chaos among party radicals.[17]

Hitler introduced the Nuremberg Laws, therefore, to placate his radical followers, but also to pressure reluctant bureaucrats to take a firmer hand with Jews.[18] Hitler himself chose the particular plan that became law.[19] This plan was the mildest of four options and was chosen because of the following advantages: (1) the party rather than the state was to decide who was a Jew; (2) Hitler rather than the SA could determine the pace and legality of anti-Semitic policy; (3) a moderate policy was designed to impress bureaucrats and to make them more willing to implement the laws; and (4) the laws were announced as definitive ones to make Hitler appear moderate and benevolent.[20] As indicated above, he was not yet willing to reveal his final intentions.

The Nuremberg Laws temporarily assuaged radical party members; however, between 1936 and 1937 their resentment rose again, exemplified by concrete anti-Semitic actions by party members and by demands from party radicals for some new anti-Semitic initiatives.[21] In Bavaria party members demanded that Jewish businesses be marked with an insignia to prevent "Aryans" from patronizing them.[22] In 1936 the Ministry of the Interior sent a letter to leading state offices throughout Germany indicating that Jews could not be denied their rights to property ownership because they were protected by law. This type of attitude enraged radical party members.[23] By the summer of 1938 Goebbels and the party radicals were once more engaging in anti-Semitic attacks, especially in Berlin.

In 1938 the third stage of persecution was initiated. In April Jews were forced to report all of their property to the government. In June fifteen hundred Jews were arrested and sent to concentration camps. During the summer Berlin was the site of sporadic violence against Jews by Nazi rowdies. Between July and September successive government decrees restricted the employment of Jewish doctors and lawyers and forced Jews to adopt the middle names "Israel" or "Sara" on passports and identity cards. These measures were followed by a forced repatriation of fifty thousand Polish Jews in October 1938. This act was particularly indicative of the vehemence of Nazi intentions, because individuals were given only a few hours' notice before they were literally dumped on the Polish-German border. This was the first precursor of the extreme violence that would later be commonplace, and was noteworthy because it illustrated the ad hoc Nazi approach to persecution. Increased willingness to use force became even clearer when a wholesale pogrom took place during the night of November 9, 1938. This is termed *Kristallnacht* because the streets were littered with broken glass from vandalized Jewish businesses.

During *Kristallnacht* over two hundred synagogues were burned, seventy-five hundred businesses were destroyed, ninety-one Jews were murdered, and twenty-six thousand Jews were arrested. Most of these were subsequently sent to concentration camps but released within a few months.[24] This violence was committed by the SA, SS, and Hitler Youth.[25] Goering, Goebbels, Heydrich, and other high officials then determined that Jews should pay a billion marks to cover damage to insured property destroyed by Nazi rowdies. The ostensible motive for *Kristallnacht* was retaliation for the murder of a German diplomat, vom Rath, by a Polish Jew. More genuine motives, however, were to justify past, current, and future expropriation of Jewish businesses, to provide an excuse for increased pressure on Jews to emigrate, and to satisfy personal ambitions of top Nazi leaders, particularly Goebbels and Streicher.[26]

Many historians believe that Goebbels, Streicher, and assorted party radicals were the main instigators behind *Kristallnacht*, but that Hitler directed Goebbels to incite demonstrations against Jews in order to justify driving them from the economy;[27] however, Adam in particular believes that Hitler was the primary architect of *Kristallnacht*.[28] But Hitler's motivations were not totally related to domestic events. After Munich he wished to show foreign powers that Jews would be future hostages for his expansion into Czechoslovakia and Eastern Europe,[29] and also possibly to "punish" the "lackey of the Jews," Britain, for caving in to his demands at Munich and preventing his hoped-for war at that time.[30]

Although from 1933 to 1937 sporadic forced sales of Jewish businesses had occurred, between 1938 and 1939 economic persecution reached a high point. Jews were systematically driven from their businesses by Hitler's party henchmen, Goering, and the SS, primarily at Hitler's prompting. This coincided with the Four Year Plan for economic autarchy and was designed to confiscate all remaining Jewish property.

Expropriation was useful to the SS because it often made emigration a necessity. The SS had long favored organized emigration in lieu of the party's piecemeal attacks on Jews. Aside from its desire to free Germany of Jews, the SS hoped to embarrass foreign governments that refused to accept Jews whose poverty was the result of Nazi persecution. Therefore, the SS cooperated with Jewish organizations to speed up emigration. In the process, of course, the SS made certain that Jewish property was heavily taxed or expropriated.

Between 1938 and 1941 an almost endless series of new restrictions was placed on every aspect of Jewish life, sometimes at the urging of Nazi party radicals, as before.[31] No indignity appeared too trivial to legislate, and Jews were almost totally isolated and reduced to a miserable subsistence level. They were denied entrance to parks, they could no longer own automobiles, and Jewish publications and associations were prohibited.[32] They could not use public telephones or automatic ticket machines, visit the countryside, restaurants, railway or bus station waiting rooms, "Aryan" hairdressers, and sleeping or dining cars on trains. They could not buy newspapers or periodicals, sell their books, buy books in bookstores, receive "smokers' cards," shop during normal shopping hours, or receive a full ration of meats, cereals, and milk. After 1942 they were no longer permitted to keep pets; they were required to turn them in to dog pounds for extermination because they had been "tainted" by "Jewish blood." Some of these measures were enacted because Hitler considered the Jews to be hostages for the good behavior of their "co-conspirators" abroad, the Jews who influenced policy in the U.S.A. and Britain. For example, after Hitler attacked Poland and received adverse publicity in the American press, he retaliated by prohibiting Jews from "going outdoors after 8 P.M. in the winter and 9 P.M. in the summer."[33] This description of persecution lists only illustrative cases. Additional measures were taken against Jews in almost every sphere of life.[34] By 1941 there were no buffers left between Jews and the Nazi state.

In October and November 1938 the Madagascar Plan (to deport Jews to Madagascar in case of war) was being seriously discussed.[35] The Madagascar Plan was still considered as late as March 1942.[36] Hitler apparently did not want an internal Jewish "enemy" to "stab Germany in the back" during wartime.[37] In October 1940 Jews were deported from Baden and the Saarpfalz

125

to concentration camps in southern France, with the intention of shipping them from there to Madagascar. Only the German navy's failure to gain control of the Atlantic temporarily halted additional plans for deportation of 270,000 Jews to France from the northern Rhineland, the East Mark, Bohemia, and Moravia.[38]

By 1939, and probably as early as 1936, Hitler *envisioned* the fourth and final stage of persecution, the concrete physical destruction of Jews.[39] Nevertheless, many historians think that the final decision for genocide was probably not made until March of 1941. At the same time that Hitler decided to invade Russia, which was in his mind a minion of "world Jewry," he introduced the fourth phase of his racial policy; Jews were not to be allowed even their meager existence: deportation, enslavement, and murder constituted the "final solution" to the "Jewish question."[40]

In October 1941 a ban on free emigration was imposed and the deportation of German Jews was resumed.[41] Some "privileged" Jews were sent to Theresienstadt, the "model" camp where killing was rare, but the majority were deported to eastern ghettos and were later worked to death, shot, or gassed.[42]

The extermination of German Jews did not occur in a vacuum but was closely tied to decisions to exterminate Jews in Poland and Russia. When Hitler invaded Poland in 1939, a few months of general confusion followed and no organized measures against Jews were undertaken; however, in December 1939 the first decisions were made to drive Jews into ghettos. These were predominately in cities, where most Polish Jews lived. The conditions endured by the Polish (and later German) Jews in ghettos were atrocious. For example, in Warsaw the Jews, who comprised a third of the population, were crowded into 2.4 percent of the city.[43] Children and parents were separated and often ran screaming through the streets to find each other, only to be drowned out by the many cries of "half a million uprooted people" and the attendant commotion.[44] Housing and food shortages were calamitous and typhoid swept the ghetto:

> Starvation and typhus quickly destroyed life in the Ghetto. Over 43,000 Jews in 1941, and over 37,000 in the first nine

months of 1942 starved to death. The mortality in 1941 was nearly five times that of 1940. Among the refugees, about 150,000 in April 1941, the number of deaths from starvation was 66 percent in May–June 1942. At the 1942 rate (26,000 deaths for the first half of the year for the entire population), the Jews of the Ghetto would have died out in eight years.[45]

The process of ghettoization continued until March 1942 when gassing began, first among Polish Jews and then among German Jews who had been transshipped to Polish ghettos.

In the meantime, in the spring of 1941 Hitler decided to invade Russia. Most probably he also made the decision to exterminate Russian Jews at this time because SS units, *Einsatzgruppen*, were specially trained in May. The initial exterminations in Russia began not with Jews, but with Communist party commissars and officials; however, they were quickly extended to include Jews as well. Mobile units of SS *Einsatzgruppen* initially followed the first wave of army troops, but later operated on the front lines so that Jews could be surprised and trapped. The procedure for shootings followed the pattern outlined by Ohlendorf, an SS major general, at his postwar trial:

> The unit selected for this task would enter a village or city and order the prominent Jewish citizens to call together all Jews for the purpose of resettlement. They were requested to hand over their valuables to the leaders of the unit, and shortly before the execution, to surrender their outer clothing. The men, women and children were led to a place of execution which in most cases was located next to a more deeply excavated antitank ditch. Then they were shot, kneeling or standing, and the corpses thrown into the ditch. I never permitted the shooting by individuals in the group D, but ordered that several of the men should shoot at the same time in order to avoid direct personal responsibility.[46]

By the end of November 1941 the *Einsatzgruppen* had shot a half a million Russian Jews. In the Baltic and other states they recruited local anti-Semites to assist in shooting Jews and to organize pogroms against them. Tens of thousands of Jews were killed by nationals of their own regions, either in spontaneous outbreaks of violence or in raids by bands of Jew-haters.

In the spring of 1942 the SS began killing Russian Jews in gas vans that were camouflaged so that their true function was not exposed. These, however, could only kill fifteen to twenty-five people at a time and the process took ten to fifteen minutes. This was clearly slower than shooting; therefore, Himmler, who had observed a special liquidation by shooting to see how it was done, asked the commander of *Einsatzgruppe* B, Artur Nebe, to consider other killing methods that would be more humane for SS troops, and faster.[47] Both Nebe and another commander, Bach-Zelewski, eventually suffered nervous breakdowns, and Himmler was always concerned that his troops not suffer undue hardships because of the "hard task" that he had assigned to them.

The *Einsatzgruppen* alone shot or gassed more than a million Russian Jews.[48] Another 400,000 or so were killed by other SS units including thousands of anti-Semitic non-German troops, as well as police units and the army.[49] In the spring of 1942 the gassing of Polish Jews was begun and the ghettos were gradually liquidated. The death camps, which were primarily in Poland, then served as execution centers for Jews from Germany and other parts of Europe. Most German Jews were killed by the middle of 1943.

## HITLER'S RESPONSIBILITY AND TIMING

What can we learn from Hitler's own words about his responsibility for the extermination of European Jewry? Hitler's speeches and comments provide some insights. He made many threatening statements about Jews beginning in 1919, when he wrote his first propaganda letter. In it he advocated rational versus emotional anti-Semitism and said: "Its final objective must unswervingly be the removal of the Jews altogether."[50] In March 1921 he declared that "One has to prevent the Jewish subversion of our people, if necessary by securing its instigating virus in concentration camps."[51] In July 1924, while he was in Landsberg prison, he said:

128

While working out my book, I have come to the realization that in the future the most severe methods of fighting will have to be used to let us come through successfully. I am convinced that this is a vital question not just for our people but for all peoples. For Juda is the plague of the world.[52]

Although Jaeckel interprets this as advocacy of extinction and extermination, the words "most severe methods of fighting" could mean many things, and to read "extermination" into them is questionable. In the numerous speeches made by Hitler in his campaigns of 1928, 1930, and 1932, no specific proposals on the "Jewish question" can be found.[53] It is clear that Hitler intended to do *something* about Jews, either by repression at home or by forcing them out of Germany, but exactly what is not spelled out anywhere. In 1934 he had a heated argument with United States Ambassador Dodd in which he said that 59 percent of all offices in Russia were held by Jews, that they had ruined that country, and that they intended to ruin Germany; he added, "If they continue their activity, we shall make a complete end to all of them in the country."[54] In 1936 he had one of many conversations with Hermann Rauschning, an acquaintance who later left Germany in disgust at Nazism and wrote his insights in many books. Hitler is reported to have said:

Do I intend to eradicate whole races? . . . Of course I do. . . . Cruelty is impressive. Cruelty and brutal strength. . . . The masses want it. They need the thrill of terror to make them shudderingly submissive. I do not want concentration camps to become old age pensioners' homes. Terror is the most effective way of politics.[55]

In April 1937 Hitler gave a speech to eight hundred Nazi district leaders, among whom were many veteran anti-Semites. An editor of a provincial newspaper had called for the introduction of a distinguishing insignia for Jewish firms. To this Hitler replied:

From whom is he demanding this? Who can give the necessary orders? Only I can give them. The editor, in the name of his readers, is asking me to act. First, I should tell you that long

129

before this editor had any inkling about the Jewish problem, I had made myself an expert in the subject. Secondly, this problem has been under consideration for two or three years, and will, of course, be settled one way or another in due course. My point is then this: the final aim of our policy is crystal clear to all of us. All that concerns me is never to take a step that I might later have to retrace and never to take a step that could damage us in any way. You must understand that I always go as far as I dare and never further. It is vital to have a sixth sense that tells you, broadly, what you can do and what you cannot do. Even in a struggle with an adversary it is not my way to issue a direct challenge to a trial of strength. I do not say "Come on and fight, because I want a fight." Instead I shout at him (and I shout louder and louder): "I mean to destroy you." And then I use my intelligence to help me to manoeuvre him into a tight corner so that he cannot strike back, and then I deliver the fatal blow.[56]

Toland comments on this speech as follows:

His last words, leaving no doubt that he meant to solve the problem by killing the Jews, were drowned out by a spontaneous mass scream of blood lust. This flesh-creeping roar was preserved on tape, a reminder to posterity of man's primal brutality and how like the shrieks of the mob in the Roman Colosseum for the death of a fallen gladiator it must have been![57]

On June 31, 1938, Hitler claimed that the Jews would be "crushed by the wheel of history."[58] On January 21, 1939, he told the Czechoslovakian foreign minister, "We are going to destroy the Jews. They are not going to get away with what they did on 9 November 1918. The day of reckoning has come."[59] And on January 30, 1939, he gave the first speech that hinted at his ultimate intention to the public via radio. The speech was delivered before the Reichstag, and because of its importance, three translations are given:

If the Jewish international financiers inside and outside Europe succeed in involving the nations in another war, the result will not be world bolshevism and therefore a victory for Judaism; it will be the end of the Jews in Europe. [Alternatively, "the annihilation of the Jewish race in Europe" and "the destruction of the Jewish race in Europe."[60] The German word was "*die Vernichtung*."]

On July 16, 1941, at a planning conference with top Nazis and an army general, Hitler discussed occupation policy as follows:

. . . we are taking all the necessary measures—shootings, deportations and so on—and so we should. . . . The whole vast area must of course be pacified as quickly as possible—and the best way to do that is to shoot anyone who so much as looks like giving trouble. . . . [Russian guerrilla warfare] is not without its advantages as far as we are concerned, since it gives us a chance to wipe out anyone who gets in our way.[61]

In the autumn of 1941 Hitler made some remarkably frank statements in the presence of his normally shielded inner circle of secretaries, aides, servants, and personal staff:

From the rostrum of the Reichstag, I prophesied to Jewry that, in the event of war's proving inevitable, the Jew would disappear from Europe. That race of criminals has on its conscience the two million dead of the First World War, and now already hundreds and thousands more. Let nobody tell me that all the same we can't park them in the marshy parts of Russia! Who's worrying about our troops? It's not a bad idea, by the way, that public rumor attributes to us a plan to exterminate the Jews. Terror is a salutary thing. . . . I have numerous accounts to settle, about which I cannot think today. But that doesn't mean I forget them. I write them down. The time will come to bring out the big book! Even with regard to the Jews, I've found myself remaining inactive. There's no sense in adding uselessly to the difficulties of the moment. One acts shrewdly when one bides one's time.[62]

On January 23, 1942, Hitler remarked at his own humaneness and pointed out that eight Jews riding donkeys were regularly led through the streets of Rome until 1830 (presumably to demonstrate their guilt for the murder of Christ). He then said: "For my part, I restrict myself to telling them they must go away. If they break their pipes on the journey, I can't do anything about it. But if they refuse to go voluntarily, I see no other solution but extermination."[63] Also, in January 1942 he made a speech at the Sports Palace to commemorate the ninth anniversary of the Nazi rise to power. The audience included forty high-ranking military officers:

> They are simply our old enemies, their plans have suffered shipwreck through us, and they rightly hate us, just as we hate them. We realize that this war can only end either in the wiping out of the Germanic nations, or by the disappearance of Jewry from Europe. For the first time, it will not be the others who will bleed to death, but for the first time the genuine ancient Jewish law, "an eye for an eye, a tooth for a tooth," is being applied. The more this struggle spreads, the more anti-Semitism will spread—and world Jewry may rely on this.[64]

In late April 1942 he made a major speech before the Reichstag in which he "denounced Bolshevism as 'the dictatorship of Jews' and labeled the Jew 'a parasitic germ' who had to be dealt with ruthlessly."[65]

In early 1942 Goebbels made the following entry in his diary:

> Beginning with Lublin, the Jews in the General Government are now being evacuated eastward. The procedure is a pretty barbaric one and not to be described here more definitely. Not much will remain of the Jews. On the whole it can be said that about 60 percent of them will have to be liquidated whereas only about 40 percent can be used for forced labor. . . . It's a life-and-death struggle between the Aryan race and the Jewish bacillus. No other government and no other regime would have the strength for such a global solution of this question. Here, too, the Fuehrer is the undismayed champion of a radical solution necessitated by conditions and therefore inexorable. Fortunately, a whole series of possibilities presents itself for us in wartime that would be denied us in peacetime. We shall have to profit by this.[66]

But Hitler's final conclusion, reached when the "Thousand-Year Reich" was collapsing under Russian bombardment, was the true measure of the man:

> I have always been absolutely fair in my dealings with the Jews. On the eve of the war, I gave them one final warning. I told them that, if they precipitated another war, they would not be spared and that I would exterminate the vermin throughout Europe, and this time once and for all. To this warning they retorted with a declaration of war and affirmed that wherever in the world there was a Jew, there, too, was an implacable enemy of National Socialist Germany.
>
> Well, we have lanced the Jewish abscess; and the world of the future will be eternally grateful to us.[67]

What can we conclude from the evidence contained in Hitler's speeches? It would appear that Hitler did not *openly* state his intention to exterminate Jews until 1936, and given his penchant for the melodramatic, even his comments at that time *might* be interpreted as wishful thinking rather than a concrete plan. But his speech before Nazi Party district leaders in April 1937 also indicates that he was contemplating a "fatal blow" to his enemy, the Jews, and one in 1938 clearly implies that the Jews were under direct physical threat.

Hitler's speech to the Reichstag in January 1939 is very important but hard to interpret because it depends upon which meanings translators give to his words. It is variously translated that World War II would mean "the end," "destruction," or "annihilation" of the Jews in Europe. Hitler deliberately chose a word (*die Vernichtung*) with ambiguous meanings because he wanted to frighten the Jews of foreign countries so that they would not encourage their governments to wage war against Germany. On the other hand, he could not directly state that he wanted to exterminate European Jewry because he wished to preserve domestic unity in the envisioned war. The public had shown after *Kristallnacht* that they did not approve of violence against the Jews, and his choice of an ambiguous word was probably a result of his uncertainty about public support for extermination. In Hit-

133

ler's later references to this speech, he alternately recalled that he had threatened destruction or annihilation, or that Jewry "would have finished playing its role in Europe.''[68] Again, ambiguity.

In Hitler's speeches and comments after 1939 he first spoke as if extermination were only a plan (fall 1941); then he spoke of telling the Jews to go away and exterminating them if they did not (January 23, 1942), and that they would disappear from Europe and be bled to death (January, 1942). And in March 1942 Goebbels reported that Hitler was the "undismayed champion" of barbarities that would cost the lives of 60 percent of Europe's Jews. In his *Testament* Hitler revealed that the real promise in his speech at the outbreak of the war was to "exterminate the vermin throughout Europe." (The speech was actually given in January 1939, but he constantly referred to it as having been delivered in September 1939.) One could not ask for a clearer statement of responsibility than Hitler gives in his *Testament*. It would hardly be necessary even to refer to his own words were it not for some misguided writers who question both that the Holocaust ever occurred and that Hitler was the prime mover behind it. Although Hitler was a deliberate liar, his wartime speeches and comments corroborate his boast that *he* decided upon the extermination of European Jewry. One wonders when he began to conceive of extermination first as an abstract, and later as a concrete possibility. Hitler wanted to rid Europe of the Jews, and this was clearly his objective in 1924 when he collected his thoughts for *Mein Kampf*; it was still his goal in 1928 when he wrote his second book. Nevertheless, extermination was not proposed in either his books or in his speeches before 1936, as we saw above.[69] One hypothesis is that he seriously thought of this possibility in 1924 when he began formulating his ethnic theory, since in *Mein Kampf* he treated the "Jewish question" as not merely a problem for Germany alone but also for the world as a whole. And if Jews were to him a problem for all the world, then simply deporting them to Palestine or some island would not suffice in the long run, because they would then constitute a territorial state that would collude with Jews in other nations and pose a severe threat of world domination to Hitler. In *Mein Kampf* Hitler adopted a

134

more radical attitude toward the Jews, linking them to foreign policy, and adding a new universalist and internationalist outlook to his discussions about them.[70] All of these were key developments in the formulation of his final ethnic theory, in which the Jews were classified as a world threat that required diligent countermeasures by all nations. Clearly, the most logical and surest way to eliminate this "threat" was to kill all Jews. The possibility of exterminating European Jews might just have simmered in Hitler's mind during the years when he was strengthening the party and fighting for power. But with his appointment as chancellor in 1933, he may have decided that the elimination of Jews from Europe was a *real* possibility, rather than just a dream that could never be actualized. The process would need slow preparation, starting with gradual measures and then harsher measures in Germany itself, and finally extending to other nations as they were conquered in the future eastern war, which Hitler had envisioned as Germany's only hope for acquiring living space and world domination (as expressed in *Mein Kampf* and in his second book). Nevertheless, he now had a strong power base that could be expanded by the destruction of domestic rivals. If he could prepare Germany to wage war successfully in the East, then he could trap the vast majority of Europe's Jews. They could be annihilated by hoarding them either into small ghettos or into one vast ghetto in the Russian Far East, where they would die of exposure, starvation, and disease; by working them to death as slave laborers; or by shooting them in mass executions. However, as Hitler discovered from the boycott in 1933, he could not act without taking both domestic and foreign opinion into consideration. His party already had a reputation for violence, which he was later forced to curb in order to retain popular support. He was anxious to gain favorable world opinion so that he could first reverse the Treaty of Versailles and then expand his domination without opposition. He therefore had to confine his attacks on the Jews to a much slower timetable than he would have hoped. He clearly thought that they were the greatest menace in the world, and the sooner they had been eliminated, the better he would have

135

liked it; however, here as in other cases, Hitler was willing to bide his time, as he told his staff in the fall of 1941.[71]

In support of the hypothesis that Hitler made concrete mental plans, rather than indulge himself in simple day dreaming, we should again refer to his comments early in 1936.[72] He said quite clearly that he intended to "eradicate whole races" in order to terrorize the population into submission. Hitler enjoyed saying outrageous things to shake people out of their complacency, but this is probably not the kind of statement that even he would have made lightly. Certainly his tying it to a purpose, rather than simply saying it in bombast, makes one suspect that he had been considering this as a real, versus wishful, possibility for some time. He may have thought of it in concrete terms even as early as 1924; but as argued above, his accession to power meant that he could actually plan for mass murder under the cover of a war, which he himself knew was certain to come. We should note that in his *Testament* Hitler specifically said that a localized war waged in 1938 might have prevented a second world war, but he was referring to a war with the West.[73] He never abandoned his "eastern aspirations," and these could only have been fulfilled through a gigantic war with Russia.[74] Thus Hitler knew when he took power in 1933 that both the conquest of Russia and the destruction of European Jewry were within his reach if only he could adequately strengthen Germany's military machine.

Hitler's decision to eradicate European Jews could thus have been made anytime between 1924 and 1936 (probably not earlier because his ethnic theory was not sufficiently developed). If one subscribes to the interpretation that Hitler was only "posing" as a man of infinite ruthlessness in 1936 and that his statements in 1937 and 1938 were ambiguous, then one might conclude that he made the mental decision only by 1939, when he promised both the Czech foreign minister and (in his own recollection) the German people that he intended to destroy the Jews. But to overlook the accumulated evidence in his speeches and conversations and to conclude that he made the abstract decision later than 1939 would require incredible gullibility.

The timing of Hitler's decisions regarding extermination has been the subject of considerable controversy among historians. Some think he made the decision in the 1920s,[75] a possibility if his plan was only abstract and not yet concrete. Others believe such a decision was made by subordinates in response to local conditions and only later approved and extended by Hitler, possibly between November 1941 and the spring of 1942.[76] Still others imply that Hitler had nothing to do with the extermination of European Jewry.[77] Over and above Hitler's own statements, what other evidence can be found in only a few secondary sources regarding Hitler's responsibility for and timing of the extermination?[78] As early as September 29, 1939, Hitler charged Himmler in a secret decree with three tasks for the "strengthening of Germanism," one of which was the "elimination of the injurious influence of those sections of the population of foreign origin constituting a danger to the Reich and the German community."[79] This decree also granted Himmler "such wide plenary powers that he was, in effect, in a position to lay down the law in the East."[80] This naturally meant that Jews, who were considered an "injurious influence," were doomed to be exploited or murdered. Himmler claimed to have thought that Goebbels had convinced Hitler "that the Jewish question could only be solved by the total destruction of the Jews."[81] However, it was only in March 1942 that Goebbels wrote of exterminating the Jews, and even by December 1941 one million Jews had been killed, mostly by Himmler's SS.[82] Given Hitler's own anti-Semitism and earlier speeches, it is doubtful that he needed anything except his own distorted mind to arrive at the decision to kill Jews. In any case, Himmler adopted the destruction of European Jewry as his own sacred task.

On April 2, 1941, Alfred Rosenberg, head of the East Ministry, visited Hitler and talked with him for two hours. The topic discussed was "something I do not wish to record today but shall never forget."[83] On June 6, 1941, General Walter Warlimont signed the notorious Commissar Order, which ordered the execution of communist political commissars who were captured during the invasion of Russia. This was extended to include "second-class Asiatics," Gypsies, and Jews.[84] The army also circulated "Guidelines for the Conduct of the Troops" in Russia beginning

June 4, 1941, in which troops were instructed that: "This struggle demands ruthless and energetic measures against *Bolshevik agitators, guerrillas, saboteurs, Jews*, and the complete elimination of every active or passive resistance."[85] On June 26, 1941, the commander of the Sixth Army, Walter von Reichenau, was overheard by Blobel, a subordinate, telling his aides that in cases of Jews, only two rifle shots rather than the customary five should be used. "While strutting about, he commented to Blobel on the 'Fuehrer Order' and the necessity for total ruthlessness."[86]

In a summary of all instructions that were given before July 2, 1941, Himmler's direct subordinate, Heydrich, made a list of those who were to be executed, and this list included "Jews in the service of the Party [Communist] or State . . . in so far as in individual cases they are not required, or are no longer required for economic or political intelligence of special importance, for future security police measures, or for the economic rehabilitation of the occupied territories."[87] In his postwar trial, Ohlendorf, an SS lieutenant general, claimed that the order for the extermination of the Jews of Russia was an oral order from Hitler to Himmler.[88] As we shall see below, Himmler frequently stated that Hitler himself had ordered the extermination of the Jews.

Rudolf Hoess, who was the commandant of Auschwitz and directed the extermination of two and a half million people, nearly all of them Jews, supported Himmler in his claim that Hitler ordered the exterminations. He said that in the summer of 1941 Himmler called him to Berlin, and "He told me something to this effect—I do not remember the exact words—that the Fuehrer had given the order for a final solution of the Jewish Question. We, the SS must carry out the order. If it is not carried out now, then the Jews will later destroy the German people."[89]

By early summer 1942 Himmler had authorized the mass extermination of Jews in a written order to Eichmann, who showed it to one of his assistants. His assistant said: "May God forbid that our enemies should ever do anything similar to the German people!" Eichmann replied: "Don't be sentimental. This is a Fuehrer order."[90] At the end of July 1942 Himmler confirmed this "Fuehrer order" in a letter to the head of the SS Main Office: "The occupied Eastern territories will be cleared of Jews. The implementation of this very hard order has been placed on my shoulders by the Fuehrer. No one can release me from this responsibility in any case. So I forbid all interference."[91]

In the spring of 1942 the first large-scale gas experiments were conducted. These had been designed by engineers at Hitler's chancellery, and it is probable that Hitler saw the designs.[92] In mid-1942 one of Himmler's most stalwart officers in the East, Bach-Zelewski, had a nervous breakdown, as mentioned earlier. When he asked Himmler if the killings could not be stopped, Himmler irately replied: "That is a Fuehrer order. The Jews are the disseminators of Bolshevism . . . if you don't keep your nose out of the Jewish business, you'll see what'll happen to you!"[93]

In July 1942 Himmler wrote to his representative at the Ministry for the Eastern Territories as follows:

> I must ask you urgently to see that no definition of the term "Jew" is published. We are simply tying our hands by dogmatizing in this stupid way. The occupied territories will be cleared of Jews. The Führer has charged me with carrying out this very difficult task. No one can relieve me of the responsibility. I cannot allow myself (sic) the luxury of discussing it.[94]

On August 15, 1942, Hitler inspected various killing apparatuses at a Polish extermination camp, and

> remarked irritably that the killings were proceeding too slowly and that "the whole operation must be speeded up, considerably speeded up." When another member of the party suggested that for reasons of concealment it might be better "to burn the corpses instead of burying them" Globocnik, who shared Himmler's visions of "racial hygiene" practised on a vast scale, replied that later generations could hardly be "so feeble and cowardly" as not to appreciate "such good and necessary work." He went on to suggest that they should also bury "bronze plaques recording that it was us that had the courage to complete this gigantic task." To this Hitler replied approvingly: "Yes, my good Globocnik . . . I think you're perfectly right."[95]

Himmler sent a report to Hitler on December 20, 1942, concerning "anti-partisan operations." His three headings were: "(a) captured . . . , (b) executed . . . , and (c) Jews executed. . . ."[96] This was his fifty-first report to Hitler; can one doubt that other reports both before and after would have contained information on shootings and extermination of Jews? Himmler also talked to Hitler on the telephone at least once and sometimes several times a day. Unfortunately, these conversations were not recorded, but obviously Hitler and Himmler were in very close communication, and they must have discussed Himmler's primary task, the destruction of European Jewry.

In the spring of 1943 Henriette von Schirach, the wife of Baldur von Schirach, the head of the Hitler Youth, described to Hitler a scene in Amsterdam where Jewish women had been rounded up in the dead of night for deportation. At first Hitler was silent, then he stared at her, and finally rose to his feet. He apparently tried to control his anger, but suddenly lost his temper and said: "You are a sentimentalist! What business of yours is it? The Jewesses are none of your business!"[97] He continued to shout until she ran out of the room. Also in the spring of 1943 Himmler was questioned by Hans Lammers, the chief of the German chancellery, about the rumors of extermination in the East. Himmler told him that only deportation was involved, but that it was a Fuehrer order.[98] In January and May 1944, Himmler gave three speeches to high-ranking army and navy officers in which he declared that Hitler had given him the mission of exterminating the Jews.[99] And finally in April 1945, when the Allies were closing in from east and west and it was decided to evacuate the remaining concentration camps so that atrocities would not be discovered, Himmler complained that "Hitler has been raging for days because Buchenwald and Bergen-Belsen were not completely evacuated,"[100] but rather fell nearly intact into the hands of the horrified Allies.

What does this evidence tell us about Hitler's responsibility for and timing of extermination? His official appointment of Himmler as law of the land in the East in September 1939 indicates that Himmler was in a position to begin extermination whenever Hitler ordered it. That Hitler did not give such an order in 1939, but waited until his invasion of Russia to start mass shootings, is at first glance surprising. Since he had repeatedly said in one form or another that he intended to destroy European Jewry, why did he not now begin shooting Polish Jews instead of crowding them into ghettos? This surely must have been due to the local situation. Most Jews lived in cities and could not be shot out-of-hand there, because word of such action would have quickly leaked to the West, and Hitler still hoped to arrange a peace treaty with Britain and to keep the United States out of the war. Ghettoization, therefore, allowed Jews to be identified and was in accord with Hitler's foreign-policy considerations.

When Hitler made the decision to have Russian Jews shot along with commissars, officers, partisans, and other "security threats," the United States was not yet in the war, Britain had proved intractable to peace overtures, and Russia was considered far enough away so that mass shootings could be conducted with more secrecy there than in Poland. Rumors of the executions did leak out, but hard evidence was scarce because of prohibitions against photographs and other revelations of these "actions." The German army first acquiesced to the shootings in Poland and later participated in them.[101] According to Streit, this "favorable" development led Hitler to conclude around mid-July 1941 that he could extend the killing operations to Jews in other parts of Europe.[102] Hilberg also believes that Hitler decided to begin the total destruction of European Jewry in the summer of 1941.[103] This is quite plausible, because as one can see from the evidence above, there are nine specific references to "*the* Führer order."[104] (The order to exterminate Jews was always referred to as *the* Führer order.) These references indicate that the order was given sometime in the summer of 1941. One can say that this testimony came only from war criminals and should therefore be open to question; but Himmler killed himself by taking poison after capture by the Allies, so his letters to the SS Main Office and to his representative in the Eastern Territories were not doctored after the fact, and also confirm the actions that had been taken. In addition, it is known that Hitler *personally* inspected killing devices at a Polish

141

concentration camp on August 15, 1942, complained that the whole operation must be considerably speeded up, and agreed that bronze plaques should be buried with the corpses to record the courageous completion of a "gigantic task," the exterminations.

It is possible that Hitler made the decision for mass extermination of Jews by the fastest possible method sometime in the summer of 1941. Since the gas chambers and crematoria at major extermination camps were already equipped during the winter of 1941–1942, and this naturally required considerable advance preparation, the decision would have to have been made some months earlier. Later evidence that Hitler gave the order for extermination is found in Report 51, in which Himmler clearly discussed killings of Jews; it confirms that Hitler indeed had knowledge of the exterminations. There were other indications that he knew: Himmler's conversation with Lammers in 1943; Henriette Schirach's experience; Himmler's speeches in 1944, and his report of Hitler's displeasure over the failure to evacuate concentration camps.

That there is no written record of *the* Führer order is entirely predictable. Hitler never signed orders when it could possibly be avoided; it was a basic principle of his not to do so, as his following statement shows: "Everything that can be discussed should *never* be put in writing, never!"[105] When his ministers pressed him to legalize euthanasia, he refused to sign such a law.[106] On important questions Hitler always liked to camouflage his actions. Therefore, when Streit and Irving imply that Hitler had no predominant role in decisions regarding Russian prisoners of war and the civil population (including Jews) because there is no written order, one can seriously question their conclusions.[107]

If none of this is convincing, then consider the following argument. Is it possible that Heinrich Himmler or Warlimont, who were Hitler's direct subordinates, would have issued orders for mass exterminations of Jews or anyone else without Hitler's approval? What would have happened to them if they had done this and word leaked back to the "humanitarian" Hitler that his top SS and army officers had given such orders without his permission? They could have counted their future lifespan in minutes,

142

not years. Hitler's state was exactly what he said it was, a "Führer" or "leader state" in which he made the critical and final decisions. The average American, or even the typical present-day German who did not experience Hitler's tyranny, has little conception of the magnitude and functions of power in a nondemocratic state. Hitler was a dictator, and although he obviously had to have faithful and acquiescent subordinates to carry out his wishes, his oral instructions were literally and unalterably *the law*. This is not to say that others may not have offered proposals or initiated small-scale individual actions on their own to impress Hitler or other superiors, or that sporadic on-the-spot executions of real or suspected partisans did not take place without Hitler's prior approval, as they would in any wartime situation. However, as we noted above, Hitler's approval of mass executions of Russian Jews was clearly indicated in mid-July 1941, when he said, "[Russian guerrilla warfare] is not without its advantages as far as we are concerned, since it gives us a chance to wipe out anyone who gets in our way."

Hitler made all major policy decisions, and he bragged about exterminating Europe's Jews in his final testament. How could this have happened had he not ordered it? Even in an earlier speech about marking Jews with an insignia, Hitler had said: "Who can give the necessary orders? Only I can give them." Can one seriously believe that despite his own ethnic theory, his speeches, and the testimony of others, Hitler was not directly responsible for the holocaust? On the contrary, all of these sources indicate that he first justified the extermination of Jews theoretically in his ethnic theory, then planned for their destruction, and finally ordered that it be carried out. That this did not happen overnight but rather over several years only illustrates Hitler's typical method of confronting all issues, whether domestic or foreign.

One cannot climb into Hitler's mind, and he was extremely proud of hiding his true intentions even from his closest associates. But it was entirely consistent with Hitler's style that he formulated a plan, took small steps toward achieving it to "test the waters," or, as he put it, used his sixth sense to tell him what he could or could not do, and then pounced upon his enemy to deliver the

143

fatal blow. There are numerous examples of this technique in both his rise to power and his conduct of foreign policy. All evidence indicates that he followed exactly this pattern in the "Jewish question." First he attempted to stir up public support for harsh measures against the Jews with the boycott in 1933; when that support was not forthcoming, he backed off and with as little fuss as possible removed the Jews from their professions. In 1935 he again tested the waters with the Nuremberg Laws and these were generally well accepted, so for the next three years he encouraged his party followers and ministers to extend them in thirteen implementing decrees. He also encouraged them to begin the "Aryanization" of Jewish property, or its forced sale to non-Jews. Again in 1938 he radicalized persecution by the deportation of Polish Jews and *Kristallnacht*. There was some public outcry over the deportation of Polish Jews, and *Kristallnacht* was a failure—he did not gain public support for violence against the Jews. Therefore, he backed away from public violence and proceeded as discreetly and secretly as possible to confiscate the remaining businesses of Jews and to impose additional restrictions on them. When he began World War II he announced his intention to eliminate the Jews from Europe. But during wartime, as Goebbels noted in his diary, opportunities presented themselves that were not available in peacetime. Hitler could proceed without regard to public opinion and cover his murderous tracks by any number of subterfuges (antipartisan activities, eliminating security risks, and so on).

How did Hitler delegate authority over racial issues? He did not authorize one central agency to handle the "Jewish question." Instead he encouraged a multitude of agencies in both party and state to dabble in racial politics. This structural fragmentation created anarchy among competing agencies and resulted in contradictory policies. Hitler chose from among these contradictory policies; his choices depended on his estimate of domestic opinion, party unity, and foreign affairs. He then allowed his many agencies to compete in implementing the approved policy. This resulted in further power struggles, after which Hitler acknowledged the emerging victor as the "primary authority" in racial matters.

Between 1933 and 1938 party agencies were "primary authorities"; between 1938 and 1939 the SS and party contested for power; and after 1939 the SS was the "primary authority." Agencies that lost out in these struggles for power were not eliminated, however; they were allowed to meddle in their role as second- and third-rate powers. Thus a hierarchy was established to handle Jewish policy.[108] The power of the party relative to the state was also enhanced because the competitive anarchy crippled conservative opposition, which bogged down in the morass of contradictory directives.

Thus, although between 1933 and 1939 party pressure, combined with Hitler's anti-Semitism, accelerated persecution, between 1940 and 1944 the actual deportations and exterminations were almost exclusively instigated by Hitler himself. Even though some historians point out the importance of the SA and radical Nazi party anti-Semites who pressed for more extreme persecution at key dates, this is, in 1933, 1935, and 1938, one should always bear in mind that all acts, decrees, laws, and other instruments of policy were approved by Hitler himself.[109] Hitler used his position as head of the party and state to get his ideas accepted among his followers and to have enforcing legislation passed by the state.[110] Yet apparently he had no highly detailed master plan for handling the "Jewish question."[111]

## SUMMARY

As we saw in chapter 2, there was a great diversity of opinion in the NSDAP about anti-Semitic goals. The leaders themselves accounted for several types of anti-Semites. Hitler, Streicher, and Goebbels represented the radical anti-Semites.[112] Rosenberg spoke for the mystical-theoretical anti-Semites; Schacht and Goering represented economic-financial anti-Semites;[113] and finally, the SS represented Nazis who advocated the systematic and orderly removal of Jews from Germany.[114]

Between 1933 and 1939 it was necessary to placate party radicals who felt the Nazis were moving too slowly on the "Jewish question." Party discontent focused upon Hitler's failure to rev-

145

olutionize German society fast enough. Anti-Semitic measures were not going to change German society fundamentally, but they did satisfy radical party anti-Semites. Yet Hitler had to provide a diversion and safety valve for discontent. Therefore, he gave the party free rein in the "Jewish question" at opportune moments, especially during the boycott of April 1933, in enforcing the Nuremberg Laws, during *Kristallnacht*, and to some extent during the "Aryanization" of Jewish property and businesses.[115]

The Nazi party was always to some degree a problem for Hitler. In order to sound out the party's mood, Hitler first set general anti-Semitic guidelines and then awaited "organic developments" at local, regional, and national party levels. His behavior appeared arbitrary, but the arbitrariness was deliberate. It allowed him to respond to the mood of the party at any given time.[116] Also, by issuing a complex series of directives rather than establishing codified laws to handle Jewish matters, he assured his future flexibility; racial policy could be changed almost instantaneously. This ability to shift policy quickly after sounding out the party allowed him to maintain his Führer image and simultaneously to unify the party behind a common purpose.

The elimination of Jews from social, political, intellectual, economic, and religious life provided a common goal that united Hitler's uneasy coalition of rival factions within the party.[117] Thus "old fighters" and contented as well as discontented Nazis competed in a joint effort. This gave at least the appearance of unanimity. If Hitler refused the "second revolution" to reorganize German society totally according to Nazi party preferences, at least he compensated the radicals by giving them a hand in the "permanent purge."[118] This, particularly during 1933, 1935, and 1938, created an image of "movement," even as the party's role in Jewish affairs declined relative to that of the SS.[119]

By the beginning of World War II, although some party radicals still competed for influence in the "Jewish question" and many undoubtedly approved of all measures including extermination, the prime mover behind extermination was Hitler himself. From Hitler's speeches and comments one can see that he took his ethnic theory seriously throughout the 1920s and 1930s and that he himself made the decision to exterminate European Jewry, most probably giving the final oral order to Himmler by the summer of 1941, at least for the Russian Jews, and possibly also for Jews in other parts of Europe, although this may have come later.

Hitler escalated persecution from 1933 to 1939 with an eye both to domestic and foreign affairs, first testing the waters and then radicalizing persecution as far as he thought he could push it. He authorized several agencies to handle different aspects of the "Jewish question" and encouraged them to compete with one another. Eventually, of course, the SS became the primary authority when deportation and extermination were adopted as the "final solution."

# Functions of Persecution and Propaganda

"Propaganda tries to force a doctrine on the whole people; the organization embraces within its scope only those who do not threaten on psychological grounds to become a brake on the further dissemination of the idea."
Adolf Hitler, *Mein Kampf*, p. 582.

Hitler's role as instigator and mediator of racial policies and the functional use of anti-Semitism to preserve party unity are now clear, but what were the other functions of persecution to enhance Nazi power and control over the population? What were the functions of Nazi anti-Semitic propaganda, and was it a success or a failure?

### FUNCTIONS OF PERSECUTION OUTSIDE THE NAZI PARTY

Hitler used anti-Semitic policies for domestic purposes other than party unity. For Nazi propaganda to retain converts to the Nazi racial view, it was important that individuals adopt anti-Semitism as the new social, political, economic, religious, and intellectual norm. Potential opponents could be neutralized, because if they criticized persecution of the Jews, they appeared to be outside the pale of social acceptability.[1] This was a very important type of "social atomization" that forced individuals to keep their real opinions to themselves. The give-and-take of normal discourse on current events was curtailed as anti-Semitic

148

measures became more extreme and Nazi terror infiltrated all personal relations.[2] Germans who disagreed with Hitler's radical policies were progressively identified and terrorized. They became examples for relatives, friends, and neighbors, even though opposition was seldom and sparingly publicized. Thus Hitler used actual persecution of Jews to terrorize the general population, but he also punished Jewish sympathizers as an example to potential opponents.[3] Two useful consequences of terror, from the Nazi point of view, were apathy and acquiescence; whenever physical threats were employed, acquiescence was the typical result.

Isolation of the individual German and his consequent ignorance was made worse by news blackouts. In the case of racial persecution, blackouts and camouflage of facts were deliberate. For example, startling and illogical as it may seem, press directives, which dictated all publishable and nonpublishable news, imposed systematic silence about all major types of persecution.[4] I shall discuss this in some detail later because it is critical to understanding public ignorance of concrete occurrences, even though rumors contributed to some knowledge of what was going on.

Rumors of extermination were useful to Hitler because they made the Germans, particularly leaders in the military, the party, and the SS, complicitors who would have to fight to the death to prevent anticipated reprisals.[5] Extermination was thus designed to gain domestic support for Hitler's war effort.

Another function of anti-Semitic measures and propaganda was to divert the population from other issues, particularly those vague promises of economic and social change that the Nazis had not fulfilled.[6] Martin Broszat considers this especially significant because the Nazis' failure to carry through the positive features of their program meant that only negative ones were left.[7] It was particularly important for party unity that some goals, even negative ones, be fulfilled.

Hitler also needed an excuse to attack rivals—for example, reactionaries, churchmen, and state officials—whose power and influence he wished to eliminate. Manifest sympathy for the Jews was a useful excuse. These groups and others that opposed his

149

policies—for example, the outlawed SPD—could be identified as Jewish sympathizers, and therefore they were fair game.[8]

Anti-Semitism served still other functions. In order to gain support for Hitler's foreign policy of expansion and war, Nazi propagandists consistently identified Germany's enemies (Britain, France, the United States, Poland, and Russia) with the "worldwide Jewish conspiracy."[9] Hitler also stepped up domestic persecution to bait foreign nations into criticizing the Nazi regime.[10] Propagandists then used the resultant foreign "atrocity propaganda" as an excuse both to initiate further draconian persecution at home and to expand their influence abroad.[11]

Moreover, in Hitler's mind Jews were hostages who guaranteed acquiescence by foreign nations when they were confronted with his expansionist moves.[12] Hitler believed that the threat of further persecution deterred foreign criticism or interference. Even during World War II he apparently thought his enslavement of millions of Jews would force Britain and the United States to sue for peace. This itself is evidence that he genuinely believed in an "international Jewish conspiracy" that could be called off at will by foreign leaders. On this issue, as on other aspects of "racial politics," he lost contact with reality, as Hanfstaengl says, "like an airman in a fog."[13]

Before and during the war, treatment of German Jews served as a prime example of what would befall both Jews and non-Jews in occupied lands. Persecution of Jews provided a striking lesson on the legal and psychological consequences of the totalitarian idea and the experimental "socialization" of human beings.[14]

## FUNCTIONS OF PROPAGANDA

Several functions of anti-Semitic measures in the Nazi state were well developed by the propaganda machine.[15] Although many historians debate the existence of a genuine "ideology" in Hitler's world view, few would dispute his intention to spread his system of ideas. Any revolutionary movement needs at least a world view (if not an elaborate ideology) to justify its politics. It also needs to compete with rival world views. Hitler needed to combat Christianity, democratic liberalism, socialism, and communism.[16] For example, Nazi "ideology" obviously replaced class struggle with race conflict, and socialist or communist Utopias with a peoples' community (*Volksgemeinschaft*).[17] His rival "ideology" was founded on the premise that Jews were an inferior race who corrupted past and present political affairs, economic life, social relations, and religious values. The Nazis harped on the theme of Jewish culpability ad nauseum, extending it from domestic to international affairs. Jews were accused of starting World War I, causing Germany's war defeat, overthrowing the monarchy, directing the revolution, dominating the "Weimar system," precipitating the Great Depression, inventing and perpetuating socialism, communism, and internationalism, and polluting the "Aryan" race.[18] These were the same themes that had been used during the years before 1933, and they never changed in substance. During World War II these ideas were buttressed by accusations that Jews caused the war, plotted Germany's destruction, and hoped to destroy European culture.[19] They also supposedly prayed for a Bolshevik victory that would mean the end of the Western world.[20] Thus the Jewish problem was treated as an international crisis.[21]

Nazi propaganda is infinitely boring because every tract merely repeats the same accusations. Regardless of minute variations, the overriding theme was always that Jews were The Enemy. According to Hagemann, who has provided the best overall analysis of Nazi propaganda, the major objective was not to incite attacks on Jews, but to create a psychological enemy, or an anti-symbol.[22] Buchheim implies the same by saying: "To the degree that propaganda is freed from legal and moral restrictions, it will not be content with interpreting events but will attempt to bring about such events as are necessary to its purposes."[23]

Several historians point out the importance of anti-Semitic measures and propaganda in making Jews a "scapegoat."[24] Others discuss the demonological content of anti-Semitic propaganda. Their analyses, particularly that of Cohn, dovetail nicely with Hagemann's theory that the purpose of anti-Semitic propaganda was to create an anti-symbol. Jews were viewed as a mythical

151

symbol of evil, while Aryans were viewed as a mythical symbol of good. This was fundamental to Nazi anti-Semitic propaganda. Both Hagemann and Cohn provide elegant analyses of the circuitous routes by which the Nazis attempted to create an image of Jews as the incarnation of evil.[25]

Had the majority of Germans regarded Jews as enemies, the Nazis would have had limited need for their endless anti-Semitic propaganda. That the entire period 1933–1945 is steeped with Nazi harangues against Jews indicates that they were attempting to instill hatred of Jews among the German people. As Hagemann says, they were trying to *create* an enemy. Jews, being a visible minority, were the most logical "enemy" from 1919 on, particularly among Nazi radicals.

In the process of "creating" an enemy, the Nazis did not rely upon logic; rather, they attempted to win converts by attitude formation, capitalizing on covert hatreds, hostilities, and tensions that they directed toward Jews.[26] In this way they hoped to secure a consensus that strong measures should be taken against Jews;[27] consensus was desired both for the populace and for the Nazi party. As we saw earlier, there were divergent attitudes toward Jews among party members, and Nazi propaganda was aimed at pockets of resistance inside as well as outside of the party.[28]

A major function of Nazi propaganda was to spread Nazi racial "ideology."[29] Thus press directives were issued to insure a discussion of racial issues on a continual basis. For example, Goebbels suggested that not a week should pass without discussion of racial-political questions in the press.[30] He meant, of course, not specific measures against Jews, but general attacks on the historical role of Jews in Germany and the world. Frequently, specific sources, including anti-Semitic speeches, publications, and films, were recommended.[31] The press was often castigated for noncompliance and was ordered to use these or other anti-Semitic materials.[32] Even terminology was dictated to the press. For example, treating the word "race" lightly by referring to a "race" (in the sense of "group") of automobiles was prohibited, and the term "German race" was to be used with care in order to avoid a "split" in public opinion.[33]

To illustrate Jewish culpability, emphasis was placed on Jewish "criminality" and the "conspiracy" of foreign Jews against Germany. This was particularly stressed at the time of *Kristallnacht*.[34] The assassination of the German diplomat vom Rath was to be followed by a "winter campaign" of "enlightenment" to demonstrate the history of Jewish "crimes" to the public.[35] A similar "enlightenment" program had been ordered before the proclamation of the Nuremberg Laws.[36] And in propaganda relating to foreign affairs, the "international conspiracy" of world Jewry was a favorite theme during World War II.[37]

What was published in the daily press on the role of Hitler and the party's radicals in formulating racial policies? Were Hitler or party leaders praised as heroes because of *Kristallnacht* and the extermination of Jews? Aside from the Nuremberg Laws, which were announced by Hitler and implemented by the party and which were viewed as moderate stabilizing legislation, very little racial persecution was attributed directly to Hitler or the Nazi party. For example, the boycott of April 1933 was ascribed to a "spontaneous reaction" by the German people for which no party responsibility was taken, even though SA men were major perpetrators of the boycott and its attendant excesses.[38] The same propaganda line was used to explain the pogrom of November 1938. The party was not blamed or praised; synagogue burnings were attributed to spontaneous combustion, as if they had burned themselves down![39] Likewise, deportation and extermination were never attributed to Hitler or the party because these events were almost totally blacked out of the news.[40] Even on a minor scale there were attempts to conceal the role of party organizations in formulating and executing racial policy. For example, as early as 1935 the daily press was ordered not to publish Himmler's directives regarding Jews.[41] Also, during Hitler's visits to various parts of Germany, no discussion of the "Jewish question" was permitted in the press.[42] Frequently, Goebbels's speeches were to be discussed only in accordance with Propaganda Ministry directives.[43] And, in order to obscure the role of the party in the racial question, no discussion of racial policies was allowed before elections.[44] All in all, these directives indicate deliberate obfuscation of Hitler's and the party's role in racial persecution.

One function of anti-Semitic measures, as already noted, was to allow the party machine to gain power over the state by associating conservative bureaucrats with Jews or reactionaries.[45] Such conflicts, however, were not played up by the press. As a common practice, leading editors and journalists were informed that conflicts existed, but they were told that news about them was not to be published in newspapers. For example, a major purpose of the Nuremberg Laws was to allow the party to formulate and execute racial policy at the expense of the unreliable "reactionaries" in the state bureaucracy. The press was instructed about this in a long and detailed information report that was to be kept strictly confidential.[46] Also, press directives intended only for private circulation attacked Schacht, the minister of economic affairs, as a reactionary and a footdragger, but these were not to be published.[47]

From these examples of press blackouts, we may hypothesize that one major function of propaganda was to camouflage reality by denying individuals the means of reaching independent conclusions. To test this hypothesis let us examine other types of blackouts.

As stated earlier, a major function of anti-Semitic measures was to resolve conflicts inside of the party. Press directives show how propaganda was directed to this goal. For the years 1933–1939 there were no press directives directly related to conflicts over racial issues within the party. The only references were indirect. For example, during the last days of the boycott of 1933 and the pogrom of 1938, the press called for a halt of "independent actions" against Jews.[48] This referred, of course, to the SA and other party rowdies who surpassed the bounds of acceptable behavior even in party circles. But in general, propaganda concealed conflicts between different party organizations despite power struggles in progress at any given time in order to hide party disunity from the public.

Blackouts of major and minor information on persecution of Jews were commonplace. Persecution was camouflaged whenever it was perceived by Hitler, Goebbels or other party leaders as going beyond the bounds of domestic or foreign support. Although some historians believe anti-Semitic measures and propaganda were orchestrated with an eye to foreign reactions, one should always bear in mind that the major audience for propaganda was German, not foreign. For example, if even small newspapers throughout Germany were ordered to black out news of events during *Kristallnacht*, this can legitimately be described as an effort to control domestic opinion. Foreign countries obtained their information about events in Germany from other sources—for example, from foreign reporters and diplomats. They did not rely upon German newspapers precisely because they knew these seldom contained the truth. Of course, the German public came to recognize the inaccuracy and the biased coverage of German media, but German newspapers and radio were still, by and large, their primary sources of information.

Since press directives were used to disseminate Nazi racial "ideology," did Goebbels and the Propaganda Ministry believe the public accepted this ideology? We can gain some insight into public attitudes as perceived by the Propaganda Ministry with its feedback system by examining the issues, events, and facts that were omitted or camouflaged in accordance with press directives. We shall examine three types of camouflage: (1) blackouts of news that would have provided information upon which individuals could have formed independent judgments; (2) blackouts of evidence of domestic opposition to Nazi racial policies; and (3) blackouts of foreign nations' reactions to persecution.

Given the dependence of Germans on their media, what blackouts were imposed on events and facts that would have allowed them to form independent judgments on the types and extensiveness of persecution? As I stated earlier, the role of the party in organizing and perpetrating the boycott of Jewish businesses, doctors, and lawyers in April 1933 was not publicized.[49] The Propaganda Ministry also heavily censored publication or discussion of the Nuremberg Laws and their enacting ordinances.[50] Lists of individuals and their families who were newly deprived of civil rights because of the Nuremberg Laws were likewise not to be

155

published.[51] Nor did the Propaganda Ministry permit accounts of events in concentration camps to be published.[52] News of arrests of Jews and plundering of Jewish property during the summer of 1938 was completely suppressed.[53] So were burnings of Jewish homes in Nuremberg during October 1938.[54] Also, Polish-Jewish problems and the forced emigration of fifty thousand Polish Jews during October 1938 were prohibited news items.[55]

The party's role in organizing and directing the pogrom during *Kristallnacht* was not made public. Instead, this event was ascribed to a "spontaneous uprising" of the German people in response to the murder of vom Rath.[56] The extensiveness of murder and property destruction during *Kristallnacht* was never reported.[57] All newspapers were ordered to describe general events at local levels only, not at regional or national levels.[58] Pictures and reports of individual burnings and lootings were prohibited, and articles were to appear on the second or third, rather than first, page.[59] When rumors abounded after the pogrom, the press was instructed to report that destruction had occurred only "here and there."[60] Publication of information on court proceedings (there were very few) against individuals who made personal attacks on Jews during *Kristallnacht* was also forbidden.[61] At Goering's request, the press was ordered not to publish information on the directors of insurance companies that would have paid off claims to Jews if Jews themselves had not been forced to pay one billion *Reichsmark* to cover the damages caused by *Kristallnacht*.[62] In November 1938 the press was directed to omit sentences such as "not a hair on the head of a German Jew was touched," and "although no Jew was injured," from its reports on *Kristallnacht*.[63] Significantly, if cynically, the Propaganda Ministry backed off from its formerly rabid and threatening posture toward Jews after *Kristallnacht*.[64] Goebbels nervously claimed that "Germany has now solved its Jewish Question."[65] This new stance was probably a reaction to both domestic and foreign criticism. Normally, however, propaganda lines and blackouts followed one upon the other, unchecked by modification.

After the pogrom of November 1938, further economic measures against Jews could be published only with restricted commentary.[66] This was not uncommon, because between 1935 and 1937 a number of restrictions on reporting "Aryanization" proceedings had already been announced.[67] Aside from *Kristallnacht*, the largest number of press directives prohibiting publication of information was related to the "Aryanization" of property. All aspects of forced sales and expropriations were banned from the press.[68] After 1939 a general ban was placed on publishing any information on anti-Jewish measures, and arrests of Jews were not to be reported during the war.[69] Even news of restricted shopping hours and food rations of Jews was suppressed, and the compulsory wearing of the six-pointed yellow star by Jews was another prohibited news item.[70] Likewise, transports of Jews were to be kept strictly secret.[71] More important, publication of the Madagascar and similar plans was absolutely forbidden.[72] The term "liquidation" was never to be used in writing or orally, except to refer to shootings of Communist party leaders in Russia.[73] Hitler himself gave a blackout order on further publication of measures against Jews on February 7, 1942.[74] Extermination in concentration camps was completely taboo news for the press.[75] A cautionary directive was sent to party offices by Bormann indicating that Hitler wanted no public treatment of the "total solution" of the "Jewish question."[76]

When publication of laws on racial policy was deemed essential to insure public compliance, this was generally done in a perfunctory manner. Laws and legal interpretations were to be published with no commentary or only with comments forwarded by the official German News Service.[77]

All major blackouts were ordered by press directives, and as the above instances demonstrate, the Propaganda Ministry deliberately concealed and camouflaged the truth about persecution of Jews.[78] That this was systematically done can hardly be doubted. Moreover, the Ministry was not content merely to suppress news about major events; it also ordered directives prohibiting publication of "minor" facts relating to Jews. For example, news that a Jew had received the Nobel Prize was not to be published, and Jewish aid to the Winter Aid, a national charity, was to be ignored.[79] Telegrams of Jews to Hitler were never to be published, the Patent Office's payment of money to the wife of a Jew was prohibited news, the dissolution of B'nai B'rith was kept secret, meetings of Jewish veterans were not to be announced, and telegrams sent by doctors' associations to newspapers indicating a shortage of doctors were expunged from the press.[80] In short, the Propaganda Ministry blacked out all events and facts both great and small that would have allowed Germans to form an accurate picture of racial persecution and to arrive at an independent judgment of it.

Another large group of blackout directives was issued with respect to the emigration of Jews and their treatment in new homelands. Silence was decreed on Jewish emigration to Palestine, Palestinian immigration agreements, any murder of Jews by Arabs in Palestine, any Jewish settlement work in Palestine, the bad job opportunities in Palestine, and the rejection of emigrant Jews by Cuba.[81] By 1939 it was forbidden to publish *any* information on troubles faced by emigrant Jews in new lands.[82] The next year a total blackout was placed on information about emigration of Jews at any time in past, present, or future years.[83]

By cutting off information about persecution, particularly the extensiveness of persecution, the Nazis attempted to create an image of Jews as mere abstractions rather than people. Of course, they were also attempting to hide Nazi brutality toward Jews, since destruction of Jewish property and physical attacks on Jews aroused sympathy for Jews rather than agreement with Nazi policies.

A second type of camouflage was to suppress evidence of opposition to racial persecution by German citizens. For example, the boycott of April 1933 was described as a "spontaneous reaction" of the German people against foreign "atrocity propaganda," even though it was almost exclusively controlled and perpetrated by the SA and other Nazi rowdies. (The population did not take an active role in the boycott except in the sense that they were reported if they did not comply with it.)[84] Those who read newspaper reports of a "spontaneous reaction" were led to believe that the boycott was inspired by the people, which it was not.

158

Another type of camouflage of opposition occurred in 1935, when the Propaganda Ministry described the possibility of public discontent over the Jewish issue (as well as policies toward churches and reactionaries) if employment and consumption should decline. The press was informed of this possibility, but discussion of this matter was of course forbidden in the press.[85] After the Nuremberg Laws were introduced, opposition to them was generally kept out of the daily press, although *Der Stürmer* and *Das Schwarze Korps* (the official SS magazine) made a fetish of publishing violations. In the daily press, details of cases in which German women consorted with Jews were not to be discussed.[86] Also, details of *Rassenschande* (sexual relations between Jews and non-Jews) were especially not to be published if they occurred in German brothels.[87] More important, *Rassenschande* by party members was strictly taboo news for the press.[88] Instances of mixed marriages were to be kept secret, as were annulments of mixed marriages.[89] It was also forbidden to discuss the ancestry of German historical figures.[90]

During *Kristallnacht* Goebbels employed the same propaganda tactics that he had used during the 1933 boycott. According to press directives, the German people had "spontaneously erupted." All other interpretations were prohibited.[91] The Propaganda Ministry knew very well that in fact the public did not support *Kristallnacht*, as indicated by its own directives. These urged the press to avoid giving the impression that a large number of Germans disagreed with measures against Jews.[92] The press was directed to encourage hostility toward "no-sayers" or opponents of persecution and to portray them as disloyal citizens.[93] According to one directive:

> One knows that anti-Semitism in Germany today is essentially confined to the party and its organizations, and that there is a certain group in the population who have not the slightest understanding for anti-Semitism and in whom every possibility of empathy is lacking.
>
> In the days after *Kristallnacht* these people ran immediately to Jewish businesses. . . .

This is so to a great extent because we are, to be sure, an anti-Semitic people, an anti-Semitic state, but nevertheless in all manifestations of life in the state and people anti-Semitism is as good as unexpressed. . . .

There are still groups of maudlin Babbits (*Spiessern*) among the German people who talk about the poor Jews and who have no understanding for the anti-Semitic attitudes of the German people and who interceded for Jews at every opportunity. It should not be that only the leadership and party are anti-Semitic.[94]

Because of this, editors were instructed to stick to directives and not to publish anything that might diminish public understanding of *Kristallnacht*, namely, they were not to foster opposition by diverging from the party line.[95] By World War II the press was well aware of its "duty" to follow directives, so directives on blackouts on deportations and exterminations were short and to the point.[96]

Another type of censorship about disapproval of Nazi racial persecution can be found in press directives for foreign news. Adverse reactions by foreign countries to Nazi persecution were either systematically ignored or described as "atrocity propaganda."[97] For example, foreign reactions to the forced repatriation of Polish Jews in 1938 were not to be published.[98] Neither were reports of the foreign press on *Kristallnacht*.[99] A similar type of blackout involved prohibitions on reporting foreign news about Jews. For example, news of the boycott of Jews in Austria and Jewish emigration from Austria was disallowed.[100]

Nazi propaganda also fostered hostility among Germans toward foreigners. For example, the leaders of the Soviet Union were labeled "Jewish" and bolshevism was treated as synonymous with Jewishness.[101] Foreign leaders were described as Jews who prevented any friendship with Germany.[102] "Hypocrisy" by foreign nations that criticized German anti-Semitism but refused entry to emigrating Jews was also emphasized, particularly after *Kristallnacht*.[103] And finally, injustices of foreign nations (British concentration camps in South Africa, American destruction of native

Indians, American slavery, immigration quotas, French colonial domination, etc.) were used not only to demonstrate the cruelty and hypocrisy of other nations, but also (by implication) to justify Germany's racial persecution.[104] Anti-Semitic countries were correspondingly praised in order to justify Germany's anti-Semitic policies.[105]

During World War II agitation by Jews in enemy countries was headlined.[106] This was also true of assassination threats in the "Jewish press" abroad.[107] The Katyn massacres were used indirectly to justify extermination of Jews even though the extermination policy was not made public in the press.[108] A similar indirect justification of extermination was sought by concentrating on an international, versus national, Jewish problem, since few German Jews were killed compared to the millions from other countries. As the war progressed, anti-Semitic propaganda was also used to inspire hostility toward Jews among foreign workers and in other countries.[109]

Although anti-Semitic propaganda was directed at foreign countries during most of the Third Reich's existence, there were respites when this policy appeared to damage Germany's diplomatic relations. For example, in May 1933 Nazi leaders called for a halt to attacks on Jewish businessmen because this was bad for Germany's foreign trade.[110] Prewar publications on the "racial demise" and racially mixed population of France were supposed to be "handled with discretion."[111] The term "anti-Semitic" was replaced by "anti-Jewish" in order not to alienate Arab countries.[112] The 1936 Berlin Olympics in particular were accompanied by a reduction in anti-Semitic attacks on other nations.[113] One press directive prohibited anti-Semitic slurs against Soviet officials unless they were of known Jewish ancestry.[114] Also, arrests of Jews with uncertain citizenship were not to be reported in the press, lest these antagonize foreign nations.[115] After *Kristallnacht* the press was advised to tone down anti-Semitic propaganda because of foreign criticism,[116] and in 1939 the press was directed neither to publish caricatures of English leaders nor to speculate on their ancestry.[117] In 1940 the most frequent causes of revisions in *Der Stürmer* were foreign-policy considerations.[118]

Regardless of these brief respites, the predominant theme of Nazi propaganda was that Jews were evil no matter where they lived. If the USSR, the United States, and Britain had important Jewish leaders, or even if they did not, accusations were made regarding their "Jewishness" in order to drum up antagonism toward these countries. This was an attempt to prepare the population for war. Thus domestic anti-Semitic propaganda was not simply confined to domestic issues and German Jews.

Why did these blackouts of domestic and foreign events occur? Two functions of anti-Semitic measures and propaganda were to establish an ideology and to give the appearance that all Germans supported this ideology. If the Nazi regime had achieved these goals, that is, if a majority of Germans believed in Nazi racial policies, why did the Nazis not relish this accomplishment and publish news of their major coups against Jews, particularly *Kristallnacht*, economic "Aryanization," forced emigration, deportation, and the "final solution?" From considering these events in themselves, one might suppose that a rabidly anti-Semitic German public systematically demanded escalation of persecution and genocide. But then why was the German public not informed of these "successes?" And even if the more controversial events such as deportation and extermination were concealed by order of the Propaganda Ministry, why were relatively less severe forms of persecution also hidden? On the basis of Goebbels's press directives, it is clear that the Propaganda Ministry deliberately concealed facts to prevent the German public from grasping the types, extent, and severity of persecution. In Goebbels's opinion, such knowledge could be counterproductive, that is, it could inspire disagreement with Nazi racial policies.

The obscurity of news coverage, the social isolation of Germans from one another, plus the physical separation of Jews from Germans made it difficult even for party members to know the true and complete state of affairs at any given time.[119] This was, of course, exacerbated by the large number of contradictory directives that governed racial policy. For the average nonparty member it was even more difficult to determine the real situation, particularly because 300,000 Jews emigrated between 1933 and 1941, and Jews were therefore less visible.[120] In any case, the Propaganda Ministry never felt confident enough of a genuine consensus of support for racial persecution to allow accurate or complete news to be published. Rather, as ever more severe measures were introduced, real information became even scarcer. Cases of blackouts and camouflage increased significantly between 1933 and 1939. During the war they were even stricter, especially when many Germans attributed Germany's war losses to "divine justice," whereby God punished Germany for exterminating Jews and other groups.[121]

It would, however, be a gross inaccuracy to conclude that Goebbles's blackouts and camouflage of racial persecution prevented the general public from perceiving that Jews were being tormented with ever-increasing cruelty.[122] All Germans knew that their media were censored, and they consequently looked to other sources for information, particularly to eyewitnesses and rumors. Yet whatever Germans discovered about persecution of Jews, it did not come from Goebbels's propaganda machine, which systematically concealed information on their treatment.

## SUMMARY

Apart from insuring party unity, Hitler used anti-Semitism to establish a new ideology, to create an illusion of consensus on racial issues, to isolate opponents by social atomization, to divert Germans from his failure to fulfill promises, to terrorize the population, to weaken the power of the state relative to the party, and to justify expansion and war. After 1939 he also satisfied personal and long-standing paranoid delusions by ordering European Jews to be slaughtered.

Anti-Semitic propaganda served almost the same political functions. However, whereas fulfilling his personal desires and insuring party unity were probably the most important functions of anti-Semitism for Hitler, the most important function of anti-Semitic propaganda was to create a consensus by proselytizing the abstract Nazi racial view and blacking out or camouflaging

163

concrete facts and events which, if known, might have fostered domestic or foreign criticism of racial persecution.

The Propaganda Ministry could not reveal harsh anti-Semitic measures without running certain risks. First, publication of details of persecution would have revealed the abrogation of law, order, and respect for life and property that were held dear by most Germans. This in turn might have delegitimized the Nazi regime and led to questioning of both its racial policies and its plebiscitory image. As Hitler claimed to represent the "peoples' will," especially in racial policies, he would have condemned out of hand any serious questioning of these policies on the basis of true facts about persecution of the Jews. Goebbels, Hitler's apt pupil, made certain that information about which questions might arise was kept to the minimum necessary to insure compliance with racial "regulations."

Terrorization was not a primary function of propaganda except in some of Streicher's issues of *Der Stürmer* and the SS's *Das Schwarze Korps*, which threatened Jews and those who sympathized with them. The Propaganda Ministry tried to create an abstract image of the Jews as demons, while the Gestapo and SS instilled terror among actual and potential opponents of persecution by interrogation, arrest, imprisonment, torture, concentration camps, and murder. In a sense both Goebbels's extensive censorship and police terror were a measure of his failure to achieve a consensus on racial policy. Had the German people accepted Nazi anti-Semitic propaganda, terror would have been unnecessary because the German population would have "spontaneously" driven Jews from Germany. In fact, they were driven out by Hitler's henchmen, particularly Himmler, Streicher, Goebbels, and radical anti-Semites in the Nazi party and its affiliated organizations.

# Public Reactions to Nazi Anti-Semitism

"The failure when the regime first sat insecurely in power to protest its inhumane measures made prevention of their logical culmination all but impossible, however unwanted and disapproved this undoubtedly was."
Lawrence Stokes, "The German People and the Destruction of the European Jews," p. 190.

Now that we have examined some of the functions of anti-Semitic measures and anti-Semitic propaganda, we should consider additional questions:

What, in the end, did all the propaganda achieve? There is no simple answer to that question. The picture that Hitler and Goebbels liked to present to the world was of a nation united in a passionate determinism to defeat the Jewish world-conspiracy. Confronted with the almost unbelieveable fact of five or six million murdered Jews, many in the outside world found it easy enough at the end of the war to accept this picture as accurate. But how accurate was it?[1]

It is well known that in Germany there never were massive and highly organized demonstrations or protests against either anti-Semitic measures or anti-Semitic propaganda. Does this mean that Nazi racial policies were favored and supported by the majority of Germans? If so, which policies were most popular? If not, which policies were unpopular?

Historians studying general levels of anti-Semitism from 1933 to 1945 point out several attitudes among the public: active agreement and support for Nazi persecution, indifference, acquiescence, and covert or overt opposition. Because many secondary works contain only generalities, it is difficult to determine whether there is a consensus on the percentage of Germans who knew about the severity of racial persecution or on their attitudes toward it; however, most historians appear to believe that the majority had some vague knowledge and were indifferent or acquiescent, whereas a minority were either supporters or opponents.[2] Nevertheless, there are significant differences of opinion. For example, Bracher claims the entire nation followed Hitler in his anti-Semitism.[3] Yet he thinks Hitler's Jewish policy was not as popular as the Nazis liked to believe.[4] George Mosse also implies that the majority of Germans avoided Jews rather than maintain contacts with them.[5] Bracher points out the failure of Germans to oppose persecution of Jews as strongly as they protested euthanasia.[6] Of course, at the time, euthanasia involved murder, while persecution of German Jews entailed segregation, expropriation, or forced emigration, so this disparity may be understandable. Other historians believe that pogroms, extermination, and violent attacks against Jews were rejected as extreme, but that legal and pseudolegal quotas and restrictions on intermarriage were popular.[7]

It is clear from the discussion in the previous chapter that reports by the press are of little value in determining the true state of public opinion. Instead of these one can use reports of the SD (*Sicherheitsdienst*), Government President's reports, court cases, internal correspondence of the NSDAP, and similar documents. One can also use the *Deutschland-Berichte*, socialist underground reports that covered a wide variety of topics, including anti-Semitism. I will comment on the reliability of these sources.

The *Deutschland-Berichte* are the most helpful source for information on attitudes toward Jews from 1935–1940 because they made a fetish of trying to report objectively on both good and bad public reactions.[8] The editors believed that the only way to fight the Nazis was to have an accurate picture of German public opinion. Their reports came from all parts of Germany, and although their major concern in reporting economic conditions was the situation of workers, their reports on reactions to persecution of Jews also included a great deal of information on the middle classes. Historians are very reluctant to use sources from organizations with a decided political bias, but the *Deutschland-Berichte* appear to have been remarkably accurate and objective, and they are well corroborated by other sources.[9] The Gestapo in particular considered these reports to be a very good reflection of public opinion, even better than their own reports in many cases.[10] This was true partly because they were often based on documents that were leaked from government agencies.[11] After 1938 the number of contacts between resident reporters and SPD emigres declined, so the number of verbatim eyewitness accounts was correspondingly reduced. Yet they are still the most fruitful source of information on public opinion during prewar years.[12]

In contrast to the *Deutschland-Berichte*, reports of the *Sicherheitsdienst* (SD) were extremely variable. They were frequently very general, offered far less extensive information on public attitudes toward Nazi racial policies, and were often doctored for political reasons. That is, they often painted rosy pictures to impress political superiors. They do, however, give a certain amount of information on middle-class attitudes because most of their reporters were from that stratum. For the war years, after the *Deutschland-Berichte* ceased publication and when the SD reports became more reliable and objective, they are a very good source of information. Therefore, I shall use these reports for information on public attitudes toward persecution during war years. The SD reports were called *Meldungen aus dem Reich* during most of the war.

Government President's reports covered a number of topics, including Jews (*Judentum*). They were designed to provide political feedback on Nazi policies and to point out opposition to those policies. Unfortunately, the sections on Jews frequently contained facts about the response of Jews to persecution rather than lengthy or informative accounts of Germans' reactions to the persecution of Jews. Nevertheless, they are sometimes of value.[13]

167

## GENERAL SOURCES

As indicated earlier, the first phase of anti-Semitic policies lasted from the boycott of April 1933 until the Nuremberg Laws of September 1935.[14] During this period there were, predictably, indications of support for anti-Semitic measures as well as opposition to them. Private protests against the boycotts by Hindenburg and the Economics Ministry were apparently effective in limiting it,[15] yet in general hardly anyone spoke up publicly in protest.[16]

Even in private correspondence, hostility toward Jewish influence in Germany surfaced. For example, a German doctor strongly supported the 1933 boycott against Jews in a letter to a Jewish colleague. He based his judgment on the previous disproportionate influence of Jews after the war. In his own case he maintained that he had been unable to secure employment at a clinic in Breslau because he was not Jewish and that a non-Jewish doctor had been forced to leave it. The German doctor also claimed that independent, generally violent personal attacks against Jews by the SA or SS did not have Hitler's approval, but that in any case the period after 1918 was filled with similar violence, presumably by Jewish revolutionaries.[17] Other letters were far harsher, and many letters denouncing Jews were sent to Prussian officals in 1933.[18] The boycott in April was occasionally successful in keeping some customers away, especially when SA men conducted themselves in an orderly fashion.[19] In Munich the boycott was more effective than in Berlin, where violence was more common.[20] In some parts of Bavaria (Middle Franconia), the boycott was actively supported by the population through acts of violence; however, Kershaw indicates that this was very uncommon and that the boycott was by and large a failure.[21] In the Rhineland and elsewhere the boycott failed to impress broad sections of the public. Even businessmen, many of whom were in direct competition with Jews, disapproved of the boycott.[22] According to some reports, a majority of the population opposed the boycott but were frightened away from Jewish stores by the SA.[23] Still, many people bought deliberately from Jews.[24] In some parts of Germany they tried to force their

168

way into Jewish shops, and even generals in uniform bought in Jewish stores.[25] In Krefeld, women responded to the call for a boycott against Jews by boycotting Christian businesses, for which they were publicly threatened by the SA.[26] A school director vehemently criticized the boycott and was duly reported by a Nazi.[27]

These instances are revealing. At several points in his writings, Kershaw argues that merely buying from Jews did not indicate opposition to Nazi anti-Semitism, but rather economic self-interest.[28] This is certainly possible if one considers the entire period 1933 to 1939, when Jews were finally driven from the German economy. Yet the experience of the boycott in 1933 might give one pause to consider whether or not this is the entire answer. The days of the boycott were not special sale days; they were ordinary days made extraordinary only by the Nazis' call for a boycott. Given this, can one ascribe the boycott's failure merely to self-interest? On the other hand, since the possible duration of the boycott was unknown, many shoppers may have rushed to Jewish stores simply because they feared that Jewish merchants would be driven out of business and their own supplies would be curtailed. The available sources permit both interpretations because in themselves they provide no clear-cut evidence for the 1933 boycott.

Between April and July 1933, many Germans aided Jews who were boycotted or otherwise harassed.[29] According to police and SD reports for Düsseldorf between 1934 and 1935, the population was either indifferent or hostile to anti-Semitism.[30] The same was true in the Government District Aachen.[31] Many letters protesting dismissals of Jewish civil servants were sent to Grauert, the state secretary of the Ministry of the Interior.[32] According to Annedore Leber, the number of those who disapproved of Nazi racial persecution was much greater than was recognized outside of Germany. She cites the anonymous distribution to 200,000 people of a leaflet protesting anti-Semitism during 1934.[33] At the end of 1934 the Gestapo noted adverse public reactions to anti-Semitic propaganda that had been published in the Nazi paper, the *Westdeutscher Beobachter*.[34] More important, the Government Pres-

169

ident's Report for the Government District Aachen bemoaned the lack of public comprehension of how the "Jewish question" had to be settled.[35]

In addition to these examples of public opposition to anti-Semitic measures, miscellaneous verbal and written criticisms came to the attention of authorities. For example, Goering received a letter on April 1, 1933, saying that it was no wonder that foreigners engaged in "atrocity propaganda" because of the year-long anti-Semitic propaganda of the NSDAP, and that if a foreigner saw the molestation of Jews during the boycott, one need not wonder why every possible "fairytale" was reported in the foreign press.[36] Another gentleman said Jews were the most honorable people in the world; he was subsequently charged with slander against the state.[37] Socializing with Jews continued and was frowned upon by the Nazis.[38] In a governmental Daily Report (*Tagesbericht*) of August 30, 1934, seizure of two letters from Innsbruck was reported. The letters announced a day of retaliation for Nazi criminality. They were written by members of the World Organization to Combat War and Race Hatred.[39] In the Government President's Situation Report (*Lagebericht*) for Aachen in November 1934, it was noted that a leading member of the Young Germanic Order protested boycotts against Jews.[40] In December 1934 the Aachen Government President's Daily Report confirmed the seizure of a publication containing an article entitled "Honorary Retirement for Jewish War Veterans"; it was considered a danger to public security and order.[41] In his Situation Report of December 18, 1934, the Aachen Government President reported that twenty handwritten notes were thrown from a train; the notes blamed *Der Stürmer*, Streicher's anti-Semitic newspaper, for damaging Germany's foreign trade.[42]

According to the American Consul at Berlin, some of the businessmen and financiers of Germany, as well as public men, realized the dangers of complete elimination of the Jews to the social and economic structure, but they were "almost without exception afraid to raise their voice. They feel and have learned by experience that doing so is only to prepare the way for their own elimination."[43]

Thus between 1933 and 1935 there was both support for and opposition to anti-Semitic measures, even though the predominant sentiment was probably indifference.[44] Between 1935 and 1938 we find a similar situation, although there appears to have been a hardening of attitudes among both supporters and opponents of anti-Semitism.

The second phase of persecution, from 1935 to 1938, was also marked by letters of denunciation against Jews.[45] The Nuremberg Laws were viewed by many Germans, probably a majority, as a stabilizing and necessary measure to limit Jewish influence and intermarriage.[46] For example, the socialist underground heard criticism leveled against the Weimar Republic for not having instituted similar measures.[47] Some Germans felt that the Nuremberg Laws did not go far enough to prosecute both Jews and non-Jews who engaged in sexual relations with one another.[48] Nazi propaganda clearly had been successful in persuading the public to recognize a "Jewish problem" during the years since Hitler took power.[49] According to some *Deutschland-Berichte*, public opinion favored exclusion of Jews from leading positions in the state and from previous positions of power. This was true of the educated, the socialists, and the workers, some of whom were unlikely to have been anti-Semitic before.[50]

According to other reports, the population was basically indifferent to the "Jewish question" except that Jews without influence or personal acquaintances were pitied.[51] Overall, between 1935 and 1938 it appears that anti-Semitic measures and propaganda received increased support, certainly more than between 1933 and 1935.

During the months preceding the introduction of the Nuremberg Laws, there had been considerable opposition to boycotts and violent attacks on Jews. This was noted by Nazi officials, foreign observers, and the socialist underground.[52] Yet several sources indicated that the public accepted the Nuremberg Laws with little discussion and less opposition, primarily because they appeared to clarify the legal position of Jews in Germany.[53] The *Deutschland-Berichte* offered only two examples of disagreement with the Nuremberg Laws.[54] Thus legal exclusion seems to have been accepted in principle and as an abstract concept.[55] Here one already discerns a peculiarly bifurcated attitude that will be discussed further below: there was much wider acceptance of anti-Semitism as an abstract concept than there was of its actual implications and real applications.

Nevertheless, the Nuremberg Laws did not satisfy all Germans. A Government President's Situation Report for October 1935 stated that the public was not in agreement with the laws except insofar as they would halt the spate of anti-Semitic excesses by the party.[56] Individuals who were arrested for violating the Nuremberg Laws were called *Rassenschänder*, or "race polluters." Their detection normally came in three ways, either from denouncement by acquaintances or "busybodies," or investigation by the police independently of denouncements. Arrests of Germans who had had long-standing relations with Jews were generally instigated by the police on their own, while less well-known *Rassenschänder* were typically reported by Nazis or acquaintances. In the early years after the Nuremberg Laws were passed the police sometimes interrogated persons whose guilt was questionable and were forced to release them. As a result, the public frequently ignored or discounted individual cases even though the Nuremberg Laws in general were accepted.[57] Evidence of disagreement with Nazi racial policies can be found in criminal statistics, which listed 1,683 cases of *Rassenschande* between 1935 and 1939.[58] Many of these cases were reported in the *Deutschland-Berichte*.[59] Government Presidents also reported cases of "racial pollution";[60] still other cases were reported in local and regional court records.[61] Since criminal sentences did arise from *Rassenschande*, and given the difficulty of hiding it from Nazi authorities, it is clear that some Germans simply chose their own partners without references to Nazi racial "ideology."

There was considerable direct aid to Jews by individual Germans during the years 1935–1938.[62] The most common contacts were business transactions. Many sources indicate that a large number of Germans maintained business contacts with Jews and patronized Jewish stores.[63] This in itself is not evidence that Germans wished to aid Jews, because Jews may simply have had lower prices and better services than their competitors. However, it is a clear indication that many did not believe continued business relations were the evil that Nazi propaganda portrayed them to be. In short, a genuine anti-Semite of Hitler's ilk would have preferred to shop in "Aryan" stores as a matter of "national honor" or "racial purity." Many sources contained direct statements that buying from Jews was deliberately chosen as an expression of opposition to racial persecution.[64]

In the Government District Aachen several seizures of publications criticizing anti-Semitic measures were reported for 1935.[65] One gentleman was arrested for condemning Streicher because of his anti-Semitic article in *Der Stürmer*.[66] On February 19, 1936, a Monthly Report (*Monatsbericht*) of the government president for Aachen reported complaints against driving Jews out of the cattle trade.[67] In December 1936 the *Deutschland-Berichte* reported a case in which a man was arrested for boxing the ears of his child, who had refused to visit a Jewess.[68]

These examples of general public opposition, *Rassenschande*, business relations between Jews and "Aryans," and verbal and written criticism of racial persecution indicate that just as some Germans hardened their attitudes against Jews, other Germans strengthened their opposition to Nazi racial policies. The majority probably remained indifferent as the advocates and opponents of anti-Semitism adopted more extreme attitudes. As the American ambassador to Germany, Dodd, noted,

> . . . It may be said that a large proportion of the adult population have ceased to be impressed by the anti-Jewish hue and cry. Being for the most part the indifferent or incompetent to express whatever sympathy they may now have for the Jews in their affliction, they have very little influence, however, upon those extremist Party elements who are pushing the anti-Jewish campaign for their own ends and who moreover may be expected to derive support from the new generation which is being educated to regard the Jews as a menace to be suppressed with all the brutality at the command of the Party and State.[69]

173

When we examine reports on public opinion for January to November 1938 (at the beginning of stage 3 of persecution), our suspicions regarding hardening of attitudes are confirmed. In March 1938 the *Deutschland-Berichte* reported that anti-Semitism was slowly taking root among the German people. It was a more kindly anti-Semitism than that preached by the Nazis, but anti-Semitism nevertheless.[70] In August the *Deutschland-Berichte* reported that anti-Semitism was growing and that those who formed their own opinions were few in number.[71] Many were reported to have become anti-Semitic as a result of anti-Semitic propaganda, and some wrote to authorities to complain of close contacts between Jews and Gentiles.[72]

Nevertheless, there were also reports that indicated opposition to anti-Semitic measures. The SS bemoaned continuing assimilation of Germans and Jews.[73] The party office in Mannheim complained to *Der Stürmer* that women were too friendly with Jews,[74] and in Karlsruhe there were also complaints of high levels of *Rassenschande*.[75] When Hitler was forced to seize an issue of *Der Stürmer* because of an article advocating the death penalty for Jews having sexual relations with ''Aryan'' women (presumably because of potentially adverse public reactions), the SD complained that liberals and reactionaries welcomed the seizure.[76] The *Deutschland-Berichte* reported that even when people approved of measures against Jews in large cities, they sympathized with local Jews and complained of the terror against them.[77] Buying from Jews also continued.[78]

In March 1938 a similar report from Bavaria indicated that the populace had not become anti-Semitic.[79] After attacks on Jews in Berlin during the summer of 1938, the *Deutschland-Berichte* reported that these measures were designed to win new converts in circles where racial measures were still not accepted because anti-Semitic propaganda alone had failed.[80] In a gesture of ironic circularity (but only in view of the official position), Germans attended funerals of Jews who committed suicide because of persecution.[81] On a more trivial level, other reports demonstrate disapproval of racial policies. For example, an older Jewish gentleman was arrested for speaking to a German lady and was ordered not to speak to her again. Afterward she greeted him with great curtsies when they met.[82] A more important example was widespread public criticism of the forceable deportation of Polish Jews in October 1938.[83]

These examples for the months of January to November 1938 indicate support for racial persecution as well as opposition. Once again, however, these were extremes of opinion; most people were indifferent to Jews, who comprised a very small percentage of the population, and who were in any case decreasing their numbers by emigration.[84]

During the latter part of stage 3, from November 1938 until October 1941, a shift in attitudes became markedly apparent. One of the *Deutschland-Berichte* indicated that there was either apathy or support for anti-Semitism by a few women and workers.[85] Rauschning also pointed out the role of callousness and fear in producing apathy during *Kristallnacht*.[86] However, these two reports are the only indications of support for the pogrom in a survey of the *Deutschland-Berichte*. Kershaw did find some isolated cases of support for *Kristallnacht* in Bavaria; however, these were apparently atypical.[87]

In contrast, there was a torrent of reports indicating public disapproval of *Kristallnacht*.[88] The British *chargé d'affaires* commented that most Germans disapproved of *Kristallnacht*, reporting as follows:

> Inarticulate though the mass of the people may have been, I have not met a single German of whatever class who in varying measure does not, to say the least, disapprove of what has occurred. But I fear it does not follow that even the outspoken condemnation of professed National Socialists or of senior officers in the army will have any influence over the insensate gang in present control of Nazi Germany.[89]

The lack of class differences was also noted by Kershaw.[90] The British consul general in Frankfurt stated: "I am persuaded that, if the government of Germany depended on the suffrage of the people, those in power and responsible for these outrages would be swept away by a storm of indignation if not put up against a wall and shot.''[91] The American consul in Leipzig described local crowds as benumbed and aghast.[92] The United States ambassador to Germany, Wilson, reported:

> In view of this being a totalitarian state a surprising characteristic of the situation here is the intensity and scope among German citizens of a condemnation of the recent happenings against Jews. This sentiment is variously based upon two considerations. One of utter shame at the action of the Government and of their fellow Germans and the other on a conviction that the happenings constitute bad policy in the internal and more particularly in the external field. Such expressions are not confined to members of the intellectual classes but are encountered here throughout all classes—taxi-drivers, servants, et cetera— and it is understood among the peasantry in the country.[93]

Because of *Kristallnacht*, Ambassador Wilson was recalled from Germany. The assistant secretary of state, Messersmith, stated that ''As to the effects of such action, I believe it will be excellent in Germany. It will give heart to the right-thinking people there who are in the majority, if impotent.''[94]

According to one report, public reaction to *Kristallnacht* was so bad that even the Sudeten conquest could not balance the harm done.[95] Also, ''. . . where we could notice excitement, insofar as it existed at all, it was directed against the SA and not against Jews.''[96] Because of the importance of *Kristallnacht*, one should reflect upon a long quotation from the *Deutschland-Berichte*:

> Goebbels has tried to persuade the world that the German people are fundamentally anti-Jewish in order to defend and to excuse the atrocities for which the state is responsible. Those who had an opportunity of watching the Berlin population during the days of the pogroms know that the people have nothing in common with this brown barbarism.
>
> The protest of the Berlin people against the looting and arson, against the ill-treatment of Jewish men, women and children of all ages was clearly noticeable. You could see the contemptuous looks of the people, you could notice movements

expressing indignation and you could even hear words of shame and drastic cursing. On Weinmeisterstrasse a police corporal and a Reichswehr sergeant protected two elderly Jewish women with their six or seven children against a party-mob and led them to a place of refuge.

The new measures against the Jews have met with general disapproval from the people. There are of course individuals, especially women, who express their satisfaction, but they are greatly outnumbered by the many Aryans who have voiced their unconditional disapproval of the pogroms and who have offered help to the persecuted Jews in spite of the dangers involved in such assistance. A number of Aryans have taken Jews into their homes during the critical days whereupon they were informed by their landlords that this meant a criminal offense.

The German people as a whole have not been greatly infected by the poison of anti-Semitism. If the anti-Semitic propaganda had produced the desired effect, this whole action would not have been necessary. If five and a half years of constant propaganda could not make the people stay away from Jewish shops, if on the contrary the number of Aryans who deliberately went to shop with Jews was still fairly large, this is at best proof of the failure of the anti-Jewish propaganda.[97]

According to Steinert, the rural population, urban Catholics, Germans living in the south and west, liberals, and pacifists were most critical of *Kristallnacht*.[98] Kershaw also confirms the unpopularity of *Kristallnacht*; however, he contrasts the Germans' acceptance of legal measures against Jews and their rejection of pogroms that destroyed property, entailed violence, and damaged Germany's reputation abroad. Although he cites some examples of humanitarian concern, he apparently does not believe that this was a primary reason for opposing the pogrom.[99] Nevertheless, the personal attitudes of those Germans who disapproved of *Kristallnacht* will never be known. Even if the majority of Germans' objections had been humanitarian, researchers can never discover this because the objectors would have taken care to camouflage

177

their actual feelings behind verbal criticisms of property damage and Germany's foreign image, since this would protect them against the rather serious charge (to Nazis) of being "Jew lovers." In any case, available data allow no definitive conclusion regarding the true feelings of the majority of Germans. What is not in doubt, however, is the fact that the majority did disapprove, whether out of concern for domestic order, foreign relations, or sympathy for individual Jews or Jews in general.

During and after *Kristallnacht*, many Germans aided Jews by forewarning them of Nazi attacks, hiding their possessions, hiding Jews in their homes, providing medical care, and giving food.[100] For this assistance a large number of Germans were arrested in a Nazi attempt to root out criticism of their racial policies.[101] The *Deutschland-Berichte* reported the following:

> Too little attention has been paid abroad to the fact that following the Jewish pogroms a great hunt for "state enemies" was started. The reliable members of the Nazi Party were instructed to mix with the people wearing no badges and to take everybody to the police or the appropriate Nazi quarters whom they overheard passing critical remarks. This led to a huge number of arrests in the streets, to an extent not experienced previously. People were arrested in the trams for no other reason than that they had talked to Jews. In Nuremberg things were particularly bad. People were arrested while travelling in the train and taken to Dachau. Most of the arrested were released after leaving names and addresses. But the population became nevertheless very frightened. Many had thought that in this case the number of grumblers was so large that nothing could be done against them. But now they saw that the Nazis went to any length in trying to fight the oppositional elements. The immediate result is that grumbling has become less pronounced. Less people dare to speak openly. Everybody realises more and more that after all the Nazis have the power to do what they like.[102]

The *Deutschland-Berichte* reported arrests of 114 people by the Hindenburg police (in Silesia); they had made critical remarks against the pogroms.[103] In the early months of 1938 a few cases of grumbling against Nazi racial policies were reported.[104] However, after *Kristallnacht* verbal complaints escalated, according to reports from a number of sources.[105] Even during World War II some complaints about *Kristallnacht* could still be heard.[106]

After *Kristallnacht* the Nazis accelerated their campaign to drive Jews out of the economy. If we attempt to discover public opinion toward this economic persecution, we are faced with almost no information. Only two reports indicated opposition to "Aryanization," and both Steinert and Kershaw claim that "Aryanization" was well received.[107] After December 1938 the public was more reluctant to buy from Jews because of increased penalties and arrests.[108] Given the large number of reports on opposition to *Kristallnacht* and the paucity of reports on opposition to "Aryanization," one might interpret the lack of evidence to mean that the German people did indeed accept economic persecution. However, one should bear in mind the comprehensive news blackout of "Aryanization," which may have successfully concealed its extensiveness.[109] In this case lack of evidence may reflect agreement with persecution, but it might also reflect genuine ignorance or simply fear in the face of increased penalties for criticizing Nazi racial policies.

Germans did not appear to have discontinued sexual relations with Jews. Criminal statistics reported 412 cases of *Rassenschande* in 1939, compared to 480 cases of 1938.[110] Sentences for *Rassenschande* were more uniformly executed and risks became more extreme for both Germans and Jews after 1938; however, this did not eliminate sexual contacts, despite the declining number of Jews between the ages of fifteen and fifty who remained in Germany.[111] There was also a new flood of verbal protests against Nazi racial policies.[112] Socializing and friendly relations between Jews and non-Jews were still a source of concern to the Nazis.[113]

As a general summary of attitudes between 1938 and 1940, we can conclude that murder, destruction of property, and violence were condemned by the minority that had earlier opposed persecution, but also by large segments of the previously indifferent

179

population. Many individuals aided Jews and were arrested for overt or covert disagreement with persecution. Public opposition to rabid anti-Semitism was at a peak after *Kristallnacht*, and it constituted a thorn in the side of the Nazi regime.[114] Large-scale arrests were used to frighten potential opponents into silence. This tactic was apparently successful, because the next, more orderly attack on Jews during "Aryanization" was never widely condemned. If anyone seriously objected, he kept his opinions to himself to avoid harassment by Nazi authorities. The Nazis were not successful in eliminating sexual contact between Germans and Jews, as the number of cases of *Rassenschande* decreased only slightly in 1939. After the furor over *Kristallnacht* died down, the majority of the population seems to have become more circumspect. Covert grumbling against racial persecution increased, and the population grew skeptical of official reports.[115] According to von Hassell, the German ambassador to Rome, the prevailing attitude was moral opposition to brutal treatment of Jews and a sense of shame.[116] After 1940 anti-Semitic propaganda became a daily deluge. Jews were held responsible for the war, and Nazis indirectly justified their attacks on Jews by accusations of an international Jewish conspiracy to defeat the Fatherland.

However, before we discuss the Germans' responses to wartime propaganda and rumors, we should consider the overall question of knowledge of persecution, deportation, concentration camps, and death factories. After *Kristallnacht*, the Nazis deliberately tried to conceal their measures against the Jews, as our examination of propaganda on blackouts revealed. During the destruction process secrecy became a *major* Nazi concern.[117] Hitler was delighted that rumors of extermination by shooting circulated because this terrorized the Germans at home; nevertheless, he did not want hard factual evidence to surface because this might have led to extensive public criticism and foreign propaganda coups.

The SD was well aware of rumors about shootings, as the following report indicates:

> Much is discussed in the population about the *Einsatz* of the Gestapo, but one is not able to form a clear picture about the

tasks of the German SS, since the wildest rumors are spread about them. Therefore it is rumored that the SS has the task of exterminating the Jews in the occupied territories. Supposedly thousands of Jews are driven together and shot after first having to dig their own graves. The shootings supposedly sometimes result in nervous breakdowns by members of the shooting commandos. These rumors have given the population occasion to form a picture of the activities of the SS which is surrounded by a gruesome nimbus. Therefore, it arouses special interest when the daily press and weeklies also report on these police formations. Since the army also very frequently reports on battles with partisans and emphasizes that these battles are led by the SS and SD, but one knows little about the characteristics of these battles, one is especially interested in reports of this type. Also, one still has a completely unclear picture of the events behind our front lines in the Soviet territories. One is very interested in credible reports on the behavior of the Soviet population in the occupied territories. This report of the VB [Nazi newspaper, the *Völkischer Beobachter*] is very informative and has also shown how important the activities of the SS are. Now one may be able to explain why so many police officials have fallen behind our lines.[118]

Whether these rumors were believed is not clear. According to the SD, other rumors were also spread by Catholics in order to heighten the effectiveness of their rumors about the transports of Jews—for example, ''that all Germans in America are supposedly forced to wear a swastika on their left breast in order to make them more recognizable. The Germans in America must suffer heavily because the Jews in Germany are supposedly so badly handled.''[119] These rumors were false, but it is not clear whether they or the rumors of mass shootings of Jews were actually believed.

With respect to deportations of the approximately 164,000 Jews left in Germany by October 1, 1941, one must realize that their removal was generally attempted during the night or early morning hours to conceal the action, and that Jews were transported in a variety of public and private vehicles, including furniture vans, to hide the operation further. The late hours and covert methods of transporting Jews to collection stations limited the number of direct observers. Jews had already been concentrated in certain geographic areas so that they were by and large isolated from non-Jews. Nevertheless, many Germans did witness the deportations, and many others learned of them from reliable acquaintances, either Jewish or non-Jewish. It was less possible to obtain eyewitness information regarding the shootings; however, accounts of shootings of Jews and Poles in the East were brought back by soldiers, even though they were under threat of execution for revealing the truth.[120] This led to widespread rumors of shootings, yet it is not possible to determine, given available evidence, whether these rumors were actually believed. Knowledge of concentration camps was common almost from their inception in Germany (1933); however, before the war there were few Jewish inmates, and these were mainly punitive institutions rather than slave labor camps. Certainly the German concentration camps from 1933 to 1939 were not death camps for Jews. Jews were arrested in large numbers (over twenty thousand) only during *Kristallnacht*, and practically all of them were released within a short period of time.[121] The camps in the occupied East, on the other hand, were in most cases out of view of soldiers and were kept strictly secret. Knowledge about them was very limited except among top officials, the resistance, and church leaders.[122]

Stokes cites examples of a select few who were highly placed in German society and presumably had good contacts and believed the rumors, as well as others who tried very hard to stay well informed but nevertheless considered the information to be rumor rather than fact.[123] It is, of course, obvious that in wartime rumors of all types are spread and most are false. That many Germans might have disbelieved them is therefore not surprising, since others who had better information also failed to comprehend their accuracy. British, American, and Vatican authorities continually discounted or rejected information that was partly, if not totally, accurate regarding the extermination of the Jews.[124] Even well-informed Jews in other countries downplayed or discountenanced the information that they received. Since what they heard was on the surface incredible by normal standards of common sense and past experience, this is not shocking; no human beings had ever had to contemplate premeditated carnage on quite so vast a scale.[125]

It is somewhat startling to learn that many Jews in Germany also refused to believe rumors of what might happen to them if they were shipped to the East. Even so prominent a Jewish leader as Leo Baeck, the head of the Berlin Jewish community, said that he did not know of Auschwitz and the systematic murder of Jews until 1943, by which time millions had already been murdered.[126] Thus one may assume that the Nazis were successful in concealing their true aims even from those Jews whose underground connections should have informed them of their fellow Jews' immediate danger.

Some historians find a continuing trend of Jewish "self-deception" about German anti-Semitism, even between 1870 and 1914.[127] Certainly, in 1933 many perceptive Jews recognized that the Nazis meant to do them harm but anticipated "normal" European discrimination—perhaps a bad period followed by Hitler's fall—but nothing vaguely similar to the unprecedented slaughter that occurred.[128] Eva Reichmann, who lived in Berlin in 1933, said: ". . . 'You never heard "Heil Hitler" in Berlin, . . . Berlin was a haven. . . . There was nothing to bother you there.' "[129] Walter Bacharach concluded that "Despite the fact that the anti-Jewish legislation and the events subsequent to January 1933 provided clear proof of the uncompromising Nazi attitude, there existed a tendency among Jews to blur the grave import of the victory of racism."[130] And as Leonard Baker, Leo Baeck's biographer, said:

This was the same problem the Jews had faced ever since Hitler had come to power: They could not believe it. They could not believe they would be stripped of their citizenship until it happened. They could not believe their houses of worship would be destroyed until it happened. They could not believe they would be torn from their homes and families until it happened. And now they could not believe they would be murdered systematically.[131]

The "creeping" nature of persecution also disarmed the Jews, who thought that each stage of persecution was the final stage.[132] Although there was much foreboding among most Jews when they were rounded up, for example, in Berlin, their fears were reduced because they were transported in an orderly fashion to the collection point, food and clothing were available, and they were allowed to take some possessions; they actually thought they were being "relocated" in the East, presumably to minimal, or worse, housing.[133] Even when they were traveling in open trains across the countryside to the East and farmers made gestures that they were dead men, they refused to believe the warnings.[134] As late as 1943, after the exterminations had been in progress for many months, Jewish victims refused to believe the rumors of death camps; this was true not only in Berlin, but also in other German cities.[135] As Kren and Rappoport write:

> Until 1943–1944, when firm knowledge of the "final solution" had leaked out to large numbers of Jews and Germans alike, many Jews accepted the relocation story as legitimate. In this connection, the sheer implausibility of massive killing as an official German policy worked to the advantage of the SS because ordinary people could not believe it.[136]

And as Leo Baeck said after learning of Auschwitz and other camps in 1943 and deciding not to inform anyone:

> If the Council of Elders were informed, the whole camp would know within a few hours. Living in the expectation of death by gassing would only be the harder. And this death was not certain for all—there was selection for slave labor; perhaps not all transports went to Auschwitz. So came the grave decision to tell no one. Rumors of all sorts were constantly spreading through the ghetto, and before long the rumors of Auschwitz spread too. But at least no one knew for certain.[137]

Without doubt, the Jews in Germany did not typically perceive the real possibility of their wholesale destruction after Hitler's election. During the years of persecution that followed, many left Germany, which indicates that they did consider the measures taken against them to be permanent or of such duration that emigration was the safest course. Those who remained behind could not comprehend the threat to their lives: not when they were transported East, not when they saw the miserable conditions in the concentration camps, not when they were transferred again to death camps; and for some, not until they actually arrived in Auschwitz or some other death camp.

If Jews who had been shipped to the East did not themselves perceive their perilous situation, can one automatically assume that German observers of transports knew the outcome that awaited them? The first Jews who were deported were not sent immediately to death camps, but to ghettos in the East or to the "model camp," Theresienstadt. Thus those witnessing their departure would have been in error to assume that the first transports necessarily meant death. It is possible to argue that both the Jews and the Germans who had heard rumors should have concluded that death awaited deportees from Germany. It is questionable to argue that Jews should have known, while Germans did not, or that Germans should have known, while Jews did not. The blindness, whether willful or not, applied to both Jews and Germans. If so principled a man as Leo Baeck felt it unwise to inform fellow inmates of their probable deaths when transported from Theresienstadt to "camps" farther east, can one realistically expect that the average German would have attempted to intervene in deportations and extermination with his family held hostage, even if he had actually *known* rather than merely suspected that death awaited deportees? This is not a frivolous question; it is also one that is very seldom asked, probably because the answer is so unfortunate not only for the Germans, but for all those who believe in the perfectibility and nobility of man. If mankind is neither perfectible nor noble, and if the Germans under Hitler were a representative sample, then one can only expect that men will typically think of themselves and their families first and others last, if at all. Certainly the bulk of research on public opinion indicates that the majority of Germans simply did not think much about Jews during the period of their deportation and extermination. Jews had in most instances already been segregated from Germans physically, occupationally, sexually, socially, and psychologically. There were only 164,000 Jews left in Germany by October 1941, and these lived in a forcibly and cruelly restricted environment. Even those Germans who helped them, however few that may have been, did so at considerable personal risk and against their own objective self-interest.

Immediately after the war Admiral Doenitz, who may himself have been unaware of the death camps, claimed that the Germans knew nothing about them and that they would be indignant to a man if they knew the camps existed.[138] However, this was either wishful thinking or self-delusion. Thousands of soldiers knew of them, thousands of bureaucrats in state and Nazi offices helped to organize and transport Jews to the East, even if they did not know but only suspected that death awaited them, and thousands of SS men participated in the killings. Hilberg is right to say that "A destruction process is not the work of a few mad minds. It cannot be accomplished by any handful of men. It is far too complex in its organizational build-up and far too pervasive in its administrative implementation to dispense with specialized bureaucrats in every segment of society."[139]

But what of those Germans who were not directly involved in the destructive process—what did they know? Evidence of knowledge during the war years is very limited; however, reports studied by Stokes, Steinert, Kershaw, and this author indicate that: (1) many Germans knew of the deportations;[140] (2) rumors of shootings in the East were rampant;[141] and (3) the majority of Germans did *not* know of the many and horrid death camps, although there was some awareness in eastern Germany.[142] With these conclusions on the Germans' knowledge in mind, let us examine evidence on public attitudes toward rumored atrocities. Since some of the evidence came from the SD and may have been designed to impress superiors, it may not always mirror the true state of public opinion; however, because evidence on the war years is otherwise thin, SD reports must be examined.

During the war years we find intensification among the German people of support for persecution as well as opposition to it. Those who participated directly in the transports, deportation, labor camps, and death camps were a minority of the population, yet there is evidence that even Germans who did not participate directly approved of the curtailed employment, residential restrictions, separate shopping hours, and imprisonment of Jews. For example, one Jewess reported that there was a minority of real Jew-baiters even though the bulk of the population was indifferent.[143] Another reported that the population had become desensitized to racial persecution because of continual anti-Semitic propaganda.[144] The SD in Minden reported public sympathy with the new policy of restricting shopping hours for Jews in 1939.[145] According to another SD report, the public liked the film *Jud Süss* and was spurred to demonstrate against Jews after viewing it.[146] There were, however, objections to showing it at youth film hours.[147] The Führer was applauded in scenes from *Der ewige Jude* in which he announced that the war would result in the destruction of Jewry.[148] Yet after its introductory showings attendance was much reduced; only very politically active Nazi supporters attended. According to the report, regular moviegoers stayed away and waged an oral propaganda campaign against the film.[149] However, another SD report claimed that films concerning imprisonment of Jews were welcomed everywhere.[150]

When the yellow star was introduced as a method of identifying Jews, it was well received except in Catholic and middle-class circles.[151] In August 1941 the SD in Bielefeld reported a popular feeling of relief that Jews in Germany should be made to wear a star, as was the case in the General Government (occupied Poland).[152] This would prevent the public from having to associate with Jews in public places from which they were restricted. The SD in Bielefeld later complained that the population was upset because Jews could still use third-class trains and other public transportation, in which soldiers and workers were also forced to travel.[153] On September 16, 1941, the same SD office reported as follows regarding the introduction of the order compelling Jews to wear the yellow star:

> The above-mentioned police order has evoked genuine satisfaction in all classes of the population. It constituted the major

topic of conversation on Saturday and Sunday. Time after time one hears the opinion that now the Jews in Germany have lost every possibility of concealing themselves. Generally it is pointed out that only through this police order will the complete effectiveness of the restrictive measures against Jewish use of cinemas, restaurants and markets be achieved. It is frequently demanded that now Jews should also be excluded from using public means of transportation such as buses and street cars. In general it is hoped that now the last Jews will soon leave the German fatherland.[154]

Public satisfaction with the star and calls for further restrictions on Jewish shopping hours were reported by government presidents in Bavaria.[155] Moreover, many reports indicated that the population did not understand why Jews who were married to Germans were not also required to wear the star, since this oversight made it possible for them to escape detection.[156]

Several special interest groups had specific complaints. For example, doctors demanded that Jews should be forbidden to use their professional titles,[157] and renters complained that Jews were still living in their flats while "Aryans" were forced to go without lodging.[158] According to the SD in Minden, still others were upset because an "Aryan" wife of a full Jew was permitted to announce her husband's death in the local newspaper.[159] On February 3, 1942, the SD reported public complaints that elderly Germans received no milk at a time when Jewish children were allowed the same ration as Germans.[160] The SD also noted popular disapproval of the remaining legal options for Jews in German courts.[161] Goebbels's diary entry for February 3, 1942, complained that the "Jewish question" was once again a headache because large sections of the population were beginning to believe that the "Jewish problem" could not be solved until all Jews had left Germany.[162] Other reports indicated that some Germans did indeed demand a radical elimination of Jews from Germany.[163]

We do not have many reports on public reactions after deportations began, but a few will be cited here. For example, documents on public opinion in Bavaria turned up only one report on

December 10, 1941, of reactions to deportation: "The population, from whom this was not concealed, took notice of the fact approvingly."[164] One SD report stated that most of the local population approved of transports of four hundred Jews from Minden in December 1941.[165] An extensive SD report for the Government District Minden has survived:

> Although this action by the state police was kept secret, the deportation of the Jews was nevertheless discussed in all circles of the population. Accordingly, a great number of comments were collected to measure public attitudes. It has been established that the action was greeted by far and away the majority of the population. Individual statements that one should thank the Führer for freeing us from the pest of Jewish blood were overheard. A worker said, for example, "that had the Jews been taken care of 50 years earlier, then we would not have had to endure either a world war or the current war." Many in the population were astounded that well-maintained city buses were made available to transport Jews to the railway station.[166]

However, there was some objection to deportations from the Government District Minden, as we shall see below.

Several German soldiers wrote letters to *Der Stürmer* praising the measures taken against Jews in occupied countries. One soldier wrote from Russia on September 21, 1941, when shootings of Russian Jews were taking place:

> Today when I think back on the days of the *Kampfzeit* [1920s and 1930's when the Nazis were attempting to take power], when we as SA-men and party members also were enthusiastic about *Der Stürmer*, and today as I think back on the battles in Poland, France, and now Russia, then I always have a very great awareness that for us there can be no greater and holier task than the ceaseless destruction of Jewry.

He then proceeded to describe the filthy habits of Jews, the political oppression of Russian farmers by Jewish commissars, and the continuing fear of Jews by Russians. He concluded, "But in

189

everything the German army will see that there is a well-deserved punishment . . ." and promised to report many interesting things about this "pest" in the future.[167] Another soldier sent pictures of Polish Jews to *Der Stürmer*, saying that there was not a soldier who had seen these Jews who did not look at them with abhorrence. He also said, "When the sword of the Führer has exterminated this pest, he will also have freed Europe and the whole world of this central seat of diseases. . . ."[168]

Just as anti-Semitism appeared to become more radical among a minority of Germans in World War II, opposition to anti-Semitism increased among another minority. Reitlinger points out mob sympathy for Jews who were arrested by the Gestapo in Berlin.[169] Goebbels complained that the best (presumably the most educated or "cultured") elements in Berlin society disapproved of these arrests and subsequent deportations.[170] Von Hassell, the German ambassador to Rome, reported widespread disgust with Nazi measures against Jews.[171] Boelcke concluded that many Germans opposed anti-Semitic excesses during the war,[172] and Pulzer stated that extermination was the choice of leaders rather than the population, even though the majority of Germans acquiesced to it.[173] According to Klepper, a German who was married to a Jewess, Hitler would have had genuine support from the German population instead of false allegiance if only he had not attacked Jews and Christianity.[174]

If we examine more specific examples of opposition, we find support for the general evidence cited above. Many Germans continued to sell to Jews despite intimidation.[175] An SD report of October 1939 complained that the public was discussing the parable of the good Samaritan in which Jews were the heroes.[176] Klepper's diary entry for December 8, 1938, emphasized the unpopularity of anti-Semitic measures.[177] According to reports of observers from neutral countries that were published in the last issue of the *Deutschland-Berichte* in 1940, the majority of Germans manifested less sympathy with anti-Semitic excesses than they ever had.[178] Else Behrend-Rosenfeld reported in October 1941 that the Nazis had not succeeded in estranging Germans and Jews,[179] and Düwell supports this interpretation by citing examples of friendly relations between Germans and Jews in the Rhineland.[180] Also, an SD report on Hitler's speech of March 26, 1942, complained of friendly relations between Germans and Jews in Erfurt.[181] Even the limitation of shopping hours for Jews was strongly opposed after its introduction, notwithstanding one SD report that the idea was popular before it was implemented.[182]

Hans Fritzsche, radio propaganda chief in the Propaganda Ministry, stated that anti-Semitic measures were not well received during the war, especially after the introduction of the star in 1941.[183] Else Behrend-Rosenfeld wrote that the population simply ignored the star,[184] and Klepper also reported that the population was exemplary in ignoring the star.[185] Leo Baeck reported that although there were some instances of harassment of Jews after they started wearing the star, the populations of Berlin and Hamburg treated them very decently.[186] The papal nuncio believed that the public attitude toward Jews was remarkably sympathetic after introduction of the star.[187] According to Gestapo reports, opposition to the star led the Gestapo to complain about lack of public understanding of National Socialist principles.[188] Some Germans continued to aid Jews, which occasioned new Nazi attacks on them.[189] It also induced the Propaganda Ministry to send out a secret guide sheet indicating that every non-Jew who publicly associated with a Jew would be arrested.[190]

Information on reactions to deportations is, as noted above, very scanty. The report for the Government District Minden quoted earlier indicated general public approval; however, both that report and the draft upon which it was based contained information that the deportations were accompanied by disapproval, particularly among Catholics, who were accused of spreading the wildest rumors. One was that

> the Jews were all deported to Russia. The transport was carried through to Warsaw with passenger trains, from which it travelled farther in cattle cars to Russia. The Führer wishes to have a report by January 15, 1942 that no more Jews live in Germany. Supposedly in Russia the Jews are enlisted to work in former Soviet factories, while the oldest and sickest are shot.

It is not understood that one could deal so brutally with the Jews; whether Jew or Aryan, everyone is still a man created by God.[191]

Another SD report from Minden on December 6, 1941, is also very informative. It is entitled "Attitude of the Population to the Evacuation of Jews." It begins by stating that

the evacuation was met with great concern by the majority of the population, from two points of view which they have very much at heart. First, Germans living abroad, particularly in America, might encounter new sufferings, since one knows that 9.11.1938 [*Kristallnacht*] damaged Germans in all foreign countries more than it helped them at home. Second, it is dangerous to transport people to the East in winter, with all of its perils. Thus it could certainly be anticipated that very many Jews would not survive the transport. Along this line comments were also heard that the recently evacuated Jews are still without exception people and have lived in this region for endless years. One hears the opinion that for many Jews this decision is too hard. Although this attitude is not detected in intense degree, nevertheless one still finds it, especially in well-off circles. Also, in this regard older people comprise the predominant number.[192]

Possibly because this was not good news for superiors, the report continued, "Nevertheless on the side of the citizens who have mastered the Jewish question, the entire action was absolutely affirmed. The German feeling of community has shown itself again as it always has."[193] The general tenor of the report, though, was echoed by one in Detmold, which was sent to the SD in Bielefeld. This was the only report that made specific reference to camps. It concerned the transport of Jews on July 28, 1942:

From Lemgo it is reported that the transport of the last Jews has excited a very great sensation among the public. The Jews assembled before the transport in the marketplace in Lemgo. This fact occasioned the population to appear in truly great numbers at the marketplace. It was observed that a large part of the older citizens, supposedly also party members, negatively criticized the transport of the Jews from Germany. A position against the transport was taken more or less openly for all possible reasons. It was said that as it was the Jews in Germany were certainly condemned to die out, and that these measures, which represented a particular hardship for the Jews, were therefore unnecessary. Even citizens who had earlier demonstrated their national socialist attitude at every suitable and unsuitable opportunity had in this respect defended the interests of the Jews, as did church-going citizens. In church circles it was said: "If only the German people did not have one day to await the punishment of God." Dyed-in-the-wool national socialists sought to make it clear to those with other opinions that this action was fully justified and also unconditionally necessary. They were told that, to the contrary, the old Jews could no longer harm us at home, because they "couldn't hurt a fly." Also, there were many Jews who had done much good and who had never been as bad as some Jews. Must we then also deport them and stick them in a camp?

A significant case of standing up for the Jews occurred during the transport of Jews in Sabbenhausen. Here the wife of a teacher attempted to give the Jews sausage and other foodstuffs. According to a communication from an *Ortsgruppenleiter*, the woman was arrested by the police. A review of this has been instituted, and a further report will follow when exact information is known.[194]

Steinert, Stokes, and Kershaw concluded that rumors of deportations and shootings on the Russian front occasioned public disapproval, especially because eyewitnesses from the Eastern front were the source.[195] A confidential Nazi party circular of October 9, 1942, reported public discussion of harsh measures against Jews as a result of accounts given by soldiers. The circular complained that all Germans might not appreciate the necessity of these measures.[196] Hitler, Goebbels, and Bormann were well aware of this disapproval, particularly among the middle classes and intellectuals.[197]

An SD report from Erfurt in April 1942 concerned a speech in which Hitler blamed the war on the "Jewish clique" in America and Britain. It stated:

> What the Führer said about the Jewish world parasite will hopefully be noticed by the still-existent friends of Jews and former lackies of Jews. There are unfortunately always those who still regard the Jews as unconditionally capable. In particular, such citizens can see no difference between the beastliness, brutality and unscrupulousness of this race and the true capability of a man of propriety and correctness. They say, stop, the Jews have in every instance been creative and advanced far. It is a matter of indifference to them with which means and under what circumstances. And that the Jew always took care only for his own advantage and his own race they do not see—he is always capable and intelligent.[198]

Other indications that some Germans disapproved of deportation can be found in strange and inelegant form. The SD at Höxter recommended the deportation from Brackel of a Jew named Stein, who was spared deportation before the 27th of February, 1943, because his wife was an "Aryan." After she died, the SD said: "It now appears that it is time to deport the Jew to a ghetto, above all because, as an anonymous letter to the *Ortsgruppenleiter* demonstrates, he still evokes a certain sympathy in the "Aryan" population."[199] The anonymous letter had run as follows:

> You are now certainly rejoicing that Mrs. Stein is dead. You old hen-farmer you. You talk big in Brackel. You should get yourself to the Russian front. Just looking at you gives one a noseful. With your poor lame arm. I would rather shit than be married to you. You have many people on your conscience. Therefore for you I will not say Heil Hitler. I would rather walk on your grave. You are as much a swine as there is in the party. Recently you are always bragging in the City Hall. Therefore, I will stand by the Jews. You should be shot until you are worth nothing. You have a face like an old sow. You certainly tormented the Jew's wife earlier. You old sow.[200]

On February 27, 1943, two thousand wives of Jews and four thousand sympathizers protested the arrest of the wives' Jewish husbands and secured their release two days later.[201] According to Bramsted, there was widespread distaste for persecution during later war years. Among 150 letters of complaint that were sent to the Propaganda Ministry, 16 or (10.7 percent) protested the reappearance of persecution on the grounds that Germany had other things to worry about and that Germans were paying for their extreme persecution because the whole world was their enemy. According to Semmler, an official in the Propaganda Ministry, anti-Semitism was unpopular and created distrust or opposition to the regime.[202]

An SD report from Stuttgart on November 6, 1943, stated that thousands and thousands of Jews had been killed and that people of all classes condemned publication of pictures showing Russian atrocities at Katyn to justify Germany's murder of Jews. Even the SS and party members shared this attitude.[203] Similarly, Steinert reported that the public did not consider the Katyn massacre of thousands of Polish officers by Russians an adequate justification for shooting Jews.[204] This was confirmed by the SD.[205]

When they heard rumors, all classes shared a widespread fear of retaliation for the deportation and murder of Jews. Many believed the Allies would not accept conditional surrender because they wished to avenge the Jews.[206] The "Jewish question" occasioned great inner uncertainty among Germans even as late as 1944, when most Jews had already been exterminated.[207]

Himmler himself was distressed that all of the Nazis' propaganda had failed to convince the Germans of Jewish perfidy. At a meeting of *Gau* leaders, head of Nazi administrative units, he said on October 6, 1943:

> Remember how many people, Party members included, send their precious plea for clemency to me or some other authority; they invariably say that all Jews are, of course, swine but that Mr. So-and-so is the exception, a decent Jew who should not be touched. I have no hesitation in saying that the number of these requests and the number of differing opinions in Germany

leads one to conclude that there are more decent Jews than all the rest put together.[208]

In another speech to SS leaders in Poznan on October 4, 1943, he said:

> I want to tell you about a very grave matter in all frankness. We can talk about it quite openly here, but we must never talk about it publicly. . . . I mean the evacuation of the Jews, the extermination of the Jewish people. It is one of the things one says lightly [!]—"The Jewish people are being liquidated," party comrades exclaim; "naturally, it's in our program, the isolation of the Jews, extermination, okay, we'll do it." And then they come, all the 80 million Germans, and every one of them has his decent Jew. Of course, the others may all be swines, but this particular one is an A-1 Jew. All those who talk like this have not seen it, have not gone through it. Most of you will know what it means to see 100 corpses piled up, or 500, or 1,000. To have gone through this and—except for instances of human weakness—to have remained decent, that has made us tough. This is an unwritten, never to be written, glorious page of our history.[209]

It is known that many Germans aided Jews during the war by providing food, clothing, shelter, false identity papers, work permits, passports, and so on. It is, of course, impossible to determine how many did this, but according to one estimate, five thousand Jews were hidden during the war in Berlin alone.[210] (Since many examples can be found in other secondary works, the reader is referred to appropriate sources.)[211] Berlin had the largest percentage of Jews during the war and was a hotbed of "submarines," or Jews in hiding. Ruth Andreas-Friedrich, who lived in Berlin, discussed many instances of aid to Jews and public opposition to persecution.[212] Most aid was either by individuals or small groups such as Uncle Emil, which was comprised of individuals from the professions plus a few artisans.[213] About two dozen people provided food, shelter, passes, and so forth for Jews.[214] Groups such as the *Rote Kapelle*, which had a generally middle-class composition, collected food and money for Jewish friends.[215] The European Union provided false documents for Jews; its members were arrested in 1943.[216] The *Bund* was also a small group that aided Jews by sending packages to concentration camps.[217] Some resistance groups made aid to Jews a major task.[218] Risks were particularly high during the war because aiders were themselves under threat of imprisonment or concentration camps if their work became known.[219] Because of their bravery, many Germans have been honored by receiving Yad Vashem's medal of honor.[220] Organized aid on a large scale was impossible because of Nazi surveillance; however, aid on an individual basis was apparently quite common.

Taken as a whole and with the knowledge that the evidence on anti-Semitism is not extensive and often represents only the lunatic fringe, these reports create the general impression that at least a minority of Germans approved of draconian measures against Jews, although there were no indications that gassing in death camps was widely known or accepted. Rumors of shootings and even lesser persecution, such as the introduction of the star, were criticized by a minority of Germans, and many Germans aided Jews on an individual basis, particularly in Berlin. In general, however, we are speaking only of minorities. The paucity of reports on majority attitudes can be interpreted in two ways: either to mean that the Germans were indifferent to persecution, or that they were silenced by fear of retribution if they were critical of persecution or aided Jews. Certainly, the prior isolation of Jews, the large number of emigrations and deportations from Germany, and the extensive news blackouts must have led many Germans to put Jews out of their minds, and rumors were not always believed even when they were in fact true.

## OMGUS SURVEYS

Another source of information regarding German attitudes toward Jews is of limited utility. After World War II the American government wished to obtain information on German attitudes toward the occupation, economy, politics, and many other topics, including German attitudes toward Jews. Therefore, the Opinion Survey Section of the Intelligence Branch of the Office of the Director of Information Control conducted seventy-two surveys from 1945 through 1948. The first surveys were done by German-speaking Americans, and late in 1945 they were replaced by specially trained German interviewers. These surveys are referred to as the OMGUS surveys.[221]

The surveys that included questions on anti-Semitism are fraught with difficulties. Although the sampling technique appears unobjectionable (random selections from food ration cards), the questions themselves and the interpretations of answers are exceedingly problematic and frequently disappointing, since they could have provided better insights into how much the Germans knew and what they thought about the concentration camps and exterminations in the East. They are by no means perfect, but other sources are scanty for the war years, so they must be examined.

There appears to have been only one occasion on which the Germans were asked directly about their attitudes toward Hitler's racial policies. Interviewees were asked to indicate their attitudes by evaluating three statements and choosing the one with which they agreed. The percentage choosing each is listed in table 6.1 with the OMGUS translation:[222] Let us consider each statement and percentage in turn. The first statement, as translated by OMGUS, appears far milder than another translation might be. The German original from the survey is: *"Mit den Juden ist es unter Hitler so gegangen, wie er Sie es verdienten."*[223] An English translation might be, "As it went under Hitler, the Jews got their

TABLE 6.1 OMGUS Questions I

| Statement | Percentage Agreeing |
|---|---|
| 1. Hitler was right in his treatment of the Jews. | 0 |
| 2. Hitler went too far in his treatment of the Jews, but something had to be done to keep them in bounds. | 19 |
| 3. The actions against the Jews were in no way justified. | 77 |

SOURCE: NA RG 260, 350/3–5, report 49, p. 3.

just deserts,'' or ''Under Hitler the Jews got what they deserved.'' In any case, the German original seems to contain a stronger implication that the Jews were responsible for Hitler's treatment of them and also that this treatment was harsh. This may account for the zero percentage of interviewees who agreed with the statement, since the death camps and other barbarous results of Hitler's policies were coming to light at this time, even before the Nuremberg trials (October 1945). The initial horror may have led many Germans to a reflex rejection of this statement; however, it is still interesting that less than one percent approved of Hitler's treatment of the Jews.

In contrast to the first statement, the second and third were translated adequately. We earlier found that the majority of Germans appeared to approve of nonviolent exclusion of Jews from German life, as indicated by their general acceptance of quotas, the elimination of Jews from the civil service and the professions, and the Nuremberg Laws. One might therefore have predicted that the majority of interviewees would have agreed with the second statement, which specifically said that something had to be done to keep the Jews in bounds, but that Hitler went too far. Thus it is surprising to find that over three-quarters of the Germans interviewed agreed with the third statement, that is, that the actions against the Jews were in no way justified. Again, this may reflect the immediate horror at the daily revelations of mass murder and extermination. One should note, however, that American instead of German interviewers may have been used in this survey, since the former director of the Opinion Survey Section stated that the Germans were trained before the end of 1945, but gives no month.[224] The interviewees may have been particularly reluctant to give ''unfavorable'' answers to Americans.

This may be of some importance because a later survey found truly shocking results, which indicated that 37 percent of the interviewees disagreed with the following statement: ''Extermination of the Jews and Poles and other non-Aryans was not necessary for the security of the Germans.''[225] Since interviewees were asked to agree or disagree with the statement by saying yes or no, and because it contained an implicit double negative, it was badly phrased and confusing. Some interviewees may have responded "no" they did not agree with the statement, when they actually did agree that extermination was not necessary. Also, the exact German word for "extermination" in the question is critical, but this was not available with the English translation.

These results are completely at odds with the 77 percent who thought that the actions taken against the Jews were unjustified.[226] It is very difficult to interpret these answers. If one believes the 77 percent, then an overwhelming majority of Germans disapproved of extermination; if one believes the 37 percent, then over a third of the Germans were willing to exterminate Poles and Jews and other non-Aryans to preserve German security. If the question on German security had been better phrased, one could feel more confident in accepting the latter interpretation.

There is, however, other information in the OMGUS surveys. Interviewees were asked whether Nazism was a good or bad idea and why; 53 percent said it was a bad idea. Among the nine possible reasons why it was bad was "race policy, atrocities, pogroms." This reason was chosen by only 3–4 percent of those who disapproved of the regime, as opposed to the 21 percent who felt that Nazism was bad because of its effects on the German people before the war.[227]

If 37 percent of the Germans interviewed approved of extermination of Jews, Poles, and others for German security and only 3–4 percent considered "race policy, atrocities, pogroms" as something bad about Nazism, then it is possible that the paucity of information on extermination in the SD reports was an accurate reflection not only of widespread indifference to these atrocities, but also possible agreement among over a third of the population. This is to interpret the data in the worst light, and we shall have to examine several other OMGUS surveys to determine whether or not this is justified.

In several surveys, interviewees were asked whether or not the postwar Nuremberg Trials (convened in November 1945) had taught them anything that they did not know before. In a survey conducted in January 1946, 30 percent said that they had learned of the extermination of Jews and the mass murders from the proceedings.[228] In a report issued shortly before (December 1945), 23 percent had answered similarly.[229] It is difficult to interpret these results. They indicate that a significant percentage of the population had no knowledge of the exterminations before the Nuremberg Trials, but this information is not too helpful. Does it mean that 70 percent had known about the exterminations prior to the trials? We do not know. We also do not know when this 70 percent first learned about the atrocities—during the war or after the war from the news media and other sources? Unfortunately, there is no way of answering these questions using the OMGUS results.

When Germans did have to face up to the postwar revelations of murder, they responded in various ways. For example, they were asked to agree or disagree with the following statement: "Research has proven that the Germans killed and tortured millions of helpless Europeans." Fifty-nine percent agreed, 20 percent disagreed, and 21 percent gave no answer.[230] Clearly, denial, disbelief, and confusion were all present at this time (December 1946), even though the majority were willing to believe that Germans had committed atrocities. Earlier (November 1945), Germans were specifically asked, "Did you know exactly what happened in the concentration camps?" Fifty-one percent said they did, 40 percent said they did not, and 9 percent had no opinion. Among those who said they knew about the concentration camps, very few associated concentration camps with Jews. When they were asked why the party sent people to concentration camps, 57 percent said "for political reasons" (being anti-Nazis, security threats); another 21 percent said "for almost no reason"; and only 4 percent said "to exterminate Jews."[231] The other options, many serious, were also chosen in very small percentages. From this one might conclude that they did not at this time fully comprehend the nature and functions of concentration camps, but persisted in thinking of them as they were *before* the war—a place for "dissidents," but not exclusively slave or death camps for Jews, Poles, Russians, and others. This naiveté is only understandable if large numbers of Germans were truly ignorant of the existence of these camps.

201

It is clear that the Germans were in favor of bringing all those who murdered civilians to trial, because they were asked to agree or disagree with the following statement (OMGUS translation): "All those who ordered the murdering of civilians or participated in the murderings, should be made to stand trial."[232] A hefty 94 percent thought that murderers should be tried, and 72 percent thought that Hitler himself should have gone to trial rather than shoot himself.[233] This is very nearly as high as the 77 percent who thought he had gone too far in his treatment of the Jews.

If we examine more subtle evidence of anti-Semitism, we find a very confusing set of surveys and dubious questions. The OMGUS authorities tried to construct a scale of anti-Semitism from none to intense. To do this they asked interviewees to agree or disagree with three and sometimes four statements: "A musical composition can be beautiful in spite of the racial background of the composer"; "A true German should be judged and condemned if he marries a non-Aryan woman"; "Jews deserve to have the same rights as members of the Nordic race"; and "Germans are generally known as the best workers."[234] Two of these questions have absolutely nothing to do with Jews. Nevertheless, if the respondents answered all four in a "non-democratic" fashion, they were classified as "intense anti-Semites," on the extreme end of the scale. Those who answered all "democratically," were given the label "lacking anti-Semitism," and were on the other end of the scale, with other classifications in between. A discussion of possible objections to these questions would be too space-consuming; however, the results of two surveys are given in table 6.2. In both cases the percentage who are classified as "clearly

TABLE 6.2 OMGUS Estimates of Anti-Semitism

|  | March 1946 | May 1948 |
|---|---|---|
| Not anti-Semitic | 33 | 55 |
| Middle level or indifferent | 43 | 27 |
| Clearly anti-Semitic | 15 | 18 |

SOURCES: March 1946: NA RG 260, 350/3–5, report 19, p. 12. May 1948: NA RG 260, 350/3–5, report 22 (May 22, 1948), p. 6.

anti-Semitic'' is very small, despite the dubious value of these questions as a measure of anti-Semitism.

There were, however, several interesting questions on the surveys that cast additional light on anti-Semitism. Only those that are directly related to Jews will be used here. The questions and answers are presented in table 6.3; when the same questions were asked in 1946 and 1948, the percentages are averaged. The results of the surveys are very interesting. To this author, the most important indicator of prejudice in any society is the unwillingness to intermarry, because this involves not only the two individuals involved, but also their families. That between 85 and 91 percent were unwilling to condemn intermarriage is startling, since we are here discussing a regime that for twelve years spread endless racial propaganda against Jews, passed laws of all types to prevent sexual contact between Jews and Germans, and imprisoned and sometimes executed both Jews and Germans for violating them. This high level of acceptance of intermarriage, therefore, certainly does not indicate rabid anti-Semitism; neither does the 85 percent who were willing to give Jews the same rights as ''Aryans.'' The same pattern is evident in the answers that showed a willingness

TABLE 6.3 OMGUS Questions II

| | Yes(%) | No(%) |
|---|---|---|
| 1. If a pure German marries a non-Aryan, should he be condemned? | | 85 |
| Should a German who marries a non-Aryan be condemned? | | 91 |
| 2. Jews should have the same rights as members of the Aryan race. | 85 | |
| 3. Would you be against having a Jew live in the same house? | | 70 |
| 4. Would you be against having a Jew live on the same street? | | 78 |
| 5. Would you work under a Jew? | 66 | |
| 6. Would you work with a Jew? | 74 | |
| 7. Should Jews be allowed to go to the same restaurants as non-Jews? | 64 | |

SOURCES: (1) HA HM 261, G 373, reel 1, survey 19, question 85, and reel 2, survey 36, question 33; (2) HA HM 261, G 373, reel 1, survey 23, question 103, and NA RG 260, 350/3–5, report 19, pp. 48, 49; (3) through (6) NA RG 260, 350/3–5, report 122, p. 10; 7) HA HM 261, G 373, reel 2, survey 36, question 29.

to maintain residential and occupational contacts with Jews. As a whole, these results indicate that Germans were remarkably free of anti-Semitism by any standard measure that could be put into meaningful questions, unless they were all consistently lying, a possibility against which the questionnaire designers took special precautions. Also, since the questions did not involve the same order of magnitude of anti-Semitism (extermination, concentration camps, etc.) as some others, the respondents may have felt less pressure to contrive false answers.

What then are we to make of the 37 percent who apparently agreed that "extermination of Jews, Poles, and other non-Aryans" was necessary for German security? Are we to believe that *German* Jews would have been tolerated and even accepted, as the responses to questions on intermarriage and other contacts with Jews would indicate, but that over a third of the Germans condoned the massacre of *foreigners* (Jews, Poles, and others) to protect German security? And what of the 77 percent who said that the actions against the Jews had gone too far? Were they again thinking only of German Jews? This might be possible, since Nazi propaganda consistently portrayed Polish and Russian Jews as partisans who were a serious danger to German troops. In any case, the atrocities in the East seem to have met with significant skepticism, since 40 percent of those interviewed expressed no opinion or disagreed that Germans had murdered helpless civilians. It may be that this disbelief was similar to the incredulity with which all peoples, including Jews, received the news of Nazi barbarities in Eastern Europe and Russia. It may also have been a denial of responsibility, since no individual likes to learn of or fully comprehend his own leaders' failures, especially unprecedented butchery, or his own unwillingness or inability to change national policies. At the very least, the recognition of what in the past has been inconceivable is not an easy mental feat.

Studies similar to the OMGUS surveys were done on German prisoners of war. The samples had the bias of including all males, mostly under thirty years of age, and predominately lower socioeconomic groups. Yet according to these studies, strong cross-sample consistencies ruled out conscious deceptions or fabrications.[235] One study, the British Military Government Public Opinion Poll, concluded:

> Those who said National Socialism was a good idea pointed to social welfare plans, the lack of unemployment, the great construction plans of the Nazis. . . . Nearly all those who thought it a good idea nevertheless rejected Nazi racial theories and disagreed with the inhumanity of the concentration camps and the "SS".[236]

A psychologist, Ansbacher, has also examined data from opinion polls among prisoners of war. He found that anti-Semitism was neither well liked nor disliked. In response to questions concerning the aspects of National Socialism most and least liked, only small numbers of prisoners listed anti-Semitism as a "most- or least-liked" feature of the Nazi regime. Only 6 percent of 517 prisoners stated that they liked anti-Semitism least of all aspects of Nazism, and only 9 percent of the 517 prisoners stated that they most liked Nazi ideology, including race and *völkisch* ideology.[237] From this, one might conclude that young male Germans from lower socioeconomic groups were by and large indifferent to racial persecution.

In 1944, when 462 prisoners of war were asked, "In your opinion has anti-Semitism been helpful to Germany or harmful?"[238] they gave more informative answers. Their estimates of helpfulness or harm are listed on table 6.4. Young German males, mostly from lower socioeconomic groups, were notably more anti-Semitic than older Germans. Among older German prisoners of

TABLE 6.4 Opinions of German Prisoners of War on Helpfulness or Harm of Anti-Semitism to Germany, 1944 (*in percentages*)

|  | Age under 30 | Age 30 and over |
|---|---|---|
| Helpful | 33 | 17 |
| Harmful | 44 | 60 |
| No answer | 23 | 23 |
| Number in sample | 215 | 247 |

war the majority clearly labeled it harmful. It is interesting, however, that among both younger and older prisoners, nearly a quarter had no opinion or gave no answer, which indicates either that they were anti-Semites, but were unwilling to respond that anti-Semitism had been helpful to Germany, or that they were confused about or more probably indifferent to racial policies. This is consistent with the paucity of reports on reactions to persecution in the wartime SD reports; the low percentage (3–4) who cited "race policy, atrocities, pogroms" as a reason why Nazism was bad (OMGUS); and the conclusions of Stokes, Steinert, and Kershaw regarding indifference to Jews, especially after their deportation.[239]

## SUMMARY

Between 1933 and 1945 German attitudes toward Jews underwent notable changes. From 1933 to 1935 attitudes toward Jews were fairly favorable compared to later years. A small minority demanded stringent restrictions, but these, even on the limited scale of a four-day boycott in April 1933, were not popular with the public. The public did, however, appear to support exclusion of Jews from the civil service as well as quotas on numbers of Jews allowed in schools and universities. There was a minority that opposed these measures, but by and large such restrictions imposed up until 1935 received much popular support.

Between 1935 and 1938 anti-Semitic propaganda had a noticeable impact. Anti-Semitic policies were accepted when introduced through legal or pseudo-legal decrees and when they involved no violence. A majority of Germans apparently viewed the Nuremberg Laws as a stabilizing influence that would end illegal violence. A minority, particularly party men and the SA, but also some nonparty members, were pleased with their new power to harass Jews. On the other hand, another minority opposed racial persecution and continued to conduct business and have sexual relations with Jews. These two minorities were probably polarized around an acquiescent majority; otherwise one could have ex-

206

pected more definite reports on the attitudes of the public at large toward the Nuremberg Laws, pro or con.

By 1938 anti-Semitism appeared to be taking root among the majority, but the pogrom of November 9 and 10, 1938, quickly shifted its attitude to disapproval of Nazi methods. The peak of opposition to anti-Semitism was reached after *Kristallnacht*, when by almost all accounts the vast majority of Germans rejected violence, destruction of property, and murder. Many Germans felt strongly enough about this to aid Jews; however, large-scale arrests and Nazi harassment of these individuals discouraged opposition to the economic ''Aryanization'' that accelerated between 1938 and 1939, as did the news blackout about it.

During the war a marked worsening of attitudes toward Jews became apparent. Before 1939 almost no reports on public opinion indicated a genuine desire for forced deportation or physical attacks on Jews; after 1939 this was not the case. Several reports indicated support for draconian measures against Jews, including forced deportation. There is no evidence that labor camps and extermination were welcomed by the general public, but a host of restrictions on the domestic activities of Jews was approved by an increasing minority of hardcore anti-Semites.

At the same time, growing numbers of Germans opposed racial persecution. When rumors of deportations and shootings in the East spread through Germany, criticism of the regime snowballed. A number of reports indicated public opposition to these measures, and extrapolating from these reports, one can probably conclude that labor camps, concentration camps, and extermination were opposed by a majority of Germans. At the same time, aid for Jews became increasingly more difficult. As the number of Jews was reduced by emigration and deportation, it became easier to root out sympathizers, and penalties for aiding Jews were a very effective deterrent to sympathetic acts. Still, some Germans did aid Jews at considerable personal risk.

We asked at the beginning of this chapter whether Nazi racial policies were favored and supported by a majority of Germans, and which racial policies were most popular. From the sources cited it would appear that a majority of Germans supported elimination of Jews from the civil service; quotas on Jews in professions, academic institutions, and commercial fields; restrictions on intermarriage; and voluntary emigration of Jews. However, the rabid anti-Semites' demands for violent boycotts, illegal expropriation, destruction of Jewish property, pogroms, deportation, and extermination were probably rejected by a majority of Germans. They apparently wanted to restrict Jewish rights substantially, but not to annihilate Jews.

The relative silence of the SD reports on public reactions to deportation may reflect either indifference to Jews because of latent anti-Semitism, preoccupation with the effects of the war, or intimidation by Nazi terror. However, if we examine the SD reports in conjunction with American surveys of German public opinion after the war (OMGUS surveys) and American government surveys of prisoners of war, we find some indications that Hitler's racial policies were simply not important to many Germans. Although the results of the surveys by OMGUS are difficult to interpret, a very large majority said that the actions against the Jews were in no way justified; in response to specific questions relating to personal contacts with Jews, large majorities also appeared exceptionally tolerant of Jews when one considers that the Germans were inundated for twelve years by Nazi anti-Semitic propaganda. On the other hand, in answering one badly phrased question, 37 percent were apparently prepared to accept the extermination of foreign Jews, Poles, and other "non-Aryans" because they ostensibly posed a threat to German security. If the Germans who tolerated extermination were not misreading the question, then their answers show the success of Hitler's and Goebbels's attempts to justify extermination on the basis that these foreigners were thought to "endanger" German troops (as partisans, saboteurs, guerrillas, etc.). Yet apparently the extensiveness of murder in labor and death camps was not perceived or known, because the majority of those interviewed by the American government had totally outdated attitudes toward the true function of concentration camps—they continued to think of them as punishment centers, as they had been from 1933 to 1939, rather than as death camps for mass murder. One should note, however, that both the OMGUS surveys (which may have contained deliberate lies despite attempts to correct for this) and the wartime SD reports (which frequently downplayed opposition to anti-Semitic measures to please superiors) have defects that make any definitive interpretations exceedingly difficult. The line between indifference and acquiescence (because of inability to alter Nazi racial policies) and generalized fear of interfering in the "Jewish question" cannot be determined from SD reports and the OMGUS surveys.

# Opponents of Persecution

"The first order of business for those planning acts of revolt
usually involves the renunciation of personal concerns,
including their own individual survival. Such total commitment
to resistance action is not accomplished easily and is virtually
never shared by large numbers of people."
George Kren and Leon Rappoport, "Resistance to the
Holocaust," pp. 202–203.

It is difficult to determine the specific motivations of Germans
who opposed Nazi anti-Semitism and followed their own consciences. There are, of course, a number of secondary works in
which non-Jewish Germans describe their reasons for helping
German or Eastern European Jews, particularly during World War
II.[1] These make fascinating reading not only because of the
horrid life and death struggle of the Jews themselves, but also because of the ingenuity and courage that were required to hide Jews
or to provide significant amounts of food, shelter, and other ne-
cessities of life in a police state. Yet discovering motivations is
problematic, especially because accounts written many years after
the fact must be considered at least partially suspect, since they
may have become colored in the interval. Case histories of Jews
who were helped by Germans are on file in a variety of institutes
in Europe and the United States. The descriptions of aid and
motivations for aid are few in number, almost without exception
unsystematic, give little detailed information, and are necessarily
impressionistic; one gets a certain "feel" for the motivations from
these sources, but not a concrete picture. They concentrate on

conditions in Germany and the various paths by which Jews were able to escape the Nazi octopus, and contain little information on socioeconomic data, for which we must look elsewhere.[2]

In 1974 I discovered very important, previously unused sources in the Hauptstaatsarchiv Düsseldorf, which contained 452 Gestapo files on individual opponents of racial persecution in the Government District Düsseldorf.[3] Since most Gestapo records for other parts of Germany were destroyed during World War II, these case records representing approximately half of the Rhineland are an invaluable primary source, because they allow us to analyze the socioeconomic characteristics of opponents. Although some files for the Government District Düsseldorf were lost in air raids and attendant fires during the war, the destruction was not systematic and the remaining sample contains no selective bias. Therefore, these Gestapo files provide as random a sample of opponents of racial persecution as we are ever likely to have, at least to the extent that this area was reflective of industrialized parts of Germany.

By examining this sample, we can first compare the chronological development of opposition in specific cases to the general sources cited in the previous chapter. Second, we can discover the socioeconomic characteristics of the Germans who opposed persecution, at least if they were arrested for their behavior between 1933 and 1944.

## PRELIMINARY COMMENTS

The Hauptstaatsarchiv Düsseldorf has 203 Gestapo files on individuals who aided Jews, 42 files on critics of racial persecution, and 30 files on individuals suspected of aiding Jews. The archive also holds 137 files on Germans who had sexual relations with Jews, 40 files on persons who were suspected of having sexual relations with Jews, and an additional 255 cases of Jews who were arrested for these reasons.[4]

Individuals who aided Jews were classified by the Nazis and are classified by the Hauptstaatsarchiv Düsseldorf as *Judenfreunde* (friends of Jews). Those who had sexual relations with Jews were

211

and are similarly classified as *Rassenschänder*. Both terms will be used in our discussion simply to differentiate the two types of opponents of Nazi racial policies. Although the term *Rassenschande* had very unattractive overtones, it will nevertheless be used because it covered a variety of sexual activities that were known to potential violators at the time, and it is therefore the term that best describes *their* conception of what the Nazis meant by sexual contacts with Jews. *Rassenschande* involved a violation of the Nuremberg Laws, and even more a contravention of Nazi ideology; but the motives might have been so mixed as to render its precise meaning questionable. Love, lust, or even prostitution were all possibilities, although no cases of open prostitution were found in the Düsseldorf data.

When couples first established contact, they may not always have known the other person's religion, so it is not clear when the decision to defy the law became conscious. *Rassenschande* may or may not have been a political act depending upon the circumstances. The reader should also bear in mind the high rate of assimilation as measured by the intermarrige statistics from the period before 1933. *Rassenschande* may have been a continuation of the normal order of things under abnormal circumstances, and this can also be said to some extent of *Judenfreundlichkeit* (friendliness to Jews). Aid to Jews, however, was clearly a more political act than *Rassenschande*. Therefore, these two groups must be treated separately.

In order to distinguish opponents by the intensiveness of their opposition, I shall classify them into three categories: high-, middle-, and low-level opponents. High-level opponents include those who received a prison sentence or were sent to concentration camps for their aid to Jews or for having sexual relations with them. Middle-level opponents were individuals who were arrested but not necessarily sentenced for concretely aiding Jews or having sexual relations with them. Most of these cases were referred to the courts, but final sentences were not traceable because a large number of court records were destroyed during the war, and no copy of the verdict was forwarded to the Gestapo. The individuals in this category of arrestees are classified as middle-level opponents because we do know that they performed some overt act on behalf of Jews. Yet they must be differentiated from high-level opponents, because the fact that sentences for high-level opponents were referred back to the Gestapo by the courts implies that their "crimes" were more severe.

Low-level opponents include two types of people: those who verbally criticized persecution and were dismissed with a strong warning (forty-two), and those who were arrested on suspicion of having sexual relations with Jews (forty). Individuals who were arrested on suspicion of aid or sexual contact were not indicted because the Gestapo could not prove its charges, whereas opponents who criticized racial persecution were clearly "guilty." The two groups are classified together because of the following three reasons, which assume that those who were accused of aiding Jews or having sexual relations with them actually did so but were able to cover their tracks well enough so that the Gestapo could not discover conclusive evidence against them.

First, in all cases they were denounced by one (and frequently two) "witness(es)," but unless three "witnesses" corroborated the charges, the Gestapo dismissed the accused with the usual stern warning and the promise (and actuality) of future surveillance.

Second, there may have been some truth in the charges against these low-level opponents because their statistical profiles were very similar to those of high- and middle-level opponents.[5] The only significant differences were that both suspected *Judenfreunde* and *Rassenschänder* had higher percentages of residents of the city Essen; suspected *Judenfreunde* had a higher percentage of individuals aged sixty and over; and suspected *Rassenschänder* had more independents (professionals, businessmen, executives, etc.) and fewer persons with no profession (persons not dependent on wages or salaries). The higher percentages of Essen residents may be due to a higher level of activity by the Essen Gestapo during the years 1935–1937.[6] The other differences are fairly minor in the light of the very great similarities between low-level opponents and high- and middle-level opponents. This similarity implies that low-level opponents were probably "guilty," but

213

were careful not to leave evidence that the Gestapo could dredge up.

Third, low-level opponents differed from the general population and labor force of the Government District Düsseldorf in almost exactly the same ways as did high- and middle-level opponents,[7] and were thus also likely to have aided Jews or to have had sexual relations with them. The differences between all levels of opponents and other Germans in the district were quite definite and could by no means be attributed to chance rather than other factors. Since low-level opponents were accused by at least one (and frequently two) "witnesses," since they were very similar to high- and middle-level opponents, and since they differed from the population and labor force in almost the same ways as opponents at other levels of opposition, they will be included in our statistical comparisons.

## TIMING OF OPPOSITION

It is interesting to compare the chronological development of opposition in the Government District Düsseldorf to the more general chronological trends of opposition that were discussed in chapter 6. Among the 452 opponents in the Government District Düsseldorf, the chronological distribution of opposition between 1933 and 1944 was as follows: 3 percent in 1933–1934, 30 percent between 1935 and 1937, 39 percent in 1938–1939, and 28 percent between 1940 and 1944. We stated in chapter 6 that opposition to Nazi measures against Jews was fairly limited between 1933 and 1934, when Jews were first excluded from the civil service and professions. The small percentage of opponents from the Government District Düsseldorf who were arrested in 1933 and 1934 is consistent with more general sources that indicated only occasional opposition during these years. One should also remember that in these first years of the Third Reich the Gestapo was still in the process of getting organized; hence, the detection of opponents was probably not so widespread as it was to become later on. Between 1935 and 1937 the general sources reported growing opposition as well as growing acceptance of anti-Semitic

214

measures. Two minorities were beginning to polarize around an indifferent majority. In the Düsseldorf files the percentage of opponents between 1935 and 1937 numbered thirty. This is consistent with the overall pattern that emerged from general reports on German public opinion, but it might also reflect increasing efficiency by the Gestapo.

Between 1938 and 1939 general sources indicated a rise in anti-Semitic attitudes before October 1938 and a sharp decline after *Kristallnacht* in November 1938. In the Düsseldorf sample, most of the aid for Jews and the verbal criticism of their persecution also followed *Kristallnacht*. The number of opponents rose to 39 percent during 1938 and 1939, the highest percentage for any phase of persecution. After 1939 our general sources indicated a very definite polarization of hardcore anti-Semites and opponents of persecution, each of whom formed the extremes of an anti-Semitic continuum in which the majority of the public was indifferent to Jews. We must also consider the factors of growing terrorization of Nazi opponents, the emigration and deportation of Jews, and the news blackouts, all of which limited opposition. Yet our data from the Government District Düsseldorf show that even though opposition declined from a peak of 39 percent during 1938 and 1939, it certainly did not disappear between 1940 and 1944, when risks were much higher. During these war years, opponents of persecution comprised 28 percent of the 452 opponents. Even as some Germans, particularly Nazis, became more rabidly anti-Semitic during the war, a small minority was willing to aid Jews and to continue personal relations with them. In summary, I conclude that general sources on the shifting public attitudes in Germany as a whole and the data for the Government District Düsseldorf are highly corroborative during all phases of persecution. It is therefore likely that these sources are an accurate reflection of shifts in public opinion toward racial persecution during the Third Reich.

It is interesting to note the years in which *Judenfreunde* and *Rassenschänder* constituted the highest percentages among opponents.[8] In table 7.1 we see that nearly the same percentage of *Rassenschänder* had sexual relations with Jews between 1935 and

215

TABLE 7.1 Percentages of *Judenfreunde* and *Rassenschänder* during Different Phases of Persecution

|  | Judenfreunde | Rassenschänder |
|---|---|---|
| 1933–1934 | 2.9 | 2.8 |
| 1935–1937 | 25.8 | 36.7 |
| 1938–1939 | 41.1 | 35.0 |
| 1940–1944 | 30.2 | 25.4 |
| Number in sample | 275 | 177 |

1937 as in 1938 and 1939. This obviously demonstrated the impact of the Nuremberg Laws, which prohibited sexual contacts between "Aryans" and Jews. In contrast, a larger percentage of all *Judenfreunde* aided Jews during 1938 and 1939, and also to a considerable extent during war years. The large percentage in 1938 and 1939 was due to an increase in arrests during and after the pogrom of November 9–10, 1938, when many Germans aided Jews and criticized persecution. The considerable percentage of *Judenfreunde* during the war years may imply that the Gestapo was more concerned with stopping aid for Jews than with *Rassenschande* during this period, or it may in fact indicate that more people were helping Jews than were engaging in sexual relations with them during the war. Certainly the aging of the Jewish population would have limited *Rassenschande*. This process is made clear in table 7.2. These figures are obviously not identical to those of the Government District Düsseldorf; however, we can safely assume that the same process was occurring there.

TABLE 7.2 Age Structure of Adult Jewish Population, 1933–1939 (*in percentages*)

| Age | Jews in Germany, 1933 | Jews in Pfalz, 1937 | Jews in Germany, 1939 |
|---|---|---|---|
| 20–39 | 39.2 | 24.7 | * |
| 40–59 | 40.1 | 44.2 | * |
| 60+ | 20.8 | 31.1 | 32.3 |

SOURCES: For the age distribution of Jews in Germany in 1933, see *Statistik des Deutschen Reiches*, vol. 451 (1933), no. 5:17. For the ages of Jews in Pfalz in 1937 and in Germany in 1939, see Kurt Düwell, *Die Rheingebiete in der Judenpolitik des Nationalsozialismus vor 1942*, 72.
* Data not available.

TABLE 7.3 Number of Jews in Germany during World War II

| Date | Number |
|------|--------|
| End of 1939 | 204,000 |
| May 1, 1941 | 169,000 |
| October 1, 1941 | 164,000 |
| 1942 | 139,000 |
| 1943 | 51,000 |
| 1944 | 14,500 |
| 1945 | 20,000–25,000 |

SOURCE: Herbert Strauss, "Jewish Emigration from Germany," 326, 341.

TABLE 7.4 Jews in Rhine Province, 1933–1944, with Estimates for Government District Düsseldorf

| | Rhine Province | | Government District Düsseldorf Estimates |
|------|--------|-----------------------------------------|------|
| Date | Number | Percentage from previous year who remained | |
| 1939 | 23,103 | | 8,762 |
| October 1, 1941 | 17,236 | .746 | 6,536 |
| January 1, 1942 | 11,061 | .642 | 4,196 |
| January 1, 1943 | 2,312 | .209 | 877 |

SOURCE: Bruno Blau, "Die Entwicklung der jüdischen Bevölkerung in Deutschland von 1800–1945," p. 320 for 1939, and p. 348 for 1941–1943. Data for 1940 were not available.

A natural decrease of both *Rassenschande* and *Judenfreundlichkeit* during the war occurred as a result of the sharp decline in the number of Jews through deportation and extermination. Table 7.3 demonstrates these losses. There were 22,240 Jews in the Government District Düsseldorf in 1933 and only 8,762 in 1939.[9] Estimates for the number of Jews remaining in the district after 1939 are not readily available; but since they comprised approximately half of the Jews in the Rhineland, we can estimate the decline in the number of Jews due to deportation, as shown in table 7.4. These are only estimates, of course, and the actual timing of deportation varied considerably on a local basis; however, the estimates show that only a small number of Jews would

217

have been in the district even in 1941. The remaining Jews were dispersed throughout many very large cities, and probably only Essen, Düsseldorf, and Wupperthal has as many as 1,000 Jews by October 1941. There were therefore fewer chances to engage in *Rassenschande* or to demonstrate sympathy for Jews.

We can roughly compare the number of opponents of persecution with the estimated number of Jews in the district for prewar and war years. In the prewar years, we estimate that there were roughly 15,501 Jews in the district, although the increase in emigration occurred primarily after 1935, and especially in 1938 and 1939, so the number of Jews in the district during these years would have been considerably smaller. Nevertheless, using this estimate, if each act of assistance (or prohibited contact) affected one Jew, then the opponents in prewar years helped (or had contact with) 2.1 percent of the Jews in the district.[10] During war years the ratio was 2.8 percent.[11] This reflected a slight increase in the ratio of opponents to Jews during war years. Obviously, the deportation reduced the number of Jews and made aid much more difficult and risky because surveillance became easier. These comparisons should not imply that the files on opponents from the district contain *all* opponents of racial persecution. These were only the opponents who were discovered and for whom Gestapo files are extant. Although we cannot accurately estimate the extensiveness of opposition to anti-Semitism in the Government District Düsseldorf by extrapolating from Gestapo arrests, we are still able to study the socioeconomic characteristics of opponents from 1933 to 1944.[12]

## CHARACTERISTICS OF OPPONENTS, 1933–1944

Comparing the total sample of 452 opponents to the population and labor force of the Government District Düsseldorf, we find that several socioeconomic groups were overrepresented among both *Judenfreunde* and *Rassenschänder*.[13] Since these comparisons are based only on those opponents who were apprehended by the Gestapo, we cannot determine whether other opponents

TABLE 7.5 Most and Least Active Opponents of Racial Persecution, 1933–1944

|  | Most | Least |
|---|---|---|
| Sex | Males | Females |
| Age | *Judenfreunde* | *Judenfreunde* |
|  | 40 and over | Under 40 |
|  | (especially 50–59) | (especially under 30) |
|  | *Rassenschänder* | *Rassenschänder* |
|  | Under 30 | Over 40 |
|  | 30–39[a] | (especially over 50) |
| Occupation | Independents | Blue-collar workers |
|  | (among |  |
|  | *Judenfreunde*) |  |
|  | White-collar workers | Farmers |
|  | (particularly |  |
|  | upper level) |  |

SOURCE: Appendix B, table B.2.

[a] In all cases except this, such high percentages of a given socioeconomic group would for all practical purposes never occur by chance in a sample of this size if the opponents directly mirrored the population of the district.

had similar socioeconomic characteristics; nevertheless, there is no reason to suppose that the Gestapo concentrated on one particular sex, age, or occupational group, so the results are our best indicators of the groups who maintained contacts with Jews.

The juxtapositions on table 7.5 may help to clarify the contrasts between socioeconomic groups that were most and least active as *Judenfreunde* and *Rassenschänder*.[14] The most overrepresented opponents were males, older Germans, independents (particularly small businessmen),[15] and white-collar workers (particularly those in upper levels).[16] The distribution of urban and rural opponents was roughly comparable to the geographic distribution of Jews and therefore will not be discussed.

One can expect *Judenfreunde* to be older on average than *Rassenschänder* because sexual activity tends to decline with age, so we shall discuss their ages separately. Opponents aged 40–59, and particularly 50–59, were overrepresented among *Judenfreunde*. Predictably, opponents aged under 30, and to a slight

219

extent those aged 30–39, were overrepresented among *Rassen-schänder* compared to the population in these age groups.

In contrast to these socioeconomic groups that were highly visible opponents, the least active opponents were considerably different. Among both *Judenfreunde* and *Rassenschänder* they were females and blue-collar workers.

An attempt to account for some of the differences between the most active and least active opponents of racial persecution in the Government District Düsseldorf follows.

*Sex*

When comparing opponents to the general population we saw that males were more likely than females to aid Jews and to have sexual relations with them. This was true at all levels of opposition.[17] In addition, Wolfson's study of seventy rescuers of Jews indicates that 60 percent of them were male and 40 percent were female.[18] Similar results were found for ninety-three additional cases from all parts of Germany, in which 38 percent were female and 62 percent were male.[19] We also know that women were very slightly overrepresented in Merkl's sample of early Nazi anti-Semites and in postwar surveys of German anti-Semitism.[20]

In fact, overrepresentation of males among other opponents of Nazism was even more extreme. For example, in a study of 355 socialists who opposed Nazism between 1933 and 1938 in the North Rhine-Westphalia and were tried before Nazi courts, William S. Allen found that only 4 percent were women.[21] Also, members of the conspiracy against Hitler on July 20, 1944, were practically all men. This leads us to suspect that males were simply more likely than females to engage in all types of political opposition, including opposition to racial persecution. War service may have prevented even many more men from aiding Jews in Germany. Because Jews were concentrated in commercial enterprises in which women were more likely to shop than were men (assuming that women typically purchased food, clothing, household goods, etc.), it is unlikely that women simply had fewer contacts with Jews.[22] On the contrary, they probably had more. Considering this, and since only 30 percent of the *Judenfreunde* were women, one can legitimately hypothesize that underrepresentation of females among opponents of racial persecution reflected easier intimidation, less frequent denunciation, political impassivity, or higher levels of anti-Semitism than existed among men. The weight of accumulated evidence, especially the consistently higher levels of anti-Semitism found in the postwar surveys, indicates that they were simply more anti-Semitic, even though these other factors may also have played a role.

## Ages

The age groups that were overrepresented among *Judenfreunde* compared to their percentage in the general population were age 40 and over, especially those aged 50–59.[23] There was also a slight tendency for Germans aged 60 and over to aid Jews in disproportionate numbers. *Judenfreunde* aged 50–59 were overrepresented at all levels of opposition, while those aged 40–49 were overrepresented among middle-level opponents, who comprised over 60 percent of the sample. *Judenfreunde* aged under 40 were less active at all levels of opposition.[24]

*Rassenschänder* were younger, particularly under 30, but also aged 30–39. Since individuals are most sexually active at younger ages, the age distribution is no surprise. The ages of Jews and non-Jews who were arrested for *Rassenschande* were very similar if we consider the entire period 1933–1944.[25] Although 36.2 percent of the *Rassenschänder* were under 30, only 23.3 percent of the *Judenfreunde* were in the same age group.[26] This leads us to ask why only older opponents were overrepresented among *aiders* of Jews, as compared to the general population. This cannot be ascribed to the age structure of the Jewish population, which contained increasingly older individuals as more younger Jews emigrated, since younger non-Jews still had sexual relations with Jews, as indicated by the high percentages of younger people among *Rassenschänder*.

The low level of opposition among younger people might be due to the fact that they were not in a position to provide secret employment, false papers, currency exchanges, hiding places, food and clothing, and so forth for Jews because they did not have the financial means, their own homes (in which it would be easier to hide Jews than in apartments), or sufficient contacts with individuals who could forge documents, transfer currency on trips abroad, or smuggle Jews out of Germany. In any case, these activities would have been all the more difficult during World War II, when so many of the young males were in the armed services. But we should also note that there were no females under 30 among aiders of Jews and critics of persecution during war years, although verbal criticism and some types of aid were free. If we compare the age distribution of male and female *Judenfreunde* during prewar and war years, we have the results shown in table 7.6. Thus among both male and female *Judenfreunde*, a significantly larger percentage of individuals was aged 50 and over during the war than in prewar years, and this probably is at least partially attributable to the aging of the Jewish population. However, it may also be that anti-Semitic propaganda was more successful among younger Germans than among older ones, as was found by Ansbacher in his study of prisoners of war and in the OMGUS surveys of Germans after the war.[27] Wolfson's study of rescuers of Jews likewise indicated a tendency for older rather than younger Germans to aid Jews.[28] As was the case with women, the accumulated evidence indicates that younger Germans in general were more anti-Semitic than older ones.

The overrepresentation of older opponents among *Judenfreunde*, particularly in the age group 50–59, is unexpected. We

TABLE 7.6 Approximate Age Distribution of Male and Female *Judenfreunde* during World War II (*in percentages*)

| Age | Females | | | Males | | |
|---|---|---|---|---|---|---|
| | *Prewar* | *War* | *Prob.[a]* | *Prewar* | *War* | *Prob.[a]* |
| Under 30 | 35.3 | 00.0 | − 5.270 | 9.3 | 3.8 | |
| 30–49 | 51.0 | 58.1 | | 47.9 | 34.0 | − .04 |
| 50 + | 13.7 | 41.9 | .003 | 42.9 | 62.3 | .01 |
| Number in sample | *51* | *31* | | *140* | *53* | |

[a] Computed using test statistic 2 for males and females separately. See appendix A for interpretations of chance probability.

saw earlier that the age groups that were most strongly overrepresented among Merkl's sample of early Nazi anti-Semites (compared to the ''no evidence'' category) were 49 and older (born 1860–1877), and that paranoid anti-Semites were most likely to be 49–55 in 1933 (born in 1878–1884).[29] We also hypothesized that most individuals form their political views in their twenties, and that the age category 56 and older was unlikely to include very many individuals aged 70 and over. Therefore, we speculated that the majority of older anti-Semites in Merkl's sample formed their political views between 1884 and 1914. We concluded that the general overrepresentation of anti-Semites aged 49 and older in Merkl's sample lent indirect support to the theory that intellectual and social anti-Semitism became more pronounced before 1914.[30] Yet, when we compare *Judenfreunde* to the early Nazi anti-Semites according to their dates of birth, we have the results shown in table 7.7. The percentage of *Judenfreunde* born between 1860 and 1883 did not compare unfavorably with the percentage of early Nazi anti-Semites born in the same years. Also, a large percentage of *Judenfreunde* were born between 1878 and 1884, and this was the most paranoid age group in Merkl's sample.[31]

Thus it appears that even if anti-Semitism were stronger among older individuals who formed their political views roughly between 1880 and 1914, opposition to anti-Semitism was also strong among these individuals. Even if we dismiss the hypothesis that most individuals form their political attitudes during their twenties as too restrictive and arbitrary, we still must point out that older Germans displayed anti-Semitism as well as opposition to it and that there was a great deal of diversity in their attitudes toward Jews. From these comparisons it appears that both racial hatred

TABLE 7.7 Percentages of *Judenfreunde* and Early Nazi Anti-Semites Born 1860–1884 (Merkl's Sample)

| Birth Date | Judenfreunde | Nazi Anti-Semites |
|------------|--------------|-------------------|
| 1878–1884 | 17.8% | 10.0% |
| 1860–1883 | 12.4% | 10.0% |

SOURCE: For age distribution in Merkl's sample, see appendix B, table B.1.

and opposition to anti-Semitism were incubated between roughly 1880 and 1914; therefore, more research should be done on opposition to intellectual and social anti-Semitism in Germany before World War I, particularly since it is clear from electoral statistics that political anti-Semitism was unsuccessful during this period.[32]

In chapter 2 we saw that even though new voters may have been younger than voters who switched from parties of the middle to the NSDAP, some of the older voters who switched parties may have been less concerned with the "Jewish question" than with other issues, since they later aided Jews disproportionately.[33]

*Occupation*

We noted earlier that both independents (particularly small businessmen) and white-collar workers (especially those in upper levels) were grossly overrepresented among *Judenfreunde*, and white-collar workers were also overrepresented among *Rassenschänder*. In contrast, blue-collar workers were extremely underrepresented among both *Judenfreunde* and *Rassenschänder*.[34] These characteristics were observed at all levels of opposition.[35]

We can gather additional information that illustrates the overrepresentation of independents by examining criminal statistics for *Rassenschänder* in 1937. Unfortunately, white-collar and blue-collar workers were lumped together, so we cannot differentiate between them to discover which group was most highly represented; however, the distribution was as given on table 7.8 for

TABLE 7.8 Occupational Distribution of German Population and *Rassenschänder* (*in percentages*)

|  | German Population, 1933 | Rassenschänder, 1937 |
|---|---|---|
| Independents | 20.6 | 30.9 |
| Blue- and white-collar workers | 73.7 | 69.1 |

SOURCES: The census year 1933 was used for the German population to eliminate territories that were added to Germany after 1933; see *Statistik des deutschen Reiches*, vol. 451 (1933), no. 5:26. See *Statistik des Deutschen Reiches*, vol. 577 (1942):296–297, for criminal statistics on *Rassenschänder* in 1937.

TABLE 7.9 Occupational Distribution of Independents Who Opposed Persecution (*in percentages*)

| | |
|---|---|
| Owners of large factories or businesses | 18.8 |
| Small businessmen and shop owners | 49.1 |
| Members of free professions | 13.4 |
| High-level civil servants and military officers | 4.5 |
| Business directors and executives, factory managers | 14.3 |

473 *Rassenschänder*. From this we see that independents were considerably overrepresented in this group.

We should note that of the 112 independents, most were small businessmen. Their occupational distribution is indicated in table 7.9. Although Gellately found that anti-Semitism was relatively unimportant to small shopkeepers,[36] Pratt found a strong correlation between them and Nazi voters.[37] The percentage of small businessmen among both Nazi voters and opponents of anti-Semitism was high. From this we infer that if small businessmen voted for the NSDAP, anti-Semitism was not their primary motive. Pratt's correlation between white-collar workers and Nazi voters was not as strong as that between small shopkeepers and Nazi voters, and this is more in accord with the fact that a large percentage of opponents of anti-Semitism were white-collar workers.

Independents and white-collar workers were overrepresented as opponents in both large urban and middle-sized areas. Blue-collar workers were underrepresented among opponents in *all* geographic areas, and this was most pronounced in large cities. Only 12.2 percent of the blue-collar opponents of anti-Semitism were from large cities, whereas 52.2 percent of the labor force in these cities were blue-collar workers. Rural areas and small towns were the most favorable locale for blue-collar opposition.[38] In short, blue-collar opponents were not typically members of the "urban proletariat."

Even though blue-collar workers were underrepresented at all levels of opposition compared to their percentage in the labor force, they did have a larger percentage among high-level opponents than among middle- and low-level opponents. This was because ten of the sixteen workers who were high-level opponents were *Rassenschänder*. In contrast, all of the independents at high levels of opposition were *Judenfreunde*.[39]

A common response to the Nazi regime among both middle and lower classes appears to have been apathy in the face of a police state and the destruction of many organizations and institutions that could have served as centers of opposition both to the Nazi state and to racial persecution. Apathy was reflected in socialist underground reports for both lower and middle classes.[40] With respect to anti-Semitism in particular, these and other sources indicate that there was a minority of both anti-Semites and opponents of persecution among both middle and lower classes.[41] However, because these sources do not give a specific and detailed picture of opponents of anti-Semitism, the results from the Government District Düsseldorf are considerably more reliable and will therefore be discussed at some length.

The large percentages of independents and white-collar workers among opponents from this district conflict with the current theory that the middle classes were more anti-Semitic than the lower classes. We saw earlier that the middle classes are assumed to have adopted intellectual and social anti-Semitism between 1870 and 1933.[42] They are also thought to have voted for Hitler in disproportionate numbers, and indeed we saw that middle-class occupational groups had a larger percentage of moderate and paranoid anti-Semites in the early Nazi party than did lower classes, even though there was considerable diversity in both groups.[43] Why, then, should we find that independents and white-collar workers were the most active opponents of racial persecution, and that this could for all practical purposes never be attributable to chance factors?

We do know that many Jews were in middle-class occupations in 1933 in Germany as a whole, and this was also true for the Rhine Province, of which the Government District Düsseldorf comprised over half. With this in mind, we should examine the comparisons in table 7.10.

It is impossible to estimate the average percentage of Jews in

TABLE 7.10 Occupational Distribution of Jews and Opponents of Anti-Semitism in Germany, the Rhine Province, and the Government District Düsseldorf (*in percentages*)

|  | Jews in Germany, 1933 | Jews in Rhine Prov., 1933 | Jews in Germany, 1939 | Opponents, GDD, 1933–1944 |
|---|---|---|---|---|
| Independents | 51.7 | 53.4 | 16.2 | 33.6 |
| Civil servants | 1.1 | 1.0 | 00.0 | 6.6 |
| White-collar | 37.5 | 35.6 | 25.5 | 44.4 |
| Blue-collar | 9.8 | 9.9 | 58.3 | 15.3 |

SOURCES: For the occupational distribution of Jews in 1933, see *Statistik des Deutschen Reiches*, vol. 470 (1937), no. 1:8; for 1939, see vol. 552 (1942), no. 4:74. For the occupational distribution of Jews in the Rhine Province in 1933, see *Statistik des Deutschen Reiches*, vol. 455 (1933), no. 16:60. For the occupational distribution of opponents of racial persecution, see appendix B,. table B.2, omitting domestic servants for comparability.

given occupations for the district from these figures, but we do know that 67 percent of the opponents from the Government District Düsseldorf were arrested in 1938 and in following years, when the occupational distribution of Jews in the district was probably closer to that of Germany in 1939 than to that of the Rhine Province in 1933. We also know that the occupational distribution of Jews in Germany and in the Rhine Province was very similar in 1933, and that the district formed a large part of the Rhine Province. It is therefore probable that the occupational distribution of Jews of the Rhine Province and the Government District Düsseldorf was similar to that of all of Germany in 1939.

Because of these considerations and because most opposition occurred between 1938 and 1944, we shall roughly compare the occupational distribution of opponents in the district to the occupational distribution of Jews in Germany in 1939. From the data in table 7.10 we see that the percentage of opponents was significantly higher than the percentage of Jews in three occupations, namely, independents, civil servants, and white-collar workers. In contrast, the percentage of blue-collar workers was lower for opponents than for Jews in Germany in 1939.

We know that independents and white-collar workers were overrepresented as members of the Nazi party and as anti-Semites

227

TABLE 7.11 Occupational Distribution of Early Nazi Anti-Semites, the Nazi Party from 1933 to 1945, and Opponents of Racial Persecution from the Government District Düsseldorf (*in percentages*)

| | Early Anti-Semites | Nazi Party, 1933–1945 | Opponents, GDD |
|---|---|---|---|
| Independents | 25.3 | 22.7 | 33.6 |
| Farmers | 5.6 | 8.6 | 00.0 |
| Other | 19.7 | 14.1 | 33.6 |
| Civil servants | 25.6 | 12.0 | 6.6 |
| White-collar | 23.6 | 20.2 | 44.4 |
| Blue-collar | 25.6 | 45.1 | 15.3 |
| Number in sample | *254* | *13,016* | *333* |

SOURCES: For numbers and percentages in Merkl's sample of anti-Semites, see appendix B, table B.1. For the Nazi party from 1933 to 1945, see Michael Kater, "Quantifizierung and NS-Geschichte: Methodologische Ueberlegungen über Grenzen und Möglichkeiten einer EDV-Analyse der NSDAP-Sozialstruktur von 1925 bis 1945," *Geschichte und Gesellschaft* 3/4 (1977): 464–465; see also Sarah Gordon, "German Opposition to Nazi Anti-Semitic Measures between 1933 and 1945, with Particular Reference to the Rhine-Ruhr Area," 287, 287A (note that table 30, p. 287 should refer to Kater's pp. 464–465). For the occupational distribution of opponents, see appendix B, table B.2 (omitting domestic servants).

NOTE: For comparability and because it is impossible to classify them by occupation, persons with no profession and *all others* are eliminated from total numbers upon which *all* percentages are based. In all cases master craftsmen are included with blue-collar workers as they were in census classifications; however, they are obviously a marginal occupational group on a social scale. Master craftsmen comprised 3.8 percentage points of the 45.1 percent of these Nazi occupational groups who were blue-collar workers, and less than 2 percentage points of the 15.3 percent of the opponents of persecution (omitting domestic servants and persons with no profession) who were blue-collar workers; therefore, their classification with blue-collar workers does not substantially alter the comparatively low representation of blue-collar workers among opponents of racial persecution.

(compared to the "no evidence" category) in the early NSDAP.[44] It is therefore interesting to discover how opponents of racial persecution differed occupationally from early Nazi anti-Semites and the Nazi party. In table 7.11 the occupational distribution of Nazi party members is determined by averaging percentages for the years 1933–1945, as given in a recent study by Kater.[45] From this comparison we see that the percentage of independents and white-collar workers was considerably higher among opponents of racial persecution from the Government District Düsseldorf than among Kater's sample of new entrants to the Nazi party or among Merkl's sample of early Nazi anti-Semites. In contrast, the percentages of opponents who were independent farmers, civil servants, or blue-collar workers were considerably smaller than comparable percentages among early anti-Semites or the Nazi party between 1933 and 1945.

Since among opponents the percentage of independents and white-collar workers was higher than their percentage in the labor force in the Government District Düsseldorf, higher than their percentage in the Jewish labor force, higher than their percentage among early Nazi anti-Semites, and higher than their percentage in the Nazi party, it is clear that they supported Jews disproportionately. There is no obvious reason why the Gestapo would have selected these particular occupational groups for harassment, particularly since they were very interested in arresting blue-collar workers on any grounds to combat socialism, and because they suspected socialists of sympathizing with Jews. Therefore, it is highly probable, given the high percentages of independents and white-collar workers who opposed racial persecution, that these occupational groups were less anti-Semitic than previous studies have implied.

Even though some members of the middle classes were anti-Semites, it is certainly not true that all of them were, or that they can be stereotyped as anti-Semites. The presence of heavy opposition to racial persecution among the middle classes is extremely revealing. The theory that the middle classes were the strongest converts to intellectual and social anti-Semitism between 1870 and 1933 should be reexamined, since they were disproportionately represented among both *Judenfreunde* and *Rassenschänder*.[46] Certainly Childers's and more particularly Hamilton's questioning of the lower-middle class base of Hitler's support would seem justified as regards anţi-Semitism, since they were strong aiders of Jews.[47] Any class interpretation of anti-Semitism should include the role of the middle classes as opponents of persecution. It should also come to terms with the fact that blue-

229

collar workers were the most underrepresented occupational group among all opponents, both *Judenfreunde* and *Rassenschänder*. Only 14.4 percent of the employed opponents in the Government District Düsseldorf were blue-collar workers, whereas blue-collar workers comprised 51.1 percent of the labor force.

We should also point out that the number of Jews in blue-collar occupations did not decrease in the 1930s. It stayed at around 20,000 between 1933 and 1939, so that there was no obvious decline in occupational contacts between Jews and German workers.[48] Also, the Jews who were too poor to emigrate from Germany probably concentrated in working-class neighborhoods out of financial necessity; more prosperous Jews left the country. Therefore, although previous close associations between middle-class Germans and middle-class Jews may account for their disproportionate aid to Jews (despite the elimination of Jews in middle-class occupations between 1933 and 1941), lack of contact between Jews and blue-collar workers probably does not explain their underrepresentation as opponents of racial persecution. We should also note that working-class Germans had more contacts with unassimilated Eastern European Jews, and that this may have fostered anti-Semitism.[49]

It is possible that reports of anti-Semitism among blue-collar workers in the *Deutschland-Berichte* were exaggerated, since the SPD-in-exile may have considered anti-Semitism atypical for workers and, therefore, newsworthy.[50] Against this, however, it can be argued that the *Deutschland-Berichte* reported workers' sympathy for and aid to Jews as well as their indifference to them or expressions of anti-Semitism, frequently noting shifts in attitudes over time. Quite often these shifts were similar among blue-collar workers and members of the middle classes, which at least indirectly indicates that the *Deutschland-Berichte* were reporting what SPD leaders thought to be true information from their underground agents rather than distorted or exaggerated versions of workers' attitudes. It is likely that they were a fairly accurate reflection of public opinion among both lower and middle classes.

Much current secondary literature, some of which has a definite Marxist or socialist bias, emphasizes general opposition to the

Nazi regime by blue-collar workers. However, blue-collar workers were so grossly underrepresented among opponents of racial persecution in our data that they can in no way be characterized as strong supporters of persecuted Jews.

There are several hypotheses that may explain the underrepresentation of blue-collar workers as opponents of racial persecution. First, the sample of working-class opponents may not reflect the behavior of workers in other parts of Germany. For example, William S. Allen suggests (private communication) that there was a higher percentage of blue-collar workers with party affiliations to the Center (rather than to the SPD or KPD) in the Government District Düsseldorf than was true in other parts of Germany. If this were true, they may have been less influenced by socialist propaganda against racial persecution than were workers elsewhere. This hypothesis, however, is made less tenable if we take into consideration the studies of opponents of persecution elsewhere in Germany.[51] The underrepresentation of blue-collar workers is simply *too* great to be explained by a somewhat stronger affiliation of blue-collar workers with the Center versus the KPD or SPD. Moreover, we should only consider affiliations with the SPD, because the KPD did not demonstrate a sympathetic attitude toward Jews. The party affiliations of different classes in the *entire* Government District Düsseldorf have not been researched, and indeed, they may not be obtainable. But at best, a higher percentage affiliation of blue-collar workers with the Center in the Government District Düsseldorf would have affected a small part of the blue-collar labor force and cannot by itself account for the underrepresentation of blue-collar workers among opponents of racial persecution.

As a second hypothesis we might speculate that the Gestapo concentrated upon socialist and communist opponents, and that they therefore ignored *Judenfreundlichkeit* among blue-collar workers. However, against this it can be argued that any excuse to root out socialists would have been welcomed by the Gestapo. That is, if a known socialist worker could not be arrested for proven underground activities, the Gestapo would not have hesitated to arrest him on another charge, that is, aiding Jews. On the other hand, since blue-collar workers were aware of their vulnerability, they may have considered aid to Jews too dangerous. In addition, earlier "weeding out" of socialists and communists who opposed the regime between 1933 and 1936 may have taught those workers who were still free to be more careful and therefore less likely to get caught. This hypothesis, though plausible, is highly speculative. As the risks and stakes increased, *all* classes presumably became more careful. Blue-collar workers had no monopoly on fear.

A more plausible explanation for underrepresentation of blue-collar workers among opponents of racial persecution is that they were not in a position to aid Jews, just as younger Germans were not. Yet it is probable that they had better possibilities of obtaining false documents simply because of their contacts with the socialist underground and "lower-class" criminal elements. However, producing and procuring documents and false passports required money; assuming that most of the Jews with whom they might have had contact were also members of the working class or were poorer retailers in working-class neighborhoods, blue-collar workers may simply have been unable to provide the ready cash to aid their Jewish acquaintances. This might have been especially true since real wages of blue-collar workers did not increase on average during Hitler's regime. Aid to Jews may have been a luxury that blue-collar workers could not afford, regardless of their feelings toward Jews. On the other hand, many types of assistance to Jews, and especially criticism of persecution, did not require money (see illustrative cases of opposition), so this explanation cannot account for the *extremity* of blue-collar workers' underrepresentation as opponents of racial persecution.

Another very plausible hypothesis to explain the less frequent arrest of blue-collar workers for *Judenfreundlichkeit* and *Rassenschande* is that members of the NSDAP and its affiliates came disproportionately from the middle classes. Therefore, Nazi agents were in a better position to observe the "crimes" of their fellow members of the middle classes, to denounce them, and to document any violations of Nazi racial policy. In contrast, fewer Nazis came from the working classes, and this may have afforded them a certain amount of protection. But again, we should note that the Gestapo was very thorough in crippling the socialist movement in Germany, using any and all means, and it stretches one's imagination to believe that aid to Jews would not have been used as a pretext for harassing blue-collar workers.

After considering these hypotheses, I think that none of them, and probably no combination of them, suffices to explain the extraordinary underrepresentation of blue-collar workers as opponents of anti-Semitism. The most convincing possibility is that workers lacked the monetary or physical means to aid Jews. A fairly large percentage of workers engaged in *Rassenschande*, and this indicates close personal associations. The percentage of blue-collar workers who engaged in *Rassenschande* with Jews was second only to that of lower-level white-collar workers (57.5 percent and 47.1 percent, respectively). From this it appears that factors other than lack of contact with Jews must account for the underrepresentation. Exactly what these factors were, and whether or not they were related to anti-Semitism among the working class, cannot be determined from the data presented here.

Many former leaders of the Social Democratic party were opponents of anti-Semitism between 1870 and 1914, but most historians would classify these leaders as members of the middle class, certainly during Weimar years. Yet opposition to anti-Semitism among SPD leaders cannot be considered synonymous with opposition by the "working class," and future interpretations should take this into account.

## ILLUSTRATIVE CASES OF OPPOSITION

Before concluding our discussion of occupational groups, it may be of some interest to look at case records of opponents in different occupations to indicate the diversity of opposition. Few names will be used since some opponents may still be living, and in these cases archive regulations forbid citing names without the permission of the individual involved.

There were a number of interesting cases of opposition among independents. In 1936 a 24-year-old female lawyer from Düssel-

233

dorf was arrested ostensibly for introducing clients to Jewish lawyers and managing legal affairs of emigrating Jews. She was a former member of the Social Democratic party, was once in love with a Jewish man, and was the daughter of an emigré SPD Reichstag delegate.[52] Another lawyer, a prominent director of an industrial concern, was arrested on suspicion of giving news of boycotts against Jews to foreigners in 1934. He was a resident of München-Gladbach, was 31 years old, was married to a Jewess, and emigrated to Basel.[53] A director of a large steel concern appealed to Pohl, an SS group leader and prominent minister in the Ministry of the Interior, to classify a number of part-Jews (*Mischlinge*) as "Aryans," and to permit them to marry non-Jews. He was in his forties at the time of his requests in 1939–1942, and he was a resident of Düsseldorf.[54] In 1943 a prominent older (aged 65) lawyer from Wupperthal was arrested for sending reports of persecution of individuals who aided Jews to the *Landesbischof* Wurm.[55]

Two examples of aid by owners of large businesses are also illustrative. A 54-year-old factory owner from München-Gladbach was sent to Sachsenhausen (concentration camp) and died there in 1943 as a consequence of aiding Jews who crossed the border illegally.[56] A 48-year-old Protestant, a female owner of a stocking factory in Düsseldorf, was arrested for sending parcels to an imprisoned Jewess. Her case was referred to the courts, but we do not know her sentence.[57]

Because about 50 percent of the independents who aided Jews were small businessman, we shall cite a few examples for this occupational group. In 1932 a 55-year-old Catholic baker from Düsseldorf praised the nineteenth-century Jewish poet Heinrich Heine in an inn. He was considered a determined opponent of the Nazi regime, and the NSDAP requested his removal as head of a local (and popular) social club.[58] Another small shopkeeper, a 64-year-old proprietor of a newspaper business in Essen, was imprisoned for selling newspapers to Jews in 1934.[59] Still another small businessman, a 57-year-old Catholic from Viersen and former functionary of the Center party, illegally gave information and advice to Jewish businesses in 1938.[60] A 53-year-old owner of a meat store in München-Gladbach was arrested in 1938 for buying a cow from a Jew and saying the entire world would be against Germany in a future war because of the persecution of German Jews.[61] A 62-year-old Catholic shopowner, a woman from Emmerich, was arrested for selling cigarettes to Jews but not to soldiers' wives in 1941.[62] A 53-year-old small businessman from Düsseldorf was arrested in 1940 for aiding Jews financially.[63]

Two examples of civil servants who aided Jews are illustrative. A 66-year-old Catholic civil servant from Cleve was arrested for subversion and friendliness to Jews in 1936. He was also investigated for other opposition in 1940, whereupon it was discovered that he had aided Jews after *Kristallnacht* by attempting to find out who had vandalized their businesses. He was imprisoned for this and other opposition and died in Sachsenhausen in 1942.[64] A 38-year-old Protestant civil servant in Duisburg was arrested and fired from his position because he interceded with officials on behalf of his Jewish doctor in 1933.[65]

White-collar workers comprised an extremely large percentage of opponents, and several examples of their opposition will be cited. A 31-year-old upper-level white-collar worker from Düsseldorf was arrested in 1938 for issuing unauthorized certificates to Jews.[66] A 36-year-old Catholic supplier of goods to small groceries was arrested in Duisburg during 1939 for aiding Jews who were illegally emigrating. He was sent to Sachsenhausen and later to Dachau. He was not released until 1942, after which he died of a stroke at the age of 39.[67] A 45-year-old teacher from Essen was arrested in 1938 for claiming that Jews were an exceptional people who had a high level of culture and art, that they only went into trade because they were persecuted, and that they should be praised for having brought Christ into the world. She maintained that the persecution of Jews was making German youths brutal and callous, and she also defended intermarriage. Her case was referred to the courts, but her sentence is not known.[68]

Among lower-level white-collar workers, three examples are interesting. In 1939 a Catholic salesman from Cleve was arrested for aiding Jews to cross the border and for his religious conviction that Jews should be treated humanely.[69] Another salesman, a 41-

year-old Catholic from Essen, was arrested after *Kristallnacht* for photographing the destruction of Jewish property.[70] Two clerks in a butcher shop in Essen were imprisoned for a month and six weeks because they gave meat to Jews in 1940.[71]

Blue-collar workers also engaged in diverse kinds of opposition. For example, in 1938 a 30-year-old Catholic worker from München-Gladbach aided Jews who were crossing the border illegally.[72] Also in 1938, a 47-year-old worker who had been an SPD functionary in Graz smuggled money for Jews. He was sent to Dachau in 1938 where he was still imprisoned in 1941.[73] A 38-year-old overseer of a mining pit was arrested after *Kristallnacht* for criticizing the persecution.[74] A former functionary of the SPD and its paramilitary organization (*Reichsbanner Schwarz-Rot-Gold*), a 47-year-old Catholic worker from Suchteln, accepted silver and linen from Jews to be sent to their Jewish daughter abroad. He was sent to Sachsenhausen where he died after three months.[75]

Among persons with no profession, several examples of opposition are illustrative. In 1939 a 29-year-old housewife from Moers was arrested for selling false passes to Jews.[76] A 41-year-old housewife from Essen was arrested in 1935 for criticizing persecution of Jews.[77] A 57-year-old housewife from Essen was arrested for verbally defending Jews and thereby "inciting public disorder" during *Kristallnacht*.[78] Still another housewife was imprisoned in Grafwegen prison during 1939 for aiding a Jewish couple who were emigrating illegally.[79]

Sexual relations with Jews were much more personal, even idiosyncratic expressions of disagreement with Nazi racial policies. We shall cite a few examples. A 35-year-old shopowner was charged with criminal procurement because he condoned his wife's sexual relations with a Jew.[80] A 40-year-old Catholic civil servant from Cleve was imprisoned for a year and a half and fined 10,000 *Reichsmark* for having sexual relations with a Jewess and aiding Jews in financial transactions.[81] A 33-year-old assistant professor was imprisoned from 1940 to 1943 for having sexual relations with a Jewess.[82] A 29-year-old seamstress was sent to Ravensbrück concentration camp in 1943 for the same "offense."[83] A blue-collar worker from Düsseldorf was sent to a forced-labor prison for three years because of *Rassenschande*.[84] And finally, a 30-year-old Catholic domestic servant from Duisburg was spared imprisonment for having an affair with a Jew only because she became pregnant.[85]

From these examples we see that there were diverse types of opposition among all occupational groups. These, of course, are only a small selection from the opponents listed in the files of the Government District Düsseldorf, and there are many more types of opposition on record. The criminal cases involving *Rassenschande* were naturally so personal and frequently so detailed that they are a positive embarrassment to human dignity, and this was particularly true of cases involving Jewish males. They were, of course, nothing in comparison to the agonies and injustices that Jews were forced to endure, but they were nevertheless traumatic to the individuals who were discovered by the Gestapo.

## SENTENCES OF OPPONENTS OF RACIAL PERSECUTION

Now that I have outlined the most important socioeconomic characteristics of opponents of anti-Semitism, it is of interest to determine what sentences were imposed for *Judenfreunde* and *Rassenschänder* in the Government District Düsseldorf. Exact sentences were given for only thirty-four of the sixty-seven high-level opponents, so unfortunately it is impossible to learn a great deal from them, and no generalizations can be made on such a small sample. The other thirty-three high-level opponents were imprisoned, but the length of their sentences was not included in their Gestapo files. Of the thirty-four opponents whose sentence is known, seventeen were sent to concentration camps and the other seventeen were sentenced separately to a total of twenty-one years in prison. The average length of their imprisonment was two years during the prewar period and one year during the war; thus the combined average for prewar and war years was one and a half years. The lesser sentences during the war are probably an inaccurate indication of the actual sentences given during the war. There were only eight cases in which the length of the sentence was given during the war years, and this is ob-

237

viously too small a number from which to generalize. It is also interesting to note that information on sentences was available for only 14 percent of the Jews who were arrested for *Rassenschande*, and only one case included a sentence to a concentration camp, which shows that the Gestapo files are a poor indicator of final sentences for *Rassenschänder*, both Jewish and non-Jewish.

It is difficult to learn much about the severity of sentences from the Düsseldorf sample; however, we do know that of the sixty-seven high-level opponents, 53.7 percent were *Judenfreunde* and 46.3 percent were *Rassenschänder*. The number who were sent to concentration camps was about equal for *Judenfreunde* and *Rassenschänder* (nine and eight, respectively). Although average sentences were almost identical for *Judenfreunde* and *Rassenschänder* during war years, there was a tendency for *Rassenschänder* to receive longer sentences than *Judenfreunde* in prewar years. These results, however, are based on very small numbers and are only of marginal value. Unfortunately, other historians and I do not have good data on sentences for *Judenfreunde* because their activities were so diverse that they were prosecuted under a large number of laws (slander against the state, treason, illegal currency transactions, etc.). Thus extensive research using court records from other parts of Germany will be necessary to clarify sentences for *Judenfreunde*.

It is possible, however, to obtain additional information on sentences for non-Jewish *Rassenschänder* by examining criminal statistics for Germany as a whole and by studying Hans Robinsohn's data for Hamburg, Cologne, and Frankfurt a.M. This data is compiled in table 7.12. Sentences to a prison involving forced labor (*Zuchthaus*) are not directly comparable, but are nevertheless interesting.

Although the years in table 7.12 overlap, and even though some of Robinsohn's cases would have been included in the data on Germany as a whole, we can learn several things from this comparison. In both cases the majority of non-Jewish *Rassenschänder* were sent to a normal prison (*Gefängnis*) rather than to a harsher establishment that entailed forced labor (*Zuchthaus*). Since a *Zuchthaus* sentence was rarely given for less than one year, we

TABLE 7.12 Prison sentences for Non-Jewish *Rassenschänder (in percentages)*

| | All of Germany,<br>1935–1939 | Hamburg, Cologne, Frankfurt a.M.,<br>1936–1943 | |
|---|---|---|---|
| *Zuchthaus*<br>(imprisonment<br>with forced labor) | 17.5 | | 34.3 |
| 1 to 3 years | 16.8 | Less than 2 years | 8.3 |
| 3 years or more | 0.7 | 2 to 4 years | 23.8 |
| | | 5 to 7 years | 2.2 |
| *Gefängnis*<br>(normal prison) | 82.4 | | 65.8 |
| 1 year or more | 37.6 | | 45.9 |
| 3 months to 1 year | 43.5⎫ | Less than 1 year | 19.9 |
| less than 3 months | 1.3⎭ | | |
| Number in sample | *627* | | *211* |

SOURCES: For Germany, see *Statistik des Deutschen Reiches*, vol. 577 (1942): 86–87, 106–107, 124–164, 174–175, 180–183, 186–187, 232–233, 236–239, 252–253, 258–259, 296–297, 316–319, 330–337, 346–347, 352–353, 358–359. For Hamburg, Cologne, and Frankfurt a.M., see Hans Robinsohn, *Justiz als politische Verfolgung*, 78.

can safely assume that the 17.5 percent of non-Jewish *Rassenschänder* from Germany as a whole, plus 37.6 percent of those sentenced to a *Gefängnis*, or 55.1 percent together, served more than one year. In Hamburg, Cologne, and Frankfurt the comparable figures are 34.3, plus 45.9, or 80.2 percent serving more than a year.

Robinsohn also indicates that the average sentences for Hamburg defendants were long enough to serve as a deterrent to opposition: 501 days (1.4 years) in a normal prison, and 894 days (2.5 years) in a *Zuchthaus*.[86] Thus data for Germany as a whole and Robinsohn's court cases from Hamburg, Cologne, and Frankfurt support and corroborate the very scant evidence from the Government District Düsseldorf. All indications are that penalties for *Rassenschande* were severe enough to serve as an effective warning or deterrent to those Germans who may have wanted to start or to continue liaisons with Jews.

It is noteworthy that in Robinsohn's court cases for Hamburg,

Frankfurt, and Cologne, which include war years, over a third of the non-Jewish *Rassenschänder* were sent to the "tougher" prisons that involved forced labor. One would suspect that this was due to more draconian sentencing during World War II, and indeed an examination of Robinsohn's other data confirms this suspicion. If we compare the duration (average days) of imprisonment during each phase of persecution to the average duration for all years, we find a revealing result. During 1936–1937, 1938–1939, and 1940–1943, 61 percent, 62 percent, and 67 percent, respectively, of the total days to which non-Jewish *Rassenschänder* from Hamburg were sentenced entailed imprisonment in a *Zuchthaus*.[87] Thus the duration of sentences to a *Zuchthaus* increased during World War II, at least in Hamburg.

Moreover, despite the evidence from table 7.12 that the majority of non-Jewish *Rassenschänder* were sent to a regular prison instead of a *Zuchthaus*, when the duration of imprisonment in each type of establishment is taken into account, it is clear (at least for the Hamburg defendants) that the majority of days (61–67 percent) in prison were in a *Zuchthaus*. Since Robinsohn does not give the *number* of non-Jewish *Rassenschänder* from Hamburg who were sentenced to a *Zuchthaus* during each year, it is not possible to determine to what extent this was a consequence of a small number of defendants being given long sentences.[88]

Another interesting aspect of Robinsohn's work is his data on "social" groups and sentences for *Rassenschande*. Although his categorization does not follow clear-cut census classifications, he does divide his sample into six groups in declining order of "social" importance based upon probable income, education, and so on. From this we find confirmation of our earlier conclusion that middle-class social or occupational groups were overrepresented as opponents of racial persecution.[89] (His sample of upper-class groups [1 and 2] is very small [9], but apparently they were acquitted disproportionately.) Categories 3 and 4, which would probably correspond to middle-class occupational groups, comprised 70 percent of the sample and were sent to prison (*Gefängnis*) in 70 percent of the cases. Thus they were very likely either to engage in *Rassenschande* or to be convicted of it, and they were

240

extremely likely to be sentenced to a regular prison for it. In contrast, categories 5 and 6 (lower classes) were a small percentage of the total sample; therefore, they were less likely either to engage in *Rassenschande* or to be convicted for it. Nevertheless, the lower classes were sent to harsher prisons in percentages that were disproportionate to other classes.[90] Since poorer defendants always fare less well than richer ones, this is in part to be expected. For example, among Jewish *Rassenschänder* richer defendants were also treated with more circumspection.[91] The lower classes also had close ties to the KPD and SPD, and were therefore more vulnerable to harsher treatment. In the Government District Düsseldorf they also tended to receive stiffer sentences than did other social groups for similar activities as *Rassenschänder* and *Judenfreunde*, and this may also have been true in Hamburg.

Finally, Robinsohn points out that individuals who were tried for *Rassenschande* (and presumably those who were acquitted) had frequently been subjected to severe interrogation, including torture.[92] Although this brutality was bound to have been much worse for Jews than non-Jews, we should bear in mind that being arrested and tried for *Rassenschande* entailed enormous costs. Not only did the final sentences serve as a deterrent to those who learned of them, but also the mere fact of an arrest by the Gestapo for this type of "crime" must have frightened relatives, friends, and neighbors of suspects. Yet arrests and sentencing may also have had the effect of encouraging individuals to report suspected *Rassenschande* in order to take their rivals or enemies out of circulation. Since *Rassenschande* was most thoroughly condemned by the Nazi party, denunciation also served to advance one's personal career. This, of course, would promote anti-Semitism, as those who denounced others for *Rassenschande* could use Nazi anti-Semitic propaganda as a rationalization. Thus the denouncers could run the entire gamut from real Jew-haters to revenge-seekers, opportunists, and even rejected lovers.

## SUMMARY

Because it is difficult to determine true motives for aiding Jews so many years after the fact, this chapter concentrates on the quantifiable socioeconomic characteristics of opponents. Fortunately, a fairly large number of records of opponents of persecution is available in the Gestapo files for the Government District Düsseldorf, and these previously unused sources give us insight into both the chronological development of opposition and the socioeconomic characteristics of opponents.

We found that the timing of opposition in this district was the same as that reported in general sources for other parts of Germany, as discussed in chapter 6. Since the general sources and the Düsseldorf Gestapo files corroborate each other, they are probably an accurate reflection of shifting public opinion toward persecution. We also discovered that whereas *Rassenschänder* were most likely to engage in sexual relations with Jews between 1935 and 1939, *Judenfreunde* supported Jews most strongly in 1938 and 1939, and to some extent during World War II. That is, sexual contacts between Jews and non-Jews continued in the wake of and in defiance of the Nuremberg Laws of 1935, while assistance to Jews (either verbal criticism of persecution or direct aid to Jews) escalated when Nazi persecution became more visible and violent. It declined during the war as Jews were deported, but did not disappear despite increased risks and penalties.

When we compared the socioeconomic characteristics of opponents to those of the population and labor force of the Government District Düsseldorf for the years 1933–1944, we saw that men were much more likely than women to aid Jews and to have sexual relations with them. Males were not only more active as socialist opponents and members of the conspiracy against Hitler in July 1944, they were also more active as opponents of racial persecution. Opponents who aided Jews or criticized persecution were older (over forty), but those who maintained sexual relations with them were younger than the general population. The underrepresentation of younger Germans among *Judenfreunde* may have been due to their lack of facilities for aiding Jews, or in the case of younger males, it may have resulted from their absence during war service. However, we noted that many types of aid did not require much money, and *criticism* of persecution was certainly "free." It is probable that younger Germans were simply more anti-Semitic, as is indicated in other sources.[93]

Noticeably higher percentages of opponents were born between 1860 and 1884, and most particularly between 1878 and 1884, than were early Nazi anti-Semites. These were also the years in which many paranoid Nazi anti-Semites were born. In comparing birth dates among opponents and early Nazi anti-Semites, we found that they formed their political views in the same years, which indicates that both acceptance and rejection of anti-Semitism were spawned before World War I. Clearly, more research should be done on sources of opposition to anti-Semitism before World War I. Also, considering the percentage of opponents and anti-Semites, if older voters from parties of the Middle switched to the NSDAP in 1930 and certainly in 1932, it is probable that anti-Semitism per se was not the major reason for this shift.

The occupations of opponents were clearly different from those of the general population of the district. Independents (especially small businessmen) and white-collar workers (particularly upper-level white-collar workers) were grossly overrepresented among opponents of persecution, whereas blue-collar workers were extremely underrepresented. This was true at all levels of opposition, and it is corroborated by criminal statistics for *Rassenschänder*. Although general sources indicated pockets of anti-Semitism as well as opposition to it among middle and lower classes, the more specific and detailed information on occupations of opponents in the Government District Düsseldorf provided clear evidence that Germans in both upper and lower middle-class occupations aided Jews in percentages that were much higher than their percentages in the labor force. Conversely, blue-collar workers were very much underrepresented compared to their percentage in the labor force, and this was especially true of urban blue-collar workers. Although blue-collar workers may have been highly active as general opponents of the Nazi regime, they certainly did not oppose racial persecution in proportion to their numbers. This should be taken into account in future studies of resistance to Nazism. In addition, the spread of opposition to intellectual and social anti-Semitism among the middle classes before 1933 should be more

243

thoroughly researched, since they later opposed racial persecution disproportionately to their numbers.

Opposition among all occupational groups was quite diverse in nature, as indicated by our short summary of a few case records. Most aid was given on an individual basis or occasionally in concert with one other person. No large-scale assistance was found in the Gestapo files for the Government District Düsseldorf.

Our information on sentences for *Judenfreunde* is very limited. In the Government District Düsseldorf, 53.7 percent of the opponents were *Judenfreunde*. Using the small numbers of those whose sentence is known, it was possible to determine that average sentences were roughly the same for *Judenfreunde* and *Rassenschänder*, but much future research needs to be done on court records to verify this marginal information. There were sixty-seven high-level opponents; thirty-three were imprisoned, but their exact sentence was not included in the Gestapo file; and of the remaining thirty-four, seventeen were sent to concentration camps, and another seventeen served an average of eighteen months in prison. The general length of sentences is confirmed by data for non-Jewish *Rassenschänder* nationwide and by Robinsohn's figures on *Rassenschande* in Hamburg, Cologne, and Frankfurt. Approximately 55 percent of the *Rassenschänder* who were included in the criminal statistics for Germany, and 80 percent of those in Robinsohn's study, spent more than one year in prison. The majority of *Rassenschänder* were sentenced to a regular prison (*Gefängnis*), but a third of those sentenced in Hamburg, Cologne, and Frankfurt were incarcerated in a prison that entailed forced labor (*Zuchthaus*). As a group, *Rassenschänder* from Hamburg spent a high percentage of their days of imprisonment in a *Zuchthaus*, rather than in a regular prison. This characteristic became more pronounced during World War II, when the duration of imprisonment in a *Zuchthaus* climbed from 62 percent to 67 percent of total days for all types of imprisonment.

Robinsohn's statistics on social classes, although not directly comparable to census data, indicate that the majority of *Rassenschänder* were from the middle classes, which confirms my earlier finding that the middle classes were overrepresented among opponents of racial persecution. The two upper classes in Robinsohn's sample were frequently acquitted. In contrast, although there were only small numbers of non-Jewish *Rassenschänder* from the lower classes, they received longer sentences in a *Zuchthaus* than did other social groups.

The careful reader may observe that the socioeconomic characteristics of opponents of racial persecution are considerably at variance with those that are commonly cited in the secondary literature, especially for years before 1933. This is not unexpected, since there have been no systematic studies of opponents of anti-Semitism during the Nazi period. The impressionistic accounts of aid to Jews are very important because they provide compelling human drama; however, this is the first study that relies upon a fairly large number of individuals who opposed anti-Semitism, and it is also the first one that compares opponents to the general population. There is no possibility that these people "colored" their stories after the fact, since they were forced to defend their activities in the years 1933–1945, and their records were not available for later "adjustments." In summary, then, the most active opponents of racial persecution, considering their numbers in the population, were males, older Germans, independents, and white-collar workers.

Other information from the Government District Düsseldorf concerns religion, a topic to which we now turn.

# Attitudes of the Churches

"The murder of six million Jews by baptized Christians, from whom membership in good standing was not (and has not been) withdrawn, raises the most insistent question about the credibility of Christianity."
Franklin Littell, *The Crucifixion of the Jews*, p. 2.

A great deal has been written since World War II on the failure of German churches to oppose anti-Semitism or publicly to condemn the atrocities against the Jews, including their final annihilation. Only a few church leaders spoke out vehemently against these measures, and no amount of research will basically alter the churches' moral responsibility for these events. Their acquiescence to murder has been well covered elsewhere, and for discussions of their culpability the reader is referred to relevant secondary works.[1] Church leaders were reluctant to speak out against racial persecution not only because of their long history of religious anti-Semitism and other subjective factors, but also because of objective factors, such as the battle with the Nazi regime for institutional autonomy and the difficulty of publicly opposing the racial policies of the regime without encountering harsh countermeasures.[2] In any case, even though they fought with the Nazis to retain their prerogatives on other issues, they did not seriously attempt to intercede in Hitler's war against the Jews.

## CATHOLICS

When we examine the behavior of the churches, we find that only a few Catholic leaders attempted to ameliorate the effects of racial persecution. Among Catholics, some of the more prominent opponents were Archbishop Bertram of Breslau, Dean Lichtenberg of St. Hedwig's Cathedral in Berlin, and Cardinal Preysing, Catholic bishop of Berlin. Dean Lichtenberg condemned the pogrom of *Kristallnacht* and prayed for Jews and prisoners in concentration camps thereafter. He also said in October 1941: "If it is said that Germans, by supporting Jews, commit treason, I enjoin you not to be misled by such un-Christian sentiments, but to act in obedience to Christ's commandment, and to love your neighbor as yourself."[3] His criticisms of genocide during World War II were considered a danger to public order, and he was imprisoned by the regime for two years. In 1943 he died en route to Dachau. He died a proud death, because as he himself said, "Nothing would be better than for an old clergyman like me to stand by baptized Jewish Christians as I die."[4]

As early as 1930 Cardinal Bertram attacked Nazi racial theories.[5] In 1933, just before the April boycott of Jewish businesses, he requested assistance for Jews from the Archbishop of Freiburg.[6] In September of 1933 he complained to Pacelli, the Vatican's secretary of state who became Pope Pius XII, regarding the concordat between the Catholic church and the Nazi state, because it endangered the rights of Jewish converts.[7] In 1941 he issued instructions for church leaders to treat Jews as they did other Christians.[8] And more important, he protested against the death of Jews in concentration camps in letters to Himmler and to the Ministry of the Interior.[9] This obviously did not have a practical effect, but it did demonstrate some moral backbone.

Bishop Preysing was not as vocal as these two men in defending Jews, but he did help baptized Jews and set up an agency that assisted them from 1941 onward.[10] Earlier he had submitted documents that inspired "With Burning Concern," the papal encyclical that criticized Nazi persecution, although it did not mention Jews specifically.[11] In 1942 he contributed to a *Hirtenbrief* (pastoral letter) of the Catholic opposition that condemned Nazi violation of God's laws, although he did not mention Jews by name.[12] And in 1943 he said: "Primitive rights, such as the right to live, to be free, to have possessions, to marry whom one chooses, etc., cannot and must not be denied even to those who are not of our blood."[13] This was hardly a blanket condemnation of genocide, but it was considerably more than many of his colleagues dared to say.

There were other Catholic clerics who raised their voices and extended aid. For example, Prelate Leffers of Paderborn spent a year and a half in prison because he criticized Rosenberg's *Myth of the Twentieth Century*, an anti-Semitic book. Two others received six and eight months in prison for the same offense.[14] Bishop Berning of Osnabruck helped baptized Jews to emigrate, and the general secretary of the St. Raphael Association (which aided Jews who were emigrating) was imprisoned for many months by the Gestapo.[15] The Archbishop of Paderborn and the Bishop of Osnabruck looked upon the bitter suffering of the Jews (during the boycott of April 1933) with deep regret, and both were later castigated by the Nazis for sympathizing with Jews.[16]

The Bishop of Münster, von Galen, also criticized Rosenberg's *Myth of the Twentieth Century* in 1934, but he did not openly attack the Nazis for racial persecution.[17] Not until 1943 did he blame German war losses on the atrocities against the Jews.[18] Still, the Gestapo realized that he opposed their policies and kept a close watch on him during the war, possibly because of his nationally known opposition to Nazi "euthanasia."[19] Cardinal Faulhaber defended Jews of the Old Testament, but could not bring himself to speak out for Jews during Hitler's Third Reich; this reticence certainly did not hurt the Nazi cause.[20] In contrast, the Jesuit Alfred Delp, a member of the anti-Nazi Kreisau Circle, excoriated the church for failing to accept its moral responsibility for racial persecution.

Even though Catholic leaders did not offer more than a pittance of support for or aid to Jews unless they were also baptized Catholics, they did consistently oppose the racial ideology of the Nazi regime, in particular Rosenberg's ideas. In part this was an institutional question, because Rosenberg's glorification of race rather than religion undermined the foundations and dogmas of the church itself. In short, Catholic leaders thought they, not Nazi racists, should determine whose soul was saved and who should therefore go to heaven. The persecution of nonconverted Jews never appeared to arouse much serious interest among Catholic leaders; however, when the Nazi party attempted to infringe upon the church's ministrations to its Jewish converts, they did manifest considerable opposition and were able to preserve the right of these individuals to participate in religious services until well into World War II. Also, although Guenther Lewy gives them little credit for saving the lives of Jews who were married to Catholics, they did make some effort in this regard.[21]

One of the most important struggles between the Catholic church and the Nazis, however, derived from Catholic disapproval of Rosenberg's racial ideology. There was considerable anti-Semitism in the church, but it was based upon religious rather than racial standards.[22] Even during the Weimar Republic, several Catholic publications had condemned Rosenberg's theories,[23] and these atttacks continued throughout the Nazi regime.[24] Insofar as the attacks were based upon moral as well as institutional considerations, they offer one of the most propitious examples of courage on the part of Catholic leaders at all levels of the church hierarchy.

Apart from ideological conflicts between the party and the Catholic church, what do we know about opposition among lesser Catholic leaders and their Catholic following? Guenther Lewy's general argument is that very few Catholics opposed racial persecution, and that this was one reason for the reluctance of Catholic leaders to speak out against it. If that had been the case, we would expect to find very few references to opposition to persecution in other sources. Yet quite a few examples of opposition among less prominent Catholic leaders and the Catholic population can be found in just a few relevant sources.[25] For example, in April of 1933 a priest published an article in the *Rheinmainische Volkszeitung* condemning violent illegal attacks on Jews.[26] In the same year another priest was brought to trial for slander against the state because he said that he did not understand the measures against the Jews, that they were also men, and that he would say so in his next sermon. He also said that good Germans should not disturb Jewish property and that there was no special type of

249

Christianity for the separate races, and he attacked Rosenberg's *Myth of the Twentieth Century*.[27] Another priest wrote a flyer in which he said, "What is going on in the church struggle? . . . Salvation comes not from the Aryans, but as Christ said, from the Jews."[28] In 1935 the police seized the Catholic weekly *Ketteler Wacht* because it contained an article entitled "Christianity and Judaism," which contradicted Nazi racial ideology.[29] In 1935 a Catholic priest from Duisburg gave a lecture condemning the anti-Semite Mückermann. The meeting was stormed by Hitler Youths, and the audience sang the *Judenlied* (Song of the Jews) in protest.[30]

A report of the government president in the Government District Aachen in 1935 indicated that strong anti-Semitic propaganda would not be well received there, since a large part of the population disapproved of it, and particularly of *Der Stürmer*. It was suggested that very serious differences with the Catholic church would result if such propaganda were continued.[31] Another of these reports for 1935 read as follows:

> The treatment of the Jewish Question in my district has in any case elicited the greatest indignation, since in their values the Catholic population appraise the Jews first as men and only secondarily judge the matter from a racial-political standpoint.[32]

Still another report quoted and commented upon an ironic sermon as typical of the sense of injustice with which racial persecution was perceived by Catholics:

> Why do many people venerate the Virgin Mary, perhaps because she is not of Aryan descent? When men are dead and buried, it is irrelevant to which race they belonged, and when they come before the divine judges, they will also not be asked: "Are you of Aryan descent or do you belong to another race?"
>
> Comment: Parson Coenen's statement produced general laughter among the congregation.[33]

Attacks on Jewish property were also condemned in this largely Catholic district.[34] Catholic publications tried to undermine Nazi racial ideology by continuing traditional references to marriages between Protestants and Catholics as *Mischehe* in order to mock the Nazi's use of the term for marriages between non-Jews and Jews.[35] The press was therefore forbidden to discuss *Mischehe* except in a racial sense to foil the Catholics. Of course, the continuance of religious intermarriage suggests that Nazi ideas were irrelevant to many Catholics since it was their *own* norms that mattered to them.

In 1936 a parson from Lauterbach made the following statement while instructing Catholic children: "*Das Schwarze Korps* and *Der Stürmer* are hateful newspapers; whoever reads them commits a sin."[36] A member of the Catholic Young Men's Association is reported to have said in March 1938, "Free Jerusalem"; the confidential agent who made the report commented that all good Nazis would agree that the Catholic man belonged in a concentration camp.[37] In 1937 the *Deutschland-Berichte* reported that priests were being attacked for their friendliness to Jews and their hostility to Rosenberg during instructional sessions.[38] Another of the *Deutschland-Berichte* made the following statement in 1937:

> In the Catholic question far-reaching decisions were awaited; instead of this the Führer denied that Jews possessed any intelligence whatsoever, which statement has but strengthened the opinion of the people that he is becoming really megalomanical.[39]

A Catholic chaplain was brought to trial in 1937 because he attacked Nazi ideology regarding "race, blood, and soil" as the worst form of materialism. He also said that Russia had given an order to publish an anti-Semitic book by Ludendorff, which represented the teaching of National Socialism very well, and that this indicated how inferior the Nazis really were.[40] Also in 1937, a report on public opinion stated that Jewish shops did well in Catholic areas because of the church's opposition to persecution.[41]

Several sources indicate that Catholics disapproved of the pogrom of November 1938. For example, a priest in Düsseldorf took in a Jew during *Kristallnacht*. The man had been stabbed, a tendon in his right hand was severed, and he could easily have bled to death.[42] The church remained critical of *Kristallnacht* long after the population had by and large accepted it as a bygone occurrence.[43] Nevertheless, even the Nazis had expected the churches to sponsor a more concerted propaganda campaign against the regime because of *Kristallnacht*; however, they did not do so.[44] Individual Catholics who aided Jews at that time were more courageous than their leaders, who lost a golden opportunity to destroy the ethical credibility of the Nazi regime. *Kristallnacht* was in all likelihood the critical occasion upon which the church could have taken a stance, because a large segment of the public appears to have opposed *Kristallnacht*. Yet the church remained silent.[45]

Even though major Catholic leaders did not speak out vehemently against persecution during World War II, there are some indications that they did disapprove of it. For example, Catholic priests condemned the treatment of Jews during the Polish campaign in 1939.[46] Also, in August 1940, an SD report on German public opinion indicated that anti-Semitic propaganda was not well received in Catholic circles.[47] There was Catholic opposition to introduction of the yellow star and to the attempt to exclude Jews from religious services in 1941.[48] The church opposed compulsory divorce of Catholics and Jews, but Cardinal Bertram insisted that letters to this effect should not be interpreted as "underrepresentation of the harmful Jewish influences upon German cultural and national interests."[49] His opposition to race theory was primarily theological, and he avoided confrontations with the Nazis over the "Jewish question" when this was expedient for the church. The Catholic church did, however, circulate *Hirtenbriefe* that criticized racial ideology, referred to Jesus as the King of the Jews, and called for the blood brotherhood of all men.[50] One of these letters, written by the bishops in the church district around Cologne, cast suspicion on the legality of the Third Reich's treatment of foreign races and claimed that the regime rested solely on power rather than on legality.[51] As further examples, the Archbishop of Cologne was known to hide Jews,[52] and a Catholic prelate spoke out very strongly in favor of equality for all races and attacked their persecution. His sermon was well attended for

252

the time of day and his collection box was unusually full of money.[53] And in 1942 the *Sicherheitsdienst* complained that Catholic leaders were still willing to marry Catholics and baptized Jews.[54]

During World War II there were a number of cases of aid to Jews by Catholics in positions of only modest authority. For example, one parson (*Pfarrer*) paid the medical bills of a Jewish cancer patient in 1941, for which he was then sentenced to two and a half months in prison and fined 2,000 marks.[55] Another attempted to help a Jewess to cross the border, and criminal proceedings were begun against him.[56] Still another parson was arrested in 1942 for saying the following: "I am a minister and in this capacity cannot adopt hostility toward any man, including Poles, Russians, or Jews."[57] In Berlin a parson was arrested in 1943 because he gave 350 marks to a Jew out of the funds of the *Caritashilfe* (the major Catholic charity fund, which secretly aided many Jews) and associated with them in public.[58] A parson was brought before the German People's Court in 1943 because of his remarks in a public shop. He had said that the Allied air forces' "terror" attacks against Cologne were revenge for the legal and illegal persecution of Jews, and referred to a picture of Hitler with the following comment: "This guy is to blame for everything."[59] In Villingen another parson spoke very admiringly of Jews. The report of his activity also said:

> The Roman Catholic Church recognizes nothing of the war against the world-enemies, Judaism and Bolshevism. Certainly she stands at the front and prays for her "believers" for peace, but never for a German victory, and many party members pray with her.[60]

In 1944 a chaplain was arrested and sent to Dachau because he secured lodging for a "submarine" (Jew in hiding) even though he knew what was involved.[61] A Catholic nun in a hospital was condemned to death in 1945 at the age of twenty-seven because she helped Jews in Germany.[62] Behrend-Rosenfeld also recounts that nuns were very helpful to Jews during World War II.[63] Catholic hospitals took in Jews for real and contrived reasons to protect them.[64]

Two Catholic women, Else Heidkamp and Gertrud Luckner, aided Jews through the St. Raphael Society and the *Caritasbund*. In one case they placed a Jewish child in a Catholic home illegally, and during the investigation it was also discovered that Gertrud Luckner had aided many Jews to cross the border into Switzerland. She spent the rest of the war in a concentration camp, while Else Heidkamp was sent to prison, where it is known that she remained until at least August 1943.[65]

These examples of opposition to anti-Semitism are, of course, few in number since they are only selections from a few primary and secondary sources. More primary research on opposition among Catholics will be necessary before we have a clear picture of opposition at lower levels of the church hierarchy and among Catholics in general. Nevertheless, if these examples are at all indicative, it appears that Lewy's assumption that the Catholic population approved of racial persecution should be scrutinized more carefully. In any case, most acts on behalf of Jews seem to have been performed by lesser clergymen and lay church members; the institution itself failed to imitate their heroism.

## PROTESTANTS

Lewy's criticisms of Catholic leaders would apply even more accurately to leaders of some of the Protestant churches. There was no national Protestant church in Germany before 1933, and during the Third Reich the Protestants split into two groups, the "German Christians" who supported Hitler's racial policies, and the "Confessing church" that did not.[66] The chief instigator of this bifurcation was Pastor Martin Niemöller, head of the Berlin-Dahlem congregation. In September 1933 sixteen Nuremberg pastors publicly rejected the application of the "Aryan paragraph" (excluding participation of Jews in religious services) to Protestant churches.[67] Subsequently, Niemöller established a Pastors' Emergency League, and every pastor who joined it had to subscribe to the following pledge:[68] "In making this pledge I testify that the application of the Aryan paragraph within the Church of Christ has violated the confessional stand.''[69] This decision to oppose the "Aryan paragraph" was the first instance of organized opposition to anti-Semitism in the Protestant churches even though, according to Wolf, it was also undertaken to preserve the independence of the Confessing church.[70] After its foundation, nine thousand clergymen joined the Confessing church; in contrast, five thousand joined the anti-Semitic German Christians.[71] Several Evangelical churches set up relief organizations for Jews and opposed the establishment of a Nazi racial research institute whose purpose was to end the Jewish influence on religious life in Germany; however, they did not publicly oppose racial persecution.[72] In 1937 Niemöller was arrested, leaving the Confessing church very weak; hence there was no organization to combat the anti-Semitism of the German Christians.[73]

Although very few Catholic leaders preached against racial persecution, even fewer Protestants did so. Among the most prominent leaders, perhaps it was Dietrich Bonhoeffer of the Confessing church who was most opposed to anti-Semitism (as early as June 1933), but he failed to enlist support from his colleagues.[74] In 1942 he showed peace terms to Dr. George Bell, the bishop of Chichester, in which he proposed the abolition of the Nuremberg Laws.[75] He also helped baptized Jews.[76] The most direct assistance to Jews, however, came from Pastor Heinrich Grüber, who set up a relief agency to assist emigrating Jews. He was arrested in 1937 for defending Jews both in and out of the church.[77] Later, he went with Leo Baeck to Nazi authorities when Jewish agencies failed to negotiate successfully with them, and in 1940 he protested the first large-scale deportation of Jews. This infuriated the Nazis, and he was arrested in December 1940. He was first taken to Sachsenhausen and later to Dachau. All of his teeth were knocked out and his life was jeopardized, but he was finally released in 1943. Most of the personnel in his relief agency were killed in concentration camps, including his part-Jewish successor, Pastor Sylten.[78] Grüber saved over one thousand lives and was able to facilitate the emigration of many more Jews.[79]

Another Evangelical leader, *Landesbischof* Wurm, appears initially to have supported racialist laws, but by *Kristallnacht* he had changed his mind. He publicly protested the pogrom in his sermons and later wrote strong condemnations of persecution to Lammers, Himmler, Goebbels, and others.[80] He also set up the *Landesverband der Inneren Mission* in Stuttgart, and this organization aided many Christianized Jews from 1938 onward.[81] Another Evangelical pastor, Harald Poelchau, was also very helpful to Jews, especially in his capacity as prison chaplain. He was a member of the Kreisau Circle and provided false papers, food, and shelter for Jews, taking great risks to assist them.[82] In addition, Bishop Meiser and Bishop Dibelius fought against attacks on Jews.[83]

Aside from a few Evangelical leaders, however, most of the Protestants who assisted Jews were at lower levels of the church hierarchy or were acting in their private capacities. For example, in 1935 a pastor in Stade pointed out that Jesus said to love one's neighbors. Local Nazis paraded him through the streets carrying the sign, "I am a slave of the Jews." The government president from Stade had to protect the pastor with a revolver and take him to his own house.[84]

At the second and third synods of the Confessing church in October 1934 and March 1935, Rosenberg's paganism was denounced, but no active support for Jews was recommended in these declarations.[85] Also, the Old Prussian Confessing Synod protested against racial ideology, which then led to the temporary imprisonment of five hundred pastors.[86] Numerous protest letters were sent on their behalf and most were released; however, twenty-seven were sent to Sachsenhausen and Dachau.[87] Also, one report indicates that a reformed church periodical carried a long article entitled, "The Jewish Question as a Church Problem." Of 2,500 printed copies, 1,650 were seized because they "endangered public security" by attacking Nazi racial measures. Following this there was a long prohibition of Protestant magazines.[88] In 1936 the confessing church directed a memo to Hitler as follows:

> When within the framework of the National Socialist doctrine an anti-Semitism is imposed on Christians which obliges them to profess Jew-hatred, then we must put before them (the Christians) the commandment: Love thy neighbor.[89]

This protest as well as his activities as head of the Council of the Provincial Administration of the Confessing church cost the life of Dr. Friedrich Weissler, who died in Sachsenhausen.[90]

Several lesser clergymen tried subterfuge to avoid Nazi racial propaganda. For example, one Evangelical clergyman refused to read anything except the advertisements from *Der Stürmer* at compulsory indoctrination sessions.[91] Another attacked *Der Stürmer* in 1935 by saying that it carried on endless Jew-hatred and that anyone who participated in Jew-hate could not be given the sacrament of confirmation by him. He also told the Gestapo that Jews gave us Christ and that therefore Jew-hate was un-Christian. He maintained that the reason the Jews were rich was that they did not drink and were diligent, and that if Christians emulated them they would be better off.[92] Interestingly, the Gestapo decided not to take any measures against him because of the then fiery battle between the state and the churches.[93] Another pastor praised the Jewish apostle Paul as the apostle of prisoners and attacked Rosenberg's ideology. His case was referred to the courts in 1937.[94] In addition, the *Sicherheitsdienst* complained about close ties between German Protestants and Jews and set up observation posts to uncover these connections.[95]

To cite further incidents, a Protestant theology student attacked Rosenberg's *Myth of the Twentieth Century* and was imprisoned for three months in 1938.[96] Another pastor of the Confessing church (with good national connections) aided Jews in Berlin.[97] Still another pastor was severely warned by the Gestapo, but not charged because there were not enough witnesses. He is supposed to have said after *Kristallnacht*: "The treatment of Jews by the population in the past week is a mark of disgrace on our German nation. If we were to go to foreign countries now, we would have to be ashamed and people would point at us with their fingers."[98] Another said: "What are we to do? Love your neighbor! It is utterly irrelevant whether the neighbor belongs to the same race, class, nation. . . ."[99] Evangelical teachers were criticized by the SS after *Kristallnacht* because they refused to discontinue religious instruction in accordance with a request of the National Socialist Teachers' Association, which was directed at ending

257

"reverence" for the "criminal Jewish people"[100] Also, the Confessing church baptized Jews when it was forbidden for them to do so. The SS deplored the close ties between the Confessing church and Jews, complaining that some parsons prayed for them and had established an agency to assist baptized Jews.[101] Some members of the Evangelical churches tried to aid Jews during and after *Kristallnacht*, and the SS described the reaction of the Confessing church as very reserved at that time, implying that it did not approve of *Kristallnacht*.[102] However, there was no public statement issued between 1938 and 1943 by the Confessing church on behalf of Jews.[103] During the war individual Evangelical ministers did pray for Jews and attempted to aid them. For example, one pastor prayed publicly for Jews in 1940.[104] Others helped Jews and were imprisoned for long terms.[105] Some Evangelical clerics in Duisburg patronized Jewish stores when this was a serious offense.[106] Thirty-four ministers of the Confessing church aided one Jewish couple during the war,[107] while an Evangelical parson from Essen hid Jews and gave them food during the war.[108] Another parson hid Jews and helped them to escape from Germany; he was arrested in 1944 and shot in 1945.[109] A pastor's widow hid Jews during the war even though she had supported Hitler ardently in 1933.[110] Three Evangelical clerics from Lübeck were tried before the People's Court and condemned to death in 1943 because they opposed racial persecution.[111] One parson, Helmut Hesse, preached vehemently against the persecution of Jews in 1943; he was arrested and sent to Dachau where he died a few days later. Among other things, he said the following:

> As Christians we can no longer tolerate the silence of the church on the persecution of Jews. What leads us to this conclusion is the simple commandment to love one's neighbor. The Jewish Question is an Evangelical, not a political, question. The church has to resist anti-Semitism in its territories. The church must stand up against the state to testify to the holy historical meaning of Israel and make every attempt to oppose the destruction of Jewry. Every non-Aryan, whether Jew or Christian, has presently fallen victim to murderers in Germany.[112]

258

Early in the war the Confessing church issued leaflets opposing the exclusion of Jews from religious services and later made public protests against persecution of Jews in 1943.[113] The Old Prussian Synod of the Confessing church wrote a pastoral letter to all congregations protesting murder as beyond the authority entrusted to the state by God.[114] These protests, however, had little effect. By and large, the very few protests of the Confessing church against persecution were too weak to be of any practical consequence.

Many other examples of opposition to racial persecution by both Catholic and Protestant churches can be found in relevant sources.[115] However, more research will need to be done in local and regional church archives and many other sources before a complete picture of opposition among German Catholics and Protestants can be obtained. We do know that the most important church leaders did not speak out, partially because of the dangers of doing so, and partially because of their desire to preserve their institutional autonomy. The Nazis were well aware that the churches did not approve of extreme racial persecution, but the churches seldom wielded their moral authority on behalf of Jews. In most cases it was the "little" men in both Catholic and Protestant churches who were courageous enough to criticize racial persecution publicly.

We do have a sample of seventy-nine opponents of racial persecution from the Government District Düsseldorf who can be identified by religious affiliation. Of these, forty-six were Catholic and thirty-three were Protestant. This means that 58.2 percent of all opponents for whom religion was given were Catholics, while 41.8 percent were Protestants. The percentages of Catholics and Protestants in the population of the district were 58.8 and 41.2 respectively, so there was obviously no larger percentage of opponents of either religion.[116] Adherence to one or the other branches of Christianity per se thus did not appear to have been the impetus to oppose anti-Semitism.

If we compare Catholic to Protestant opponents, we note that there were significantly more of the following groups among Catholics than among Protestants: opponents aged 50–59, females,

259

blue-collar workers, small shopkeepers, and, to a moderate extent, high-level opponents.[117] In contrast, among Protestants there were significantly more opponents aged 40–49 and 60 or over, males, upper-level white-collar workers, and low-level opponents. There were no significant differences in place (urban/rural) of residence. It is not clear why one finds the differences in socioeconomic groups. It may have been that there were more of these two groups in the Catholic and Protestant populations of the district, but census data do not give these characteristics for religious groups, so we cannot determine whether or not this was so. The moderately higher percentage of high-level opponents among Catholics may indicate that Catholics in general were somewhat more likely to take serious risks to aid Jews than were Protestants; this conclusion is supported by the general sources on opposition among Catholics and in one OMUGUS survey. We should note, however, that there was a tendency for all church-going Catholics and Protestants to be more anti-Semitic than were those who no longer attended services regularly. Certainly religion, per se, was no antidote to anti-Semitism.[118]

## SUMMARY

The voting record over the last three years of the Weimar Republic shows clearly that Catholic areas gave less support to the Nazis than the national average, while Protestant districts gave more. Most historians attribute this to the role of the Catholic Center party in retaining its electorate. However, the nearly perfect correspondence between religious affiliations of opponents and the general population in the Government District Düsseldorf suggests, at the very least, that Protestant votes for the Nazis during Hitler's rise to power were not necessarily motivated by anti-Semitism, and it also suggests that further research is needed on the relationship between religion and support for Nazism. The basic conclusion one can draw from our statistical analysis here is that religious affiliation was not a decisive factor for opponents of racial persecution. Other motivations were at work, or else

260

religious motivation was so evenly dispersed among both Catholics and Protestants that it had little differential significance.

It is, of course, obvious that the anti-Semitic stance of the German Christian movement reflected considerable prejudice among those particular church leaders. Yet some pastors joined the German Christians in hopes of either "modernizing" their church or reacquiring a mass basis. Some undoubtedly joined out of fear, ignorance, or weakness; not enough is known about their motivations to determine the importance of anti-Semitism to them. Despite the disapproval of anti-Semitism among Confessing church leaders, the Protestant churches as a whole were less helpful to Jews than was the Catholic church. In any case, the concern of both churches was mainly for baptized Jews—an indication that their concern was primarily institutional rather than humanitarian or moral. The failure of German churches to speak out against racial persecution is a disgrace second only to that of the German military, especially since they had a unique platform from which to speak. Because the Nazis feared the propaganda or political power of the churches, it is almost certain that church leaders could have spoken out more vehemently against racial persecution. The most favorable interpretation one can give to their silence is that the risks were considerably higher for them because they had no effective military power to counter the Nazis. Also, the Catholic church was still under suspicion as a minority group in Germany, and public protestations against persecution would have made it much easier for Nazi radicals to brand them as traitors to the German nation. Nevertheless, the Catholic church has survived for approximately two thousand years by protecting its institutional prerogatives even at the expense of Christian morality when and if necessary; therefore its performance on the "Jewish question" is not too surprising.

In contrast, it is somewhat surprising that the Confessing church was as vocal as it was in breaking with the anti-Semites among the German Christians. The Protestant churches had traditionally been bulwarks of support for the state, and their rejection of the "Aryan paragraph" was courageous. Still, the Confessing church was as interested in maintaining its independence as was the Catholic church, so it provided no strong protests against racial persecution on the basis of Christian ethics until these were by and large useless. Thus, for the non-converted Jews in Germany, both German churches may as well have been nonexistent as institutions. It was the ordinary "little" people who helped Jews.

Although most historians would place much responsibility for failure to protest the destruction of the Jews on the churches, John Conway provides a less critical interpretation:

> The problem of how to take up arms against injustice and violence in a totalitarian state remains unresolved. If the religious communities still have, or still claim, a special advantage and a special responsibility in this regard, we cannot forget that the moral force of Christianity (as well as Judaism) is no longer the dominant ethical motivator in contemporary society. Any attempt to make the churches a scapegoat for the moral failure of the Germans, especially for the tragedy of the Holocaust, overestimates the effectiveness of the churches' position then and now.[119]

On the other hand, the church leaders' failure to protest such immorality can hardly have strengthened their position in contemporary society.

CHAPTER NINE

# Pockets of Opposition

". . . there has always got to be somebody to go on first;
nobody will do it alone."
Michael Balfour and Julian Frisby, *Helmuth von Moltke*,
p. 175.

As we saw earlier, there was considerable diversity of opinion
toward Jews not only in the population, but also in the Nazi party
itself, both among Nazi leaders and the early party membership.[1]
Therefore, despite the popular image of all Nazis as rabid anti-
Semites, we are not too surprised to find that a minority of Nazis
did express opposition to racial persecution. Also, there were
pockets of resistance to anti-Semitism among the conservatives,
military, bureaucracy, socialists, and press. In this chapter I shall
discuss these groups to determine how they opposed anti-Semitism.[2]

## NAZIS

One of the most interesting, if numerically limited, studies of
the attitudes of Nazis toward racial persecution was done by Müller-
Claudius in 1938 and 1942. After *Kristallnacht* and during World
War II, he had conversations with Nazi party members from all
occupations to discover their opinions on racial persecution. There
were only forty-one cases for 1938 and sixty-one for 1942, but
they are informative,[3] as shown in table 9.1. Of the Nazis with
whom Müller-Claudius conversed in 1938, a clear majority expressed extreme indignation at the treatment of Jews. By 1942

263

TABLE 9.1 Attitudes of Nazis toward Racial Persecution (*in percentages*)

|  | *1938* | *1942* |
|---|---|---|
| Extreme indignation | 63 | 26 |
| Noncommital or indifferent | 32 | 69 |
| Approval | 5 | 5 |

the percentage expressing disapproval of racial persecution had dropped to 26, but this figure is hard to interpret simply because it was not very healthy for Nazis to verbalize their criticism of Nazi racial policies by 1942. If one were discovered, the penalties could be quite high. Those who were noncommittal or expressed indifference to racial questions rose from 32 to 69 percent in 1942, and this probably also reflects the increased risk of airing one's true opinions. Nevertheless, had these Nazis been extreme anti-Semites, they could quite safely have said so. In both years we find only 5 percent of the Nazi party members expressing approval of racial persecution, which indicates that extreme anti-Semitism was certainly not the norm for all Nazis.

From Merkl's data on the early Nazi party members we saw that 33 percent gave no evidence of prejudice.[4] This was obviously lower than the 63 percent of Müller-Claudius's sample who disapproved of racial persecution after *Kristallnacht*, which may reflect the difference between anti-Semitic abstractions and concrete examples of persecution. Also, although 13 percent of Merkl's sample were paranoid anti-Semites in 1933, both in 1938 and 1942 only 5 percent of Müller-Claudius's sample approved of racial persecution. Of course, one reason for these differences is certainly the large influx of "fellow-travelers," opportunists, and those compelled to join the Nazi party between 1933 and 1942. Nazi party membership was only about 850,000 on January 30, 1933, about 2.5 million in 1935, and about 6 million in 1942.[5] We can safely assume that paranoid anti-Semites were drawn to the party in great measure because of their anti-Semitism, whereas "fellow-travelers" joined for a wide variety of reasons quite apart from anti-Semitism. Nevertheless, as I indicated earlier, if anti-Semitism had been important to them, they certainly would have had no fear of expressing this in the Third Reich to Müller-Claudius.

Even before *Kristallnacht* there were indications that Nazi racial policies were not totally accepted by party members. The violence against Jews that preceded the introduction of the Nuremberg Laws was opposed by many party members.[6] Some Nazis rejected the Nuremberg Laws themselves as the wrong solution to the "Jewish question."[7] *Rassenschande* among party members could often bring severe penalties since the party courts were determined to use the NSDAP as a model of racial purity for German society as a whole.[8] Still, *Rassenschande* by party members continued in prewar and even war years.[9] Among sixty-five Nazi opponents of anti-Semitism in the Government District Düsseldorf, 18.5 percent were *Rassenschänder*.

Penalties for *Rassenschande* were severe if cases were tried in either party or nonparty courts. Of the twelve Nazi *Rassenschänder* in the Government District Düsseldorf, six were sent to prison. Other sentences for *Rassenschande* across the country were also fairly high, averaging four and a half years in prison for four Nazis in various parts of Germany, the highest sentence being eight years.[10] Another Nazi was put to death for *Rassenschande*.[11] Normally, unless one were an "old fighter" who joined the party early, expulsion from the party and imprisonment followed *Rassenschande*.[12] The exact sentences for large numbers of Nazi *Rassenschänder* require future research; however, if the above cases are indicative, penalties were fairly severe.

Personal (nonsexual) relations between Nazis and Jews were also maintained despite party disapproval.[13] Sentences for socializing with Jews could likewise be fairly steep. For example, an SS *Stürmann* (U.S. Private First Class) was expelled from the SS and sentenced to six months in prison for drinking schnapps with Jews.[14] Another SS member danced with Jewesses and was sentenced to seven months in prison in 1941.[15] An SS *Oberscharführer* (U.S. Technical Sergeant) was given one year in prison for his friendly relations with Jews.[16] A cell leader of a party office was removed from his post because he attended a Jewish wedding in 1935.[17] A party member in Koblenz lost his membership for three years because he talked to a Jew for "no reason."[18] An SS member was expelled from both the SS and the Nazi party because he accepted cake and coffee from a Jew in 1939.[19] In other cases Nazis were strongly warned and put under surveillance if they had had social relations with Jews.[20] A number of Nazis not only socialized with Jews, but undertook considerable risks to aid them.[21]

A very common type of opposition to racial persecution was the maintenance of business contacts and commercial relations with Jews. Many Nazis were purged from the party for these activities.[22] Many others who maintained business contacts or bought from Jews retained their party membership but were warned and put under surveillance.[23] Of course, many of these Nazis may have bought from Jews simply because they offered better services and not because they wanted to help Jews, but in any case, they did not accept Nazi regulations against these activities.

Actually, Müller-Claudius's findings for 1938 are more illuminating than those from 1942 because *Kristallnacht* offered the first example of the wholesale destruction of Jewish lives and property that was later to become so commonplace. We saw earlier that widespread disapproval of *Kristallnacht* was found in the general population, and it was apparently also found within the Nazi party, as a number of sources indicate. Several *Gauleiter* and deputy *Gauleiter* (heads of Nazi party districts) refused to obey orders to destroy Jewish property and issued counterorders to prevent this destruction.[24] In some areas of Germany there were insufficient volunteers for attacks on Jewish property and many SA and Hitler Youth leaders expressed disgust with the entire operation.[25] Many SS and SA leaders openly refused to obey orders during the pogrom.[26] According to the *Deutschland-Berichte*, even Nazis said, "What shall we do if such things are tolerated? Is there no legal security left?"[27] Disapproval of the pogrom led many Nazis to put away their party badges and to declare that they had nothing in common with these affairs, and that what was going on was not worthy of a true Germany.[28] Indeed, many Nazis aided Jews in escaping from the SA, SS, and Hitler Youth during *Kristallnacht*.[29]

In general, the *Deutschland-Berichte* and Müller-Claudius's findings are corroborative in indicating that opposition to racial persecution was strong among Nazis after *Kristallnacht*.[30] This evidence should not be taken to imply that Jewish lives and property were lost through "spontaneous combustion" of buildings or a "spontaneous uprising" of the population. Even though many Nazis, perhaps even a majority (according to Müller-Claudius), opposed *Kristallnacht*, this obviously did not prevent the lesser number of rabid anti-Semites or morally indifferent thugs in the Nazi party from carrying out the pogrom. Also, Müller-Claudius points out that some party members were thoroughly anti-Semitic in an abstract sense, but that they spent a great amount of time and trouble to help Jews who were known to them personally.[31] And some simply put *Kristallnacht* out of their minds by reciting Nazi racial propaganda to themselves.[32] The overall impression, however, is that many Nazis did not wholeheartedly support the pogrom.

During World War II many rabid anti-Semites approved of exclusionary measures against the Jews, but would not go further; they were still opposed to annihilation.[33] Disapproval of extermination was found even in the SS. As a former prisoner in Auschwitz said:

> I know hardly a single SS man who could not say that he had saved someone's life. There were few sadists. No more than five or ten percent were criminals by nature. The others were perfectly normal men, fully alive to good and evil. They all knew what was going on.[34]

Of course, direct aid to Jews was difficult because Nazi party members were under closer surveillance than the population at large. No systematic study has been made of Nazi aiders of Jews during World War II, but the following miscellaneous examples of Nazis and the SS came to light. Kersten, Himmler's masseur, was instrumental in saving Finland's Jews.[35] A Nazi party member was sentenced to death for declaring that no one believed in victory and that "By murdering a million Jews, we have taken a heavy burden on our shoulders."[36] An SS functionary aided Jews to

267

cross the border and was given two years in prison in 1942.[37] An SS quartermaster-sergeant warned Jews of their impending arrest and was sentenced to a year at forced labor.[38] Another SS quartermaster-sergeant advised Jews on how to hide and warned them about their danger; he was expelled from the SS and sentenced to one year in a forced-labor prison.[39] A Nazi shopowner employed Jews in lieu of non-Jews and had nothing but praise for them. He was expelled from the party in 1936.[40] An SS man had an affair with a Jewess for several months and was sentenced to two years and three months in a forced-labor prison.[41] An SS sergeant propositioned a Jewess while he was drunk and was sentenced to six months in prison plus expulsion from the SS.[42] A member of the German Labor Front saved Jews by employing them in special offices in 1940.[43] A Nazi block leader allowed a crippled Jewish tailor to hide in his attic for many months.[44] The head of the Nuremberg police sabotaged the use of Jews in forced labor and prevented the incarceration of Jews from mixed marriages in Theresienstadt.[45] An SS lieutenant, Gerstein, had joined the SS to learn about persecution of Jews and tried to end extermination by interceding with papal representatives.[46] The *Landeshauptmann* of the Rhine Province asked the Ministry of the Interior to save a Jewish acquaintance, but was turned down by Himmler.[47]

One Nazi in particular attempted to aid Jews in Minsk. This was Wilhelm Kube, who had formerly been a writer in Berlin. Between 1920 and 1923 he was a general secretary in the DNVP, and from 1924 to 1928 he was a Nazi delegate in the Reichstag. He subsequently became *Gauleiter* for the Kurmark, but he was removed from his post in 1936.[48] Although he was an early anti-Semite, he appears to have modified his stance in later years. Kube sent an anonymous letter to Bormann's father-in-law, ex-Major Buch, accusing his wife of being half Jewish. He was angry at Buch because he objected to the fact that Kube kept a mistress. His anonymous letter states:

> You are mainly charged with having condemned hundreds of people for the same tragic fate that has befallen your wife. What conclusions do you draw, you wise and unbiased judge! We are happy that you may count yourself one of us.
>
> Signed: Some Berlin Jews[49]

Kube probably lost some of his sense of humor however, because he was interned in a concentration camp until 1940, when his release was secured by Himmler.[50] How he subsequently became general commissar for White Ruthenia is not clear.

Nevertheless, while he was in this position he was a constant menace to Nazi authorities because he interceded for Jews and refused to implement their "special handling" (i.e., extermination). In 1941 he wrote another letter (this time signing his own name) to the German commissar for the *Ostland* in Riga, in which he protested liquidation of Jewish ex-front fighters and part-Jews.[51] Again, in 1943 he ran into difficulties with the SS because he objected to extermination of Jews and demanded a written order for this brutality. He said this procedure was unworthy of Germans and of the Germany of Kant. He also claimed that these policies destroyed Germany's reputation throughout the world and that he had ordered his men not to take part in the executions. He called executioners "pigs" in an interview with the SS commander in Minsk. He was reprimanded by Heydrich in sharp language, but he managed to save seventy Jews from being transported to other areas that had more genocidally cooperative commanders. Also, he harassed local SS leaders within earshot of prisoners, called them "pigs" to their faces, and distributed candy to Jewish children. Kube was in charge of five thousand Jewish prisoners and was able to obtain false passes for a large number of them. He bemoaned the persecution and murder of Jews and defended their contributions to music and the arts. It was finally recommended that he be relieved of his post. In September 1943 he was killed by a bomb planted by his maid, a partisan agent.[52]

We can glean more information about the Nazi opponents of racial persecution from Gestapo files for the Government District Düsseldorf. With respect to the chronological development of opposition, we know that most arrests occurred in the prewar years.[53] Of the sixty-five Nazi opponents in the Düsseldorf sample, 80 percent were arrested in prewar years. The smaller wartime figure is not surprising given the harshness with which Nazis would have been treated for aiding Jews during the war. Nazi opponents were more likely to receive stiffer sentences than non-Nazi opponents, so one can anticipate a lower percentage of Nazi opponents during the war years. There was no significant difference in the percentage of Nazi and non-Nazi opponents during 1938–1939. This is consistent with Müller-Claudius's findings, which indicated widespread opposition by Nazis to racial persecution after *Kristallnacht*. A significantly larger percentage of Nazi opponents were active in 1935–1937, as compared to non-Nazi opponents. This was only true of *Judenfreunde*, so it was not due merely to the introduction of the Nuremberg Laws. Rather, it was probably due to the attempt of the party to purge unreliable Nazis once the party had initially organized its policing apparatus; hence, aiding Jews was more closely watched.

We saw earlier that 18.5 percent of all the Nazi opponents in the Düsseldorf district were *Rassenschänder*, which means that the remaining 81.5 percent either aided Jews or were critics of persecution. In contrast, 42.6 percent of the non-Nazi opponents were *Rassenschänder* and 57.4 percent were *Judenfreunde*.[54] This was probably because Nazis could not arrange meetings with Jews as easily as non-Nazis without drawing attention to themselves. Also, Nazis were more likely to be caught for *Rassenschande* than were non-Nazis, since even those opposed to the regime would denounce them more frequently. In other words, they might let the Nazis stew in a pot of their own making.

The socioeconomic characteristics of Nazi opponents of racial persecution were quite similar to those of the total sample of opponents discussed in chapter 7. For example, when we compare Nazi opponents to the general population of the Government District Düsseldorf, we find that the following groups were overrepresented among Nazi opponents: males, independents (especially small businessmen), white-collar workers (particularly upper-level white-collar workers), and opponents aged 50–59 at the time of their opposition.[55] Correspondingly, the underrepresented groups were females, blue-collar workers, and opponents aged under 30. In sum, the same socioeconomic groups that were overrepresented among non-Nazi opponents were even more strongly overrepresented among Nazis.

Given this, we are interested in knowing how Nazi opponents differed from Merkl's early Nazi anti-Semites.[56] When we compare the two groups we find that the percentages of males and females were not significantly different. Also, the ages of early Nazi anti-Semites and Nazi opponents of racial persecution were not significantly different. There was only a slightly lower percentage of Nazi opponents aged under thirty. This tends to confirm our earlier hypothesis that coming to political maturity between roughly 1880 and 1914 may have resulted in both support for and opposition to anti-Semitism.[57]

Comparing occupations of early Nazi anti-Semites and later Nazi opponents, we find that independents and white-collar workers comprised higher percentages among opponents than among early Nazi anti-Semites, whereas blue-collar workers represented a lower percentage. Independents and white-collar workers were clearly the occupational groups most likely to oppose anti-Semitism among both non-Nazi and Nazi opponents. These groups were also overrepresented compared to the percentage of independents and white-collar workers in the Nazi party in 1935 and for the years 1933–1945, while blue-collar workers were underrepresented.[58]

After making all of these comparisons of Nazi opponents to other groups, we can conclude that the strongest Nazi opponents were males, older individuals, independents, and white-collar workers. Because independents and white-collar workers had higher percentages among Nazi opponents than in any other group, we shall now look at some types of opposition in these occupational groups, and cite examples for others as well.

Opposition among Nazis who aided Jews or criticized persecution was similar to that among non-Nazis, as the following examples demonstrate. Two middle-aged (in their forties) Protestant lawyers who employed Jews in Düsseldorf were purged from the NSDAP for this activity.[59] Another lawyer, a 35-year-old Catholic from Essen, lost his party membership in 1937 because he opposed Nazi racial ideology.[60] Still another lawyer, a 55-year-old resident of Essen, was dropped from party membership because he defended a Jewess in 1936.[61] A 54-year-old small businessman, a Catholic from Düsseldorf, also lost his party membership because he rented to Jews and hid Jews during *Kristall-*

*nacht.*[62] A 39-year-old small businessman in Essen was a member of the SS and had an affair with the non-Jewish wife of a Jew; he too was kicked out of the party and was prohibited from later marrying the German woman because she was "tainted" by having been married to a Jew.[63] Another independent shopkeeper, a 34-year old Catholic from Essen, was given strong warnings against further purchases from Jews.[64] A 60-year-old small businessman in Essen was kicked out of the party and indicted by the public prosecutor's office because he and his wife hid Jews in 1938 and sold securities to them.[65] A 59-year-old shopkeeper from Essen had extensive business relations with Jews, rented to Jews, warned Jews of deportations, and offered to hide Jews during World War II; he was imprisoned for three months.[66] Another shopkeeper, a 53-year-old Catholic from Essen, gave potatoes and vegetables to Jews during the war; for this she was imprisoned for two weeks.[67]

A 53-year-old Catholic civil servant from Düsseldorf refused to participate in expropriation of Jewish property before deportation of Jews. He cooperated only after strong remonstrances from his superior, but appears to have retained his party membership.[68] A 65-year-old criminal court counsel from Duisburg was fired from his job and thrown out of the party in 1939. He had refused to consider mere Jewishness justification for legal persecution and ruled in favor of Jews a number of times. Only the fact that he had ten children saved him from further retribution.[69] Another civil servant, a 44-year-old director of police and passport controls in Wupperthal, had an affair with a Jewess and issued false passes to Jews. For this he was imprisoned from 1939 to 1944 and was finally sent to Sachsenhausen.[70] Dr. Paul Karrenbrock, a 47-year-old director of the *Institut für Ständewesen*, was expelled from the NSDAP in 1935 because he disputed Rosenberg's racial theories. He had distributed eight hundred copies of an article contesting these theories, which were confiscated by the Gestapo. His expulsion from the party was upheld by the *Gau* court.[71]

There were several kinds of opposition among upper-level white-collar Nazi workers. One 38-year-old Protestant white-collar worker from Essen was purged from the SA and NSDAP in 1936 because he socialized with Jews.[72] Another, a 42-year-old white-collar worker from Essen, was also expelled from the party for socializing with Jews in 1937. He was also given nine months in prison in 1943 for making a critical remark about the Nazi regime.[73] A 25-year-old SA brigade leader from Hagen lost his party membership because he bought from Jews while in uniform.[74] Still another SA man, a 36-year-old electrician from Essen, was expelled from the party because his wife had sexual relations with a Jew, a man with whom he himself was on friendly terms.[75] Yet another upper-level white-collar worker, a 49-year-old from Düsseldorf, applied for party membership even though it was known that he had hidden a Jew and offered to refurbish paintings owned by Jews. His application was naturally denied.[76]

A blue-collar worker, a 36-year-old Catholic from Leverkusen, was expelled from the party for criticizing the persecution of Jews during *Kristallnacht*.[77] A 58-year-old blue-collar worker from Duisburg, a member of the SD (*Sicherheitsdienst*), was given one week in prison for buying from Jews while in uniform during 1942. No further action was taken because he was declared to be mentally incompetent after announcing to a trainful of Germans that Hitler should be hanged for starting the war![78] A 23-year-old blue-collar worker from Anrath was purged from the NSDAP for having sexual relations with a Jewess and was imprisoned for two years.[79] Another blue-collar worker, a 27-year-old from Schweinfurt, was imprisoned for a year for *Rassenschande*.[80] Still another worker was given a forced-labor prison sentence of two years for *Rassenschande*.[81] These cases demonstrate the Nazis' desire to prevent all contacts between Jews and the Nazi party members, and that measures taken against Nazis were often capricious.

## OTHER OPPONENTS

Now that we have some inkling of the pockets of opposition among the Nazis, we shall examine certain identifiable political-military and other groups who appear to have given support to Jews or opposed racial persecution. Actually, they were similar

TABLE 9.2 161 Opponents of Hitler Who Were Murdered or Committed Suicide after the Attempted Coup d'Etat, July 20, 1944 (*in percentages*)

| | |
|---|---|
| Officers | 48.4 |
| Diplomats | 7.5 |
| High-level civil servants | 14.3 |
| Independents and leading white-collar workers | 11.8 |
| Politicians | 3.7 |
| Trade unionists | 6.8 |
| Clerics | 3.1 |
| Scholars | 4.3 |

SOURCE: Wolfgang Zapf, *Wandlungen der deutschen Elite*, 162.

in many respects to those Germans who were murdered or committed suicide across the country after the assassination attempt on Hitler in July 1944. The percentage breakdown of these groups is presented in table 9.2.[82]

Most of the groups listed in the table were represented in the Kreisau Circle that was headed by Count Helmut von Moltke, the great-grandnephew of General Helmut von Moltke (who had been instrumental in the conquests that resulted in the unification of Germany in 1870).[83] Moltke's estate was the meeting place for many opponents of persecution. Among the conservatives-military we find Adam von Trott zu Solz, Carl Dietrich von Trotha, Hans von Dohnanyi, Claus Schenk von Stauffenberg, and several young officers. Among religious opponents were Eugen Gerstenmaier, Harald Poelchau, Alfred Delp, and a few others. Among socialists were Julius Leber, Carlo Mierendorff, and Theo Haubach. A prominent left-wing intellectual was Adolf Reichwein. There were others in the Kreisau Circle, but these were some of the leading members.

Apparently Moltke himself set the tone for the Kreisau Circle's discussions of racial persecution. He was a determined opponent of racial persecution, as demonstrated by the following comments on the collection of Jews for deportation in Berlin during October 1941:

The authorities want to spare us the sight of how they are left to perish in hunger and cold, so arrange this in Litzmannstadt and Smolensk. A friend of Kieps saw a Jew collapse in the street; when she wanted to help him, a policeman intervened, prevented her, and kicked the body as it lay on the ground so that it rolled in the gutter. Then he turned to the lady with a last vestige of shame and said "Those are our orders." How can one know things like this and yet walk about a free man? What right has one to do so? Isn't it inevitable that, if one does, one will one day find oneself in that position and be rolled into the gutter? This is all summer lightening, for the storm has yet to come.[84]

What war breeds is cowardice, cant and mass psychosis. To give you an example, yesterday I was at a meeting of the Foreign Office about the Jewish persecutions. It was the first time that I had been involved with this question officially. I attacked an ordinance and for the time being held it up after it already had the approval of all ministers and of the Chief of the OKW (High Command of the German Armed Forces). And then I came back and the responsible official in the OKW asked me, "Why have you done that? You can't change anything about it now; naturally all these measures lead to catastrophe." I am not insensitive to the charms and qualities of people like that but their actions are determined by expediency and have no moral basis.[85]

Later, in November, Moltke had the following to say:

A difficult day. In the fight against the latest Jewish order (probably an order about the handling of Jews who came into German hands in Russia), I have at any rate achieved getting the three most important generals in the OKW to write to the fourth (Reinecke) to say he must withdraw forthwith the approval which he gave on behalf of the Chief of the OKW. The next stage is therefore to see whether he does this. The real battle will then begin. Wouldn't this be a wonderful issue on which to be thrown out of this outfit (sacked from the German Military Intelligence Service)?[86]

275

> Meanwhile I've actually succeeded in putting a few obstructive spokes in the wheel of the Jewish persecution. My self-assumed representation of the rights of the *Wehrmacht* has been backed by Canaris (head of German Intelligence) and Thomas (head of the Munitions Division of the OKW). I dictated letters for each of them to sign and both were obviously pleased just as in general a number of people are willing to make a stand as soon as anyone else does. But there has always got to be somebody to go on first; nobody will do it alone.[87]

Moltke not only intervened officially to save Jews, he also acted personally by helping them to get to London. His various kinds of aid eventually got him into trouble with the Nazi Legal Association (*Juristenbund*).[88] Discussion of persecution and aid to Jews was common also among other members of the Kreisau Circle.[89]

Carl Goerdeler, a former mayor of Leipzig, was an early and determined opponent of racial persecution. He resigned from his office in 1936 when a statue of the Jewish composer Mendelssohn was removed from public view by Nazi authorities, and even as early as 1933 Goerdeler protected Jews from plundering SA men.[90] Goerdeler was, of course, active in all types of opposition to the Nazi regime, but he was particularly opposed to anti-Semitism. Goerdeler assisted Beck (chief of the Army General Staff until 1938 and later leader of the opposition to Hitler) in drawing up a declaration that was to be broadcast as soon as the *coup d'état* succeeded in 1944. By this declaration they would have prohibited persecution of Jews and promised to punish those who had gotten rich at their expense.[91] The chief of the Central Division of the German Intelligence Service, Colonel Hans Oster, also aided Jews.[92]

Among diplomats, von Hassell, the German ambassador to Rome, State Secretary Weizsäcker, and Albrecht Graf von Bernstorff were all opponents of persecution.[93] For example, Count Ciano, Mussolini's brother-in-law, made the following entry concerning von Hassell in his diary on October 30, 1937:

> Hassell is really hostile to Fascism and an enemy of the Rome-Berlin Axis. He goes about telling a story that Streicher,

when passing through Rome, visited a German school and showered praises on a girl whom he picked out as the most intelligent and best-looking. She was the only Jewish girl in the school.[94]

One of the high-level civil servants who attempted to halt the economic measures against Jews was Schacht, Hitler's economic "wizard," who was not an anti-Semite either in public or in private.[95] He attempted to have a special edition of the *Westdeutscher Beobachter* (which attacked Jews) seized in 1935.[96] He also sent a letter to Hitler requesting clarification of the legal rights of Jews, but it was never properly answered.[97] He particularly emphasized the crippling effect of anti-Semitic measures on Germany's economy.[98] Schacht's resignation speeded up the process of "Aryanization" because he had previously opposed these measures.[99]

Among the major leaders of the assassination attempt against Hitler and of opposition in general were General Ludwig Beck and Count von Stauffenberg, chief of staff to General Fromm, commander-in-chief of the Reserve Army; both thoroughly disapproved of anti-Semitism. Beck and his colleagues opposed racial persecution as early as 1938, and Stauffenberg (who placed the bomb in Hitler's bunker in July 1944) also maintained that his initial negative reaction to Hitler resulted from *Kristallnacht*.[100]

Even though many prominent leaders of the resistance to Hitler during war years were officers, secondary sources indicate both support for and opposition to anti-Semitism in the Germany army. We saw earlier that von Moltke had difficulty persuading certain members of the *Wehrmacht* to protect Jews.[101] Army leaders had always been somewhat anti-Semitic because they considered acceptance of Jews contradictory to pure German nationalism. We are not surprised to learn, therefore, that the army supported boycotts of Jewish businesses in 1933 and 1935.[102] Also, the *Deutschland-Berichte* contain evidence that anti-Semitism was present in military circles.[103] To be certain, it is known that ten generals voiced their opposition to *Kristallnacht* to Brauchitsch, commander-in-chief of the army.[104] Still, Messerschmidt, Streit,

Krausnick, and Wilhelm are unanimous in their well-documented opinion that the *Wehrmacht* contained wild-eyed proponents of gigantic wars of racial hatred, and that officers who failed to oppose anti-Semitism regarded their genocidal instructions as a bureaucratic matter.[105] As early as March 1941, the army command was notified of Himmler's "special assignments," but they did not seriously attempt to prevent them.[106] To the contrary, they cooperated very closely with the SS. General Field Marshall von Küchler demanded that his officers and soldiers abstain from all criticism of the treatment of Jews.[107] Although some officers opposed shooting Jews in the German occupied territories in December 1941, others approved of it.[108]

That high-ranking generals such as Field Marshal von Manstein and von Reichenau accepted Nazi racial ideology is indisputable. For example, von Manstein declared that "The Jewish-bolshevik system must be exterminated once and for all," and von Reichenau spoke of German soldiers in the East as "carriers of an inexorable *völkisch* idea and as avengers of all bestialities to which the Germans and racial brothers had been subjected."[109] Streit and Krausnick are particularly critical of army cooperation. In their opinion, many high-ranking officers, but also their immediate subordinates and common soldiers, were so ideologically in accord with Nazi racial theories that they became morally desensitized, and in the case of soldiers, brutalized.[110] The leaders of the army clearly attempted to make the requests of the political leadership (which mainly meant Hitler and Himmler, although Streit does not say so) more palatable to their subordinates and troops.

Streit also attributes the increased radicalization of the army to bureaucratic rivalries between the Armed Forces High Command (OKW) and the Army General Staff (OKH) to demonstrate loyalty and initiative. The OKW and OKH tried to outdo each other in anticipating harsher measures, and "careerism" took over.[111] Even the conservative officers who hoped to keep in step and later get rid of national socialism in Germany were dragged along in this process.[112] And with the ascendancy of the SS and the appointment of genuinely national socialist officers, by 1942 the army was totally subject to the dictates of others.

Streit believes that the army's toleration of the first shootings of Russians and Jews in the summer of 1941 meant that the army had compromised itself to the point of no return. He thinks that Hitler decided in July 1941 to exterminate Jews because the army first acquiesced to and later cooperated with the SS. Since the army did not seriously oppose SS atrocities either on jurisdictional grounds (army rights versus those of the SS) or because of army traditions, Hitler could extend extermination beyond Russia.[113] Thus Hitler's actualization of his ethnic theory had become an imminent and practical option for all of Europe.

Close cooperation between the German army and the SS existed in Russia, where the army was extremely concerned about partisans and guerrilla warfare, in which Jews were ostensibly quite active. In some cases the army even encouraged the SS to undertake "cleansing actions" against Jews as partisans or potential guerrillas. In the bureaucratic contest between the SS and the army in Poland, the army attempted to protect civilians, presumably including Jews, although this was not stated clearly in the army's proclamation to the Poles: "The *Wehrmacht* does not regard the civil population as enemies. All provisions of international law will be respected."[114] The SS, of course, simply overrode such assurances and killed both Poles and Jews indiscriminately. That the army was of two minds about atrocities in Poland, even occasionally refusing to cooperate with the SS, was later admitted by Heydrich:

> . . . directives governing police activity were exceptionally far-reaching—for instance, the liquidation of numerous Polish leading circles running into thousands of persons was ordered; such an order could not be divulged to the general run of military headquarters, still less to members of the staffs; to the uninitiated, therefore, the action of the police and SS appeared arbitrary, brutal and unauthorised.[115]

In Poland several high-ranking army officers did attempt to protect Jews, using the argument that Jewish workers were needed in the

279

armaments industry; however, they were countermanded by Field Marshal Keitel, who ordered that Jews be replaced by Polish workers in September 1942.[116] When General Gienanth, commander-in-chief of the Polish Army District, protested this decision, Himmler stormed:

> "I have ordered that ruthless steps be taken against all those who think that they can use the interests of war industry to cloak their real intention to protect the Jews and their own business affairs." The intimidated Keitel hardly waited for Himmler's reaction but, via his staff, cracked down on the rebels in Poland. General von Gienanth was relieved at once.[117]

Other reports attest to considerable antipathy toward the exterminations among many officers and in the army as a whole.[118] Höhne states that the SS faced serious problems in recruiting personnel for service in the East, so that it was necessary to enlist voluntary foreign "assistants."[119] A notable opponent was the commander-in-chief of the East, Colonel-General Johannes Blaskowitz, who compiled reports of SS crimes in Poland. His summary memorandum was on Hitler's desk by the 19th of November 1939. Hitler spurned both Blaskowitz's "childish ideas" and Blaskowitz himself and suggested that it was high time to relieve him of his appointment. Blaskowitz's "childish ideas" had entailed great concern about illegal shootings, arrests, and confiscations, and a request for a return to the rule of law.[120] He was not dismissed, however, and continued to compile reports on indiscriminate public shootings and atrocities against Jews. General Ulex, commander-in-chief of the Frontier Section South, wrote a report to Blaskowitz on February 2, 1940, stating:

> The recent increase in the use of violence by the police shows an almost incredible lack of human and moral qualities; the word "brutish" is almost justified. The only solution I can see to this revolting situation which sullies the honour of the entire German people, is that all police formations together with all their senior Commanders . . . should be dismissed in a body and the units disbanded.[121]

In summarizing this and other reports, Blaskowitz said: "The attitude of the troops to the SS and Police alternates between abhorrence and hatred. Every soldier feels disgusted and repelled by these crimes committed in Poland by nationals of the Reich and representatives of our State."[122] Blaskowitz's complaints drew support from other army officers; however, he was finally foiled by the governor general of Poland, Hans Frank, who demanded his dismissal. Three months later Blaskowitz was transferred to the Western front; otherwise, he, like Gienanth, would almost certainly have been dismissed from the German army.

Lieutenant Colonel Groscurth also vehemently opposed anti-Semitic measures in Poland early in the war. In particular he protested the killing of Jewish children; his objections were overruled, and his continued protests were to no avail.[123] The army had so emasculated itself that it could not prevent the extermination of approximately three million Polish Jews and three million Polish non-Jews. In countries such as France, and Belgium the army was not wholly cooperative in carrying out orders, so the Jews fared somewhat better;[124] yet in the Balkans the army was an outright complicitor in the execution of both Jewish and non-Jewish "partisans."[125]

In Russia, when an army chaplain witnessed the execution by the SS of hundreds of Jewish men, women, and children, he noted the revulsion of German soldiers who turned away from this scene of mass murder. He reported what he had seen to a general, who was shocked. However, when the chaplain demanded that the general intercede, he replied:

> What do you propose that I should do? You have too great an estimate of my authority: Don't you think what you have told me has caused me grave concern? But what shall I do? I cannot give orders to the SS squads, which are not under my command, to suspend their criminal acts. I cannot wage a private war against commands which originate at the highest source.[126]

The theologian who published the chaplain's diary concluded that attempts by the chaplain or the general "to prevent the SS execution squads from carrying out their order could have only re-sulted in martyrdom for the general and the chaplain.''[127]

Without denigrating the sympathy and aid for Jews that were rendered by leading members of the conservative-military resistance to Hitler, one must still affirm that the majority of the German military leaders bear a great responsibility for the murder of Jews (and others) in Europe. They were the only group that could feasibly have deposed Hitler or refused to tolerate genocide, simply because they were the only genuine counterweight to the armed power of the SS.[128] Although one would expect church leaders, for example, to have spoken out against racial persecution, it is understandable that they were not more vocal because they were unarmed and quite literally could not defend themselves. The military officers, however, possessed arms, were in positions of great authority, commanded troops who would follow their orders, and had ample organizational structures through which to plot a successful *coup d'état.*

Although all soldiers swore a personal oath to Hitler declaring their loyalty, it is highly doubtful that he could have revealed his orders for handing Jews over to the SS to these soldiers without the cooperation of leading army officers. And given the natural rivalry between members of the SS and the *Wehrmacht,* army officers might have successfully ordered their men *not* to turn their prisoners over to the SS. This decision would have required a large-scale conspiracy, very adeptly and secretly organized, because the Gestapo's job was to be watchful for signs of opposition. However, how watchful was the Gestapo? If the many officers who were involved in the conspiracy against Hitler in 1944 were able to maintain contacts with each other and with many different centers of resistance, it appears that it was relatively easy for men in authority to escape detection, at least *before* the attempted coup. The lack of large-scale opposition in the army probably had more to do with anti-Semitism than with the difficulty of organizing a conspiracy. When some officers, in conjunction with some church leaders and socialist trade union leaders, finally decided to act resolutely, they came very close to assassinating Hitler. With a little more luck and an earlier decision to act, they might have saved millions of lives, not only Jewish, but also German, Polish, Russian, and a great number of others.

The *Wehrmacht* could have refused to turn over prisoners, basing this refusal on institutional prerogatives, which they cited on many other occasions. Even the threat of widespread conflict between the *Wehrmacht* and the SS in wartime might have resulted in some moderation of Hitler's nihilistic rampage in occupied territories, especially after the defeat at Stalingrad. On the other hand, Hitler would have punished any widespread army refusal to follow his orders to hand over Jews to the SS as treason; all participants would most likely have been shot and reprisals would have been taken against their families. Hitler did not want experienced and knowledgeable generals if their loyalty were in any way questionable; instead he wanted generals who would follow his dictates in technical operations, while he planned the major campaigns. Thus he could have replaced the experienced army generals with loyal junior officers, whose cooperation would have been insured by the example of their predecessors' executions. Even without any rebellion on the Jewish issue, most of Hitler's senior officers met their downfall because he was dissatisfied with them. These included every commander-in-chief in the army, eleven of eighteen field marshals, twenty-one of thirty-seven colonel-generals, and others.[129] It stretches one's imagination to think that Hitler would have tolerated large numbers of generals who interfered in any serious way with his racial policies, whether these entailed deportation, shootings, concentration camps, labor camps, or death camps.

Given the ease with which the generals could have been replaced, a halt to extermination would have also required a massive refusal of soldiers to obey Hitler's orders while their "defecting" generals were still at their posts. The U.S. army rewrote certain passages of its training manual in the closing days of the war when mass shootings and other German atrocities were coming to light, presumably to place the moral blame for these atrocities more easily and squarely on the shoulders of German soldiers. However, this last-minue "revision" does not change the fact that until then both American and German soldiers were supposed to obey all orders of their superiors. The oath of personal loyalty to Hitler taken by German soldiers, as well as army regulations that demanded unconditional obedience, would have sufficed to prevent the average soldier from joining in any massive disobedience to his country's leader in wartime. And even if this had happened, which is almost inconceivable, the SS, which comprised a private army loyal to Hitler alone, would have undertaken brutal reprisals that almost certainly would have ended the ''revolt.''

None of this discussion obviates the fact that some officers approved of extermination or that others were more interested in their careers and bureaucratic feuds with the SS than with the welfare of the Jews (or other victims). It does, however, indicate that had all leading army officers been well disposed toward protecting Jews, sympathy alone would have been insufficient to effect this goal. Even massive resignations would have achieved little, as Hitler would have simply replaced his officer corps. As it was, most generals kept silent, protected their careers, and did nothing that would jeopardize their own or their families' safety.

At levels of authority lower than the German military, we know that the bureaucracy was also very heavily involved in the machinery that made Jewish exclusion from public life and deportation possible. The civil service had traditionally been a center of anti-Semitism, partially because the low-level aristocrats who manned these posts were very jealous of their traditional prerogatives and regarded Jews as newcomers who threatened their private preserve. According to Mommsen, there was not much serious opposition to excluding Jews from the civil service in the early 1930s. The bulk of the civil service were also very instrumental in the effective functioning of the Nazi state, even though the Nazis considered them reactionaries who were constantly impeding their directives.[130]

According to Christopher Browning, bureaucrats

> . . . wished to discriminate, not exterminate, but once in motion the bureaucratic machine escaped their control, driven onward by the lower-echelon Jewish experts and Party infil-

284

trators. The old guard, hopelessly compromised by its earlier complicity, stood by passively.[131]

Why they participated in the destruction is complicated and speculative. For many, such as Eichmann and others in the SS or Nazi party, Foreign Office, and Ministry of the Interior, the primary motive may have been career advancement. In the Ministry of the Interior, for example, increasingly tough regulations were proposed as soon as it was suspected that the leaders were entertaining harsher measures.[132] Much of the escalation appears to have resulted from professional rivalry between state, Nazi party, and SS offices for increased responsibility and power. In chapter 4 I stated that Hitler determined the broad outlines of Jewish policy; however, his bureaucrats in all agencies were quick to discover and sometimes to anticipate his next move. In short, radical approaches to Jewish affairs offered "career advancement." This was true even for many who were either indifferent toward or sympathetic to Jews. Browning summarizes their actions as follows:

> Though the state secretaries created the ministerial Jewish desks, the Jewish experts increasingly received their guidance and inspiration from another source. As events outran the naïve hopes of the disillusioned old guard, it became increasingly passive and ineffectual. Leadership in the bureaucracy passed to Party infiltrators, dynamic and ambitious men who had fought their way into influential positions. Although committed Party men, they nevertheless sought to preserve their own power by defending their ministries against Party encroachment. This was best done by insuring that the ministries stayed abreast of political developments and fully participated in what they perceived to be the essential programs of the Third Reich, which inevitably included the Final Solution.[133]

There were, however, some civil servants who were anti-Nazi. We find that German bureaucrats were well represented among opponents who took part in the plot against Hitler in 1944. Their numbers comprised the second-highest percentage of opponents

285

who died during and after the July 20, 1944, plot to assassinate Hitler, and although this was only 14.3 percent, it was not negligible.[134] But once again, the majority of the bureaucracy went along with the measures against the Jews, and in the degree to which they had real power to oppose Nazi intentions, their guilt for genocide is clear. Their circumstances, however, were somewhat different from those of military officers, since any rebellion on their part would have lacked the force of arms. Because of this, most of their opposition took the form of footdragging and individual acts, which they attempted to conceal from their colleagues and police authorities. This was true of Bernhard Lösener at the Ministry of the Interior, Wilhelm Melchers at the Foreign Office, and Walter Funk, the economics minister.[135]

Some judges, as well, were opposed to racial persecution. For example, Schorn cites a number of cases in which judges reversed attempts to apply economic pressure on Jews or in which judges simply refused to consider such cases in the courts.[136] And in seventy cases of *Rassenschande* the German Supreme Court (*Reichsgericht*) overturned judgments of the more tolerant State Courts (*Landesgerichte*) because it considered their sentences too lenient.[137] In some cases judges simply refused to change their very lenient verdicts in cases of *Rassenschande*, and again these had to be reviewed by higher courts.[138] And the *Schwarze Korps* (the SS publication) objected bitterly because the State Court in Leipzig lifted an arrest order against the heads of a Jewish firm.[139] Furthermore, according to the *Deutschland-Berichte*, only 10 percent of the German judges took the "German greeting" (introduced by the Nazis) seriously. Also, some judges disliked taking cases of *Rassenschande* and even apologized to the defendant's lawyer for having to do so.[140] In many cases judges simply ruled that being Jewish was no grounds in itself for legal prosecution for political unreliability.[141] An occasional judge appealed to higher authorities on behalf of Jews.[142] Apparently, a fair number of judges were married to Jewesses, and naturally the Nazis drove them from their professions.[143] Even in 1941 and 1942 some judges continued to protect Jewish legal rights. For example, a Nazi agency fined sixty-five hundred Berlin Jews for having registered for a special coffee ration from which Jews were excluded. Of these, five hundred refused to pay the fine and requested a court decision. The judge in one case handed down a seventeen-page decision that there was no legal basis for imposing such a fine. His decision was referred up through channels, whereupon Freisler, state secretary of the Ministry of Justice, reprimanded the judge, transferred him to another office, and withheld his pending promotion. His case was then submitted to the Nazi party court.[144] Further, in November 1942 a district party leader in Allgau wanted to intern half-Jews (*Mischlinge*) in a ghetto and requested an authoritative statement from the *Oberlandesgericht* on its permissibility. Without it, he claimed, judges would give vague opinions as to whether the Jews were protected by rental decrees.[145] There were many other complaints against the laxity of judges toward Jews (and Poles).[146] Since the judges were under great pressure to comply with Nazi regulations on the ''Jewish question,'' these examples indicate a considerable amount of courage on their part.[147]

Civil servants other than judges also tried to help Jews.[148] Some of them continued to associate with Jews on a personal basis, and of course, many of these individuals consequently lost their jobs.[149] Ilse Staff presents a number of interesting cases of lawyers who were disbarred and lost their employment for such activities.[150] Some officials, however, were more successful. For example, in 1933 an official in the Foreign Office, Stieve, was able temporarily to prevent the introduction of the ''Aryan paragraph'' (which excluded Jews from Christian religious participation) into the by-laws of the German Christians, the pro-Nazi Protestant church.[151]

We saw earlier that one of the reasons for the introduction of the Nuremberg Laws was that they allowed the party rather than state officials to decide who was Jewish and how Jews should be treated. We also saw the antipathy with which party officials regarded civil servants.[152] Therefore, it is not surprising that the *Deutschland-Berichte* indicated a continuing battle between older civil servants and the newer Nazi civil servants. The traditional civil servants apparently dragged their feet in implementing directives unless they were given direct orders.[153] This was thought

287

to be especially dangerous among railway officials, so they were thoroughly "coordinated" (replaced by reliable Nazis) to insure their smooth functioning.[154] Of course, this was later an absolute necessity in order to transport Jews to death camps during World War II. Heydrich complained that many other civil servants opposed the deportations in 1941.[155] Some ministries were relatively more difficult to take over, for example the Ministry of the Interior, the War Ministry, and the Ministry of Labor, but the attack on civil servants continued throughout the Third Reich.[156]

Even the police occasionally aided Jews. For example, in Eichstatt the police refused to arrest ten Jewish families who were attacked by the local Nazi party.[157] The police in Freiburg prevented boycotts against a prominent Jewish business during 1935.[158] One police official insisted on sending his sick child to a Jewish doctor and was threatened with dismissal. The authorities told him he could only send his child to that doctor if the doctor received no payment, to which he agreed. One hopes that he paid the Jewish doctor under the table.[159] The president of the police in Breslau was instrumental in demanding the seizure of an issue of *Der Stürmer*, Streicher's anti-Semitic publication, which charged Jews with ritual murder.[160] The Berlin Criminal Police apparently kept many Jews alive by concealing their whereabouts from the Gestapo during World War II, which indicates that passive resistance was possible even for officials in fairly touchy political positions.[161]

Other groups that were active in the conspiracies against Hitler were socialists and trade unionists. Therefore, we would expect the secondary works on socialist opponents to contain numerous examples of socialists who aided Jews and of an underground network that smuggled them out of Germany or provided food, clothing, documents, and so forth. Surprisingly, in a survey of tens of books on the socialist resistance to Hitler, very few references were made specifically to opposition to racial persecution.

We do know that some workers aided Jews in the Government District Düsseldorf and elsewhere, and there are reports from Berlin of workers' sympathy for Jews. Workers shouted words of encouragement to Jews, and working-class women vehemently protested deportations in 1943.[162] The exiled leaders of the Social Democratic party were sympathetic to Jews, as indicated by their coverage of racial persecution in *Deutschland-Berichte*. However, one conference report of the SD concluded that Nazi propaganda had created some understanding among former Marxists, even formerly leading functionaries, "who did not defend the Jews and recognized that national socialist domestic and foreign policy had solved the social problem which the German social democrats had vainly sought to correct for years."[163]

However, the more general works on socialist resistance by and large ignore this important aspect of opposition to the Nazi regime. In fact, *Widerstand* (opposition) has come so much to mean membership in left-wing underground groups that Hochmuth and Meyer point out the number of Jews who were active in the socialist opposition and do not even mention the number of socialists who tried to help Jews![164] Also, Pätzold does not mention one KPD (Communist party) member who helped Jews, but he says the KPD clearly opposed anti-Semitism because it opposed the Nazi regime.[165] Likewise, Mohrmann says the KPD opposed anti-Semitism but cites only a miniscule number of cases to justify this conclusion.[166] Clearly, this is a topic that deserves more primary research.

Kahn does cite two interesting examples of opposition to racial persecution by the Communist pary in 1938. One flyer of November 15, 1938 (right after *Kristallnacht*), calls for solidarity of all Germans to oppose such measures.[167] Another says: "Down with the abominable pogrom against the Jews, which dishonors Germany. If the Jews in Germany are subjugated, then the entire German nation will not be free."[168] Also after *Kristallnacht*, the KPD published an issue of the *Red Flag* (*Rote Fahne*) in which they appealed for the strongest solidarity against the persecution of the Jews as part of their general opposition to the Nazi regime.[169]

One group of opponents, the members of the press, was not specifically active in the conspiracies against Hitler; but it was constantly trying to minimize the effects of anti-Semitism among party radicals. From the press directives of the Propaganda Ministry we find that many editors attempted to avoid publishing racial propaganda.[170] Before the press was "coordinated" (lost most of its freedom) many newspapers dared to oppose the boycott of April 1933.[171] But by the end of 1933, when most press freedom had been lost, only passive resistance was possible. The Propaganda Minister was already complaining in the middle of December 1933 that many editors had a total lack of sensitivity to the "Jewish question." He bemoaned the fact that some reports of Jewish criminality, which were in dispatches circulated by the German News Service, were so altered that one could not even discern the fact that the criminal was Jewish. He requested that the Jewishness of criminals be indicated in the future,[172] but the same complaint was still being made in December 1935.[173]

In January 1935 the press magazine *Deutsche Presse* emphasized the fact that not enough was being written on racial propaganda and recommended that the press turn questions over to Dr. Gross of the Nazi Racial-Political Office.[174] This same refrain was repeated a few weeks later along with the comment that journalists should think of the racial pollution that would occur in one thousand years if they did not act to prevent it at once.[175] The press directive for August 2, 1935, indicated that the *Kölnische Zeitung* had been severely warned because the editors had ignored an instruction not to publish information about the preparation of the Nuremberg Laws.[176]

In June 1936 the Propaganda Ministry complained that some newspapers were publishing information on the murder of Jews by Palestinian Arabs when it was forbidden to do so.[177] Apparently some editors also published articles in which it was suggested that Wagner's musical works should not be performed henceforth because so many Jewish conductors had played them. The Propaganda Ministry labeled these suggestions "destructive of Germany."[178] Also, some periodicals were discussing which famous German historical figures had been married to Jews, and naturally, strong measures were being taken against these publications.[179] In no case did the Propaganda Ministry wish the close historical ties of Germans and Jews to receive journalistic attention.

In November 1936 the *Berliner Tageblatt* praised a young man who engaged in a quarrel with Streicher. The Propaganda Ministry thereupon called the editors "spiritual Jews" who did not realize that times had changed.[180] Also in November 1936, the press published stories of Polish students attacking Jews under the title, "Persecution of Jews in Wilna." This occasioned Goebbels to send instructions to state press offices in which he demanded that such offenses against the most simple fundamentals of National Socialism be met with the expulsion from their profession of those responsible.[181] The ministry also objected to the attention that German publishers gave to Rudi Ball, a Jewish ice-hockey player, and suggested that his prominent coverage be stopped.[182] In 1937 the ministry noted that despite a recent warning, a weekly magazine had renewed business with a Jewish agency abroad. This was naturally frowned upon.[183]

After *Kristallnacht* the Propaganda Ministry complained that the regulation that prohibited publication of news about damage to Jewish property had been broken by two newspapers, including Berlin's *Morgenpost*, which had a large circulation. The ministry said that it was uncomradely for these two papers to dish out this sensationalist news. Future obedience to press regulations was requested.[184] Later in November 1938, the ministry complained about the "overdrawn" picture of persecuted Jews that had crept into German publications.[185] It also bemoaned the fact that many newspapers reported neutrally about Jewish issues when they had been instructed to use anti-Jewish commentary.[186]

Again in January 1940, the press directives denounced publishers who had not learned how to stress anti-Semitic themes, and claimed that only by the closest attention on the part of editors could Jewish-capitalist propaganda achieve the desired long-term effect.[187] This particular admonition had to be repeated throughout the war.[188] During the later war years, when the press was constantly forced to publish denunciations of Jews, a special report of the SD complained that this was merely defamation, but did not constitute true enlightenment on the "Jewish question," and that the press and radio were very lax in this regard.[189] In 1943 the Propaganda Director in the *Gau* Hessen-Nassau said that the lack of propaganda on Jews in wartime must be corrected, and that one could not speak of war without speaking of Jews, even if the German "Jewish problem" had been solved (by deportation and extermination, although he did not say so).[190] Hagemann also cites a number of press directives during later years that indicate that the press was very reticent about publishing anti-Semitic propaganda and did so under compulsion.[191]

## SUMMARY

The diversity of opinion regarding Jews, which was present among Nazi party leaders and the rank and file before Hitler's rise to power, continued to exist during the Third Reich. Müller-Claudius's sample of Nazis in 1938 and 1942 demonstrated that some Nazis were willing to express a fair amount of opposition to racial persecution despite the risks of doing so, particularly during World War II. When we compared his results to those for Merkl's early anti-Semites, we saw a decrease in the percentage of paranoid anti-Semites in the Nazi party after 1933. Of course, the party more accurately reflected the composition of the German population in later years than it did before 1933.

Even before *Kristallnacht* there were a few indications of overt opposition to racial persecution. The Nuremberg Laws received some criticism, and *Rassenschande* continued in prewar and even war years. Personal relations between Nazis and Jews also continued, and some Nazis took considerable risks to aid Jews despite penalties for such activities. Many Nazis maintained business contacts with Jews, patronized their stores, and were expelled from the party for these activities.

We found indications other than those in Müller-Claudius's study that many Nazis opposed the pogrom of *Kristallnacht* and attempted to aid Jews. This was the first example of extreme and widespread physical brutality against Jews, and it was rejected even by confirmed Nazis. Our sources for war years were limited, but they also indicated that some Nazis aided Jews despite increased risks during these years.

When we examined Nazi opponents from the Government District Düsseldorf, we saw that a larger percentage of Nazis were

*Judenfreunde* than were *Rassenschänder*, and this was particularly evident when we compared them to non-Nazi opponents. Also, there were proportionately fewer Nazis among opponents during war years than was the case for non-Nazi opponents. The percentages of Nazi and non-Nazi opponents were very similar in 1938–1939, but Nazis had a higher percentage of opponents apprehended in 1935–1937 than did non-Nazis. This may have been due to the purge of "unreliables" from the party during these years—in other words, the *identification* of opponents.

The socioeconomic characteristics of Nazi and non-Nazi opponents differed in the same ways from the socioeconomic profile of the population in the Government District Düsseldorf. The socioeconomic groups that were overrepresented among Nazis (compared to the general population and labor force) were males, independents (particularly small businessmen), white-collar workers (especially upper-level white-collar workers), and opponents aged 50–59 at the time of their opposition.

The ages of early Nazi anti-Semites and Nazi opponents were very similar. Also, Nazi opponents were somewhat older than the NSDAP at the time of their opposition. These comparisons support the hypothesis that the years before World War I bred both anti-Semitism and opposition to it. There was a higher percentage of independents and white-collar workers among Nazi opponents than among Nazi anti-Semites or in the NSDAP in 1935, which indicates that these occupational groups were the most active Nazi opponents of anti-Semitism.

From these various comparisons, I concluded that the most active Nazi opponents of racial persecution were males, older Nazis, independents, and white-collar workers. Different occupational groups engaged in different types of opposition, which was also true of non-Nazis, as we saw in chapter 7. There was considerable diversity in the Nazis' attitudes toward Jews, and only a small percentage appear to have been paranoid anti-Semites of Hitler's ilk. Even though a minority were fanatics, many were either indifferent to racial questions or disagreed with persecution. Many criticized racial persecution verbally, continued personal contacts with Jews in a variety of ways, or aided Jews despite

293

fairly severe penalties. Yet the extensiveness of Nazi opposition to anti-Semitism is hard to measure from these sources, and future research will be necessary to determine how pervasive this opposition actually was. In any case, it certainly did not prevent the minority of fanatical Nazi anti-Semites from murdering millions of Jews.

Aside from small pockets of opposition among Nazi party members, other groups disapproved of anti-Semitism. Among these were members of the Kreisau Circle, some of whom participated in the assassination attempt against Hitler in 1944. They were led by Count von Moltke, whose adamant opposition to racial persecution appears to have set the tone for the group as a whole. Other sympathizers were Goerdeler, Beck, Oster, Schacht, Stauffenberg, and a few diplomats.

Although some of the opponents of racial persecution were military officers, and even though there was some disaffection with racial persecution in the army, in Russia, Poland, and the Balkans, the army acted as a complicitor by either accepting or sometimes even requesting the liquidation of Jewish (and other) "partisans" and "guerrillas." Some top army officers adopted Hitler's racism wholesale and others went along in order to demonstrate their loyalty to the Führer and to advance their personal careers. Although any large-scale opposition to Hitler's plans to exterminate Jews would probably have failed and merely resulted in a purge of the top army officers, this possibility was apparently not even entertained. After its initial cooperation in the executions of Russian Jews and others, the army was too weak relative to the SS to change its position on the "Jewish question." Those officers who did protest the shootings as barbaric acts were ineffective because of the racial views and ambitions of their superiors.

Opponents of persecution were also found among the German bureaucracy, although civil servants did, in general, cooperate grudgingly with Hitler and made his reign of terror possible. Some judges appear to have ameliorated a number of injustices against Jews, and this was also true of several lawyers, quite a few of whom continued to treat Jews equitably within the Government

District Düsseldorf as well as in other parts of Germany. The police were also occasionally helpful to Jews, as were miscellaneous other civil servants.

The role of socialists as opponents of racial persecution is yet to be explored. Since secondary works seldom refer to the "Jewish question" but rather concentrate on other types of resistance by socialists, additional primary research needs to be done to light up this shadowy area. We do know that the socialists in exile were sympathetic to the plight of Jews in Germany, and we also saw that some prominent socialists were in the Kreisau Circle, a group of opponents of persecution. The paucity of information on aid by workers, however, may reflect a tolerance of Nazi anti-Semitic propaganda.

Members of the press had a running battle of passive resistance against the Propaganda Ministry's press directives. Where possible they tried to soften them by changing the context, and in many cases they simply violated the directives. It would be interesting to know how many journalists and editors lost their jobs and were subjected to further retribution for these deliberate expressions of disapproval of anti-Semitism.

From this discussion of opponents of anti-Semitic persecution it is clear that we are dealing with a small minority of Germans. Because of the danger to themselves and their families, only a few people were willing to take the considerable risks involved in aiding Jews. Their fears were very real and should not be dismissed lightly. On the other hand, as von Moltke pointed out, many individuals found the courage to join in attempts to thwart persecution of Jews once someone else initiated action. Years of living in a police state and the atomization which that entailed probably prevented a large number of Germans from perceiving just how strongly other individuals shared their own disapproval of racial oppression.

# Conclusions and Implications

"The ultimate fact staring all of us in the face is that starting with nothing except personal determination, Hitler could mobilize enough of the elements of modern civilization subsumed under the headings religion, law, and science to create a human inferno, a hell on earth."
George Kren and Leon Rappoport, *The Holocaust and the Crisis of Human Behavior*, p. 143.

## CONCLUSIONS

Because fairly complete summaries of conclusions are available at the end of each chapter, I shall review here only the major findings of this study and their implications.

Jews represented only a small percentage of the German population in the period 1870–1933, but they were highly visible because of their concentration in large cities, in specific occupations (particularly trade, commerce, free professions, and cultural fields), in higher income brackets, and in political parties of the Middle and later the Left. This exposure made their numbers seem much greater than they were. Both German and immigrating Eastern European Jews attempted to reduce their specific differences from the population by abandoning their customs and even their religion, and through intermarriage. By 1933 Jews in Germany had achieved levels of integration that were indeed impressive, considering that large percentages of them were first-generation immigrants or recent migrants to new cities. Nevertheless, continuing objective differences between Jews and non-Jews made it easy to stereotype Jews as aliens who did not fit into German

296

society. This was standard propaganda for anti-Semites between 1870 and 1945.

Many historians think that intellectual and social anti-Semitism increased during these years in response to the rise of the *"völkisch"* ideology, Social Darwinism, "social conservatism," nationalism, and imperialism. Still, some political parties were at least initially sympathetic to Jews and attempted to insure their fair treatment. Before 1928, parties whose major appeal was anti-Semitism were clearly an electoral failure; no major or minor rights of Jews were rescinded before Hitler came to power, despite the adoption of anti-Semitism around 1930 by some parties that had previously been neutral or sympathetic to Jews. Anti-Semitism does not appear to have been significant as an electoral issue for non-Nazi parties that advocated it sporadically before Hitler's election in 1933.

The Weimar years were marked by extreme and sudden outbreaks of anti-Semitism in Germany, primarily because Jews were blamed for Germany's defeat in World War I, the fall of the monarchy, the attempted socialist revolution, and the establishment of the Weimar Republic. Yet there was a considerable diversity of attitudes toward Jews even among the leaders of the Nazi party, as was also shown in Merkl's study of early Nazi party members. About one-eighth of Merkl's sample were paranoid anti-Semites who threatened obscure countermeasures against Jews, although they did not appear to have envisioned the expulsion of Jews from Germany, much less genocide or extermination. About 40 percent were moderate anti-Semites, including 28 percent whose hatred of Jews heightened suddenly during the "Jewish" revolution of around 1918–1919. Approximately 14 percent demonstrated only mild verbal anti-Semitism or spouted party clichés, while one-third demonstrated no evidence at all of anti-Semitic prejudice. Thus approximately one-half of the sample were indifferent to racial issues or were mild anti-Semites. Most of the remainder were moderate anti-Semites, many of whom were highly critical of the role of Jews during the immediate postwar years. This evidence of diversity is quite astounding since the early party members included the hard core of Germany's anti-

297

Semites. The Nazi party clearly appealed to many sentiments other than hatred of Jews. Certain groups, however, were more likely to be anti-Semites than were others: Germans aged forty-nine and over, urban residents, white-collar workers, military-civil servants, sons of military-civil servants, individuals with secondary education, and to some extent females, Protestants, business-professionals, and university graduates.

According to some social scientists, Nazi voters shared many of these characteristics, that is, they also included high percentages of Protestants, white-collar workers, business-professionals, and military-civil servants. Those who shifted from parties of the Middle to voting Nazi were probably also older than those who voted for other parties. Protestants and members of some middle-class occupations were also more likely to be paranoid anti-Semites in the early Nazi party than were other groups. We inferred from this that at least a minority of Protestants and members of the middle class were paranoid anti-Semites who may have voted for the Nazi party primarily because of its anti-Semitism. This supports the widely held theory that the German middle classes were more anti-Semitic than others. There was, however, considerable diversity of attitudes toward Jews among the middle classes, so that they cannot be stereotyped as universally anti-Semitic. Also, recent electoral studies by Childers, and more particularly by Hamilton have seriously questioned the lower-middle class base of Nazi electoral support. We speculated that most of the middle classes who supported Hitler did so for reasons other than anti-Semitism—for example, because they feared communism, because other political parties had previously failed to represent their disparate political and economic interests, and because they lacked a viable alternative to the Nazis.

Since extreme anti-Semitic propaganda often alienated potential voters, Hitler tempered his rhetoric after around 1925 and instead associated Jews with everything that the Nazis themselves disliked or that they assumed the population resented; however, he never outlined his concrete plans for the future treatment of Jews. Since Nazis associated Jews with every conceivable "evil" (internationalism, socialism, communism, parliamentary democracy,

298

Germany's defeat in World War I, the Weimar system, finance capitalism, "interest bondage," reparations, the depression, etc.), the adjective "Jewish" served to focus resentment of these "evils" on a common enemy. This kept the appeal of anti-Semitism at a fairly abstract level of resentment and hostility, which undoubtedly relieved some of the tensions brought on by the depression and attendant political crises and helped to cement the heterogeneous elements within the Nazi party. Nevertheless, Nazi anti-Semitism per se does not appear to have been a major campaign issue except for a minority of voters.

Hitler developed an ethnic theory encompassing all of human history, which he defined as the struggle between nations for living space and world domination. He believed that Jews comprised a nation, albeit one spread out among other nations, and that they participated in the fight for world domination, but not for living space. In his ethnic theory all "subhumans" (including Poles and Russians) must be conquered and their leaders exterminated to prove the historical superiority of "Aryans." All Jews ("nonhuman parasites") must be exterminated because they occupied living space in the East and posed a racial "threat" to other nations, which Hitler thought they were attempting to overthrow from within. He actualized his ethnic theory in World War II when conquered "Aryan" nations were given special privileges, the leadership of "subhuman" nations was murdered, and most European Jews were exterminated.

His attitudes toward Jews also influenced domestic events in Germany before the war. All institutions and political parties that were "tainted" by "Jewish influence" were taken over and those that were suspected of opposing his racial and expansionist goals were purged.

Hitler's psychology was dominated by his misperceptions of the "Jewish threat" and his belief that Jews and all "Jewish inventions" must be "resisted" at all costs. His paranoia was clearly reflected in his ethnic theory, which accounts for his demonic destruction of millions of Jews. His murder of millions of non-Jews, however, did not result so much from paranoia as from his belief that "subhumans" who had been conquered in the past

299

did not deserve anything better than enslavement and selective extermination.

Between 1933 and 1939 Hitler adopted a piecemeal policy to exclude Jews gradually from the political, economic, institutional, educational, social, and religious life of Germany. During the war he exterminated about 130,000 Jews who had remained in Germany and 30,000 who had emigrated to other parts of Europe, along with over five million other European Jews. It is argued here that despite Hitler's consideration of the effects of domestic and foreign opinion, including the attitudes of rabid anti-Semites within the Nazi party, he himself decided upon the timing of persecution and the extermination of Jews and others, because this was a logical consequence of his ethnic theory.

Hitler utilized anti-Semitism for several political purposes: to insure party unity by giving the party a role in racial policies, to dampen party criticism of his failure to implement the socio-economic aspects of his program, to establish a new racial ideology, to terrorize the population and thus to atomize them socially, to divert Germans from his failure to effect a genuine social revolution, to weaken the power of "reactionaries" in the state bureaucracy, to justify expansion and war against other states that were allegedly dominated by Jews, and, finally, during the war, to include the SS, army, and bureaucracy as complicitors who would have to fight to the bitter end to prevent reprisals.

Anti-Semitic propaganda served many of the same functions, but its most important role was to create a consensus on anti-Semitism by spreading Nazi ideology and blacking out all facts or information about deportation and extermination, as well as other types of persecution, that would have led to questioning of that world view. As it became obvious that this attempt was only partly successful, tighter proscription of news and increased terror became necessary to ferret out real and potential opponents. This was most dramatically demonstrated after *Kristallnacht*, the burning of the synagogues and the general pogrom of November 1938, which was by and large a failure because ordinary Germans now widely questioned the morality and legality of the regime.

There were, of course, shifts in public attitudes toward the Nazi

300

persecution of Jews, and these are reflected in general reports on public opinion. Certain types of measures, particularly legal or pseudo-legal exclusion of Jews from positions of prominence, authority, or economic power, appear to have been fairly well received, although some Germans attempted to aid individual Jews who were friends or neighbors. Before *Kristallnacht* even the Nuremberg Laws were acceptable to many, probably a majority, of Germans. However, the physical violence and brutality of *Kristallnacht* were clearly rejected by the same majority. Apparently anti-Semites and determined opponents of anti-Semitism were polarized around an indifferent or apathetic majority, yet one that was increasingly sympathetic to Jews during and after *Kristallnacht*. Public opinion reports indicate that widespread rumors of shootings in Poland and Russia were badly received by the public, which sometimes even attributed Germany's war losses to Hitler's rumored slaughter of Jews.

There are many possible reasons why so few Germans publicly protested these wholesale murders. Knowledge or even rumors of gassings, which were deliberately kept secret, were extremely rare outside of eastern Germany, so we have little information on German attitudes toward the death camps. Even though shootings of Russians, Poles, and Jews were widely rumored, their extensiveness was not grasped. Moreover, the rumors were apparently discounted as too fantastic to be believed; even if they had been believed, there was little that an individual or small groups of like-minded Germans could have done to halt the destruction. Only the churches and the army might have been able to interfere, and it is very doubtful that their intervention would have resulted in anything more than arrests and executions of protestors and their families. Thus an individual could act on his own, but he could not rely on higher institutions for additional support.

Opposition to racial persecution was fraught with considerable risks to one's own livelihood and freedom, and the most surprising result of this study in some ways is the number of ordinary Germans who actually did something for Jews in the face of Hitler's police state. I have avoided mentioning this factor at critical points in this study lest it imply an apology for Germans as a whole,

301

whereas I have cited only around three thousand cases of Germans—out of a population of around sixty million—who aided Jews or who were arrested for violating Nazi laws regarding Jews. At the beginning of this study I cautioned against any unwarranted generalizations from the behavior of a minority of Germans, and this caution will not be ignored here. Similarly, the findings here can by no means be construed as showing the total extent of aid to Jews. I should point out, however, that any decision to violate Nazi racial regulations, whether premeditated or impulsive, placed a stigma upon oneself and one's family. Arrest or loss of Nazi party membership, for example, frequently meant loss of one's job, retaliation against one's spouse or children, and social exclusion (often compulsory).

The individual took a very considerable risk in Nazi Germany for even the most elementary acts of human kindness toward Jews. Two years of imprisonment in a country like America is not comparable to a two-year term in one of the Nazi prisons or concentration camps, where calculated brutality often led either to death or permanent physical or psychological disability. Furthermore, it was entirely within the power of the Gestapo to remand individuals to concentration camps after coercing judges to impose harsh sentences, or arbitrarily after their completion of a prison term. In looking at aggregate numbers, one must remember that they refer to people living in a terrorist society in which any person who violated the Nazi rules could find himself and his family completely at the mercy of men whose power over the individual was rarely tempered by either conventional morality or legal restrictions. Finally, we should remember that the risks of being caught or punished rose steadily in the Third Reich, a feature of the progressive radicalization of the regime of which the general population was well aware. Only with all of this in mind do the terms *Judenfreunde* (friends of Jews) or *Rassenschänder* (race defilers) acquire full significance. Few Germans were willing to act because the risks were substantial and the probability of success was dim. As Kren and Rappoport point out, resistance is rarely encountered among large numbers of people because it threatens their own survival.[1] Only a few men are heroes, and it is utopian to hope that the average human being will risk his security, much less his life for others, especially in wartime, when bombings and shortages of food and shelter drain psychological reserves of good will.

In chapter 7 we saw how opponents of persecution differed from the general population and labor force. In the Government District Düsseldorf, which comprised over half of the Rhineland, the socioeconomic groups that were the strongest opponents of racial persecution were males, white-collar workers (especially at upper levels), and among *Judenfreunde*, independents. Least active opponents were females and blue-collar workers. *Judenfreunde* were disproportionately older (aged 40 and over, particularly 50–59), whereas *Rassenschänder* were predictably younger (mostly under 30 or between 30 and 39).

These results diverge from current interpretations of anti-Semitism in Germany. First, females were not great aiders of Jews, and this is consistent with Merkl's data, which indicated that females were slightly more likely than males to be anti-Semites in the early Nazi party. This could have been due simply to greater political passivity among women, but the accumulated and corroborative evidence indicates that females were indeed more anti-Semitic than were males.

Second, the high percentage of older individuals among opponents of racial persecution is corroborated by Ansbacher's data and data from the surveys by the American occupational forces after the war. This has considerable ramifications. It may be that intellectual and social anti-Semitism gained ground in the years before 1914, as indicated by the large percentages of older Nazis in Merkl's sample of early anti-Semites. But a competing sentiment was also developing, one which was much more favorable toward Jews and which probably led to disproportionate aid for them in later years by this same generation.

Third, the extremely high percentages of white-collar workers and independents among opponents of racial persecution indicates that even if a minority of the middle classes voted for Hitler or joined the party primarily because of anti-Semitism, another minority of the middle classes also opposed persecution. Any image of the middle classes as a universally hate-filled group who supported the Nazis in order to persecute Jews is mistaken. Also, although blue-collar workers were active in general opposition to the Nazi regime, on the whole they were unlikely to aid Jews, and it is important that scholars take these findings into account.

Aside from these socioeconomic groups, there were minorities of religious Germans, Nazis, conservatives, military officers, civil servants, socialists, and the press who sympathized with and aided Jews. The sources cited indicate that opposition to anti-Semitism was very limited within these groups; however, they do illustrate the diverse types of Germans who were willing to take risks on behalf of Jews. Of these groups, though, the church leaders, Nazis, military leaders, and civil servants who either adopted Hitler's delusions and goals or cooperated in the destruction of European Jewry shared in an ineradicable guilt that far overshadowed the occasional assistance to Jews by their colleagues.

In examining records of Germans who aided Jews it is seldom possible to determine their precise motivations, but a number of values appear to have been at play: patriotism, respect for law, order, and private property, conservatism, religious belief, socialism, and humanitarianism. Although some anti-Semites considered Jews to be totally alien foreigners who had never belonged in Germany in the first place and who had betrayed the country during World War I, some patriots, including Hindenburg, recognized that Jews had contributed to World War I both as leaders of great importance, such as Rathenau, and as front fighters. Moreover, many German Jews were well assimilated into German economic, political, social, and intellectual life; others had even converted and were religiously integrated. Significant numbers of Polish, Russian, and other Eastern European Jews had come to Germany, and they were not as well regarded either by Germans or German Jews. It is conceivable that those Germans who accepted German Jews would nevertheless have favored restrictions on immigration by Eastern European Jews, yet this does not mean that they wanted to expel all Jews from Germany.

Another aspect of patriotism that may have played a role in opposition to Nazi racial policies was the significant contribution of

Jews to German intellectual life. Not only had they brought honor to Germany by winning a large number of Nobel prizes, they were also very active in all scientific and cultural fields. Even Goebbels was slow to sever his ties with Jewish artists and performers who were considered first-rate in Germany. Jewish cosmopolitanism (which anti-Semites castigated as internationalism) also extended to their contacts with foreigners, primarily through trade, commerce, and banking. Germans who were not confirmed bigots could easily recognize the importance of Jewish entrepreneurship and international contacts for the German economy. Thus they did not necessarily perceive Jewish contacts abroad as treacherous.

Still another aspect of German patriotic values could also cut two ways. Although it became popular to excoriate "liberal" values after 1890–1900, not everyone believed they were evil. There was considerable diversity on this issue among the middle classes, and the lower classes (which represented almost 50 percent of the population) were in some ways more "liberal" than "socialist." Their complaint was that the "liberal" constitutional monarchy that Bismarck established, and which Jews supported strongly between 1871 and 1918, was not quite "liberal" enough.

In some ways Germany had been a pioneer in granting Jews rights and privileges. German universities had admitted Jews on an equal footing since 1790, and by 1909 and later they had a large percentage of Jewish professors when, for example, American and Canadian universities considered them anathema. Insofar as some Germans still believed the "liberal enlightenment" brought honor to the nation, and insofar as fair treatment of Jews was considered part of that enlightenment, some Germans viewed Hitler's attacks on Jews as a blight on national honor. Many of them equated Nazi violence against Jews with "primitive" countries and Bolshevik Russia. They complained that one might expect pogroms in "backward nations" such as Poland and Russia, but how could they happen in the land of Kant?

Closely related to the question of patriotism is the concept of a nation under law, because there can be no genuine national community without the assurance that laws will provide a stable

305

political and economic order. In most societies law becomes a principle unto itself precisely for this reason. Germans have always had a healthy respect for a nation under law (a *Rechtsstaat*), and this is probably one reason the fall of the monarchy was a traumatic shock. The Weimar government had an entirely new legal foundation, one which challenged and changed past traditions and rights that had become ensconced in the law. The new state was a potential threat simply because it could and did change the law; therefore, it was viewed with fear. Some of this fear was quite rational, and some was hysterical; yet tampering with the monarchy and the old order could only have been expected to produce such fears.

When Hitler came to power, he made certain that his takeover had the appearance of legality; this was his craftiest political maneuver. It prevented the average German from perceiving that he would alter the entire legal system of Germany. Revolutionaries have never been popular in Germany, and Hitler would never have had the full aura of legitimacy he needed had he taken power by force. Accordingly, Nazi violence and illegality after Hitler became chancellor were widely condemned. Likewise, violence against Jews during the boycott of 1933, the summer riots in Berlin in 1935, and the pogrom of 1938 was condemned by many Germans on the traditional grounds that it violated the law. If the state itself authorized wanton illegality in one sphere, such as anti-Jewish measures, how could it maintain its image as defender of the law in other spheres? Sporadic violent attacks on Jews before 1939 had to be curtailed because the public expected the state to perform its function of maintaining law and order. With the beginning of World War II and the attendant power it gave to Hitler, public indignation at violence against Jews in European lands could no longer have serious consequences. Germans who protested openly about persecution of Jews were treated as criminals because the traditional legal system was destroyed by Hitler, and his war powers could be terminated only with his death.

A value that is closely related to respect for the law is respect for legal rights over private property. When the Nazis attacked Jewish property during riots, boycotts, and *Kristallnacht*, they were also attacking the sanctity of private property. Some Germans opposed them on this ground alone, because their behavior was reminiscent of either bolshevism or anarchy.

Respect for law, for the order that law brings, and for private property were firm tenets of conservative thought. The wholesale denial of legal rights to Jews and the destruction of their property were antithetical to these values. Moreover, many conservatives were also religious because religion, as well as the state, the army, and the monarchy, was a traditional institution. It is not surprising that conservatives condemned persecution of Jews because it violated the proper functions of the state and Christian ethics. And even the anti-Semitism of the conservative movement after 1870 was rooted in religion rather than in racism. That is, conservatives might be antagonistic toward Jews because they would not convert to Christianity, but they had coexisted with Jews for centuries in the "Christian" belief that toleration offered the best route to future conversions.

Of course, conservatives were not the only Christians in Germany. Devout Christians, whether or not they belonged to the church in any formal sense, were appalled by Nazi persecution of Jews for the same Christian and humanitarian reasons. Moreover, Catholics in particular were in favor of religious toleration because they were also a minority in Germany. For the Nazis to attack Jews as a religious as well as a racial group implied real threats to both Catholics and Protestants in Germany. If religious freedom no longer existed, what protection did *they* have in the long run? Since Hitler did attack the churches well before World War II, it is doubtful that the churches would have survived as independent institutions had he won the war. Some church leaders perceived attacks on Jewish synagogues and other religious symbols as a potential threat to them, and they opposed persecution of the Jews for this reason.

Protestants and Catholics were also indignant at the "immoral" pornographic anti-Semitism in publications such as *Der Stürmer*. Even party members condemned Streicher's brand of anti-Semitism as a disgrace to the party; it was considered unrespectable to use pornographic sensationalism in a semiofficial publication.

The socialist movement was not free of anti-Semites, but its leaders upheld an ideal of equal treatment for everyone. Socialist leaders in particular, who were more familiar with socialist doctrine than the average rank-and-file member of the SPD or KPD, were sympathetic to the plight of Jews as underdogs, especially since they themselves were often treated as second-class citizens, despite their large following. Their adoption of "middle-class lifestyles" did not entirely remove this stigma, any more than it removed it for Jews. Moreover, massive Nazi campaigns against socialists throughout the Third Reich reinforced their conviction that the Nazi system was evil. In their socialist underground reports they continually held up the Nazi persecution of Jews as a prime example of this evil.

Humanitarians had similar attitudes. The basic conception that every human has worth and should be treated with respect caused some Germans with no particular political bent to criticize persecution of the Jews. If offended their sense of fair play and human dignity to see Jews manhandled or humiliated in public, let alone put into concentration camps and murdered. If such atrocities were tolerated, what would differentiate the civilized man from the most savage cannibal? The cannibal could at least make the excuse that, after all, he had never known any other way of life; the civilized man could not.

Any one of these values or any combination of them led some Germans to oppose Hitler's persecution of Jews. That only a minority of Germans acted openly to aid Jews or to oppose Nazi racial policies concretely, implies that these values were neutralized by the fear of reprisals and the improbability of evading detection.

IMPLICATIONS

What light does this study shed on current theories of anti-Semitism and Nazism? The most important theories of anti-Semitism are based primarily on psychoanalytic or psychological interpretations.[2] As we have seen, it is very difficult to determine the precise motivations, let alone the other psychological characteristics, of the Germans who supported or opposed racial persecution. We cannot develop a prototype of "bad guys" and "good guys" from the data presented in this study. Moreover, the psychological interpretations of "bad guys" that emerge from studies of such phenomena as the "authoritarian personality" have been subjected to serious, thoughtful, and probably justified attacks.[3] Any attempt to explain complex sociological and political phenomena on the basis of *attributed* or *assumed* psychological characteristics of large numbers of unknown and unknowable individuals is doomed to inaccuracy and irrelevance. One can speak at great length about supposed psychological characteristics of anti-Semitic Germans and the "German mind," but that will not get us closer to reality or to serious explanations of the role of anti-Semitism within Nazism or any other political movement.

According to Marxist historians and social scientists who have borrowed heavily from Marxist or socialist ideology, anti-Semitism is the result of psychological scapegoating that serves as a vent for distorted personalities. Also within Marxist dogma, the decline of capitalism results in fascist mass movements of the middle classes in which they unleash their frustrations over the failures of capitalism against Jews, who are falsely made its symbol. Again, this is a form of scapegoating. Reichmann found long-term historical reasons for the scapegoating of Jews and thought that by 1933 anti-Semitism had more to do with subjective attitudes of Germans than with objective differences between Jews and Germans. Hitler himself subscribed to a version of the scapegoat theory by repeatedly emphasizing the necessity to channel the hatreds and frustrations of any mass movement against a visible and common enemy. The scapegoat theory could conceivably explain support for Hitler among the "masses" or the middle classes before 1933 (though the best available evidence does not support this interpretation); however, it is certainly of limited value in explaining the functions of anti-Semitism after Hitler became chancellor, because his most well-known attacks on Jews (boycotts, *Kristallnacht*, and shootings in the East) were not popular. Had the "masses" or the middle classes simply wanted a scapegoat for their frustrations, they would have hailed these

309

events as glorious achievements. That this did not happen indicates that anti-Semitism served other functions, as we saw in chapters 4 and 5. Moreover, from our study of Nazi restrictions on published information, it is clear that the rulers of the Third Reich never intended that the German public should even know about the extent of Nazis persecution of Jews either at home or abroad. I point this out simply to indicate that any comprehensive theory of the role of anti-Semitism within Nazism cannot rely solely on psychological scapegoating as a *deus ex machina*.

Aside from the psychological and sociological interpretations of anti-Semitism, surprisingly few theories treat it as an absolutely integral part of the Nazi system, whether one considers it a form of modern authoritarianism or totalitarianism. Totalitarian theories imply that there will be a domestic enemy who is the ultimate victim of attempts to create a "new man"; however, they do not indicate specifically who the target will be. It could be Jews, "reactionaries," church leaders, or any other group that is defined as a foe of the absolute claims of the state or a movement. This does not tell us much about anti-Semitism except to echo the scapegoat theory. Likewise, interpretations of fascism as modern authoritarianism do not specifically show that anti-Semitism is essential to that political system.

Ernst Nolte, despite his analyses of Hitler's racial theories, does not explain how anti-Semitism was a necessary part of fascism.[4] Indeed, Mussolini's Italian fascism generally dispensed with it altogether. It was only Hitler's racism in the 1930s that enlisted support from Mussolini for anti-Semitism, and it was unpopular among many Italian fascists. His references to anti-Semitism within Nazism, as a specific form of fascism, likewise concentrate on Hitler's consistent racial theory without explaining how anti-Semitism was essential. Similarly, theories of Bonapartism, when they do speak to the importance of anti-Semitism, are indistinguishable from those that subscribe to the scapegoat theory alone.[5]

There is, then, no satisfactory theory of anti-Semitism as an integral part of Nazism. We have, of course, indicated some of the functions that were served by anti-Semitism both before and

310

after Hitler's rise to power (see chapters 2 to 5); these could not, however, be glorified by being called a theory. Anti-Semitism served many and important functions in the Nazi state, but it was not logically necessary to Nazism. One can, for example, imagine that Hitler could have succeeded almost solely with other types of propaganda. His anti-Semitic propaganda was neither necessary nor sufficient for his success, since there were many other problems facing Germany between 1928 and 1933, and there was certainly no lack of enemy targets (the Western democracies, communists, labor unions, socialists, etc.) to serve as a scapegoat before and after 1933. Since relatively few Nazis were extreme bigots in the early party and since anti-Semitism was most probably not crucial to Hitler's electoral success, he might have dispensed with anti-Semitic propaganda without serious political losses.

Had Hitler simply ignored the Jews in Germany, he might have alienated the radical anti-Semites in the Nazi party; however, it is unlikely that his regime would have suffered for this. Most probably it would have appeared to be more respectable and lawful. Hitler had little hesitation to purge the SA and socioeconomic radicals in the party in 1934, and it is interesting to speculate on how a purge of radical anti-Semites would have been received. Certainly it would have altered the early composition of the SS, but Himmler himself was a romantic whose ideas could have been changed with relatively little effort. Also, many of the SS were careerists and opportunists who would have bent with the wind, had Hitler chosen to change its direction. Later, the course of World War II could have progressed almost unchanged had he simply treated the Jews as he did other foreigners in occupied lands. Of course, given his treatment of all foreigners to the east, this would still have meant death for millions of Jews.

This of course reads like a fairytale, simply because Hitler's ethnic theory, especially its anti-Semitic component, was unalterable; he thought that in it he had found the explanation for all human history, and he was adamantly determined to play the role of "savior" for the "misguided" Europeans who had not perceived his "eternal truths" about the "Jewish world conspiracy." Yet it was only World War II that allowed him to act upon his

311

exterminatory visions in relative secrecy and with impunity. There were, of course, thousands of Germans in the party, SS, army, and bureaucracy who aided him in his war against the Jews by offering wholehearted support or simply by acquiescing to it, but it was Hitler himself who instigated the holocaust against the Jews and genocide against "subhumans"; Himmler and his other lackies would never have dared to initiate a policy of such magnitude without his authorization. Only Hitler had both the convictions of such obsessional ferocity and the iron-willed ruthlessness to envision and to order mass extermination; more important, only Hitler's decisions were the ultimate law of the land.

Hitler's central role in the persecution and mass murder of Jews cannot be overestimated. We have seen that his ethnic theory, properly understood, explains not only the destruction of European Jewry, but also the essential cause of World War II, as well as his treatment of other "races" in a hierarchy of satellite states whose ranking in his ethnic theory determined their actual status after his conquest. Moreover, even in prewar Germany the crippling or destruction of all significant institutions and power centers was motivated by their supposed ties to Jews or their willingness to engage in passive resistance against his racial and expansionist plans. Nevertheless, those historians who stress the role of bureaucratic careerism and interagency rivalries as accelerators in the destructive process are also on target.

In the Third Reich intuition was a necessity. The Nazis', military officers', and bureaucrats' intuitions regarding Hitler's next measures resulted in the radicalization of anti-Semitic policies at every successive stage of persecution. For personal advancement, it was far better to be an innovator who accurately anticipated Hitler's next anti-Semitic attack than to be a mere follower whose loyalty could be questioned. And of course, each successive radicalization made one a complicitor who could hardly deny his culpability to the Allies if Germany were defeated. Thus Globocnik, who suggested to Hitler that a bronze plaque be buried to honor the extermination of Jews, confided to a friend late in the war: "My heart's no longer in it but I am so deeply involved in these things that I have no alternative but to ride to victory with Hitler or go under.''[6] Also, General Governor Frank, who administered occupied Poland, commented at a police conference in January 1943 that all present were on Mr. Roosevelt's war-criminals list and were accomplices.[7]

Refusing to carry out orders or even dropping out of the race for bureaucratic prestige would have served no purpose. In the twisted logic of bureaucratic and careerist thinking, the only hope was for a German victory, and if this occurred, individuals and institutions could only maximize their futures by guessing at Hitler's intentions, drawing up anticipatory plans, and implementing these with efficiency and determination at the first sign that Hitler would opt for more radical attacks on Jews. Of course, in some cases these plans reflected the anti-Semitic hatreds of leading officers and bureaucrats, especially dyed-in-the-wool Nazi fanatics. Yet many who were not of this ilk nevertheless initiated independent anti-Semitic actions. They wanted to advance their institution's reputation with Hitler, and therefore their own careers, salaries, and prestige in the ever-shifting hierarchy of state and party organizations.

This type of process is probably common to all bureaucracies; those who do not participate in these rivalries must either resign or accept reductions in power and prestige in favor of more militant and shrewd institutional competitors. The disturbing feature of it, apart from the waste of manpower and efficiency, is that the *ends* that these bureaucracies serve appear to have very little impact on their decisions and actions. They are conveyor belts for almost *any* policies, particularly if these are adopted piecemeal. For example, had Hitler decided in 1933 after his appointment as chancellor to round up and gas all Jews in Germany, he would probably have been met with an outright refusal and mass resignations from all branches of the government and even from party agencies. However, by gradually escalating persecution, Hitler allowed himself time to replace the most uncooperative bureaucrats with reliable Nazis and to intimidate or woo the remaining ones. By 1939 the SS clearly had the controlling voice in the ''Jewish question''; the civil bureaucrats offered very little opposition. For most practical purposes they merely engaged in a futile end run to protect

313

their turf on Jewish issues thereafter; by 1941, when the military bureaucracies had also caved in, there was little to impede Hitler.

Of course, many types of rationalizations were necessary for those who understood that they were participating in a process of mass murder. Hilberg has analyzed these as obedience to superiors' orders, impersonal duty, shifting moral standards, arguments of powerlessness, and feelings that one must fight partisans and guerrillas, as Jews were labeled, or die.[8] Also, John Steiner, a survivor of many concentration camps, interviewed 229 SS men over a twenty-year period and found that many were motivated by the desire for their superiors' approval, over and above their wanting to foster their careers. They enjoyed their roles as powerful authority figures and played those roles despite personal revulsion at the consequences of their deeds.[9] For example, this was typical of Höss, the commandant of Auschwitz, who complained that "Nothing is more difficult than to have to make one's way through this business cold, unsympathetic and without pity."[10] Steiner concluded that much of the "role playing" was situational, that is, SS men would behave barbarically or without conscience when they felt that this was expected of them, but in other situations they would act as perfectly normal men. In other words, in a moral state, they would behave morally, but in an immoral one, they would go along with evil without any moral qualms. This is of course very disturbing, because it illustrates the "sleeper" in all human beings—the potential for violence and evil that can be triggered in any man in specific situations.[11] The Milgram experiments, in which normal human beings were willing to administer high electrical voltages to experimental subjects for giving wrong answers to questions, demonstrates the same phenomenon. If fairly ordinary men such as Eichmann and Himmler could direct mass murder, and if thousands of others were willing to carry out their orders, then unless one assumes that Germans are somehow different from other humans, one cannot anticipate that many men in any evil state will act upon their own consciences rather than upon expediency and rationalizations of cruelty.

Both before and after Hitler's Third Reich, Germans have lived basically within the deficient but lamentably average standards of civilized behavior. That this was not true during Hitler's regime should serve as the most forceful argument against the acquisition of inordinate power in the hands of the state or of any movement that claims to represent the "will of the people." Certainly, the accumulation of power by governments in both the Eastern and Western hemispheres during this century should be noted with unprecedented alarm and fear. Once citizens allow their freedom, whether political, economic, religious, social, or intellectual, to fall victim to a state or a movement, they cannot expect to defend themselves, let alone to protect Jews or other minorities who dangle on a short string in all societies.

Kren and Rappoport provide some sobering conclusions on the modern state:

> . . . within certain limits set by political and military power considerations, the modern state may do anything it wishes to those under its control. There is no moral-ethical limit which the state cannot transcend if it wishes to do so, because there is no moral-ethical power higher than the state. Moreover, it seems apparent that no modern state will ever seriously interfere with the internal activities of another solely for moral-ethical reasons. Consequently, in matters of ethics and morality, the situation of the individual in the modern state is in principle roughly equivalent to the situation of the prisoner in Auschwitz: either act in accord with the prevailing standards of conduct enforced by those in authority, or risk whatever consequences they may wish to impose. Just as there was no higher moral authority outside Auschwitz to which the prisoner could appeal, there is no such authority available to citizens of the modern state. If they are critical of the dominant ethos, they can only express this criticism within the limits permitted by the state.[12]

What should be emphasized here is the simple fact that for all practical purposes Hitler *was* the state, in a sense that Louis XIV of France could never have dreamed of. By destroying power centers in the traditional bureaucracy and army, by placing Nazis in critical positions, and by granting the Nazi party and SS authority at the expense of the traditional state, Hitler created what was in effect a *new* state, in which legality was redefined according to *his* world view and predilections. In that event, Hitler came as close as any man in history to playing God. And when the millions of Jewish and other victims pondered their own imminent deaths and wondered "Why must I die, since I have done nothing to deserve it?" probably the simplest answer would have been that power was totally concentrated in one man, and that man happened to hate their "race." Those who assisted Hitler in extermination craved power, not morality, and those who could have opposed him were normal men, not heroes. Once the police and military are coopted, possibilities for successful resistance are few, and normal men, who by definition are not heroes, will compete for power without regard to the catastrophic effects of their immoral actions. Therein lies a tragedy of the human, and not only the German, condition.

# Appendixes

## Appendix A
## Calculations of Chance Probability

Probabilities of obtaining a given percentage or more and a given percentage or less are calculated according to the following test statistics: test statistic A is used to compare one sample to a given "population"; test statistic B is used to compare two samples within a given "population."

| | Test statistic A | Test statistic B |
|---|---|---|
| $1.00 - z =$ | $\dfrac{p_1 - p_2}{\sqrt{\dfrac{p_2 q_2}{N}}}$ | $\dfrac{p_1 - p_2}{\sqrt{\dfrac{p_1 q_1}{N} + \dfrac{p_2 q_2}{N}}}$ |

$z$ = standard score on a cumulative normal curve
$p_1$ = actual percentage, for example in Merkl's sample or from the Government District Düsseldorf
$q_1 = 1.00 - p_1$
$p_2$ = expected percentage
$q_2 = 1.00 - p_2$
$N$ = number in sample

To illustrate the meaning of probabilities, a probability of 0.01 means that a given percentage difference would occur due to chance alone one time in 100. Probabilities of 3.00 or more indicate that a given percentage difference would almost never be due to chance alone. Minus signs before probabilities only mean that the actual percentage is less than the expected percentage.

These test statistics do not include a correction for continuity. Ideally, if we wish to determine the probability of obtaining a given percentage or more, we should lower our actual percentage

317

by subtracting 0.5 from the number upon which the actual percentage is based to make a correction for continuity. Conversely, if we wish to determine the probability of obtaining a given percentage or less, we should add 0.5 to the number upon which the actual percentage is based. Since this does not make a difference of more than 1 chance in 100 (0.01), we will simply add 1 chance in 100 to our significance levels. There is also no adjustment for sampling from a finite population in the above test statistics, and again, since this makes a difference of no more than 1 chance in 100, we will add 1 chance in 100 to our significance levels. Thus we have significance levels of 7 or less chance occurrences in 100 (0.07 or less) and 12 or less chance occurrences in 100 (0.12 or less).

The probability of obtaining a given percentage or more by chance will be significantly affected by sample size. The probability of obtaining a given percentage or more, for example 30 percent, will be very different in samples of 100 and 300. Most accurate estimates of probability occur when we have samples of 100 or more. In some of my calculations this is not the case; however, the above test statistics give rough estimates. They are used only to eliminate test results that could easily occur by chance within a sample of a given size.

## Appendix B

TABLE B.1 Percentages and Probabilities for Comparisons of Anti-Semites in Merkl's Sample to the "No Evidence" Group (in percentages)

| Group | No Evidence | Mild | Prob. | Moderate | Prob. | Paranoid | Prob. | Total Anti-Semites | Prob. |
|---|---|---|---|---|---|---|---|---|---|
| *Age* | | | | | | | | | |
| 17–31 | 37.7 | 46.0 | .13 | 25.7 | −.01 | 30.4 | | 31.0 | −.08 |
| 32–38 | 30.8 | 25.4 | | 24.6 | −.11 | 28.6 | | 25.5 | −.13 |
| 39–48 | 20.5 | 15.9 | | 25.7 | | 25.0 | | 23.4 | |
| 49–55 | 6.2 | 1.6 | −.04 | 12.3 | .03 | 12.5 | .10 | 10.0 | .08 |
| 56+ | 4.8 | 11.1 | .07 | 11.7 | .01 | 3.6 | | 10.0 | .02 |
| N | *146* | *63* | | *171* | | *56* | | *290* | |
| *Sex* | | | | | | | | | |
| Male | 93.0 | 90.9 | | 90.6 | | 92.0 | | 90.9 | |
| Female | 7.0 | 9.1 | | 9.4 | | 8.0 | | 9.1 | |
| N | *143* | *55* | | *149* | | *50* | | *254* | |
| *Residence* | | | | | | | | | |
| Urban | 44.8 | 68.3 | 3.28 | 58.2 | .008 | 64.3 | .005 | 61.6 | −.0004 |
| Middle-sized | 20.7 | 9.5 | −.01 | 14.1 | −.06 | 17.9 | | 13.8 | −.04 |
| Rural | 34.5 | 22.2 | −.03 | 27.6 | −.09 | 17.9 | −.005 | 24.6 | −.02 |
| N | *145* | *63* | | *170* | | *56* | | *289* | |
| *Religion* | | | | | | | | | |
| Protestant | 64.3 | 86.4 | .02 | 64.3 | — | 77.3 | .13 | 72.0 | .19 |
| Catholic | 35.7 | 13.6 | −.02 | 35.7 | — | 22.7 | −.13 | 28.0 | −.19 |
| N | *42* | *22* | | *56* | | *22* | | *100* | |

| Group | No Evidence | Mild | Prob. | Moderate | Prob. | Paranoid | Prob. | Total Anti-Semites | Prob. |
|---|---|---|---|---|---|---|---|---|---|
| **Religious Area of Residence** | | | | | | | | | |
| Protestant | 63.1 | 63.3 | | 67.3 | | 65.5 | | 66.1 | |
| Catholic | 19.1 | 16.7 | | 17.6 | | 9.1 | −.03 | 15.7 | |
| Mixed | 17.7 | 20.0 | | 15.2 | | 25.5 | .12 | 18.2 | |
| N | 141 | 60 | | 165 | | 55 | | 280 | |
| **Occupation** | | | | | | | | | |
| Military-CS | 20.8 | 16.4 | | 29.5 | .05 | 24.0 | | 25.6 | .14 |
| Business-Prof. | 15.2 | 14.5 | | 20.1 | .14 | 24.0 | .10 | 19.7 | .13 |
| White-collar | 14.4 | 30.9 | .004 | 20.8 | .03 | 24.0 | .06 | 23.6 | .01 |
| Blue-collar | 37.6 | 30.9 | −.19 | 23.5 | −.006 | 26.0 | −.06 | 25.6 | −.01 |
| Farmers | 12.0 | 7.3 | −.15 | 6.0 | −.04 | 2.0 | −.002 | 5.5 | −.02 |
| N | 125 | 55 | | 149 | | 50 | | 254 | |
| **Father's Occupation** | | | | | | | | | |
| Military-CS | 24.8 | 39.1 | .04 | 25.2 | | 41.7 | .02 | 31.4 | .10 |
| Business-Prof. | 11.1 | 15.2 | | 12.6 | | 12.5 | | 13.1 | |
| Artisans | 20.5 | 15.2 | | 20.7 | | 16.7 | | 18.8 | |
| Blue- and white-collar | 19.7 | 10.9 | −.07 | 21.5 | | 20.8 | | 19.2 | |
| Farmers | 23.9 | 19.6 | | 20.0 | | 8.3 | −.003 | 17.5 | −.09 |
| N | 117 | 46 | | 135 | | 48 | | 229 | |

*Education*

| | | | | | | | | | |
|---|---|---|---|---|---|---|---|---|---|
| Primary | 69.6 | | 62.1 | −.13 | 61.1 | −.06 | 54.9 | −.03 | 60.1 | −.03 |
| Secondary | 19.3 | | 17.2 | | 27.2 | .05 | 25.5 | .19 | 24.7 | .10 |
| University | 11.1 | | 20.7 | .05 | 11.7 | | 19.6 | .10 | 15.1 | .13 |
| N | *135* | | *58* | | *162* | | *51* | | *271* | |

SOURCE: Data sheets provided by Merkl.

NOTE: Probabilities computed using test statistic B (see appendix A).

TABLE B.2 Comparison of *Judenfreunde* and *Rassenschänder* to the Population and Labor Force of the Government District Düsseldorf[a] (*in percentages*)

| | GDD[a] | Judenfreunde and Rassen- schänder | | Jundenfreunde | | Rassen- schänder | |
|---|---|---|---|---|---|---|---|
| | | | Prob. | | Prob. | | Prob. |
| *Sex* | | | | | | | |
| Male | 47.9 | 63.5 | 6.64 | 70.2 | 7.40 | 53.1 | .08 |
| Female | 52.1 | 36.5 | −6.64 | 29.8 | −7.40 | 46.9 | −.08 |
| N | | 452 | | 275 | | 177 | |
| *Age in 1939* | | | | | | | |
| Under 30 | 23.3 | 21.5 | −.18 | 10.5 | −5.02 | 36.2 | 4.06 |
| 30–39 | 26.6 | 25.2 | | 22.2 | −.05 | 30.0 | .15 |
| 40–49 | 19.2 | 22.1 | .06 | 26.2 | −.002 | 18.1 | |
| 50–59 | 15.3 | 17.0 | .16 | 22.9 | 3.50 | 7.9 | −.003 |
| 60+ | 15.7 | 14.2 | −.19 | 18.2 | .13 | 7.9 | −.002 |
| N | | 452 | | 275 | | 177 | |
| *Occupation* | | | | | | | |
| Independent | 17.3 | 31.6 | 7.11 | 40.1 | 8.88 | 18.2 | .63 |
| Civil servant | 6.4 | 6.2 | | 8.3 | | 2.9 | |
| White-collar | 19.4 | 41.8 | 10.66 | 35.9 | 6.15 | 51.1 | 9.38 |
| Blue-collar | 51.1 | 14.4 | −13.81 | 12.4 | −11.40 | 17.5 | −7.86 |
| Domestic | 5.7 | 5.9 | | 3.2 | | 10.2 | |
| N | | 354 | | 217 | | 137 | |

SOURCES: For sex and age, see *Statistik des Deutschen Reiches*, vol. 555 (1939), no. 2:145. For occupations, see ibid., vol. 455 (1933), no. 16:60–64.

NOTES: For socioeconomic characteristics of separate categories of independents and persons with no profession, see Sarah Gordon, "German Opposition to Nazi Anti-Semitic Measures between 1933 and 1945, with Particular Reference to the Rhine-Ruhr Area," appendix H, table 61, pp. 447–448. For the same information on Nazi opponents and religious groups, see appendix B, tables B.4 and B.5 below.

All chance probabilities are based on test statistic A (see appendix A).

[a] GDD is the Government District Düsseldorf. Sex and age are for the population; occupation is for the labor force.

TABLE B.3 Occupational Distribution of the Government District Düsseldorf and the Rhine Province: Comparison of White-Collar Workers to the Labor Force of the Rhine Province (*in percentages*)

|  | GDD | Rhine Province | Opponents | Prob.[a] |
|---|---|---|---|---|
| Independents | 17.3 | 16.8 | 31.6 | |
| Civil servants | 6.4 | 4.9 | 6.2 | |
| Upper-level white-collar | | 5.5 | 21.2 | 14.64 |
| Lower-level white-collar | 19.4 | 11.6 | 20.6 | 5.98 |
| Blue-collar | 51.1 | 56.4 | 14.4 | |
| Domestics | 5.7 | 4.7 | 5.9 | |
| Number in sample | | | 452 | |

SOURCES: See appendix B, table B.2 for sources on the occupational distribution of the Government District Düsseldorf and of opponents from that district.

See *Statistik des Deutschen Reiches*, vol. 455 (1933), no. 16:6–7, for the occupational distribution of the Rhine Province.

[a] All calculations of probability based on test statistic A (see appendix A).

TABLE B.4 Socioeconomic Characteristics of Catholic and Protestant Opponents in the Government District Düsseldorf (*in percentages*)

| | Catholics | Protestants | Prob.[a] |
|---|---|---|---|
| *Sex* | | | |
| Male | 76.1 | 87.9 | .08 |
| Female | 23.9 | 12.1 | − .08 |
| *Age* | | | |
| Under 30 | 10.9 | 9.1 | |
| 30–39 | 26.1 | 21.2 | |
| 40–49 | 17.4 | 30.3 | .09 |
| 50–59 | 34.8 | 18.2 | − .04 |
| 60 + | 10.9 | 21.3 | .11 |
| *Occupation* | | | |
| Independent | 34.8 | 30.3 | |
| Small shop owner | (21.7) | (12.1) | (− .13) |
| Civil servant | 8.7 | 9.1 | |
| Upper-level white-collar | 17.4 | 36.4 | .03 |
| Lower-level white-collar | 8.7 | 9.1 | |
| Blue-Collar | 19.6 | 9.1 | − .09 |
| *Levels of Opposition* | | | |
| High | 37.0 | 24.2 | − .11 |
| Middle | 50.0 | 45.5 | |
| Low | 13.0 | 30.3 | − .03 |
| Number in sample | *46* | *33* | |

[a] For calculations of the significance of percentage differences, see appendix A, test statistic B.

324

TABLE B.5 Comparison of Nazi Opponents of Racial Persecution to the Population and Labor Force of the Government District Düsseldorf and Rhine Province (*in percentages*)

| | GDD | Nazi Opponents | Prob.[a] |
|---|---|---|---|
| *Sex* | | | |
| Male | 47.9 | 92.3 | 7.17 |
| Female | 52.1 | 7.7 | −7.17 |
| N | | 65 | |
| *Age* | | | |
| Under 30 | 23.3 | 9.3 | −.004 |
| 30–39 | 26.6 | 29.2 | |
| 40–49 | 19.2 | 23.1 | |
| 50–59 | 15.3 | 26.3 | .007 |
| 60 + | 15.7 | 12.3 | |
| N | | 65 | |
| *Occupation* | | | |
| Independent | 18.4 | 34.9 | 3.38 |
| Civil servant | 6.8 | 11.1 | .09 |
| White-collar | 20.6 | 41.3 | 4.06 |
| Blue-collar | 54.2 | 12.7 | −6.61 |
| N | | 63 | |
| *Rhine Province* | | | |
| *White-collar* | | | |
| (upper level) | 5.5 | 26.2 | 7.21 |
| White-collar | | | |
| (lower-level) | 11.6 | 13.8 | |
| N | | 63 | |

SOURCES: For GDD (Government District Düsseldorf), see appendix B, table B.2. For the occupational distribution of the Rhine Province, see appendix B, table B.3.

[a] Chance probability calculated using test statistic A (see appendix A).

# Notes

1. The Government District Düsseldorf comprised over one-half of the Rhineland and many large industrial cities including Düsseldorf, Essen, München-Gladbach, Solingen, Wupperthal, and others.

CHAPTER ONE

1. There is, unfortunately, no complete analysis of the situation of German Jews for the years 1870–1914; the following discussion represents only their outstanding characteristics.

2. Statistisches Amt, *Statistik des Deutschen Reiches*, vol. 451 (1933), no. 5:7.

3. Ibid., 13.

4. Ibid., 7.

5. Walter Mohrmann, *Anti-Semitismus: Ideologie und Geschichte im Kaisserreich und in der Weimarer Republik*, 173; Salomon Adler-Rüdel, *Ostjuden in Deutschland 1880–1940*, 60, 164.

6. Adler-Rüdel, *Ostjuden*, 120.

7. LBI, Miscellaneous Microfilm Collections, R 154, F 214–215.

8. Ismar Schorsch, *Jewish Reactions to German Anti-Semitism, 1870–1914*, 14.

9. *Statistik des Deutschen Reiches*, vol. 451 (1933), no. 5:9.

10. Ibid.

11. Ibid., 12, and *Statistik des Deutschen Reiches*, vol. 401, no. 1:359.

12. *Statistik des Deutschen Reiches*, vol. 451, no. 5:15. The large cities with the highest percentages of foreign-born Jews were: Leipzig, 73%; Dresden and Chemnitz, 61%; Kiel, 57%; Altona, 56%; Remscheid and Plauen, 54%; and Duisburg, 46%.

13. Ibid.

14. Lucy Dawidowicz, *The War Against the Jews, 1933–1945*, 172.

15. Gordon Morck, "German Nationalism and Jewish Assimilation: The Bismarck Period," 83–84.

16. Walter Zwi Bacharach, "Jews in Confrontation with Racist Antisemitism, 1879–1933," 205; Rosemarie Leuschen-Seppel, *Sozialdemokratie und Antisemitismus im Kaiserreich: Die Auseinandersetzungen der Partei mit den konservativen und völkischen Strömungen des Antisemitismus 1871–1914*, 198. Vernon Lidtke, "Social Class and Secularisation in Imperial Germany: The Working Classes," 33; Donald Niewyk, *The Jews in Weimar Germany*, 16, 114–120; Carl J. Rheins, "The Verband Nationaldeutscher Juden 1921–1933," 256.

NOTES TO CHAPTER ONE

17. John Toland, *Adolf Hitler*, 365.

18. LBI, AR 7183, box 10, no. 11, folder 1, K 3, pp. 109, 142; Bacharach, "Jews in Confrontation," 208; Kurt Pätzold, *Faschismus, Rassenwahn, Judenverfolgung: Eine Studie zur politischen Strategie und Taktik des faschistischen Imperialismus 1933–1935*, 18; Rheins, "The Verband Nationaldeutscher Juden," 256.

19. Adler-Rudel, *Ostjuden*, 25–26; Niewyk, *The Jews in Weimar Germany*, 120; Leonard Baker, *Days of Sorrow and Pain: Leo Baeck and the Berlin Jews*, 50.

20. Adler-Rudel, *Ostjuden*, 25–26.

21. Ibid., 120.

22. Rheins, "The Verband Nationaldeutscher Juden," 255, note 79.

23. Helmut Genschel, *Die Verdrängung der Juden aus der Wirtschaft im Dritten Reich*, 21.

24. *Statistik des Deutschen Reiches*, vol. 451 (1933), no. 5:23.

25. Ibid. Among foreign Jews, 28 percent were in industry and crafts, versus 22 percent for German Jews.

26. LBI, AR 7183, box 10, no. 11, folder 1, K 3, p. 221.

27. Ibid., 222.

28. Esra Bennathan, "Die demographische und wirtschaftliche Struktur der Juden," 113–114; Kurt Düwell, *Die Rheingebiete in der Judenpolitik des Nationalsozialismus vor 1942*, 75; Genschel, *Die Verdrängung*, 22–23; *Statistik des Deutschen Reiches*, vol. 451 (1933), no. 5:22.

29. Bennathan, "Die demographische und wirtschaftliche Struktur," 114–115. The following figures represent the percentage of firms owned by Jews in selected retail trades, 1928–1932: Textile dealers, 40%; Clothing trades, 62%; Warehouse sales, 79%; Corn dealers, 23%; Hops dealers, 56%; Department stores, 79%.

30. Ibid.

31. Genschel, *Die Verdrängung*, 286. The percentage distribution of incorporated banking concerns was as follows in 1930: anonymous banks of a non-Jewish character, 62.2%; anonymous banks of a Jewish character, 0.3%; private banks of a non-Jewish character, 19.1%; private banks of a Jewish character, 18.4%. Before World War I, in ten main branches of the *Aktiengesellschaften*, Jews held 13.3 percent of the directorships; they also represented 24.4 percent of the supervisory personnel (see Genschel, *Die Verdrängung*, 25–26). Some of these positions were lost between 1928 and 1930, but not at the highest levels; see Bennathan, "Die demographische und wirtschaftliche Struktur," 115–116.

32. Bennathan, "Die demographische und wirtschaftliche Struktur," 118.

33. Genschel, *Die Verdrängung*, 26.

34. Bennathan, "Die demographische und wirtschaftliche Struktur," 119–120.

35. Ibid.

36. *Statistik des Deutschen Reiches*, vol. 451 (1933), no. 5:26.

37. LBI, AR 7183, box 10, no. 11, folder 1, K 3, p. 227.

38. Genschel, *Die Verdrängung*, 24. The following information on Jews in Prussia, as percentages of total employed in each area, indicates their significant numbers

in leading positions in 1925: banking and stock market, 6.23%; mediation, administration, consulting, 7.76%; insurance, 3.95%; tailoring and manufacture of clothing, 23.09%; lending and auctioneering, 19.05%; book and art dealerships, loan libraries, 9.45%.

39. Genschel, *Die Verdrängung*, 25–26.

40. E. H. Lowenthal, "Die Juden im öffentlichen Leben," in Werner Mosse, ed. *Entscheidungsjahr 1932*, 59.

41. LBI, AR 7183, box 10, no. 11, folder 1, K 3, p. 228.

42. U.S. Department of State, *Foreign Relations of the United States: Diplomatic Papers* (Washington: Government Printing Office, 1933), 2:363, The Consul General at Berlin (Messersmith) to the Secretary of State, November 1, 1933.

43. *Statistik des Deutschen Reiches*, vol. 451 (1933), no. 5:26.

44. Ibid., 22, 26.

45. Bennathan, "Die demographische und wirtschaftliche Struktur," passim; Düwell, *Die Rheingebiete*, 73; Lowenthal, "Die Juden im öffentlichen Leben," 57; Ernst Hamburger, *Juden im öffentlichen Leben Deutschlands: Regierungsmitglieder, Beamte und Parlamentarier in der monarchistischen Zeit*, 44, 63; Karl Thieme, ed., *Judenfeindschaft: Darstellung und Analysen* (Frankfurt a.M.: Fischer Bücherei, 1963), 246; Jacob Toury, *Die politischen Orientierungen der Juden in Deutschland von Jena bis Weimar*, 38, 44, 63, 67, 325; Herbert Strauss, "Jewish Emigration from Germany—Nazi Policies and Jewish Responses (I)," 340.

46. Niewyk, *The Jews in Weimar Germany*, 31.

47. Peter Pulzer, "Why Was There a Jewish Question in Imperial Germany?" 142.

48. Strauss, "Jewish Emigration," 340.

49. Peter Pulzer, *The Rise of Political Anti-Semitism*, 25.

50. Fritz Ringer, "The Perversion of Ideas in Weimar Universities," 53; Alan Beyerchen, "The Physical Sciences," 151.

51. Leuschen-Seppel, *Sozialdemokratie und Antisemitismus*, 62.

52. Gert Brieger, "The Medical Profession," in Friedlander and Milton, *The Holocaust*, 145.

53. Pulzer, *The Rise of Political Anti-Semitism*, 12; *Statistik des Deutschen Reiches*, vol. 451 (1933), no. 5:10.

54. William Shirer, *The Rise and Fall of the Third Reich*, 251, on Jewish recipients; see Hana Umlauf Lane, ed., *The World Almanac and Book of Facts 1983*, New York: Newspaper Enterprise Association, 1983, 410–411, for total German recipients.

55. LBI, AR 7183, box 10, no. 11, folder 1, K 3, p. 231.

56. Leuschen-Seppel, *Sozialdemokratie und Antisemitismus*, 57.

57. Niewyk, *The Jews in Weimar Germany*, 33, 37–38.

58. Toury, *Die politischen Orientierungen*, 243.

59. Schorsch, *Jewish Reactions*, 15–16; Arthur Ruppin, *The Jews in the Modern World*, 151.

60. Schorsch, *Jewish Reactions*, 15–16.

61. Ruppin, *The Jews in the Modern World*, 152.

62. For additional information on the high percentage of taxes paid by Jews in these cities, see Genschel, *Die Verdrängung*, 27–28, and Düwell, *Die Rheingebiete*, 75.

63. Ruppin, *The Jews in the Modern World*, 151; Düwell, *Die Rheingebiete*, 75; and Schorsch, *Jewish Reactions*, 16.

64. Genschel, *Die Verdrängung*, 27–28.

65. Bennathan, "Die demographische und wirtschaftliche Struktur," 91, 93.

66. Genschel, *Die Verdrängung*, 258.

67. Pulzer, *The Rise of Political Anti-Semitism*, 26; Genschel, *Die Verdrängung*, 17, 19, and passim; Bennathan, "Die demographische und wirtschaftliche Struktur," passim; Donald Niewyk, *Socialist, Anti-Semite, and Jew: German Social Democracy Confronts the Problem of Anti-Semitism, 1918–1933*, 163.

68. Ruppin, *The Jews in the Modern World*, 330.

69. Genschel, *Die Verdrängung*, 20, note 23; Johan Snoek, *The Grey Book: A Collection of Protests against Anti-Semitism and the Persecution of the Jews Issued by non-Roman Catholic Churches and Church Leaders during Hitler's Rule*, 24; Fritz Stern, *The Politics of Cultural Despair: A Study in the Rise of the Germanic Ideology* (Berkeley: University of California Press, 1963), 140.

70. Almost two-thirds of these occurred after 1900. Bruno Blau, "Die Entwicklung der jüdischen Bevölkerung in Deutschland von 1800–1945" (unpublished manuscript held at the Leo Baeck Institute, New York), 308–309. See also *Statistik des Deutschen Reiches*, vol. 451 (1933), no. 5:8.

71. For 1901–1905, and 1926–1932, computations are based on absolute numbers in *Statistik des Deutschen Reiches*, vol. 451 (1933), no. 5:8; computations for 1933–1938 are based on absolute numbers given in the *Statistisches Jahrbuch für das Deutsche Reich* as follows: 44% for 1933, *Statistisches Jahrbuch*, 1935, p. 41; 24% for 1934, *Statistisches Jahrbuch*, 1936, p. 41; 22% for 1935, *Statistisches Jahrbuch*, 1937, p. 37; 3% for 1936, *Statistisches Jahrbuch*, 1938, p. 46; 2% for 1938, *Statistisches Jahrbuch*, 1938–1940, p. 42. See also BA, ZSg 116/646, Blatt B (November 14, 1935).

72. Ruppin, *The Jews in the Modern World*, 324; Düwell, *Die Rheingebiete*, 71, note 47.

73. Ruppin, *The Jews in the Modern World*, 325.

74. Ibid.

75. Hamburger, *Juden im öffentlichen Leben*, 120.

76. Toury, *Die politischen Orientierungen*, 242.

77. Hamburger, *Juden im öffentlichen Leben*, 253.

78. The average percentage of Jews in the German population between 1867 and 1916 was 0.9 percent (computed from figures given for *Glaubensjuden* in *Statistik des Deutschen Reiches*, vol. 451 [1933], no. 5:7, and the total German population given in *Statstik des Deutschen Reiches*, vol. 470 [1937], no. 1:5).

79. Jews represented 129 out of 5,736 delegates between 1867 and 1912 (see Hamburger, *Juden im öffentlichen Leben*, 251–253). During Weimar years the

average percentage of Jewish Reichstag delegates was 2.8 percent (see Lowenthal, "Die Juden im öffentlichen Leben," 58, and Hans-Helmuth Knütter, *Die Juden und die Deutsche Linke in der Weimarer Republik*, 110).

80. See Hamburger, *Juden im öffentlichen Leben*, passim, and Toury, *Die politischen Orientierungen*, passim. Toury gives a brief description of shifts in Jewish attitudes toward politics, which indicates their general passivity around 1849, increasing interest in national integration around 1871, and forceful activism during Wilhelminian years (see his p. 245).

81. See also Knütter, *Die Juden*, 110.

82. Hamburger, *Juden im öffentlichen Leben*, 147, 251, 254, 338, 405; see also Toury, *Die politischen Orientierungen*, 131, note 45, and pp. 193, 235, 245; Golo Mann, "Der Antisemitismus; Wurzeln, Wirkung und Ueberwindung," *Vom Gestern zum Morgen* 3 (1960):22; Paul Massing, *Rehearsal for Destruction: A Study of Political Anti-Semitism in Imperial Germany*, 272, note 28; Rudolf Schay, *Juden in der deutschen Politik* (Berlin: Welt Verlag, 1929), 243, 307; see also Niewyk, *The Jews in Weimar Germany*, 30, for connections between Zionists and communism.

83. See table 1.2 for Toury's estimate that only 19 percent of the Jewish population supported the Social Democratic party in immediate prewar years. Hamburger, on p. 147 of *Juden im öffentlichen Leben*, estimates that only 30,000 to 40,000 out of 150,000 Jews in the electorate voted for the SPD. This would have represented around 23 percent of Jewish voters, far from a majority. See also, Knütter, *Die Juden*, 64, 67, 89.

84. Calculated from the number of Jews in the SPD according to Hamburger, *Juden im öffentlichen Leben*, 251–253.

85. Ibid., 254.

86. Ibid.; for the percentage of Jews in the population see *Statistik des Deutschen Reiches*, vol. 451 (1933), no. 5:7; see also Lowenthal, "Die Juden im öffentlichen Leben," 58, for the percentage of Jews in the SPD during Weimar years.

87. Toury, *Die politischen Orientierungen*, 325; also see p. 235. For additional information on Jews affiliated with socialist publications, see Lowenthal, "Die Juden im öffentlichen Leben," 61–63; Pulzer, *The Rise of Political Anti-Semitism*, 13. For the large percentage of Jewish socialists in the SPD and KPD during the Weimar Republic, see Knütter, *Die Juden*, 109–122; Niewyk, *Socialist, Anti-Semite*, 17–19; H. G. Sellenthin, *Geschichte der Juden in Berlin und des Gebäudes Fasanenstrasse 79/80: Festschrift anlässlich der Einweihung des jüdischen Gemeindehauses*, 62; F.O.H. Schulz, *Jude und Arbeiter* (Berlin: Niebelungen, 1934), 64–74.

88. See Max Kele, *Nazis and Workers: National Socialist Appeals to German Labor, 1919–1933*, 116, regarding Jewish financial backing for the SPD publication *Vorwärts*; for close ties between the *Reichsbanner* and the Jewish *Centralverein*, see Werner Mosse, "Der Niedergang der Weimarer Republik und die Juden," 33; Knütter, *Die Juden*, 213; Niewyk, *Socialist, Anti-Semite*, 190. For general close affiliations between the *Centralverein* and the SPD, see Knütter, *Die Juden*, 90–91, and Schorsch, *Jewish Reactions*, passim.

89. See A. J. Nicholls and Erich Mathias, comps., *German Democracy and the Triumph of Hitler: Essays in Recent German History*, 244–245.

90. Ernst Hamburger, "Jews, Democracy and Weimar Germany," Leo Baeck Institute *Memorial Lecture* 16 (1973):2–27; Niewyk, *The Jews in Weimar Germany*, 25–26.

91. Dawidowicz, *The War Against the Jews*, 172–173; Niewyk, *Socialist, Anti-Semite*, 192.

92. Niewyk, *Socialist, Anti-Semite*. In 1932, 67 percent of the Jewish electorate voted for the SPD; see also Arnold Paucker, *Der jüdische Abwehrkampf gegen Antisemitismus und Nationalsozialismus in den letzten Jahren der Weimarer Republik*, 29.

93. George Mosse, *The Crisis of German Ideology: The Intellectual Origins of the Third Reich*, passim; see also Robert Cecil, *The Myth of the Master Race: Alfred Rosenberg and Nazi Ideology*, 68–69; Massing, *Rehearsal for Destruction*, 8; Geoffrey Pridham, *Hitler's Rise to Power: The Nazi Movement in Bavaria, 1923–1933*, 25–33; Pulzer, *The Rise of Political Anti-Semitism*, 328.

94. George Mosse, *Germans and Jews: The Right, the Left, and the Search for a "Third Force" in Pre-Nazi Germany*, 34–77; see also Massing, *Rehearsal for Destruction*, 78.

95. Norman Cohn, *Warrant for Genocide: The Myth of the Jewish World Conspiracy and the Protocols of the Elders of Zion*, passim; also Cecil, *The Myth of the Master Race*, 61–81.

96. Hans Buchheim et al., *The Anatomy of the SS State*, 1–19; Cecil, *The Myth of the Master Race*, 68–69; Dawidowicz, *The War Against the Jews*, 36; Massing, *Rehearsal for Destruction*, 78; George Mosse, *Germans and Jews*, 34–77; Pulzer, *The Rise of Political Anti-Semitism*, 26–27, 31, 248, 328; Eva Reichmann, *Hostages of Civilization: The Social Sources of National Socialist Anti-Semitism*, 65–96; Stern, *The Politics*, xxvi; Andrew Whiteside, "Comments on the Papers of William A. Jenks and Donald L. Niewyk," 174.

97. Karl Dietrich Bracher, *The German Dictatorship: The Origins, Structure, and Effects of National Socialism*, 37–38; Buchheim, *Anatomy*, 10–19; Reichmann, *Hostages*, passim.

98. For a discussion of nationalism and imperialism, see Hanna Arendt, *The Origins of Totalitarianism* (New York: World Publishing, 1972), pp. 3–305; Bracher, *The German Dictatorship*, 13, 34–45; Pulzer, *The Rise of Political Anti-Semitism*, 57–58, 226, 333; Reichmann, *Hostages*, 80–93.

99. Herman Lebovics, *Social Conservatism and the Middle Classes in Germany, 1914–1933* (Princeton: Princeton University Press, 1969), passim; Stern, *The Politics*, passim.

100. Bracher, *The German Dictatorship*, 34–45; Cecil, *The Myth of the Master Race*, 68–69; George Mosse, *The Crisis* and *Germans and Jews*, passim; Pulzer, *The Rise of Political Anti-Semitism*, passim; Reichmann, *Hostages*, passim; Shirer, *The Rise and Fall*, passim; Peter Viereck, *Metapolitics: The Roots of the Nazi Mind* (New York: Capricorn Books, 1965), passim.

101. Wanda Kampmann, *Deutsche und Juden: Studien zur Geschichte des deutschen Judentums*, 293–363, has a good discussion of German intellectuals' theories of anti-Semitism.

102. Richard Hamilton, "Some Difficulties with Cultural Explanations of National Socialism" (unpublished article, March 1975), 17; see also George Mosse, "Discussion," in *The Holocaust as Historical Experience*, edited by Bauer and Rotenstreich, 264, for his conclusion that Jews were generally portrayed favorably in German literature.

103. Hamilton, "Some Difficulties," 18, 20.

104. Ibid., 19.

105. Ibid., 20.

106. Niewyk, *The Jews in Weimar Germany*, 9, discusses Jewish optimism.

107. Marjorie Lamberti, "Liberals, Socialists and the Defence against Anti-Semitism in the Wilhelminian Period," 150–151. See also Massing, *Rehearsal for Destruction*, 107; he describes the League of Notables that attempted to combat anti-Semitism between 1884 and 1892; see also Uriel Tal, *Christians and Jews in Germany: Religion, Politics, and Ideology in the Second Reich, 1870–1914*, 49.

108. Richard Levy, *The Downfall of the Anti-Semitic Political Parties of Imperial Germany*, 146.

109. Ibid., 150.

110. See also the Leo Baeck Institute's *Yearbook*, which frequently contains articles on Weimar years.

111. See table 1.3.

112. Koppel Pinson, *Modern Germany: Its History and Civilization*, 572–575.

113. Despite the low support for anti-Semitic parties, approximately 15 percent of all national politicians interested themselves in specifically Jewish affairs (see Toury, *Die politischen Orientierungen*, 245).

114. Kampmann, *Deutsche und Juden*, 254; Levy, *The Downfall*, 21; Pulzer, *The Rise of Political Anti-Semitism*, 76.

115. Levy, *The Downfall*, 18, 27.

116. Pinson, *Modern Germany*, 573.

117. Ibid.

118. Calculated from ibid., 252–253.

119. Leuschen-Seppel, *Sozialdemokratie und Antisemitismus*, 187, and Eugene Davidson, *The Making of Adolf Hitler* (New York: Macmillan, 1977), 294.

120. Martin Broszat, *German National Socialism, 1919–1945* (Santa Barbara, Calif.: Clio Press, 1966), 3; Bracher, *The German Dictatorship*, 45; Massing, *Rehearsal for Destruction*, 197; Albert Tyrell, *Führerbefiel: Selbstzeugnisse aus der Kampfzeit der NSDAP; Dokumente und Analyse* (Düsseldorf: Droste Verlag, 1969), 76, 381.

121. Massing, *Rehearsal for Destruction*, 104; Pinson, *Modern Germany*, 168; Pulzer, *The Rise of Political Anti-Semitism*, 122.

122. Quoted in Levy, *The Downfall*, 83; see also Kampmann, *Deutsche und Juden*, 286–287; Pulzer, *The Rise of Political Anti-Semitism*, 79.

123. Levy, *The Downfall*, passim; Massing, *Rehearsal for Destruction*, 104–106; Pulzer, *The Rise of Political Anti-Semitism*, 122.

124. Pulzer, *The Rise of Political Anti-Semitism*, 191–193; Tal, *Christians and Jews*, 128.

125. George Mosse, *The Crisis*, 243; idem, "Die deutsche Rechte und die Juden," 228–230, 245; Lewis Hertzman, *DNVP: Right-wing Opposition in the Weimar Republic, 1918–1924* (Lincoln, Nebraska: University of Nebraska Press, 1963), passim; see also Pulzer, *The Rise of Political Anti-Semitism*, 303; for Wiener's opinion, see P. B. Wiener, "Die Parteien der Mitte," 344; see also Knütter, *Die Juden*, 104–105.

126. Pulzer, *The Rise of Political Anti-Semitism*, 226.

127. Levy, *The Downfall*, 181–183.

128. Pulzer, *The Rise of Political Anti-Semitism*, 195.

129. Schorsche, *Jewish Reactions*, 61.

130. Bruce Frye, "The German Democratic Party and the 'Jewish Problem' in the Weimar Republic," Leo Baeck Institute *Yearbook* 21 (1976):143–172.

131. Wiener, "Die Parteien der Mitte," 289, 292–293, 295.

132. Ibid., 298, 295 (note 23), 305, 315, 318.

133. Rheins, "The Verband Nationaldeutscher Juden," 263.

134. Guenter Lewy, *The Catholic Church and Nazi Germany*, 268-274.

135. Levy, *The Downfall*, 4, 5, 13, 14, 183–190; Pulzer, *The Rise of Political Anti-Semitism*, 274–275; Tal, *Christians and Jews*, 81–120.

136. Levy, *The Downfall*, 183–190; Wiener, "Die Parteien der Mitte," 308; Pulzer, *The Rise of Political Anti-Semitism*, 88.

137. Werner Jochmann, "Struktur und Funktion des deutschen Antisemitismus," in *Juden im wilhelminischen Deutschland 1890–1914*, edited by Werner Mosse, Leo Baeck Institute, Schriftenreihe wissenschaftlicher Abhandlungen, no. 33 (Tübingen: Mohr, 1976), 399.

138. See Levy, *The Downfall*, 184–186; see also Hamburger, *Juden im öffentlichen Leben*, 143; Kampmann, *Deutsche und Juden*, 257; Massing, *Rehearsal for Destruction*, 47.

139. Lamberti, "Liberals, Socialists," 160–161.

140. Pulzer, *The Rise of Political Anti-Semitism*, 271–278; Massing, *Rehearsal for Destruction*, 151–206.

141. Wiener, "Die Parteien der Mitte," 308.

142. Ibid., 313.

143. Ibid., 311.

144. Ibid., 307, 310; according to Knütter, Jews turned to the Center party after the DDP broke up in 1930 and again when the Staatspartei split apart in 1932 (*Die Juden*, 119).

145. Hans-Helmuth Knütter, "Die Linksparteien," 338.

146. Lewy, *The Catholic Church*, 268–274.

147. Pinson, *Modern Germany*, 575.

148. Massing, *Rehearsal for Destruction*, 159; see also Kampmann, *Deutsche*

*und Juden*, 335; Niewyk, *Socialist, Anti-Semite*, 20–21, 26–27; Pinson, *Modern Germany*, 81; Edmund Silberner, *Sozialisten zur Judenfrage; ein Beitrag zur Geschichte des Sozialismus vom Anfang des 19. Jahrhunderts bis 1914*, 124–125.

149. Silberner, *Sozialisten zur Judenfrage*, 124.

150. William S. Allen, *The Nazi Seizure of Power: The Experience of a Single German Town, 1930–1935*, 52, 213; Kampmann, *Deutsche und Juden*, 335; Knütter, "Die Linksparteien," 344.

151. Knütter, "Die Linksparteien," 341; George Mosse, "German Socialists and the Jewish Question in the Weimar Republic," Leo Baeck Institute *Yearbook* 16 (1971):123; Silberner, *Sozialisten zur Judenfrage*, 124.

152. Kampmann, *Deutsche und Juden*, 336–337; George Mosse, "German Socialists."

153. For anti-Semitism rooted in anticapitalist sentiment in the Left, see Niewyk, *Socialist, Anti-Semite*, 5, 26, 27; Leuschen-Seppel, *Sozialdemokratie und Antisemitismus*, passim; Silberner, *Sozialisten zur Judenfrage*, 124.

154. George Mosse, "German Socialists," 138.

155. Lamberti, "Liberals, Socialists," 156.

156. Quoted in ibid., 157, note 45.

157. Leuschen-Seppel, *Sozialdemokratie und Antisemitismus*, 274–275, 278, 287.

158. Massing, *Rehearsal for Destruction*, 325.

159. Niewyk, *Socialist, Anti-Semite*, 98–99.

160. Ibid., 101–103, 202–223; see also Niewyk, *The Jews in Weimar Germany*, 25–26.

161. Niewyk, *Socialist, Anti-Semite*, 105, 111, 113–114, 184, 208-209, 216–218; for other views on the levels of anti-Semitism among socialists, see Knütter, *Die Juden*, 75–87, 121, 123–136, 165–218, 222; idem, "Die Linksparteien," 324–338, 341, 344; George Mosse, "German Socialists," 131–132; Pinson, *Modern Germany*, 405; Schulz, *Jude und Arbeiter*, 67, 70.

162. Niewyk, *Socialist, Anti-Semite*, 37, 133–134, 216.

163. Knütter, *Die Juden*, 69, 217.

164. Walter Gross, "Das politische Schicksal der Juden in der Weimarer Republik," in *In Zwei Welten*, edited by H. Tramer (Tel Aviv: Bitaon, 1962), 548.

165. Ibid.

166. George Mosse, "German Socialists," 128; see also Knütter, "Die Linksparteien," 330, 336–337; Knütter, *Die Juden*, 205, 217 (Knütter indicates on p. 218 that although the KPD was opportunistic on the Jewish question, the *Rote Hilfe*, a subsidiary organization, was philo-Semitic).

167. Reichmann, *Hostages*, 1–39.

168. Ibid., 6, 37.

169. Ibid., 53, 60–64, 169, 236–243.

170. For indications of tension between German and Eastern European Jews, see Bennathan, "Die demographische und wirtschaftliche Struktur," 122, 126; Kurt Loewenstein, "Die innerjüdische Reaktion auf die Krise der deutschen Demokratie," 403; Fritz Marburg, *Der Antisemitismus in der deutschen Republik* (Vi-

enna: Kommissions Verlag, 1931), 58; Massing, *Rehearsal for Destruction*, 143; Arnold Paucker, "Der jüdische Abwehrkampf," 409; Reichmann, *Hostages*, 27–64; Stern, *The Politics*, 64, note 4; George Mosse, *Germans and Jews*, 24; Niewyk, *The Jews in Weimar Germany*, passim.

171. Pulzer, *The Rise of Political Anti-Semitism*, 15.

172. Levy, *The Downfall*, 6.

173. Pulzer, *The Rise of Political Anti-Semitism*, 248; Stern, *The Politics*, xxvi.

174. Hans Peter Bleuel and Ernst Klinnert, *Deutsche Studenten auf dem Weg ins Dritte Reich: Ideologien-Programme-Aktionen, 1918–1935* (Gütersloh: Mohn, 1976), 18–25, 130–153, 166–169; Bracher, *The German Dictatorship*, 165; Dawidowicz, *The War Against the Jews*, 284–285; Heinz David Leuner, *When Compassion Was a Crime: Germany's Silent Heroes, 1933–1945*, 39; Manfred Priepke, *Die evangelische Jugend im Dritten Reich* (Hannover and Frankfurt a.M.: Norddeutsche Verlagsanstalt, 1960), 41–42; George Mosse, *Germans and Jews*, 19, and *The Crisis*, passim. For indications that students were friendly rather than hostile toward Jews, see Albert Speer, *Inside the Third Reich*, 45.

175. Bracher, *The German Dictatorship*, 45; Pulzer, *The Rise of Political Anti-Semitism*, 189, 219; Reichmann, *Hostages*, 169.

176. Pulzer, *The Rise of Political Anti-Semitism*, 71, 96.

177. Bleuel, *Deutsche Studenten*, 135; Hamburger, *Juden im öffentlichen Leben*, 10–16; Massing, *Rehearsal for Destruction*, 108, 198.

178. Davidson, *The Making of Adolf Hitler*, 39; George Kren and Leon Rappoport, *The Holocaust and the Crisis of Human Behavior*, 3.

179. Davidson, *The Making of Adolf Hitler*, 295.

180. Kren and Rappoport, *The Holocaust*, 3.

181. Davidson, *The Making of Adolf Hitler*, 374.

182. Baker, *Days of Sorrow*, 221.

183. Claude R. Foster, Jr., "Historical Antecedents: Why the Holocaust?" 16.

184. Niewyk, *The Jews in Weimar Germany*, 165–177, 198–199.

185. Foster, "Historical Antecedents," 16.

186. Niewyk, *The Jews in Weimar Germany*, passim.

187. Quoted in Baker, *Days of Sorrow*, 124.

CHAPTER TWO

1. Wolfgang Sauer, "Comments on the Paper of Donald L. Niewyk," 178–181.

2. Hans P. Bahrdt, "Soziologische Reflexionen über die gesellschaftlichen Voraussetzungen des Antisemitismus in Deutschland," in *Entscheidungsjahr*, edited by Werner Mosse, 14; Z. Barbu, "Die sozialpsychologische Struktur des Nationalsozialistischen Antisemitismus," in *Entscheidungsjahr*, edited by Werner Mosse, 166; Else Behrend-Rosenfeld, *Ich stand nicht allein: Erlebnisse einer Jüdin in Deutschland*, 122; Bennathan, "Die demographische und wirtschaftliche Struktur," 128, 131; Bracher, *The German Dictatorship*, 39; Dawidowicz, *The War Against the Jews*, 35, 42–43; Theodor Geiger, *Die soziale Schichtung des*

*Deutschen Volkes* (Stuttgart: F. Enke, 1932), passim; Genschel, *Die Verdrängung*, 37, 40–42; Emil Lederer and Jacob Marschak, "Die Klassen auf dem Arbeitsmarkt und ihre Organisationen," *Grundriss der Sozialökonomik* 9, part 2, passim; Buchheim et al., *Anatomy*, 5–6; Lebovics, *Social Conservatism*, passim; Massing, *Rehearsal for Destruction*, 47, 75; Jeremy Noakes, *The Nazi Party in Lower Saxony, 1921–1933*, 86, 112, 124, 129; Dietrich Orlow, *The History of the Nazi Party, 1918–1933*, vol. 1, passim; Paucker, *Der jüdische Abwehrkampf*, 145, 147; Pulzer, *The Rise of Political Anti-Semitism*, 27; Reichmann, *Hostages*, 101–105; idem, "Diskussionen über die Judenfrage 1930–1932," 529; Ernst-August Roloff, "Wer wählte Hitler? Thesen zur Sozial- und Wirtschaftsgeschichte der Weimarer Republik," 299; Karl Schleunes, *The Twisted Road to Auschwitz: Nazi Policy toward German Jews, 1933–1939*, 58–60; David Schoenbaum, *Hitler's Social Revolution: Class and Status in Nazi Germany, 1933–1939*, 152; Marlis Steinert, *Hitlers Krieg und die Deutschen: Stimmung und Haltung der deutschen Bevölkerung im zweiten Weltkrieg*, 53–54; Heinrich Winkler, "Extremismus der Mitte? Sozialgeschichtliche Aspekte der nationalsozialistischen Machtergreifung," passim.

3. Dietrich Uwe Adam, *Judenpolitik im Dritten Reich*, 21; Ernst Hanfstaengl, *Unheard Witness* (New York: Lippincott, 1957), 31; Werner Jochmann, *Nationalsozialismus und Revolution; Ursprung und Geschichte der NSDAP in Hamburg, 1929–1933* (Hamburg: Forschungsstelle für die Geschichte des Nationalsozialismus in Hamburg, 1963), 5–8, 25–27; Buchheim, *Anatomy*, 19; George Mosse, "Die deutsche Rechte und die Juden," 235; Paucker, *Der jüdische Abwehrkampf*, 27; Pulzer, *The Rise of Political Anti-Semitism*, 229–306.

4. For numbers of Jews in World War I, see Hamburger, *Juden im öffentlichen Leben*, 101; Sellenthin, *Geschichte der Juden in Berlin*, 52. See also Niewyk, *The Jews in Weimar Germany*, 47, and Otto Armin, *Die Juden im Heere: Eine statistische Untersuchung nach amtlichen Quellen* (Munich: Deutsches Volksverlag, 1919).

5. Robert Waite, *Vanguard of Nazism: The Free Corps Movement in Postwar Germany, 1918–1923* (New York: Norton, 1969), 30; for accusations of Jewish treachery, see Erich Eyck, *A History of the Weimar Republic*, 2 vols. (New York: Atheneum, 1970), 1:135.

6. Davidson, *The Making of Adolf Hitler*, 177.

7. Wiener, "Die Parteien der Mitte," 309; Hamburger, "Jews, Democracy and Weimar Germany," 1–6.

8. Peter Merkl in comments on this book manuscript, 1982.

9. Gross, "Das politische Schicksal der Juden," 541, 545; Knütter, *Die Juden*, 68–110; Lowenthal, "Die Juden im öffentlichen Leben," 56; Fritz Marburg, *Der Antisemitismus in der Deutschen Republik* (Vienna: Kommissions Verlag, 1931), 45; Kurt Meier, *Kirche und Judentum: Die Haltung der evangelischen Kirche zur Judenpolitik des Dritten Reiches*, 9; Niewyk, *Socialist, Anti-Semite*, 49.

10. Knütter, *Die Juden*, 75; George Mosse, "Die deutsche Rechte," 230; Nicholls and Mathias, *German Democracy*, 108.

11. Dawidowicz, *The War Against the Jews*, 47; Hanfstaengl, *Unheard Witness*, 35–61.

12. Robert Weltsch, "Entscheidungsjahr 1932," in *Entscheidungsjahr*, edited by Werner Mosse, 548; see also Niewyk, *The Jews in Weimar Germany*, 36–38.

13. Hanfstaengl, *Unheard Witness*, 243; see also Peter Merkl, *Political Violence under the Swastika: 581 Early Nazis*, passim.

14. Adam, *Judenpolitik*, 15; Ernst K. Bramsted, *Goebbels and National Socialist Propaganda, 1925–1945* (East Lansing: Michigan State University Press, 1965), 378; Alan Bullock, "The Theory of Nazism: Hitler's Basic Ideas," 63.

15. Hermann Rauschning, *The Voice of Destruction*, 233–234; for attitudes of party members in Hamburg toward Streicher and other rabid anti-Semites in the NSDAP, see Albert Krebs, *Tendenzen und Gestalten der NSDAP: Erinnerungen an die Frühzeit der Partei*, 203.

16. Broszat, *German National Socialism*, 41, and Ian Kershaw, "Antisemitismus und Volksmeinung: Reaktionen auf die Judenverfolgung," 346.

17. Cecil, *The Myth of the Master Race*, 261–265; Krebs, *Tendenzen*, 16, 151; Barbara Lane, "Nazi Ideology: Some Unfinished Business," *Central European History* 7 (March, 1974), passim; Nicholls and Mathias, *German Democracy*, 136–138; Niewyk, *Socialist, Anti-Semite*, 146; George Mosse, "Die deutsche Rechte," 238; Reichmann, *Hostages*, 190.

18. Niewyk, *Socialist, Anti-Semite*, 200.

19. Merkl, *Political Violence*, passim; an earlier study by Theodore Abel, *Why Hitler Came to Power: An Answer Based on the Original Life Stories of Six Hundred of His Followers*, was not nearly as comprehensive or systematic as Merkl's work. Although Merkl's book contains a self-selected data base, his selections conform to common sense and practical necessity; for limitations of his sample, see his pp. 5–11.

20. Merkl, *Political Violence*, 499–500.

21. Ibid., 499.

22. Merkl's comments on this book manuscript, 1982.

23. Merkl, *Political Violence*, 660–710.

24. For a more detailed analysis of Merkl's results, see my "German Opposition to Nazi Anti-Semitic Measures Between 1933 and 1945, with Particular Reference to the Rhine-Ruhr Area," chapter 3. See also appendix A for methods used.

25. See appendix B, table B.1 for the data on which these results are based.

26. See appendix B, table B.1 for numbers and percentages on which age comparisons are based.

27. Merkl, *Political Violence*, 501.

28. See table 2.1.

29. Ages of party members may vary slightly in different sources.

30. See chapter 2, note 2.

31. See appendix B, table B.1 for numbers and percentages upon which sex comparisons are based.

32. Ibid., for numbers and percentages on which residential comparisons are based.

33. Merkl, *Political Violence*, 501.

34. Seymour Martin Lipset, *Political Man: The Social Bases of Politics*, 144; see also Pridham, *Hitler's Rise*, 237–244; Rudolf Heberle, *From Democracy to Nazism: A Regional Case Study on Political Parties in Germany* (Baton Rouge: Louisiana State University Press, 1945), passim.

35. Heberle, *From Democracy to Nazism*.

36. Pridham, *Hitler's Rise*, 240; Allen, *The Nazi Seizure*, 77; for the percentage of paranoid anti-Semites from Berlin, see Merkl, *Political Violence*, 501.

37. Lipset, *Political Man*, 148.

38. Statistisches Amt, *Wirtschaft und Statistik* 19 (1934):658.

39. See appendix B, table B.1, for religion, which was given for only one hundred anti-Semites.

40. See ibid., for numbers and percentages on which occupational comparisons are based; see also Merkl, *Political Violence*, 500.

41. See this chapter, note 2.

42. See Appendix B, table B.1, for numbers and percentages on which comparisons of fathers' occupations are based.

43. Farmers are normally classified as members of the "old middle class" versus the "new middle class" (white-collar workers).

44. See appendix B, table B.1 for numbers and percentages on which educational comparisons are based.

45. There were 295 anti-Semites from the middle class and 112 from the lower class.

46. See appendix B, table B.1 for numbers of urban residents in Merkl's sample.

47. See appendix A or a discussion of chance occurrences.

48. See *Statistik des Deutschen Reiches*, vol. 451 (1933), no. 5:26, for the percentages of the Jewish and non-Jewish labor force in blue-collar occupations.

49. Ibid., for percentages of the labor force in middle-class occupations.

50. Cecil, *The Myth of the Master Race*, 21–36; Werner Maser, *Die Frühgeschichte der NSDAP: Hitlers Weg bis 1924*, 97, 121; Orlow, *The History*, 1:47; Noakes, *Hitler's Rise*, passim; Schoenbaum, *Hitler's Social Revolution*, 40.

51. See Wolfgang Schäfer, *Entwicklung und Struktur der Staatspartei des Dritten Reiches*, 17, for NSDAP membership; for additional membership figures, see also Michael Kater, "Quantifizierung und NS-Geschichte; Methodologische Ueberlegungen über Grenzen und Möglichkeiten einer EDV-Analyse der NSDAP-Sozialstruktur von 1925 bis 1945," *Geschichte und Gesellschaft* 4 (1977):453–484; for *völkisch* influences in the early NSDAP, see Merkl, *Political Violence*, 498–517; for anti-Semitism in the *völkisch* movement, see George Mosse, *The Crisis*, passim.

52. Merkl, *Political Violence*, 508, 694.

53. Ibid., 481.

54. Ibid., 508, 694.

55. See table 2.1 and ibid., 499.

56. Merkl, *Political Violence*, 476.

57. Ibid., 322, 343, 355, 365, 380, 443, 506, 677, 679, 688, 693.
58. Ibid., 473, 376.
59. Ibid., 476.
60. Ibid. and see Kershaw, "Antisemitismus und Volksmeinung," 345, 347.
61. See table 2.1.
62. Ernst Nolte, *Three Faces of Fascism: Action Française, Italian Fascism, National Socialism,* 387; Wiener, "Die Parteien der Mitte," 320–321; Marburg, *Der Antisemitismus,* 58–59.
63. Dawidowicz, *The War Against the Jews,* 48; Ambrose Doskow and Sidney Jacoby, "Anti-Semitism and the Law in Pre-Nazi Germany," *Contemporary Jewish Record* 3, no. 5 (1940):498–509.
64. Pulzer, *The Rise of Political Anti-Semitism,* 326; Erick Eyck, *A History of the Weimar Republic,* 2 vols. (New York: Atheneum, 1970), 1:271, 2:261.
65. Dorothee Linn, *Das Schicksal der jüdischen Bevölkerung in Memmingen von 1933 bis 1945,* 18; Düwell, *Die Rheingebiete,* 78–81; Pridham, *Hitler's Rise,* 52.
66. Bracher, *The German Dictatorship,* 253; Düwell, *Die Rheingebiete,* 56; Reichmann, *Hostages,* 53; Hans-Gunther Zmarlik, "Der Antisemitismus im Zweiten Reich," 273.
67. Bracher, *The German Dictatorship,* 39.
68. Pridham, *Hitler's Rise,* 58–59, 177.
69. Noakes, *The Nazi Party,* 103.
70. Reichmann, *Hostages,* 166–167, 198, 234.
71. For tactical advantages of this ploy, see Horst Gies, "The NSDAP and Agrarian Organizations in the Final Phase of the Weimar Republic," in *Nazism and the Third Reich,* edited by Henry Turner, Jr., 56; for a similar tactic with regard to wartime enemies from 1939 to 1944 see Ernst Kris and Hans Speier, *German Radio Propaganda: Report on Home Broadcasts during the War* (New York: Oxford University Press, 1944), 215ff, 231ff.
72. Wiener, "Die Parteien der Mitte," 320–321.
73. George Mosse, "Die deutsche Rechte," 230.
74. David A. Hackett, "The Nazi Party in the *Reichstag* Election of 1930" (Ph.D. dissertation, University of Wisconsin, 1971), 290; Orlow, *The History,* 1:170–187; see also Barbara Lane and Leila Rupp, trans., *Nazi Ideology before 1933: A Documentation* (Austin: University of Texas Press, 1978), 45, for the absence of virulent anti-Semitism in Nazi writings from 1923–1933.
75. Hackett, *The Nazi Party,* 285; Golo Mann, "Der Antisemitismus: Wurzeln, Wirkung und Ueberwindung," *Vom Gestern zum Morgen* 3 (1960):34; Noakes, *Hitler's Rise,* 148–150.
76. Hackett, *The Nazi Party,* 16.
77. Ibid., 285, 291.
78. Ibid., 303, 306.
79. Ibid., 227.
80. Norman Baynes, ed., *The Speeches of Adolf Hitler: April, 1922–August, 1939,* 727; for Hitler's denials of Nazi attacks on Jews after the 1930 election, see Eyck, *A History,* 2:290.

81. Adam, *Judenpolitik*, 27.
82. Düwell, *Die Rheingebiete*, 82.
83. Max Domarus, ed., *Hitler Reden und Proklamationen 1932–1945*, vol. 1 (1932–1934):57–188.
84. Ibid., 25, and Baynes, *The Speeches of Adolf Hitler*, 72.
85. Adam, *Judenpolitik*, 25–26; Schoenbaum, *Hitler's Social Revolution*, 27.
86. Martin Broszat, "Soziale Motivation und Führer-Bindung des Nationalsozialismus," *Vierteljahrshefte für Zeitgeschichte* 18, no. 4 (October 1970):400; Wilhelm Hoegner, *Die verratene Republik: Geschichte der deutschen Gegenrevolution* (Munich: Isar Verlag, 1958), passim; Reichmann, *Hostages*, 166–167, 198, 234; Noakes, *Hitler's Rise*, 209; James Rhodes, *The Hitler Movement: A Modern Millenarian Revolution*, 3; Toland, *Adolf Hitler*, 329; Davidson, *The Making of Adolf Hitler*, 294–295, 365.
87. Barbu, "Die sozialpsychologische Struktur," 160; Kele, *Nazis and Workers*, 145; Paucker, *Der jüdische Abwehrkampf*, 16; Werner Mosse, "Der Niedergang," 45; Schleunes, *The Twisted Road*, 44.
88. Pridham, *Hitler's Rise*, 244; see also Allen, *The Nazi Seizure*, 77; Richard Hamilton, *Who Voted for Hitler?*, 605–607, note 46.
89. Martin Needler, "Hitler's Anti-Semitism: A Political Appraisal," 669; see also Arendt, *The Origins of Totalitarianism*, 76; Werner Mosse, "Der Niedergang," 29; Reichmann, "Diskussionen," 530.
90. Schoenbaum, *Hitler's Social Revolution*, 42.
91. Cohn, *Warrant for Genocide*, 198–199; George Mosse, "Die deutsche Rechte," 243; Niewyk, *Socialist, Anti-Semite*, 122; Reichmann, *Hostages*, 5, 65; Davidson, *The Making of Adolf Hitler*, 195–365; Kershaw, "Antisemitismus und Volksmeinung," 345.
92. Allen, *The Nazi Seizure*, 77–78, 210, 281; Düwell, *Die Rheingebiete*, 56; Knütter, *Die Juden*, 104–108; Kurt Lowenstein, "Die innerjüdische Reaktion auf die Krise der deutschen Demokratie," 378; Werner Mosse, "Der Niedergang," 39–40; Arnold Paucker, "The Diaries of Ernst Feder," Leo Baeck Institute *Yearbook* 13 (1968):161–234; Eva Pfeifer, *Das Hitlerbild im Spiegel einiger konservativer Zeitungen in den Jahren 1929–1933*, 189–190; Kershaw, "Antisemitismus und Volksmeinung," 345; Reichmann, "Diskussionen," 506; Lawrence Stokes, "The *Sicherheitsdienst* of the *Reichsführer* SS and German Public Opinion, September, 1939–June, 1941" (Ph.D. dissertation, Johns Hopkins University, 1972), 527; Weltsch, "Entscheidungsjahr 1932," 561–562; Wiener, "Die Parteien der Mitte," 320; the Boxheim Papers did, however, reveal Nazi plans to exclude Jews from Nazi-controlled food distribution (see Eyck, *A History*, 2:337).
93. See this chapter, "Anti-Semitism in the Early Nazi Party."
94. Pinson, *Modern Germany*, 575.
95. Lipset, *Political Man*, 139.
96. Ibid., 138, 151.
97. Hackett, "The Nazi Party," 347, 353–356, 427, 429; Karl O'Lessker, "Who Voted for Hitler? A New Look at the Class Basis of Nazism," 63, 65; Noakes,

*The Nazi Party*, 152–153; for Lipset's recent remarks, see *Political Man*, 440–495.

98. O'Lessker, "Who Voted for Hitler?" 65; see also a reply to O'Lessker by Allen Schnaiberg, "A Critique of Karl O'Lessker's 'Who Voted for Hitler?' " 734. Schnaiberg disputes O'Lessker's attribution of NSDAP gains to increased electoral turnout of new and previous nonvoters.

99. Heinrich A. Winkler, *Mittelstand, Demokratie und Nationalsozialismus: Die politische Entwicklung von Handwerk und Kleinhandel in der Weimarer Republik*, 177–178, 180.

100. Alexander Weber, *Soziale Merkmale der NSDAP-Wähler* (published dissertation, Freiburg: University of Freiburg, 1969), 162–163, 165. See also Larry Jones, "The Dying Middle: Weimar Germany and the Fragmentation of Bourgeois Politics," *Central European History* 5, no. 1 (May 1972), passim, for a discussion of the difficulties of middle-class parties in forming stable coalitions. For the middle classes and the 1932 elections see Samuel Alexander Pratt, "The Social Basis of Nazism and Communism in Urban Germany: A Correlational Study of the July 31, 1932 Reichstag Elections in Germany," 63, 261–266; see also Winkler, *Mittelstand*, 260–261, notes 45–48; Lipset, *Political Man*, 138–152; Geiger, *Die soziale Schichtung*, 109–122; Noakes, *The Nazi Party*, 119; Weber, *Soziale Werkmale*, 96–99, 159–160, 164; Roloff, "Wer wählte Hitler?" 294; Hamilton, *Who Voted for Hitler?*, 413, 421, 435.

101. Hackett, "The Nazi Party," 356.

102. Ibid.

103. Ibid., 353–356.

104. Thomas Childers, "The Social Bases of the National Socialist Vote," 36, note 37.

105. Hamilton, *Who Voted for Hitler?*, 61.

106. The DNVP is normally considered a party of the right; the DVP, DDP, WP, and smaller regional parties constituted the middle for most historians.

107. DNVP 0.32; NSDAP 0.34; see Childers, "The Social Bases," 41, table 4.

108. Hackett, "The Nazi Party," 353–357; see also Weber, *Soziale Merkmale*, 161.

109. Walter Dean Burnham, "Political Immunization and Political Confessionalism: The United States and Weimar Germany," *Journal of Interdisciplinary History*, 3/1 (Summer 1972):13.

110. See discussion earlier in this section.

111. See *Statistik des Deutschen Reiches*, vol. 451 (1933), no. 5:26.

112. Pratt, "The Social Basis," 63, 261–266; Heberle, *From Democracy to Nazism*, passim; Lipset, *Political Man*, 138-152; Winkler, *Mittelstand*, 177; Weber, *Soziale Merkmale*, 96–99; Hackett, "The Nazi Party," 417, 420–421.

113. Merkl, *Political Violence*, 668.

114. Childers, "The Social Bases," 40, table 2B.

115. Pratt, "The Social Basis," 63, and also pp. 261–266.

116. Winkler, *Mittelstand*, 177.

117. Weber, *Soziale Merkmale*, 416.
118. Childers, "The Social Bases," 40, table A.
119. Ibid., 36, notes 35, 36. In 1932: r = 0.67 for self-employed Protestants and NSDAP votes; r = 1.13 for Protestants in handicrafts and NSDAP votes; r = 0.83 for Catholics in handicrafts and NSDAP votes.
120. Ibid., 38, note 51.
121. Ibid., 41, table 6.
122. Ibid., 40–41, tables 2–6.
123. Ibid., 24.
124. Ibid., 27.
125. Ibid., 36, note 37; 41, table 4.
126. See this section, below.
127. Hamilton, *Who Voted for Hitler?*, 25–26, 39; see also his critique of existing theories, pp. 26–36.
128. Ibid., 56–57.
129. Ibid., 390.
130. Ibid.; for platforms of political parties, see Hamilton's chapter 10; for stances of newspapers, see his pp. 393, 414–419.
131. Ibid., 417.
132. Ibid., 370.
133. Hackett, "The Nazi Party," 342–343; see also Lipset, *Political Man*, 148, note 29.
134. Hamilton, *Who Voted for Hitler?*, 391.
135. Ibid., 392.
136. Ibid.; for a discussion of blue-collar workers, see pp. 387–390.
137. Ibid., 387.
138. Ibid., 390.
139. Ibid., see chapter 10.
140. Ibid., 231.
141. Ibid., 388.
142. Childers, "The Social Bases," 28–29.
143. Hamilton, *Who Voted for Hitler?*, 39–41.
144. See ibid.
145. George Mosse, *The Crisis*, 243, and his "Die deutsche Rechte," 228–230.
146. Jones, "The Dying Middle," passim; Weber, *Soziale Merkmale*, 162–163; Winkler, *Mittelstand*, passim; Robert Gellately, *The Politics of Economic Despair: Shopkeepers and German Politics, 1890–1914*, covers the problems of some middle-class occupational groups before World War I; see also Heinrich August Winkler, "From Social Protectionism to National Socialism: The German Small Business Movement in Comparative Perspective," *Journal of Modern History* 48 (1976):1–18.
147. Allen, *The Nazi Seizure*, 130-131; Noakes, *The Nazi Party*, 209; Hamilton, *Who Voted for Hitler?*, 418–419; Kershaw, "Antisemitismus und Volksmeinung," 346.

148. By 1933 *Mein Kampf* had sold 300,000 copies, but it is not known how many of these were sold to the Nazi party for compulsory purchase by its members and affiliates; see Bracher, *The German Dictatorship*, 129.

149. For example, in the United States, Democrats frequently enact Republican programs and vice versa.

150. Hanfstaengl, Rauschning, and other perceptive critics of Hitler's policies frequently had greater insight because they had close personal contacts with Hitler. For unawareness of Hitler's intentions, see Bauer, *The Holocaust*, 7, and Kershaw, "Antisemitismus und Volksmeinung," 347.

151. See chapter 1, "Political Parties."

152. Pinson, *Modern Germany*, 574.

153. See table 2.6.

154. See this section above.

155. See Gordon, "German Opposition," appendix F, 424–426, for a comparison of civil servants, white-collar workers, and blue-collar workers according to their wages or salaries and unemployment during Weimar years. Also see Winkler, *Mittlestand*, 36–37, and 206–209, notes 66–101, for data on the economic situation of artisans, small businessmen, and farmers.

156. Pratt, "The Social Basis," chapter 8; Weber, *Soziale Merkmale*, 96–99, 159–160, 164.

157. Weber, *Soziale Merkmale*, 164.

158. See *Statistik des Deutschen Reiches*, vol. 451 (1933), no. 5:7, for the percentage of Jews in the German population in 1933.

159. See this chapter, "Anti-Semitism in the Early Nazi Party."

160. For anti-Semites, see ibid.; for voters, see Lipset, *Political Man*, 127–154.

161. Lipset, *Political Man*, 140.

162. Ibid., 144, 148; Roloff, "Wer wählte Hitler?" 294.

163. Lipset, *Political Man*, 142–143.

164. Merkl's comments on this book manuscript, 1982.

CHAPTER THREE

1. Eberhard Jaeckel, *Hitler's Weltanschauung: A Blueprint for Power*, and Sebastian Haffner, *The Meaning of Hitler: Hitler's Use of Power: His Successes and Failures*.

2. Quoted in Werner Maser, *Hitler*, 251.

3. See Jaeckel, *Hitler's Weltanschauung*, 52, for Hitler's comments on the "Jewish spirit" in 1923.

4. Adam, *Judenpolitik im Dritten Reich*, 118.

5. Haffner, *The Meaning*, 81. (In this chapter Haffner's summaries and quotations will be used because his book is accessible to general readers.)

6. Ibid., 78–79.

7. Ibid., 83.

8. Ibid., 81.

9. Ibid., 82; my parentheses.
10. Quoted in ibid.
11. Ibid., 84.
12. Ibid., 85.
13. See Adolf Hitler, *The Testament of Adolf Hitler: The Hitler-Bormann Documents, February–April, 1945*, 114, on the "Jewish influence" that resulted in the "unnatural" entry of the United States into World War II. See also his comments on "Nature" decreeing German eastward expansion, p. 54.
14. Quoted in Haffner, *The Meaning*, 82.
15. See Saul Friedländer, "On the Possibility of the Holocaust: An Approach to a Historical Synthesis," 8.
16. See chapter 4, "Functions of Anti-Semitism inside the Nazi Party."
17. Hitler, *Testament*, 38, 42, 60, 100, 119, 121.
18. Quoted in Haffner, *The Meaning*, 78, and see Hitler, *Testament*, 45.
19. Hitler, *Testament*, 31–32.
20. Ibid., 48.
21. Ibid., 63.
22. Quoted in Toland, *Adolf Hitler*, 951.
23. Hitler, *Testament*, 85.
24. Ibid., 41.
25. Ibid., 45.
26. Jaeckel, *Hitler's Weltanschauung*, 50, 61.
27. Allan Mitchell, "Polish, Dutch, and French Elites under the German Occupation," 235.
28. Ibid., 228, 239.
29. David Calleo, *The German Problem Reconsidered: Germany and the World Order, 1870 to the Present* (Cambridge: Cambridge University Press, 1978), 119; Bauer and Feingold also make this point with respect to Jewish victims; see Yehuda Bauer, "Genocide: Was it the Nazis' Original Plan?" *Annals of the American Academy of Political and Social Science* 450 (July 1980):40, 44, and Henry Feingold, "The Government Response," 256.
30. Quoted in Pierre Ayçoberry, *The Nazi Question: An Essay on Interpretations of National Socialism (1922–1975)* (New York: Pantheon Books, 1981), 89.
31. Quoted in Michael Balfour, *Propaganda in War, 1939–1945: Organisations, Policies and Publics in Britain and Germany* (London and Boston: Routledge, 1979), 304; see also a similar report in Steinert, *Hitlers Krieg*, 256.
32. Quoted in Heinz Hoehne, *The Order of the Death's Head: The Story of Hitler's SS*, 336.
33. Quoted in Robert Waite, *The Psychopathic God: Adolf Hitler*, 475.
34. On Czechs, see Hoehne, *The Order*, 335; the August quotation is from his p. 336.
35. Hoover Institution, "Anti-Nazi Propaganda Leaflets," PaM DD253.3 An, library (one envelope), press directive of October 24, 1939.
36. Quoted in Hoehne, *The Order*, 339.

37. Ibid.

38. Kren and Rappoport, *The Holocaust*, 55.

39. Ibid., 55.

40. Quoted in Hoehne, *The Order*, 332.

41. Quoted in ibid., 332–333.

42. Quoted in ibid., 357.

43. Ibid., 354.

44. Norman Stone, *Hitler*, 128; Haffner, *The Meaning*, 132; Robert Payne, *The Life and Death of Adolf Hitler*, 462. The higher estimate of 275,000 is made by Frederic Wertham in *A Sign for Cain* (New York: Macmillan, 1966), 156–158.

45. Christian Streit, *Keine Kameraden: Die Wehrmacht und die sowjet Kriegsgefangenen 1941–1945*, 10, 228.

46. See Bauer, "Genocide," 42, on Russian prisoners of war; see Raul Hilberg, "The Nature of the Process," in *Survivors, Victims and Perpetrators: Essays on the Nazi Holocaust*, edited by Joel E. Dimsdale, M.D. (New York: Hemisphere Publishing Corp., 1980) 11, on ugly prisoners.

47. NA, T-175, R 502, F 9366335, *SD Hauptaussenstelle Bielefeld an III B 1*, 8.5.41.

48. NA, T-175, R 502, F 9365693, *SD Hauptaussenstelle Erfurt*, 19.6.42.

49. NA, T-175, R 271, F 2767377, *SD Hauptaussenstelle Bielefeld an III A 3*, 10.12.42. This was probably a typical attempt of the SD to generalize public attitudes from those of the Nazi party radicals.

50. YIVO, G-157, no. 113, no date.

51. YIVO, G-96a 1, *Propaganda Parole* 43, 9.12.43.

52. YIVO, G-76, no. 71, *Informationsdienst: Rassenpolitischesamt der NSDAP, Reichsleitung*, no. 140, 8.20.43.

53. Bauer, *The Holocaust in Historical Perspective*, 10.

54. Kren and Rappoport *The Holocaust*, 36.

55. Bauer, *The Holocaust in Historical Perspective*, 10.

56. Reinhard Henkys, *Die nationalsozialistischen Gewaltverbrechen: Geschichte und Gericht* (Stuttgart: Kreuz Verlag, 1964), 167; Streit, *Keine Kameraden*, 10.

57. Henkys, *Die nationalsozialistischen*, Lothar Berthold, "Das System des faschistischen Terrors in Deutschland und die Haltung der einzelnen Klassen und Volksschichten," *Zeitschrift für Geschichtewissenchaft* 1/1 (1964):6.

58. See also Bauer, "Genocide," 39, on extermination as the logical conclusion of Nazi ideological developments.

59. Ibid.; see also Andreas Hillgruber, "Die 'Endlösung' und das deutsche Ostimperium als Kernstück des rassenideologischen Programms des Nationalsozialismus," *Vierteljahrshefte für Zeitgeschichte* 20/2 (April 1972):133–153.

60. Quoted in Toland, *Adolf Hitler*, 836.

61. Quoted in ibid., p. 848; see also Hitler, *Testament*, 41, 95.

62. Hitler, *Testament*, 86, 99.

63. Ibid., 94.

64. Quoted in Toland, *Adolf Hitler*, 1056–1057.

65. Bauer, *The Holocaust in Historical Perspective*, 36.
66. Bracher, *The German Dictatorship*, 389, 390.
67. Donald McKale, *The Nazi Party Courts: Hitler's Management of Conflict in his Movement, 1921-1945*, 156-157.
68. See chapter 5, "Functions of propaganda."
69. For example, see Waite, *The Psychopathic God*.
70. George Kren and Leon Rappoport, "Resistance to the Holocaust: Reflections on the Idea and the Act," 196-197.
71. Ibid., 197.
72. Ibid.
73. Ibid., 198.
74. Ibid., 200.
75. Ibid., 203.
76. Ibid.
77. Ibid., 205.
78. Ibid., 208.
79. Quoted in ibid., 209.
80. Ibid., 216.
81. Ibid., 217.
82. Hitler's fear of Stalin was somewhat diminished when he examined a photograph taken during the signing of the Nazi-Soviet Pact and discovered to his relief that Stalin's earlobes were not "Jewish"—to Hitler this meant that Stalin would not be as difficult an opponent. His respect decreased, however, because Stalin had allowed pictures to be taken while he was smoking; Hitler considered this unworthy of a great leader. See Toland, *Adolf Hitler*, 754.

CHAPTER FOUR

1. For general discussions of this process, see Adam, *Judenpolitik im Dritten Reich*; Dawidowicz, *The War Against the Jews*; Düwell, *Die Rheingebiete*; Schleunes, *The Twisted Road*; Raul Hilberg, *The Destruction of the European Jews*; Buchheim, *Anatomy*, 1–73.
2. *Statistik des Deutschen Reiches*, vol. 451 (1933), no. 5:7; also see Strauss, "Jewish Emigration," 326.
3. Strauss, "Jewish Emigration," 327. Strauss indicates that between 270,000 and 300,000 Jews emigrated from Germany, but the 300,000 figure appears more probable because he estimates that 247,000 emigrated between 1933 and December 31, 1939, and that an excess of 47,500 Jews died due to old age during the same period (p. 326). But if the Jewish population was 204,000 at the end of 1939 (p. 341), then another 26,500 must have emigrated between 1933 and 1940 for the numbers to tally.
4. Ibid., 326–327.
5. Ibid; the final estimate includes 134,000 deportees from Germany plus 30,000 German Jews in other countries, minus 5,000 camp survivors.

6. Adam, *Judenpolitik*, 35; Rauschning, *Voice of Destruction*, 89.

7. Düwell, *Die Rheingebiete*, 81.

8. Schleunes, *The Twisted Road*, 68–75, 81.

9. Genschel, *Die Verdrängung*, 54–56; Leuner, *When Compassion was a Crime*, 20.

10. Adam, *Judenpolitik*, 63, note 196; Jürgen Hagemann, *Die Presselenkung im Dritten Reich*, 120; Schleunes, *The Twisted Road*, 90–91; BA ZSg 116/69/5—25.3.33.

11. Strauss, "Jewish Emigration," 340; around 30,000 Jews were affected.

12. Meier, 12–13.

13. Adam, *Judenpolitik*, 120, 142, 163; Düwell, *Die Rheingebiete*, 171; Orlow, *The History*, 2:163; Edward Peterson, *The Limits of Hitler's Power*, 134–170; *DB* II/8 (August 1935):B-13–B-15.

14. Adam, *Judenpolitik*, 114, 119, 120; Genschel, *Die Verdrängung*, 108; *DB* II/9 (August 1935):A-12.

15. Adam, *Judenpolitik*, 114–115.

16. Ibid., 142; Peterson, *The Limits*, 134–140; Schleunes, *The Twisted Road*, 102–103.

17. Adam, *Judenpolitik*, 118.

18. Ibid., 129.

19. Ibid., 128.

20. Ibid., and 129–130; Hagemann, *Die Presselenkung*, p. 121; Hans Mommsen, "Der nationalsozialistische Polizeistaat und die Verfolgung vor 1938," 76; Jeremy Noakes and Geoffrey Pridham, *Documents on Nazism, 1919–1945*, 257; Steinert, *Hitlers Krieg*, 57; *DB* II/8 (August 1935):B-1, B-2.

21. *DB* III/1 (January 1936):A-6, A-16, A-17b; *DB* III/7 (July 1936):A-21, A-22; *DB* IV/4 (April 1937):A-3; *DB* IV/6 (June 1937):A-10, A-11; *GR* IV/10 (November 1937):11; *GR* IV/11 (December 1937):40; Adam, *Judenpolitik*, 114, 119–120, 142; Orlow, *The History*, 2:163; Peterson, *The Limits*, 134–140; Schleunes, *The Twisted Road*, 135.

22. Kershaw, "Antisemitismus und Volksmeinung," 454.

23. LBI, AR 7183, box 4, no. 4, folder 2, part 1, pp. 229-230, *Der Reichs- und Preussische Minister des Innern*, 21.4.36.

24. Meier, *Kirche und Judentum*, 13; Nora Levin, *The Holocaust: The Destruction of European Jewry, 1933-1945*, 80.

25. On Hitler Youth participation, see *GR* V/15 (January 1939):A-20.

26. Goebbels was particularly anxious to gain power at the expense of Himmler, whose role in the Jewish affairs was steadily increasing.

27. For comments on instigators, see Adam, *Judenpolitik*, 206, 208; Bracher, *The German Dictatorship*, 367; Hermann Graml, *Der 9. November 1938, "Reichskristallnacht,"* Schriftenreihe der Bundeszentrale für Heimatdienst (1957), vol. 2, no. 2:18, 20–21; Genschel, *Die Verdrängung*, 178; Orlow, *The History*, 2:241–251; Peterson, *The Limits*, 220; Schleunes, *The Twisted Road*, 240; Speer, *Inside the Third Reich*, 162. For economic motivations, see Adam, *Judenpolitik*, 165–

166; Genschel, *Die Verdrängung*, 138, 141, 151, 177, 180; Gerhard Reitlinger, *The Final Solution: The Attempt to Exterminate the Jews of Europe, 1939–1945*, 12; BA ZSg 102/10/123—17.5.38; Schleunes, *The Twisted Road*, 135; Frank Tennenbaum, *Race and Reich: The Story of an Epoch*, 47, note 16.

28. Adam, *Judenpolitik*, emphasizes Hitler's final responsibility; his view is shared by Bramsted, *Goebbels and National Socialist Propaganda*, 384. Schleunes, *The Twisted Road*, 20, places more responsibility on party radicals.

29. McKale, *The Nazi Party Courts*, 161; Reitlinger, *The Final Solution*, 8.

30. Hitler, *Testament*, 95.

31. NA T-175, R 577, F 653, and Kershaw, "Antisemitismus und Volksmeinung," 480.

32. Meier, *Kirche und Judentum*, 14.

33. Toland, *Adolf Hitler*, 784.

34. See bibliographies in Düwell, *Die Rheingebiete*, 21–30, and Schleunes, *The Twisted Road*, 263–271.

35. Willi Boelcke, *The Secret Conferences of Dr. Goebbels: The Nazi Propaganda War*, 93; Genschel, *Die Verdrängung*, 185.

36. Genschel, *Die Verdrängung*; see also Louis Lochner, ed. and trans., *The Goebbels Diaries*, 134-135.

37. *GR* V/11 (December 1938):A-4.

38. LBI, AR 7183, folder 3, box 13, 30.10.40: Karlsruhe, *Bericht über Verschickung von Juden deutscher Staatsangehörigkeit nach Südfrankreich*; see also Buchheim, *Anatomy*, 57; Dawidowicz, *The War Against the Jews*, 375; Düwell, *Die Rheingebiete*, 273, 488; Lawrence Stokes, "The German People and the Destruction of the European Jews," 180, note 55.

39. Adam, *Judenpolitik*, 248–250; Bracher, *The German Dictatorship*, 368.

40. Boelcke, *The Secret Conferences*, 93; Dawidowicz, *The War Against the Jews*, 119, 121; Hoehne, *The Order*, 368, 400; Jaeckel, *Hitler's Weltanschauung*, 79; Noakes and Pridham, *Documents*, 468; Steinert, *Hitlers Krieg*, 204.

41. Meier, *Kirche und Judentum*, 15; Hans-Josef Steinberg, *Widerstand und Verfolgung in Essen 1933–1945*, 167.

42. Meier, *Kirche und Judentum*, 14; Wolfgang Scheffler, *Judenverfolgung im Dritten Reich 1933–1945*, 114 (Reitlinger's estimates); see also Dawidowicz, *The War Against the Jews*, 403, for the total number of Jews killed in Europe; for years of deportation and numbers deported, see Strauss, "Jewish Emigration," 326–327.

43. Levin, *The Holocaust*, 207.

44. Ibid., 208.

45. Quoted in ibid., 230.

46. Quoted in ibid., 243.

47. Ibid., 244.

48. Ibid., 267.

49. Ibid., 268.

50. Quoted in Dawidowicz, *The War Against the Jews*, 17.

51. Quoted in Jaeckel, *Hitler's Weltanschauung*, 52.

52. Quoted in ibid., 57.

53. See Domarus, *Hitler Reden*; and Baynes, *The Speeches of Adolf Hitler*.

54. U.S. Department of State, *Foreign Relations* (1934) 2:220, Memorandum by the Ambassador in Germany (Dodd), no date, but the next report is dated April 7, 1934.

55. Quoted in Waite, *The Psychopathic God*, 46.

56. Quoted in Buchheim, *Anatomy*, 34.

57. Quoted in Toland, *Adolf Hitler*, 563.

58. Quoted in Adam, *Judenpolitik*, 35.

59. Quoted in Buchheim, *Anatomy*, 44.

60. For translations of three quotations, see ibid., 45; Lochner, *The Goebbels Diaries*, 171; Dawidowicz, *The War Against the Jews*, 106.

61. Quoted in Buchheim, *Anatomy*, 65.

62. Quoted in Toland, *Adolf Hitler*, 960.

63. Quoted in ibid., 964.

64. Quoted in ibid.

65. Quoted in ibid., 970.

66. Lochner, *The Goebbels Diaries*, 170–171.

67. Hitler, *Testament*, 66.

68. Quoted in Dawidowicz, *The War Against the Jews*, 110–111.

69. See this section above.

70. Jaeckel, *Hitler's Weltanschauung*, 56-57.

71. See this section, above.

72. Ibid.

73. Hitler, *Testament*, 94.

74. Ibid., 97.

75. Dawidowicz, *The War Against the Jews*, 17; Jaeckel, *Hitlers Weltanschauung*, 50, 57, 58.

76. Martin Broszat, "Hitler und die Genesis der 'Endlösung': Aus Anlass der Thesen von David Irving," 739ff; see also Streit, *Keine Kameraden*, 126; Adam, *Judenpolitik*, 305ff.

77. See, for example, Arthur Butz, *The Hoax of the Twentieth Century* (Richmond, England: Historical Press Review, 1974) and the implications in David Irving's *Hitler's War*, 2 vols. (New York: The Viking Press, 1977), vol. 1: xiv, xv, 270ff, 326, 330–331, 392, 427, and vol. 2:505, 575, 601–602, 858; for West German sources, see Ino Arndt and Wolfgang Scheffler, "Organisierter Massenmord an Juden in Nationalsozialistischen Vernichtungslagern: Ein Beitrag zur Richtigstellung apologetischer Literatur," *Vierteljahrshefte für Zeitgeschichte*, 24/2 (April 1976):105–135. For rebuttals, see C. Aronsfeld, "A Propos of a British 'Historical Review': Facts of the Holocaust," *Patterns of Prejudice*, 8/4 (July-August 1974):11-16; Broszat, "Hitler und die Genesis," 739-775; and Charles W. Sydnor, Jr., "The Selling of Adolf Hitler; David Irving's *Hitler's War*," *Central European History* 12/2 (1979):169–199; see also Gerald Fleming, *Hitler und die Endlösung: "Es ist des Führers Wunsch"* (Munich: Limes Verlag, 1982).

78. See chapter 9 for the role of the military, SS, and bureaucracy.

79. Quoted in Hoehne, *The Order*, 351.

80. Quoted in ibid.

81. Quoted in George Bailey, *Germans: Biography of an Obsession* (New York: Avon Books, 1972), 170.

82. Lochner, *Goebbels Diaries*, 159, 171.

83. Quoted in Maser, *Hitler*, 215.

84. Dawidowicz, *The War Against the Jews*, 124; Buchheim, *Anatomy*, 62.

85. Quoted in Dawidowicz, *The War Against the Jews*, ibid.

86. Levin, *The Holocaust*, 254.

87. Quoted in Buchheim, *Anatomy*, 62.

88. See Hoehne, *The Order*, 406, and Robert Wolfe, "Putative Threat to National Security as a Nuremberg Defense for Genocide," *The Annals of the American Academy of Political and Social Science* 450 (July 1980):55.

89. Quoted in Payne, *The Life and Death*, 465; see also Toland, *Adolf Hitler*, 959.

90. Quoted in Toland, *Adolf Hitler*, 974; see also Jochen von Lang, *Das Eichmann-Protokoll: Tonbandaufzeichnungen der israelischen Verhöre* (Berlin: Severin und Siedler, 1982), passim, on The Führer Order.

91. Quoted in ibid.

92. Payne, *The Life and Death*, 467.

93. Quoted in Hoehne, *The Order*, 411.

94. Quoted in Buchheim, *Anatomy*, 69.

95. Quoted in Maser, *Hitler*, 246–247.

96. Quoted in Buchheim, *Anatomy*, 73.

97. Quoted in Toland, *Adolf Hitler*, 1016.

98. Ibid., 1038.

99. Ibid., 1057; see also Bradley Smith and Agnes Peterson, eds. *Himmler, Heinrich: Geheime Reden 1933 bis 1945* (Frankfurt a.M.: Propyläen Verlag), 202–203.

100. Quoted in Toland, *Adolf Hitler*, 1188.

101. See chapter 9 on the army's role.

102. Streit, *Keine Kameraden*, 298.

103. Raul Hilberg, "The Anatomy of the Holocaust," 91.

104. See this section, above.

105. Quoted in Dawidowicz, *The War Against the Jews*, 158.

106. Ibid., 106.

107. Streit, *Keine Kameraden*, 299, and Irving, *Hitler's War*, 1:xiii, xiv, 270ff, 326, 391–392, 427, and passim; 2:505, 858, and passim.

108. Adam, *Judenpolitik*, 107–108, 111–112, 243–246, 357; Mommsen, "Der nationalsozialistische Polizeistaat," 68.

109. Adam, *Judenpolitik*, 47, 60–61, 91–92, 96; Geoffrey Barraclough, "Farewell to Hitler," *New York Review of Books* 22/5 (April 3, 1975):11; Genschel, *Die Verdrängung*, 47; Schleunes, *The Twisted Road*, 75, 122.

NOTES TO CHAPTER FIVE

110. Adam, *Judenpolitik*, 47, 60–61, 91–92, 96; see also BA ZSg 110/10/173—21.12.35.

111. Adam, *Judenpolitik*, 35, 68, 355, 357; Broszat, "Soziale Motivation," 405–407, 437; Mommsen, "Der Nationalsozialistische Polizeistaat," 68, 76; Schleunes, *The Twisted Road*, 70, 92, 257–258; Peterson, *The Limits*, 10–11, 450.

112. BA ZSg 101/2/49—24.1.33.

113. Adam, *Judenpolitik*, 86, 139; see George Mosse, "Die deutsche Rechte und die Juden," 239, for Reventlow's attitudes; G. M. Gilbert, *Nuremberg Diary* (Toronto: New American Library of Canada, 1971), 23; Krebs, *Tendenzen und Gestalten*, passim; BA ZSg 110/5/115—23.6.37; *DB* II/8 (August 1935):A-10.

114. For diversity of opinion in the party, see Adam, *Judenpolitik*, 96; Eric Boehm, *We Survived: The Stories of Fourteen of the Hidden and Hunted of Nazi Germany*, 289; Düwell, *Die Rheingebiete*, 272; Joachim Fest, *The Face of the Third Reich: Portraits of the Nazi Leadership* (New York: Random House, 1970), 334; Gilbert, *Nuremberg Diary*, 28, 33, 43, 168; Graml, *Der 9. November*, passim; Hoehne, *The Order*, 369–387; McKale, *The Nazi Party Courts*, x; Noakes and Pridham, *Documents*, 462; Peterson, *The Limits*, 138–142, 144–145, 206; Rauschning, *The Voice of Destruction*, 234–235; Steinert, *Hitlers Krieg*, 236–237; *DB* II/9 (September 1938):A-26.

115. Alexander Hardy, *Hitler's Secret Weapon: The "Managed" Press and the Propaganda Machine of Nazi Germany* (New York: Vantage Press, 1968), 188; Hagemann, *Die Presselenkung*, 6; Hoehne, *The Order*, 383–387; Peterson, *The Limits*, 447; *DB* III/1 (January 1936):A-6.

116. Adam, *Judenpolitik*, 112, 219, 359.

117. Mommsen, "Der nationalsozialistische Polizeistaat," 69–70.

118. Jochen Klepper, *Unter dem Schatten deiner Flügel: aus den Tagebüchern der Jahre 1932-1942*, 270–271.

119. Adam, *Judenpolitik*, 360; Peter Hüttenberger, *Die Gauleiter: Studie zum Wandel des Machtgefüges in der NSDAP*, Schriftenreihe der Vierteljahrshefte für Zeitgeschichte, no. 19 (Stuttgart: Deutsche Verlagsanstalt, 1969): 212; Mommsen, "Der nationalsozialistische Polizeistaat," 69–70; Schleunes, *The Twisted Road*, 260.

CHAPTER FIVE

1. Harold Nicolson, *Diaries and Letters: The War Years, 1939-1945*, 2 vols. (New York: Atheneum, 1967) 2:388; Noakes and Pridham, *Documents*, 235; Max Seydewitz, *Civil Life in Wartime Germany: The Story of the Home Front*, 344; *DB* II/9 (September 1935):A-18.

2. For examples of social atomization, see Allen, *The Nazi Seizure of Power*, 209–266.

3. Hagemann, *Die Presselenkung*, 5, 15.

4. For examples of press directives, see Willi Boelcke, ed., *Kriegspropaganda 1939-1941: Geheime Ministerkonferenzen im Reichspropagandaministerium*; Ha-

gemann, *Die Presselenkung*, passim. Erich Goldhagen, "Weltanschauung und Endlösung: Zum Antisemitismus der nationalsozialistischen Führungsschicht," 395–396.

5. Erich Goldhagen, "Weltanschauung und Endlösung: Zum Antisemitismus der nationalsozialistischen Führungsschicht," 395–396.

6. Bracher, *The German Dictatorship*, 330–335; Schoenbaum, *Hitler's Social Revolution*, 126, 129–143; Steinert, *Hitlers Krieg*, 62–65; *DB* III/1 (January 1936):A-6; *DB* II/8 (August 1935):A-12; *DB* III/6 (June 1936):A-15; *GR* III/3 (August 1939):A-21; *GR* V/11 (January 1939):A-25.

7. Broszat, "Soziale Motivation," 404–405.

8. Bracher, *The German Dictatorship*, 254; BA ZSg 101/28/221 to 227 = 12.7.35 to 20.7.35; BA ZSg 101/26/225-1.3.33; BA ZSg 110/3/97-2.11.36.

9. Adam, *Judenpolitik*, 360; Hagemann, *Die Presselenkung*, 9.

10. Domarus, *Hitler Reden* 1:27–28; Hanfstaengl, *Unheard Witness*, 222.

11. Bracher, *The German Dictatorship*, 250; Dawidowicz, *The War Against the Jews*, 86–106; Hagemann, *Die Presselenkung*, 5; Franz Neumann, *Behemoth: The Structure and Practice of National Socialism*, 125.

12. Domarus, *Hitler Reden*, 27–28; Hanfstaengl, *Unheard Witness*, 222.

13. Hanfstaengl, *Unheard Witness*, 230, 267.

14. For the view that treatment of Jews was a model for Nazi policies in occupied lands, see Gilbert, *Nuremberg Diary*, 40; Speer, *Inside the Third Reich*, 16; for comments on socialization see Allen, *The Nazi Seizure*, 209; Bracher, *The German Dictatorship*, 365, 431; Hans Buchheim, *Totalitarian Rule: Its Nature and Characteristics* (Middletown, Conn.: Wesleyan University Press, 1968), 49; Orlow, *The History* 1:4.

15. Press directives were issued on all aspects of German life, including the "Jewish question." Although copies were supposed to be destroyed, a few editors kept and hid some; they were recovered after the war and are now held by the Bundesarchiv in Koblenz, West Germany. Those salvaged by Brammer are designated ZSg 101; those saved by Sänger are designated ZSg 102; others, frequently duplicates, are designated ZSg 110 and ZSg 116. Almost all the directives were confidential, and the editors of newspapers faced severe penalties for leaking information or printing material that was not approved in the directives.

16. Neumann, *Behemoth*, 125; Jaeckel, *Hitler's Weltanschauung*, 52, 98–105; Steinert, *Hitlers Krieg*, p. 578.

17. Neumann, *Behemoth*, 121; Orlow, *The History* 2:486.

18. For a good discussion of propaganda themes, see BA ZSg 110/10/125—17.11.38.

19. Dawidowicz, *The War Against the Jews*, 94; Tennenbaum, *Race and Reich*, 43.

20. Bramsted, *Goebbels and National Socialist Propaganda*, 400–402; Steinert, *Hitlers Krieg*, 259–260, notes 211–213.

21. Boelcke, *The Secret Conferences*, 87; Hardy, *Hitler's Secret Weapon*, 190.

22. Hagemann, *Die Presselenkung*, 6–7, 120; see also Adam, *Judenpolitik*, 360;

Broszat, "Soziale Motivation," 403; Needler, "Hitler's Anti-Semitism," 668; Schleunes, *The Twisted Road*, 57.

23. Buchheim, *Totalitarian Rule*, 31.

24. For interpretations of anti-Semitism that emphasize the role of Jews as scapegoats, see Adam, *Judenpolitik*, 360; Bracher, *The German Dictatorship*, 47; Fest, *The Face of the Third Reich*, 142; Hagemann, *Die Presselenkung*, 6, 120; Buchheim, *Anatomy*, 22; Reichmann, "Diskussionen," 526; idem, *Hostages*, 37, 164; Speer, *Inside the Third Reich*, 46; Paul Tillich, "The Jewish Question: Christian and German Problem," *Jewish Social Studies* 33 (October 1971):266; Melvin Tumin, "Anti-Semitism and Status Anxiety: A Hypothesis," *Jewish Social Studies* 33 (October 1971):315.

25. See Hagemann, *Die Presselenkung*, passim, and Norman Cohn, "The Myth of the Jewish World Conspiracy, A Case Study in Collective Psychopathology," *Commentary* 41/6 (1965–1966):35–42; see also Cohn's *Warrant for Genocide*, passim, for particularly good insights into concrete circumstances under which the myth of Jewish demonism helped the Nazis to organize their paranoid ideas.

26. Hagemann, *Die Presselenkung*, 12–124; Steinert, *Hitlers Krieg*, 35.

27. Steinert, *Hitlers Krieg*, 30.

28. Orlow, *A History*, 1:6.

29. See this section, above.

30. BA ZSg 101/1/103—21.9.33.

31. BA ZSg 110/1/105—20.7.35; ZSg 110/1/175—28.12.35; ZSg 110/3/415—1.10.36; ZSg 101/8/329—19.11.36; ZSg 110/3/165—14.12.36; ZSg 101/9/267—12.4.37; ZSg 102/5/295—10.5.37; ZSg 101/11/25—12.1.38; ZSg 102/11/35—16.6.38; ZSg 110/9/2—1.7.38; ZSg 102/3/3 2.11.38; ZSg 102/13/15—9.11.38; ZSg 102/13/38–39—17.11.38; ZSg 116/203/31—22.11.38; ZSg 102/13/43—18.11.38; ZSg 102/13/54—23.11.38; ZSg 110/10/152—23.11.38; ZSg 102/13/118—9.12.38; ZSg 102/13/149—19.12.39; ZSg 110/10/70—19.1.39; ZSg 102/14/189—28.2.39; ZSg 102/15/392—27.4.39.

32. BA ZSg 110/10/125–132—17.11.38; ZSg 102/13/47—22.11.38; ZSg 110/10/148—22.11.38; ZSg 110/10/157–159—24.11.38; ZSg 102/13/61—25.11.38; ZSg 102/15/3—2.5.39.

33. BA ZSg 102/4/39—14.1.37.

34. BA ZSg 102/13/33–35—15.11.38; ZSg 102/13/94—2.12.38; ZSg 102/13/10—14.1.37.

35. BA ZSg 110/10/38—19.11.38; ZSg 110/10/125–132—17.11.38; ZSg 102/13/43—18.11.38; ZSg 102/13/157–159—24.11.38.

36. BA ZSg 101/28/221–223 between 12.7 and 20.7.35.

37. Boelcke, *The Secret Conferences*, 87; Bramsted, *Goebbels and National Socialist Propaganda*, 400–402; Lochner, *The Goebbels Diaries*, 373; Hardy, *Hitler's Secret Weapon*, 190; Steinert, *Hitlers Krieg*, 256, notes 195–196; 259–260, notes 211–213; BA ZSg 102/13/35—15.11.38; ZSg 102/14/2—2.1.39.

38. BA ZSg 116/69/12—28.3.33; ZSg 116/69/4—27.3.33.

39. BA ZSg 102/13/19—10.11.38; ZSg 102/13/18—10.11.38.

40. See this section below.
41. BA ZSg 101/8/65—28.7.36.
42. BA ZSg 101/11/329—2.5.38.
43. BA ZSg 110/8/228—21.6.38.
44. Hagemann, *Die Presselenkung*, 120–121; BA ZSg 101/11/221—19.3.38; ZSg 101/27/301—19.3.38; ZSg 101/27/301—11.8.34.
45. See chapter 4, "Functions of Anti-Semitism inside the Nazi Party."
46. BA ZSg 101/28/221-227-—12.7 to 20.7.35.
47. Ibid.
48. BA ZSg 102/13/119—10.11.38; ZSg 102/13/28—13.11.38.
49. Hans-Peter Görgen, *Düsseldorf und der Nationalsozialismus: Studie zur Geschichte einer Grosstadt im* "Dritten Reich" (Düsseldorf: Schwann, 1969), 86; BA ZSg 116/69/12—28.3.33.
50. BA ZSg 101/6/144—16.10.35; ZSg 101/6/185—16.11.35; ZSg 110/1/142—26.11.35.
51. Hagemann, *Die Presselenkung*, 144, notes 41–42.
52. BA ZSg 101/8/407—11.12.36.
53. BA ZSg 102/10/193—17.6.38; ZSg 102/10/196—18.6.38; ZSg 102/10/200—20.6.38; ZSg 102/10/205—22.6.38.
54. BA ZSg 102/12/340—25.10.38.
55. BA ZSg 110/3/19—5.10.36; ZSg 101/33/339—28.10.38.
56. BA ZSg 102/13/19—10.11.38; also see *GR* V/12 (January 1939):A-18; *GR* V/11 (December 1938):A-19.
57. *GR* V/11 (December 1939):A-18, A-28, A-29.
58. BA ZSg 110/10/112—10.11.38.
59. Ibid.
60. Ibid.
61. BA ZSg 102/13/75—30.11.38.
62. Hagemann, *Die Presselenkung*, 143 note 34.
63. BA ZSg 102/13/107—6.12.38.
64. BA ZSg 102/13/19—10/11/38; ZSg 116/204/32–35—12.11.38; ZSg 102/13/24—12.11.38.
65. BA ZSg 110/10/125–132—17.11.38.
66. BA ZSg 102/13/26—12.11.38.
67. For blackouts on Aryanization before 1938, see: BA ZSg 101/3/78—16.2.34; ZSg 101/28/263—24.9.35; ZSg 101/6/224—12.12.35; ZSg 101/7/413—29.6.36; ZSg 101/29/321—24.8.36; ZSg 110/2/54—3.9.36; ZSg 101/9/469—July 1937; ZSg 101/10/435—18.12.37.
68. BA ZSg 101/11/173—25.2.38; ZSg 110/7/287—23.3.38; ZSg 102/10/31—9.4.38; ZSg 116/17/4—5.1.38; ZSg 102/10/189—16.6.38; ZSg 101/33/347–349—9.11.38; ZSg 116/204/33—12.11.38; ZSg 102/13/45—21.11.38; ZSg 102/13/48—22.11.38; ZSg 102/13/66—25.11.38; ZSg 102/13/83—1.12.38; ZSg 102/13/84—1.12.38; ZSg 102/13/85—1.12.38; Zsg 102/13/92—2.12.38; ZSg 102/13/132—13.12.38; ZSg 102/14/117—23.2.39; ZSg 102/18/289—19.7.39. For black-

outs on rental assistance for Jews, see BA ZSg 102/13/96—3.12.38; ZSg 110/10/186—3.12.38; ZSg 110/10/213—13.12.38; ZSg 110/10/215—13.12.38; ZSg 102/13/132—13.12.38; ZSg 110/11/20—7.1.39; ZSg 101/12/66—7.3.39.

69. Hagemann, *Die Presselenkung*, 123, 180, notes 73–78; 144–145, notes 44–52; Boelcke, *Kriegspropaganda*, 268.

70. Hagemann, *Die Presselenkung*, 144, note 49; 147, note 76.

71. Boelcke, *Kriegspropaganda*, 342, 355, 361, 367; Steinert, *Hitlers Krieg*, 101.

72. Hagemann, 146, note 66; 146, note 173; 147, note 74.

73. NA T-175, R 577, F 751, F 752; Ohlendorf (*Reichssicherheitshauptamt* to all of its offices), 19.10.42.

74. Adam, *Judenpolitik*, 330–340; Hagemann, *Die Presselenkung*, 224; Steinert, *Hitlers Krieg*, 257.

75. Boelcke, *The Secret Conferences*, 185; Broszat, "Soziale Motivation," 400; Hardy, *Hitler's Secret Weapon*, 185; Peterson, *The Limits*, 444–445; for penalties for reporting activities in the camps, see Steinert, *Hitlers Krieg*, 249.

76. Steinert, *Hitlers Krieg*, 257.

77. BA ZSg 102/13/24—12.11.38.

78. Executions of Jews in Warsaw were inadvertently published by the SD; the publication was seized. The Propaganda Ministry confirmed the authenticity of the story but disallowed its publication in Germany. See YIVO G-125 (I), no. 82, containing *Geheiminformation*, nr. 81, from the Propaganda Ministry, December 1939.

79. BA ZSg 110/3/20—13.11.36; BA ZSg 101/6/125—28.9.35; BA ZSg 101/9/37—14.1.37.

80. BA ZSg 101/4/71—23.8.34; ZSg 101/6/36—31.7.35; ZSg 101/9/287—19.4.37; ZSg 101/11/Anw. 46—10.1.38; SK 403, 16825; ZSg 110/10/187—3.12.38 and ZSg 102/13/69—3.12.38, respectively.

81. BA ZSg 110/2/80—27.6.36; ZSg 101/8/35—16.7.36; ZSg 101/7/409—27.6.36; ZSg 101/8/251—19.10.36; ZSg 101/13/25—19.5.39; ZSg 101/5/89—14.3.35; and ZSg 102/17/145—8.6.39, respectively.

82. BA ZSg 102/17/155—10.6.39; ZSg 102/18/377—16.8.39.

83. Boelcke, *Kriegspropaganda*, 513.

84. PGA Rep. 77/31 (11.4.33).

85. BA ZSg 101/28/221–227 between 12.7 and 20.7.35.

86. BA ZSg 101/10/63—29.7.37; ZSg 102/17/324—10.11.37; ZSg 102/17/226—28.6.39; ZSg 110/9/189—14.8.38.

87. BA ZSg 101/9/113—11.2.37.

88. BA ZSg 101/1/112—27.7.35; ZSg 101/6/32—27.7.35; ZSg 110/1/129—8.11.35; ZSg 101/6/177—8.11.35.

89. BA ZSg 102/14/130—7.2.39; ZSg 110/11/239—4.3.39.

90. BA ZSg 101/8/274—28.10.36; ZSg 101/11/265—13.5.38.

91. BA ZSg 102/13/19—10.11.38.

92. BA ZSg 110/10/138—19.11.38; ZSg 102/13/43—18.11.38; ZSg 110/10/125–132—17.11.38.

93. BA ZSg 110/10/125–132—17.11.38.

94. BA ZSg 110/10/157–159—24.11.38.

95. BA ZSg 110/10/119—14.11.38.

96. Hagemann, *Die Presselenkung*, 146, note 67; 224, notes 173–177.

97. BA ZSg 101/1/55—10.7.33; ZSg 101/1/84—between 14.8 and 18.8.33; ZSg 102/1/ Anw. 608—13.5.38 for blackouts; see BA ZSg 116/69/4—27.3.33; ZSg 102/13/19—10.11.38 for atrocity propaganda.

98. BA ZSg 101/12/47—9.6.39.

99. BA ZSg 102/13/27—12.11.38; see Hagemann, *Die Presselenkung*, 224, notes 73, 76.

100. BA ZSg 101/11/31—23.4.38; ZSg 101/32/301—30.4.38; ZSg 101/11/361—12.5.38.

101. BA ZSg 101/9/115—11.1.37; ZSg 102/4/39—26.2.37; ZSg 110/4/289—24.4.37.

102. BA ZSg 110/10/125–132—17.11.38; ZSg 110/10/152—23.11.38.

103. BA ZSg 102/13/35–37—15.11.38; ZSg 102/13/38–39—17.11.38; see Hagemann, *Die Presselenkung*, 2, 17; Steinert, *Hitlers Krieg*, 34.

104. BA ZSg 110/10/125–132—7.11.38; ZSg 102/13/29—13.11.38; ZSg 102/13/38–39—17.11.38; see also YIVO G-52, no. 46, December 1938: "*Wenn Englands Soldaten Araber zusammenschiessen. . . .*"

105. BA ZSg 102/12/166—12.4.37; ZSg 102/13/61—25.11.38.

106. Boelcke, *The Secret Conferences*, 268 (11.8.42).

107. Steinert, *Hitlers Krieg*, 474 (20.7.44, after the assassination attempt against Hitler by Count Stauffenberg).

108. Heinz Boberach, ed., *Meldungen aus dem Reich: Reichssicherheitshauptamt; Auswahl aus den geheimen Lageberichten des Sicherheitsdienstes der SS 1939–1944*, 385.

109. Bramsted, *Goebbels and National Socialist Propaganda*, 400–402.

110. Genschel, *Die Verdrängung*, 79.

111. BA ZSg 101/2/72—16.12.33.

112. BA ZSg 101/6/64—22.8.35.

113. BA ZSg 101/6/64—22.8.35; ZSg 110/2/36—21.2.36; ZSg 101/7/129—21.2.36; ZSg 110/2/105—12.8.36.

114. BA ZSg 101/7/275—24.4.36.

115. BA ZSg 101/9/407—4.6.37.

116. BA ZSg 102/13/134—14.12.38.

117. BA ZSg 102/18/317—25.7.39.

118. YIVO G-34, G-35, no. 33 (October 1–December 27, 1940).

119. Behrend-Rosenfeld, *Ich stand*, 67; Buchheim, *Anatomy*, 31; Peterson, *The Limits*, 444–445; Steinert, *Hitlers Krieg*, 41, note 84.

120. Steinert, *Hitlers Krieg*, 237; DB III/9 (September 1936):A-2.

121. Blackouts were not more numerous, but covered more extensive persecution; see Steinert, *Hitlers Krieg*, 52–53.

122. Stokes, "The German People," 175, 181 (note 57), 190.

CHAPTER SIX

1. Cohn, *Warrant for Genocide*, 209–210.
2. Buchheim, *Anatomy*, 388.
3. Bracher, *The German Dictatorship*, 63; see also Steinert, *Hitlers Krieg*, 12, note 25.
4. Bracher, *The German Dictatorship*, 365.
5. George Mosse, "Die deutsche Rechte und die Juden," 243, note 219.
6. Bracher, *The German Dictatorship*, 384.
7. Hans-Joachim Fliedner, *Die Judenverfolgung in Mannheim 1933–1945*, 2 vols. (Stuttgart: W. Kohlhammer, 1961) 1:228–229; see also Konrad Heiden, *Der Führer: Hitler's Rise to Power* (New York: Howard Fertig, 1968), 587, and Stokes, "The German People," 175.
8. Lewis Edinger, *German Exile Politics: The Social Democratic Executive Committee in the Nazi Era* (Berkeley and Los Angeles: University of California Press, 1956), 137.
9. Steinert, *Hitlers Krieg*, 82–87.
10. Edinger, *German Exile Politics*, 213.
11. Ibid., 270, note 17.
12. Ibid., 213.
13. The reports themselves were sent to the *Oberpräsidenten* of each Provinz and to the *Geheimen Staatspolizei* (Gestapo). *Regierungspräsidenten-Berichte* for *Regierungsbezirk* Aachen (Government District Aachen) are relied upon for the years 1934–1936. Excerpts of some of these may be found in Vollmer's *Volksopposition im Polizeistaat*, but many of the sections on Jews were omitted; therefore, the original reports at the Staatsarchiv Düsseldorf are more informative; see Bernhard Vollmer, *Volksopposition im Polizeistaat*, passim. For similar reports from Bavaria, see Martin Broszat et al., eds., *Bayern in der NS-Zeit: Soziale Lage und politisches Verhalten der Bevölkerung im Spiegel vertraulicher Berichte*. See also all of Kershaw's publications on extant records from Bavaria; these are very comprehensive and enlightening. The Gestapo reports for Prussia, mainly 1933–1937, in the PGA (Rep. 90p) were seen too late for inclusion here, but they are in all cases similar in substance to others examined by Kershaw and me.

There is also considerable information about public attitudes in court records and internal correspondence of the NSDAP. For this study, court records of the *Oberlandesgericht* Düsseldorf and subsidiary courts are used. Miscellaneous party correspondence can be found at the Bundesarchiv and the Staatsarchiv in Koblenz, as well as at the National Archives in Washington and on microfilm from the Hoover Institution.
14. For phases of anti-Semitic persecution, see chapter 4.
15. Schleunes, *The Twisted Road*, 140.
16. Kurt Pätzold, *Faschismus, Rassenwahn, Judenverfolgung: Eine Studie zur politischen Strategie und Taktik des faschistischen deutschen Imperialismus*, 79.
17. LBI, letter (uncatalogued August 1981) to *Kollege* Meyer, Arnsdorf/Rsgb, dated 23.IV.33.

18. PGA Rep. 77 (*Preussisches Ministerium des Innern*), no. 31, Berlin, 20.3.33.
19. BA ZSg 101/26/231—4.4.33.
20. Genschel, *Die Verdrängung*, 52–53.
21. Kershaw, "Antisemitismus und Volksmeinung," 296.
22. Düwell, *Die Rheingebiete*, 82, 89; see also Stokes, "The German People," 173, notes 27, 28, 30.
23. Kommission zur Erforschung der Geschichte der Frankfurter Juden, ed., *Dokumente zur Geschichte der Frankfurter Juden 1933–1945* (Frankfurt a.M.: M. W. Kramer, 1963), 26.
24. For socialists buying from Jews, see Allen, *The Nazi Seizure*, 213; see also Schleunes, *The Twisted Road*, 88–89; Vollmer, *Volksopposition*, 70 (*Reg. Präs. Lagebericht* 6.8.34); HSD Rep. 21/5, 30655b, p. 4 (*Reg. Präs. Tagesbericht*, no. 158); LBI Wiener Microfilm, reel 32, no. 22, article from the *Westdeutscher Beobachter*, 1.6.33, and AR 7183, box 11, folder 5, letter to Dr. Kahn of June 1933, p. 5.
25. Genschel, *Die Verdrängung*, 52.
26. Ibid., 69, note 40; see also Maria Zelzer, *Weg und Schicksal der Stuttgarter Juden: Ein Gedenkbuch*, 59–82.
27. LBI Wiener Microfilm, reel 32, no 27: *Gauleitung* Koblenz-Trier to *Kreisleitung* Kreuznach, 18.4.33.
28. Kershaw, "Antisemitismus und Volksmeinung," 301, 308. See also his "The Persecution of the Jews and German Popular Opinion in the Third Reich," 266–268; "Popular Opinion in the Third Reich," in *Government, Party, and People in Nazi Germany*, edited by Jeremy Noakes, 70; and O. D. Kulka, " 'Public Opinion' in National Socialist Germany and the 'Jewish Question,' " *Zion, Quarterly for Research in Jewish History* 40 (1975):260–290 (in Hebrew).
29. Behrend-Rosenfeld, *Ich stand*, 17.
30. Görgen, *Düsseldorf und der Nationalsozialismus*, 183.
31. Vollmer, *Volksopposition*, 323.
32. PGA Rep. 77 (*Preussisches Ministerium des Innern*), no. 9:23–80.
33. Annedore Leber, ed., *Conscience in Revolt: Sixty-Four Stories of Resistance in Germany* (London: Vallentine, 1957), 92.
34. Vollmer, *Volksopposition*, 113 (*Reg. Präs. Lagebericht*, 4.11.34—*Judentum*).
35. Ibid., 131 (5.12.34—*Judentum*).
36. HSD G/20/14, 23886 (letter to Goering, April 1, 1933).
37. HSD G/90/21/38 (*General Staatsanwaltschaft Köln, Beleidigung*), 4.5.33.
38. Fliedner, *Die Judenverfolgung*, 2:368–372.
39. HSD G/21/5, 30655a—30.8.34 (*Reg. Präs. Tagesbericht—Judentum*).
40. HSD G/20/2, 1025—5.12.34 (*Reg. Präs. Lagebericht—Judentum*).
41. HSD G21/5, 30655b—13.12.34 (*Reg. Präs. Tagesbericht—Judentum*).
42. HSD G/21/5, 30655d—18.12.34 (*Reg. Präs. Lagebericht—Judentum*).
43. U.S. Department of State, *Foreign Relations* (1933) 2:361, The Consul General at Berlin (Messersmith) to the Secretary of State, Berlin, November 1, 1933.
44. Sources are not extensive on protests before 1935 because the *Deutschland-*

*Berichte* and SD reports were not in full operation until August 1935 and 1936, respectively.

45. PGA Rep. 77 (*Preussisches Ministerium des Innern*), no. 31 (April 24, 1935); Fliedner, *Die Judenverfolgung*, 2:370 (May 23, 1935).

46. Buchheim, *Anatomy*, 30; Robert Thevoz et al., eds., *Pommern 1934/35 im Spiegel von Gestapo-Lageberichten und Sachakten*, vol. 1, *Quellen*, 196; Kershaw, "Antisemitismus und Volksmeinung," 297.

47. *DB* III/1 (January 1936):A-5.

48. Broszat, *Bayern in der NS-Zeit*, 455, 460.

49. *DB* III/1 (January 1936):A-17, A-27; see also Thevoz, *Pommern*, 187–188.

50. *DB* III/1 (January 1936):A-18, A-19.

51. *DB* III/8 (August 1935):A-37; *DB* III/12 (December 1936):A-17.

52. HSD G/20/2, 1026—6.2.35 (*Reg. Präs. Lagebericht*, 25); G/20/2, 1039—29.7.35 (*Reg. Präs. Lagebericht*, 123); SK Abt. 441, no. 35464, *Bericht des Landrats von Bad Kreuznach* 6/35 (*Judentum*); *DB* II/8 (August 1935):A-3, A-31, A-34, A-35; *DB* II/9 (September 1935):A-11, A-21, A-25, A-30, A-37.

53. HSD G/20/2, 1039—28.9.35 (*Reg. Präs. Lagebericht—Judentum*); G/20/2, 1059—12.10.35 (*Reg. Präs. Lagebericht—Judentum*); G/20/2, 1047—14.12.35 (*Reg. Präs. Lagebericht—Judentum*); *DB* III/1 (January 1936); see also Hagemann, *Die Presselenkung*, 121; Leuner, *When Compassion*, 38.

54. *DB* III/1 (January 1936):A-18; *DB* V/2 (February 1938):A-67; see also Karl Ludwig Günsche, *Phasen der Gleichschaltung: Stichtags-Analysen deutscher Zeitungen 1933–1938* (Osnabrück: Fromm, 1970), 61–71.

55. Vollmer, *Volksopposition*, 323 (*Reg. Präs. Lagebericht* 9.12.35—*Judentum*).

56. Ibid., 285 (*Reg. Präs. Lagebericht* 7.10.35—*Judentum*); see also Kershaw, "Antisemitismus und Volksmeinung," 294.

57. *DB* II/8 (August 1935):A-32, A-39; *DB* II/9 (September 1935):A-25.

58. *Statistik des Deutschen Reiches*, vol. 577 (1942); see p. 22 for 1935 and 1936, p. 238 for 1937, p. 28 for 1938 and 1939.

59. *DB* II/8 (August 1935):A-30–A-45; *DB* II/9 (September 1935):A-25; *DB* III/1 (January 1936):A-33, A-34–A-36; *DB* III/9 (August 1936):A-28–A-34, A-124, A-127; *DB* V/7 (August 1938):A-76; *DB* VI/7 (August 1939):A-98; *GR* IV/10 (August 1937):5, 128; *GR* IV/11 (December 1937):30; *GR* V/1 (March 1938):18.

60. HSD G/20/2, 1033—7.11.35 (*Reg. Präs. Lagebericht—Judentum*); G/20/2, 1035—7.1.36 (*Reg. Präs. Lagebericht—Judentum*; G/20/2, 1036—10.2.36 (*Reg. Präs. Lagebericht—Judentum*; G/20/2, 1037—5.3.36 (*Reg. Präs. Lagebericht—Judentum*); SK Abt. 662.7—11.5.37 (Gestapo *Lagebericht*).

61. HSD G/90 Rep. 17 (*Staatsanwaltschaft Kleve, Strafakten*), no. 43; Rep. 14 (Staatsanwaltschaft Born, Strafsachen), no. 46; G/90 Rep. 27 (*Staatsanwaltschaft beim Oberlandegericht Düsseldorf, Strafsachen*), nos. 124–127 (1936–1940); box 55, 4KLs 1/38—2AR 302/38; box 56, 4KLs 4/38—2AR 394/38; box 53, 16Js 151/38—2AR 217/38; box 54, 16Js 334/38—2AR 278/38; box 55, 18Js 648/38—2AR 306/38; box 55, 6KLs 6/38—2AR 325/38; box 56 2KLs 22/38—2AR 415/38; box 59, 5Js 724/38—2AR 44/39; box 59, 18Js 1272/38—2AR 46/39.

62. *DB* III/1 (January 1936):A-9–A-27; *GR* IV/8 (August 1937):9–10.

63. HSD G/21/5, 30655c—25.2.35 (*Reg. Präs. Lagebericht—Judentum*); G/21/ 5, 20655d—6.5.35 (*Reg. Präs. Lagebericht—Judentum*); G/20/2, 1028—8.5.35 (*Reg. Präs. Lagebericht—Judentum*); G/20/2, 1029—June 1935 (*Reg. Präs. Lagebericht—Judentum*); G/20/2, 1030—July 1935 (*Reg. Präs. Lagebericht—Judentum*); *DB* II/8 (August 1935):A-30, A-31; HSD G/20/2, 1034—9.12.35 (*Reg. Präs. Lagebericht*, 70–72); *DB* II/9 (September 1935):A-24, A-29, A-36; *DB* III/ 1 (January 1936):A-19, A-30, A-33; HSD G/20/2, 1040—3.4.36 (*Reg. Präs. Lagebericht—Judentum*); *DB* III/12 (December 1936):A-121; SK Abt. 662.6, no. 407—Gestapo *Lagebericht* 2.2.37; NA T-175 III, R 271, F 2767873 (*SS Unterscharführer Koblenz-Trier, Lagebericht*); *GR* IV/11 (December 1937):31; *DB* V/ 2 (February 1938):A-69–A-74; *GR* V/2 (March 1938):A-27; *DB* V/7 (August 1938):A-83. See also LBI Wiener Microfilms, which contain several additional reports: reel 32, no. 22, article from *Frankische Tageszeitung* 17.5.35; *Befehle*, July 1935; *Monatsbericht der Gestapo* (Berlin) 18.10.37; also at LBI, see AR 7183, no. 37, box 19, folder 9, pp. 11, 12: *Lagebericht der Abteilung II 112*, April–May 1936. For others, especially farmers, buying from Jews, see Kershaw, "Antisemitismus und Volksmeinung," 301, 308; Thevoz, *Pommern*, 73, 82, 103–104, 173, 177; Broszat, *Bayern*: 1:462, 464, 467, 469.

64. HSD G/21/5, 30655c—25.2.35 (*Reg. Präs. Lagebericht—Judentum*); G/20/ 2, 1028—8.5.35 (*Reg. Präs. Lagebericht—Judentum*); *DB* II/8 (August 1935): A-30, A-31; *DB* II/9 (September 1935):A-29, A-36; *DB* III/1 (January 1936):A-19, A-30, A-33.

65. HSD G/21/5—30655c—2.2.35 (*Reg. Präs. Lagebericht—Judentum*); G/21/ 5, 30655d—14.5.35 (*Reg. Präs. Lagebericht—Judentum*); G/21/5 30655e—3.6.35 (*Reg. Präs. Tagesbericht*, 12); G/21/5, 30655e—4.6.35 (*Reg. Präs. Tagesbericht*, 15).

66. HSD G/21/5, 30655e—22.5.35 (*Reg. Präs. Tagesbericht*, 18).

67. SK Abt. 662.3/125 (*Monatsbericht, Ortsgruppe Clüsserrath an der Kreisleitung Trier-Land-West*, 103).

68. *DB* III/12 (December 1936):A-122.

69. U.S. Department of State, *Foreign Relations* (1936)2:205, Extract from Report of the Ambassador in Germany (Dodd) sent in his despatch no. 3095, received October 24, 1936.

70. *DB* V/2 (March 1938):A-60: *GR* V/1 (March 1938):23.

71. *DB* V/7 (August, 1938):A-85.

72. Ibid., A-89; SK Abt. 662.7/5 (see comments in letters of 22.6.38 and 13.8.38, *Gauleitung Hessen-Nassau an der Kreisleitung Rheingau-St. Goarshausen*).

73. Boberach, *Meldungen aus dem Reich*, 274.

74. Fliedner, *Die Judenverfolgung*, 2:374.

75. Joerg Schadt, *Verfolgung und Widerstand dem Nationalsozialismus in Baden: Die Lageberichte des Generalstaatsanwalts Karlsruhe 1933–1945*, 270.

76. SK Abt. 662.6/408--10.2.38 (*SD—Koblenz-Trier an der Dienststelle Kochem, Neuwied*).

77. *DB* V/2 (February 1938):A-67.

78. *DB* V/2 (February 1938):A-67; LBI Wiener Microfilm, reel 23, no. 22, 29.7.38, *Amtsgerichts Karlsruhe.*

79. *GR* V/2 (March 1938):24; for low levels of anti-Semitism in Bavaria, see also Nicholls and Mathias, *German Democracy*, 104.

80. *DB* V/7 (August 1938):A-76.

81. Ibid., A-94.

82. Ibid., A-96.

83. *GR* V/11 (December 1938):A-11.

84. *DB* V/7 (August 1938):A-90.

85. *GR* V/11 (December 1938):A-30; *GR* V/11 (January 1939):A-25, A-26.

86. Rauschning, *The Voice of Destruction*, 235.

87. Kershaw, "Antisemitismus und Volksmeinung," 328–329.

88. *GR* V/11 (December 1938):A-6, A-19, A-28, A-29, A-30, A-31; *GR* V/12 (January 1939):A-3, A-16, A-18, A-22–A-24, A-27, A-28, A-30; *DB* VI/2 (January 1939):A-26; *DB* VI/2 (February 1939):A-95; *DB* VI/7 (August 1939):A-99; for secondary sources see Bracher, *The German Dictatorship*, 367; Eugene Davidson, *The Trial of the Germans* (New York: Collier Books, 1972), 47; Düwell, *Die Rheingebiete*, 187; Philip Friedman, *Their Brothers' Keepers* (New York: Holocaust Library, 1978); Genschel, *Die Verdrängung*, 201; Görgen, *Düsseldorf*, 172; Graml, *Der 9. November*, 10, 16, 43; Klepper, *Unter dem Schatten*, 675; Leber, *Das Gewissen*, 60; Leuner, *When Compassion*, 43–44; Melita Maschmann, *Account Rendered: A Dossier of My Former Self* (London: Abelard-Schuman, 1965), 56–57; Noakes and Pridham, *Documents*, 473; Peterson, *The Limits*, 220, 269; Hans Rothfels, *German Opposition to Hitler*, 31–33; Karl Schabrod, *Widerstand am Rhein und Ruhr 1933–1945* (Herne: A. Nierhoff, 1969), 107, for leaflets protesting persecution; Steinert, *Hitlers Krieg*, 74–75; Kershaw, "Antisemitismus und Volksmeinung," 318–335.

89. Foreign Office, *Documents on British Foreign Policy* (London: Her Majesty's Stationery Office), series 3, vol. 3 (1938–1939):277.

90. Kershaw, "Antisemitismus und Volksmeinung," 331.

91. Quoted in Rothfels, *German Opposition*, 31–32.

92. Noakes and Pridham, *Documents*, 475.

93. U.S. Department of State, *Foreign Relations* (1938) 2:400, The Ambassador in Germany (Wilson) to the Secretary of State, Berlin, November 16, 1938.

94. Ibid., 397–398, The Assistant Secretary of State (Messersmith) to the Secretary of State, Berlin, November 14, 1938.

95. *GR* V/11 (December 1938):A-6.

96. Ibid.

97. Ibid., A-29, A-30.

98. Steinert, *Hitlers Krieg*, 74–75; see also Kershaw, "Antisemitismus und Volksmeinung," 330, 334.

99. Kershaw, *Antisemitismus und Volksmeinung*, 332, 334–335; idem, "The Persecution," 275–281.

100. *GR* V/11 (December 1938):A-5, A-29; *DB* VI/7 (August 1938):A-106; *GR* VI/1 (January 1940):A-12; Behrend-Rosenfeld, *Ich stand*, 65; Görgen, *Düsseldorf*, 170; Helmut Krausnick, "Vorgeschichte und Beginn des militärischen Widerstandes gegen Hitler," *Vollmacht des Gewissens* 1 (1960), passim; NA T-175, R 237 (misscellaneous letters to Goering on behalf of Jews), F 2726268; SD XXIII J8 (26.2.60, letter of a former resident of Düsseldorf).

101. *GR* V/12 (January 1939):A-18, A-23, A-26, A-49; *DB* VI/2 (February 1939):A-99; Hans-Josef Steinberg, *Widerstand und Verfolgung*, 170–173; see also HSD G/90 Rep. 27 (*Staatsanwaltschaft beim Oberlandegericht Düsseldorf, Strafsachen*), box 57, 5Js 119/38—2AR 450/38.

102. *GR* V/11 (December 1938):A-29.

103. Ibid., A:31.

104. HSD G.90 Rep. 27 (*Staatsanwaltschaft beim Oberlandegericht Düsseldorf, Strafsachen*), box 52, 5Js 150/14—2AR 146/38; NA T-580, Ordner 20, R 112 (no frame number), 21.3.38 (NSDAP (*Schutzpolizei an der Kreisleitung Nordlingen*); SK Abt. 662.7/5—22.6.38, 13.8.38 (*Gauleitung an der Kreisleitung Rheingau-Hesse-Nassau*).

105. HSD G/90 Rep. 27 (*Staatsanwaltschaft beim Oberlandegericht Düsseldorf*), box 57, 18Js 864/38—2AR 439/39; 5Js 119/38—2AR 450/38; 6Js 1217/38—2AR 472/38; box 60, 2AR 57/39—26.1.39; box 58, 18Js 1196/38—2AR 528/38; G/90 Rep. 88 (*Justizvollzugsanstalt Düsseldorf*), box 1, 18KMs 38/39; SD XXII J8, XII J8, XXIII 778 (personal accounts of residents of Düsseldorf); *GR* V/11 (December 1938):A-30, A-31.

106. T-175 R 502, F 9366551—report of wartime conversation in Borgenstreich 8.8.41; T-175 R 575, F 1107—report of arrest of man who demanded the release of Jews during *Kristallnacht*.

107. Steinert, *Hitlers Krieg*, 75.

108. *GR* V/11 (December 1938):A-5.

109. See chapter 5, "Functions of Propaganda."

110. *Statistik des deutschen Reich*, vol. 577 (1942):28.

111. HSD G/90 Rep. 27 (*Staatsanwaltschaft beim Oberlandegericht Düsseldorf, Strafsachen*), box 59, 6KLs 1/39—2AR 16/39; box 60, 16Js 13/39—2AR 89/39; 3Js 36/39—2AR 100/39.

112. HSD G/90 Rep. 27 (*Staatsanwaltschaft beim Oberlandegericht Düsseldorf, Strafsachen*), box 52, 6Js 120/38—2AR 146/38; box 57, 18Js 864/38—2AR 439/39; 5Js 119/38—2AR 450/38; 6Js 1217/38—2AR 472/38; 18Js 1196/38—2AR 528/38; box 60, 2AR 57/39 (26.1.39); G/90 Rep. 88 (*Justizvollzugsanstalt Düsseldorf*), box 1, 18KMs 38/39; B/90 Rep. 21 (*Generalstaatsanwaltschaft Köln, Beleidigung*), box 39, 20KMs 39/40.

113. LBI AR 1570, 3959, V a2; letters of complaint to *Der Stürmer* because of continuing socialization: 10.9.39, 13.9.39, 4.10.39, 7.10.39, 10.10.39, 16.10.39, 18.10.39.

114. See Kershaw, "Antisemitismus und Volksmeinung," 336–337, for arrests for criticizing persecution 1938–1939.

115. *GR* V/3 (October 1938):A-21.

116. Ulrich von Hassell, *The Von Hassell Diaries, 1938–1944*, 76–77.

117. On secrecy, see Kershaw, "Antisemitismus und Volksmeinung," 338, 339, 346, 347; Toland, *Adolf Hitler*, 975, 1037; Steinert, *Hitlers Krieg*, 101, 257–258; Goldhagen, "Weltanschauung," 396; Stone, *Hitler*, 130; LBI AR 7183, box 13, folder 1, p. 3; NA T-175, R 577, F 675, F 751; YIVO, G96aI, *Propagandaparole No. 1 (Geheim!)*, 2, no date, but after the introduction of the star; see also Stokes, "The German People," passim.

118. NA T-175, R 268, F 2763310: *Sicherheitsdienst RFSS, Beobachter 11, Steiger, an die SD Hauptaussenstelle*, Erfurt, 30.4.42; my parentheses.

119. Ibid.

120. Stokes, "The German People," 176; Steinert, *Hitlers Krieg*, 249, 257; Kershaw, "Antisemitismus und Volksmeinung," 339.

121. Stokes, "The German People," 175.

122. Kershaw, "Antisemitismus und Volksmeinung," 285.

123. Stokes, "The German People," 181, note 57.

124. See Walter Laquer, *The Terrible Secret: Suppression of the Truth about Hitler's "Final Solution"*; Bernard Wasserstein, *Britain and the Jews of Europe, 1939–1945*; Arthur Morse, *While Six Million Died: A Chronicle of American Apathy* (New York: Random House, 1967); Henry Feingold, *The Politics of Rescue: The Roosevelt Administration and the Holocaust, 1938–1945* (New Brunswick, N.J.: Rutgers University Press, 1970); see also idem, "Failure to Rescue European Jewry: Wartime Britain and American," *Annals of the American Academy of Political and Social Science* 450 (July 1980); John Morley, *Vatican Diplomacy and the Jews during the Holocaust, 1939–1943*.

125. For discussion of the various types of knowledge, see Laquer, *The Terrible Secret*, passim.

126. Baker, *Days of Sorrow*, 272.

127. For an extreme view, see Sidney Bolkosky, *The Distorted Image: German-Jewish Perceptions of Germans and Germany, 1918–1935* (New York: Elsevier Scientific Publishing Co., 1975). For others, see Jehuda Reinharz, *Fatherland or Promised Land: The Dilemma of the German Jew, 1895–1914* (Ann Arbor: University of Michigan Press, 1975), and Stephen Poppel, *Zionism in Germany, 1897–1933: The Shaping of a Jewish Idenitity* (Philadelphia: Jewish Publication Society of America, 1977).

128. Bauer, *The Holocaust in Historical Perspective*, 7.

129. Quoted in Baker, *Days of Sorrow*, 196.

130. Quoted in Walter Zwi Bacharach, "Jews in Confrontation," 216.

131. Baker, *Days of Sorrow*, 273.

132. Werner Angress, "The German Jews, 1933–1939," 70.

133. See LBI AR 7183, box 13, folder 1, pp. 3, 8, 21; see also Levin, *The Holocaust*, 230, and Yitzhak Zuckerman, "From the Warsaw Ghetto," *Commentary* 67/6 (December 1975):65, for similar Jewish acceptance of "relocation" despite warnings of its true meaning; see also Bauer and Rotenstreich, *The Holocaust*, passim.

134. LBI AR 7183, box 13, folder 1, p. 31: report of a Jewish survivor from Berlin; see also Baker, *Days of Sorrow*, 270.

135. LBI AR 7183, box 13, folder 1, p. 25 (on back): *Begleitbericht von Ball-Kaduri*.

136. Kren and Rappoport, *The Holocaust*, 87; for Jewish denial, see also Laquer, *The Terrible Secret*, chapter 5, pp. 123-156.

137. Quoted in Baker, *Days of Sorrow*, 137; see also Hilberg, "The Anatomy of the Holocaust," 97–98.

138. NA T-77, R 859, F 5605179: *Doenitz an den leitenden Minister der geschäftsführenden Reichsregierung*, 15.5.45.

139. Hilberg, "The Anatomy of the Holocaust," 99.

140. Stokes, "The German People," 181; Kershaw, "The Persecution of the Jews," 283; Steinert, *Hitlers Krieg*, 243.

141. Stokes, "The German People," 186; Kershaw, "The Persecution of the Jews," 285, and "Antisemitismus und Volksmeinung," 339; Steinert, *Hitlers Krieg*, 261.

142. Stokes, "The German People," 185, 186; Kershaw, "The Persecution of the Jews," 285; Steinert, *Hitlers Krieg*, 261.

143. Behrend-Rosenfeld, *Ich stand*, 28.

144. Leber, *Das Gewissen*, 60.

145. NA T-175, R 270 (*Meldungen aus dem Reich*), F 2766261 (26.7.41).

146. Boberach, *Meldungen*, 115 (20.11.40).

147. NA T-175, R 260 (*Meldungen aus dem Reich*), F 275303 (20.1.41).

148. Ibid., F 275304 (4.3.41).

149. Ibid., F 275305 (3.4.41).

150. Boberach, *Meldungen*, 165–166 (26.7.41).

151. Steinert, *Hitlers Krieg*, 239–241; Kershaw, "The Persecution of the Jews," 282–283.

152. NA T-175, R 502, F 9366337: *SD Hauptaussenstelle Bielefeld an II A 3*, 9.8.41.

153. NA T-175, R 577, F 647: *SD Aussenstelle Bielefeld an III A 3*.

154. NA T-175, R 502, F 9366509: *SD Hauptaussenstelle Bielefeld an III A 3*, 16.9.41.

155. Broszat, *Bayern*, 1:483.

156. NA T-175, R 577, F 627: *SD Aussenstelle Höxter*, 25.9.41; F 629: *SD Aussenstelle Minden*, 26.9.41; F 679-680: *SD Aussenstelle Minden*, 21.2.42; F 624–625: *SD Aussenstelle Bielefeld an III A 3*, 30.9.41.

157. NA T-175, R 577, F 699: *SD Hauptaussenstelle Bielefeld*, 3.3.42.

158. NA T-175, R 577, F 757: *SD Aussenstelle Herford*, 3.12.42.

159. NA T-175, R 577, F 754, 11.12.42.

160. NA T-175, R 270 (*Meldungen aus dem Reich*), F 2766125.

161. Boberach, *Meldungen*, 216 (29.1.42).

162. Lochner, *The Goebbels Diaries*, 83.

163. BA R 58/165 (*Meldungen aus dem Reich*—9.10.41).

164. Broszat, *Bayern*, 1:482; see also Kershaw "Antisemitismus und Volksmeinung," 338, and "The Persecution of the Jews," 283.

165. NA T-175, R 270 (*Meldungen aus dem Reich*), F 2766261 (16.12.41).

166. NA T-175, R 577, F 675: *SD Hauptaussenstelle Bielefeld an III B 1*, 16.12.41.

167. LBI, *Stürmer* Collection, 3959, no. 9, 21.9.41; my parentheses.

168. LBI, *Stürmer* Collection, 3959, no. 10, 10.2.42; for additional letters to *Der Stürmer*, see Fred Hahn, *Lieber Stürmer: Leserbriefe an den NS-Kampfblatt 1924–1945* (Stuttgart-Degerloch: Seewald, 1978).

169. Reitlinger, *The Final Solution*, 171.

170. Lochner, *The Goebbels Diaries*, 261–262, 294; see also Buchheim, *Anatomy*, 542; Stokes, "The German People," 181, note 60.

171. von Hassell, *The von Hassell Diaries*, 92.

172. Boelcke, *The Secret Conferences*, 21.

173. Pulzer, *The Rise of Political Anti-Semitism*, 70.

174. Klepper, *Unter dem Schatten*, 760.

175. NA T-175, R 502, F 4366661: SD Bielefeld, 7.10.41.

176. NA T-175, R 258: *SD Bericht zur innen-politische Lage*, 23.10.39.

177. Klepper, *Unter dem Schatten*, 825 (8.12.39).

178. *GR* VI/4 (April 1940):A-42, A-43.

179. Behrend-Rosenfeld, *Ich stand*, 114.

180. Düwell, *Die Rheingebiete*, 248.

181. NA T-175, R 267, F 2763316 (*Stimmung zur Führerrede*—26.4.42).

182. Ibid.; see also this section, above.

183. Hans Fritzsche, *Hier spricht Hans Fritzsche* (Zurich: Interverlag, 1948), 241.

184. Behrend-Rosenfeld, *Ich stand*, 114–115.

185. Klepper, *Unter dem Schatten*, 970, 972–973, 1015–1017 (1941).

186. Boehm, *We Survived*, 288.

187. Steinert, *Hitlers Krieg*, 248; see also Stokes, "The German People," 182, note 61.

188. Steinert, *Hitlers Krieg*, 242.

189. Behrend-Rosenfeld, *Ich stand*, 114–115.

190. YIVO, G 96aI, *Propagandaparole No. 1*, no date, but after the introduction of the star.

191. NA T-175, R 577, F 675: *SD Hauptaussenstelle Bielefeld an III B 1*, 16.12.41, and F 674: *SD Aussenstelle Minden an III B*, 12.12.41.

192. NA T-175, R 577, F 664: *SD Aussenstelle Minden*, 6.12.41; my parentheses.

193. Ibid.

194. NA T-175, R 577, F 736: *SD Aussenstelle Detmold an die SD Hauptaussenstelle Bielefeld*, 31.7.42.

195. Steinert, *Hitlers Krieg*, 256; see also Stokes, "The German People," 178–179, notes 48, 51, 52.

196. Leuner, *When Compassion*, 68; see also Stokes, "The German People," 187, notes 83–85, and p. 89, notes 90, 91, for Germans' responses to the revelation

of the Katyn massacre. Goebbels's anti-Russian propaganda did not assuage those Germans who claimed that the Nazis had done worse things to Jews.

197. Boelcke, *The Secret Conferences*, xv; Lochner, *The Goebbels Diaries*, 261–262, 294; Steinert, *Hitlers Krieg*, 256–257.

198. NA T-175, R 268, F 2763316: *SD RFSS Aussenstelle Erfurt*, 29.4.42.

199. NA T-175, R 577, F 773: *SD Aussenstelle Höxter an die SD Hauptaussenstelle Bielefeld*, 27.2.43.

200. Ibid.

201. Düwell, *Die Rheingebiete*, 249; see also Levin, *The Holocaust*, 497.

202. Bramsted, *Goebbels and National Socialist Propaganda*, 400–404.

203. Noakes and Pridham, *Documents*, 669.

204. Steinert, *Hitlers Krieg*, 555.

205. Boberach, *Meldungen*, 383; see also ibid., 242.

206. Heinrich Hermelink, ed., *Kirche im Kampf: Dokumente des Widerstandes und des Aufbaus in der Evangelischen Kirche Deutschlands von 1933 bis 1945*, 467, 657; Peterson, *Limits*, 367; Seydewitz, *Civil Life in Wartime Germany*, 344; Günther Weisenborn, ed., *Der lautlose Aufstand: Bericht über die Widerstandsbewegung 1933-1945*, 35; Stokes, "The German People," 189, note 90; see also Kershaw, "Antisemitismus und Volksmeinung," 341–342; Michael Balfour, *Propaganda in War, 1939-1945: Organisations, Policies and Publics in Britain and Germany* (London: Routledge, 1979), 304.

207. Max Weinreich, *Hitler's Professors: The Part of Scholarship in Germany's Crimes Against the Jewish People*, 238.

208. Quoted in Hoehne, *The Order*, 413–414.

209. Quoted in Bracher, *The German Dictatorship*, 423.

210. Leuner, *When Compassion*, 161; it should be noted that since more than one person aided "submarines," this number would represent a much larger number of opponents of racial persecution.

211. Leuner, *When Compassion*, passim; Kurt Grossman, *Die unbesungenen Helden: Menschen in Deutschlands dunklen Tagen*, passim; Franz-Josef Heyen, *Nationalsozialismus im Alltag*, 127–163; Klepper, *Unter dem Schatten*, passim; Otto Kopp, ed., *Widerstand und Erneuerung: Neue Berichte und Dokumente vom inneren Kampf gegen das Hitler-Regime* (Stuttgart: Seewald, 1966), passim; Heinz Leipman, "Ein deutscher Jude denkt über Deutschland nach," *Vom Morgen zum Morgen* 5 (1961):1–21; Sellenthin, *Geschichte der Juden in Berlin*, passim; Steinberg, *Widerstand und Verfolgung*, 172; for a recent study, see Leonard Gross, *The Last Jews in Berlin* (New York: Simon and Schuster, 1982); for personal cases in this book, see chapters 7 and 9.

212. Ruth Andreas-Friedrich, comp., *Berlin Underground, 1938-1945* (New York: Holt, Rinehart and Winston, 1947), 70–78, 118.

213. Reitlinger, *The Final Solution*, 171.

214. Andreas-Friedrich, *Berlin Underground*, 312; see also Willi Bohn, *Stuttgart Geheim! Ein dokumentärischer Bericht* (Frankfurt a.M.: Röderberg, 1969), 219.

215. Boehm, *We Survived*, 194; see Hans-Robert Buck, *Der kommunistische*

367

*Widerstand gegen Nationalsozialismus in Hamburg*, Veröffentlichungen des Se-
minars für Geschichte Osteuropas und Südeuropas an der Universität München
(Munich: Universität München), 194, for occupations in the *Rote Kapelle*.

216. Weisenborn, *Der lautlose Aufstand*, 168.

217. Ibid., 102.

218. Ibid., 104, 317.

219. *GR* V/12 (January 1939):A-21; SD XXII J8 (personal accounts of residents
of Düsseldorf); HSD G/90 Rep. 88 (*Justizvollzugsanstalt* Düsseldorf), box 1,
18KMs 43/40, 18KMs 80/40; box 4, 18KMs 35/34; prisoners received sentences
of six months to one year for casual criticism of Nazi racial views.

220. Arieh Bauminger, *Roll of Honour* (Jerusalem: Cooperative Press, 1970),
passim.

221. These surveys will be referred to as OMGUS surveys. Footnotes to these
surveys will be of three types: (1) information from Anna and Richard Merritt,
*Public Opinion in Occupied Germany: The OMGUS Surveys, 1945–1949*, will
be referred to by pages; (2) references to the Hoover Institute microfilm with
results for specific questions will be cited under HA; (3) references to reports on
the surveys, which are actually condensations, will be referred to under NA.

222. NA RG 260, 350-3/5, Rep. 49 for October 1945, p. 3.

223. For the peculiar German translation, see HA HM 261, G 373, reel 1, survey
1, question 14.

224. See Merritt, *Public Opinion*, xviii.

225. NA RG 260, 350-3/5, Rep. 19, p. 47, question 81.

226. See this section, above.

227. HA HM 261, G 373, reel 2, survey 29, question 18B.

228. HA HM 261, G 373, reel 1, survey 10, question 11.

229. HA HM 261, G 373, reel 1, survey 9, no question number.

230. HA HM 261, G 373, reel 2, survey 36, question 22c.

231. HA HM 261, G 373, reel 1, survey 4, question 9.

232. HA HM 261, G 373, reel 1, survey 19, question 47.

233. Merritt, *Public Opinion*, 31.

234. NA RG 260, 350/3-5, Rep. 19, p. 11.

235. Heinz Ansbacher, "Attitudes of German Prisoners of War: A Study of the
Dynamics of National-Socialistic Followership," 4, 34.

236. Ibid., 39.

237. Ibid., 24–25.

238. Ibid., 32.

239. Ian Kershaw, "Alltägliches und Ausseralltägliches: Ihre Bedeutung für die
Volksmeinung 1933–1939"; see also his "Antisemitismus und Volksmeinung,"
339.

CHAPTER SEVEN

1. See chapter 6, note 211.

2. See Manfred Wolfson, "The Subculture of Freedom: Some People Will Not";

idem, "Der Widerstand gegen Hitler: Soziologische Skizze über Retter (Rescuers) von Juden in Deutschland," *Aus Politik und Zeitgeschichte: Beilage zur Wochenzeitung Das Parlament*, Bonn, 15/71 (April 10, 1971):32–39, presents some data.

3. The boundaries of *Gestapostelle* Düsseldorf-West were almost identical to those of the Government District Düsseldorf, which contained Düsseldorf, Essen, and several other large urban areas. For brief descriptions of these areas and voting patterns in some major cities, see Hamilton, *Who Voted for Hitler?*, 156–198.

4. In 1974, 75,000 of the 100,000 Gestapo files in this archive had been indexed. Its 452 files on opponents of persecution form the basis for discussion in the remainder of this chapter. (An additional 20,000 Gestapo files are in Würzburg, but they are not yet completely indexed.)

5. For comparisons of high- and middle-level opponents to low-level opponents, see my "German Opposition," appendix G, table 44, p. 427.

6. See ibid., 225–226.

7. Ibid., 257, and appendix H, table 57, p. 440.

8. For data on years of opposition of both Jewish and non-Jewish *Rässenschander* in Hamburg, see Hans Robinsohn, *Justiz als politische Verfolgung: Die Rechtsprechung in "Rassenschandefällen" beim Landegericht Hamburg 1936–1943*, 18, 52. Since data include both Jewish and non-Jewish *Rässenschander* they cannot be used for comparison here.

9. *Statistik des Deutschen Reiches*, vol. 451 (1933), no. 5:3; vol. 552 (1939), no. 3:12.

10. Calculated as follows: 321 divided by 15,501 equals 2.1 percent.

11. Calculated as follows: 131 divided by 4,748 equals 2.8 percent.

12. Scholars who wish to know which socioeconomic groups were most active during each phase of persecution are referred to Gordon, "German Opposition," 223–248.

13. See appendix B, table B.2, for socioeconomic groups that were over- and underrepresented compared to the population and labor force of the Government District Düsseldorf.

14. For the socioeconomic characteristics of Catholics and Protestants, see chapter 8; for those of Nazis, see chapter 9. For characteristics of persons with no profession, see Gordon, "German Opposition," appendix H, table 61, p. 447. Civil servants were probably overrepresented among *Judenfreunde*, and domestic servants were probably overrepresented among *Rassenschänder*, but their percentages in the population and labor force as well as among opponents were too small for reliable statistical comparisons to be made. Also, note that the percentage of non-Jewish *Rassenschänder* who were domestic servants was somewhat higher than the percentage of the Jewish labor force who were domestic servants and were arrested for *Rassenschande* (see Gordon, "German Opposition," appendix H, table 54, p. 437).

15. Independents were overrepresented among *Judenfreunde* but not among *Rassenschänder*. Also note that there were only two farmers among the independents,

369

NOTES TO CHAPTER SEVEN

who therefore included owners, managers, business executives, leading civil servants, and a large percentage of small businessmen. Even though this was an industrial area, underrepresentation of farmers was extreme. Although Merkl found that farmers were underrepresented among early anti-Semites in the Nazi party, the OMGUS surveys of Germans after World War II found that farmers consistently demonstrated more anti-Semitism than did any other occupational group. (For Merkl's results, see appendix B, table B.1; for the OMGUS results, see NA RG 260, 350-3/5, Rep. 19, p. 13, and Rep. 49, p. 10.)

16. It was not possible to obtain separate percentages of upper- and lower-level white-collar workers for the district; however, since the occupational distribution of the Government District Düsseldorf was very similar to that of the Rhine Province as a whole (of which the district comprised 53.4 percent), it is probable that the percentage of upper- and lower-level white-collar workers in the Rhine Province was also similar. If that were the case, we would note that both upper-level and lower-level white-collar workers were overrepresented among opponents, and that this overrepresentation was most extreme among upper-level white-collar workers. See appendix B, table B.3, for comparisons of the occupational distribution in the Rhine Province and the Government District Düsseldorf. Also see *Statistik des Deutschen Reiches*, vol. 455 (1933), no. 16: 60, for comparisons of the size of the Government District Düsseldorf and the Rhine Province.

17. See Gordon, "German Opposition," appendix H, table 57, p. 440.

18. Wolfson, "The Subculture," 7.

19. See Gordon, "German Opposition," 257. The study of ninety-three additional cases was conducted by this author but not included with the data from the Government District Düsseldorf because it was not a random sample. Note that 81.2 percent of the Jews arrested for *Rassenschande* in the district were males who consorted with non-Jewish women (see Gordon, "German Opposition," appendix H, table 54, p. 437). This probably reflects the Gestapo's harsher treatment of Jewish males, and the fact that they did not arrest similar percentages of non-Jewish women indicates that many Jewish males were probably falsely accused, which comes to no surprise. The underrepresentation of women as opponents of anti-Semitism conflicts with Leuner's impression that women were highly visible aiders of Jews (see Leuner, *When Compassion*, 54).

20. See appendix B, table B.1 for Merkl's data. The postwar OMGUS surveys clearly indicated higher levels of anti-Semitism among women (see NA RG 260, 350-3/5, Rep. 19, p. 13; Rep. 49, pp. 2, 9; Rep. 112, p. 2).

21. See William S. Allen, "Eine statistische Analyse der sozialistischen Untergrundbewegung in Nordrhein-Westfalen 1933–1938," in *Widerstand, Verfolgung und Emigration 1933–1945*, edited by Helmut Esters. Studien und Berichte aus dem Forschungsinstitut der Friedrich-Ebert-Stiftung (Bad Godesberg: Friedrich-Ebert-Stiftung, 1967), 26.

22. See *Statistik des Deutschen Reiches*, vol. 451 (1933), no. 5:23 for the percentage of Jews in commerce and trade.

23. See appendix B, table B.2.

24. See Gordon, "German Opposition," appendix H, table 57, p. 440.

25. Ibid., table 54, p. 437.

26. Ibid., table 53, p. 435.

27. See chapter 6.

28. Wolfson, "The Subculture," 7; for comparisons to the German population in 1933, see *Statistik des Deutschen Reiches*, vol. 451 (1933), no. 5:7. This year is used rather than 1939 to eliminate territories that were added to Germany after 1933.

29. See chapter 2, "Anti-Semitism in the Early Nazi Party."

30. See chapter 1, "Anti-Semitism, 1870–1933," and chapter 2, note 2.

31. The oldest Nazi anti-Semite in Merkl's sample was born in 1860, and the oldest opponent of racial persecution from the district was born in 1863. In the sample from the district, opponents aged 50–59 were the only age group that was overrepresented among high-level opponents (see Gordon, "German Opposition," appendix H, table 57, p. 440). It was not possible to obtain the percentage of Merkl's sample who were aged 50–59, but there was clearly considerable overlap between those aged 49–55 and those aged 50–59 in the district.

32. See chapter 1, "Anti-Semitism, 1870–1933."

33. See chapter 2, "Nazi Voters."

34. See appendix B, table B.2. For very similar results among non-Jewish *Rassenschänder*, see Robinsohn, *Justiz als politische Verfolgung*, 70. Since his occupational scale does not follow the census format, his results are not directly comparable. However, using a "social" scale of 1–6 (upper to lower classes), he found that among 102 non-Jewish *Rassenschänder*, 9 percent were levels 1–2, 65 percent were levels 3–4, and 25 percent were levels 5–6.

35. The only exception was that there was no significant difference between the percentage of independents who were high-level opponents and the percentage of independents in the labor force (see Gordon, "German Opposition," appendix H, table 53, p. 435).

36. Gellately, *The Politics of Economic Despair*.

37. Lipset, *Political Man*, 146, citing Pratt, pp. 148, 171.

38. See Gordon, "German Opposition," appendix H, table 60, p. 446, for the percentages of occupational groups in different geographic areas.

39. Ibid., appendix H, table 57, p. 441.

40. For apathy in the middle classes, see *DB* II/8 (August 1935):A-7, A-10–A-14; *DB* III/2 (February 1936):A-1, A-2; *DB* III/7 (July 1936):A-1, A-2; *DB* III/10 (October 1936):A-8, A-11; *GR* V/4-5 (May–June 1938):56; for apathy in working classes, see *DB* II/10 (October 1935):A-4–A-6; *DB* II/11 (November 1935):A-24; *DB* III/2 (February 1936):A-5; *DB* III/4 (April 1936):A-2; *DB* III/6 (June 1936):A-17a; *DB* III/12 (December 1936):A-19; *GR* IV/5 (May 1937):4; *GR* IV/6 (June 1937):8; *GR* IV/10 (October 1937):9–13; *GR* IV/11 (December 1937):6; *GR* IV/12 (January 1938):8; *GR* V/5 (June 1938):50–55, 58; *GR* VI/6 (July 1939):A-24; Steinert, *Hitlers Krieg*, 62.

41. For working-class anti-Semitism, see *DB* II/9 (September 1935):A-12; *DB* II/

11 (November 1935):A-24, A-25, A-64–A-69; *DB* III/2 (February 1936):A-4–A-6; *DB* III/4 (April 1936):53; *DB* III/6 (June 1936):A-14; *DB* IV/3 (March 1937):A-28; *DB* IV/11 (November 1937):A-51; *DB* V/7 (August 1938):A-10; *GR* V/12 (January 1939):A-25; *GR* VI/2 (March 1940):A-23; see also NA T 175, R 267, F 2763333 (*SD Aussenstelle Erfurt-Weisensee* to *SD-Hauptaussenstelle Erfurt*, April 27, 1942), for ascriptions of guilt for World War II to Jews among former SPD and KPD members; for anti-Semitism among working-class women in World War II, see Boehm, *We Survived*, 71–95; for political motives for participation of workers in *Kristallnacht*, see Graml, *Der 9. November*, 45–46; for opposition to anti-Semitism among workers, see *DB* II/8 (August 1935):A-32; *DB* II/9 (September 1935):A-11, A-22, A-29; *DB* III/1 (January 1936):A-18, A-19, A-31; *DB* V/7 (August 1938): A-99, A-100; see also Buchheim, *Anatomy*, 26, and Noakes and Pridham, *Documents*, 461, for workers' opposition to the boycott of April 1933; see Boehm, *We Survived*, 288, for opposition among workers during the war; for anti-Semitism among the middle classes, see Genschel, *Die Verdrängung*, 49–50, 123, 267, and Schleunes, *The Twisted Road*, 86, 142–143, 164, 261–262; for opposition to anti-Semitism among the middle classes, see Buchheim, *Anatomy*, 26; Noakes and Pridham, *Documents*, 46; Pätzold, *Faschismus*, passim; see also *DB* II/8 (August 1935):A-35–A-37; *DB* II/9 (September 1935):A-10, A-11; *DB* II/11 (November 1935):A-29; *DB* III/1 (January 1936):A-6, A-7, A-19, A-20; *DB* IV/11 (November 1937):A-51; *GR* V/11 (December 1938): A-29; *DB* VI/1 (January 1939):A-1, A-2; see also HSD G/20/2, 1039—27.5.35 (*Reg. Präs. Lagebericht*, 10).

42. See chapter 2, note 2.

43. See chapter 2, "Nazi Voters" and "Anti-Semitism in the Early Nazi Party."

44. See appendix B, table B.1 and chapter 2, "Anti-Semitism in the Early Nazi Party."

45. For a detailed analysis of the occupational and other socioeconomic characteristics of the Nazi party between 1933 and 1945, see Kater, "Quantifizierung und NS-Geschichte," 453–484.

46. See chapter 1, "Anti-Semitism, 1870–1933" and chapter 2, "Anti-Semitism in the Early Weimar Years."

47. Hamilton, *Who Voted for Hitler?*, 423–433.

48. Calculated from *Statistik des Deutschen Reiches*, vol. 470 (1937), no. 1:8 for 1933 and vol. 552 (1942), no. 4:74 for 1939.

49. Cities in the Government District Düsseldorf had very large percentages of foreign Jews. For example, in 1933 Jews with foreign citizenship and those born outside of Germany represented the following percentages of all Jews: Remscheid 47%, Duisburg 46%, Dortmund 36%, Essen 35%, Düsseldorf 27%, Wupperthal 22%, Solingen 19%. Also, even in 1933, before large-scale Jewish migration from small towns to cities, in the cities listed above an average of 74 percent of the Jewish population was born outside of the census city; see LBI, Bruno Blau, "Die Entwicklung der jüdischen Bevölkerung in Deutschland von 1800–1945," (unpublished manuscript), 52, *Tabelle 7*. In short, a majority were "newcomers" rather than assimilated long-term residents.

50. For anti-Semitism among workers, see note 40. See also NA RG 260, 350-3/5, Rep. 19, p. 13; rep. 49, pp. 2, 7, 8, 10; Merritt, *Public Opinion in Occupied Germany*, 147.
51. See Gordon, "German Opposition," 275–278.
52. HSD *Gestapoakten*, file 7,535.
53. Ibid., file 1,776.
54. Ibid., file 13,441.
55. Ibid., file 1,437.
56. Ibid., file 17,402.
57. Ibid., file 11,293.
58. Ibid., file 1,798.
59. Ibid., file 21,810.
60. Ibid., file 4,377.
61. Ibid., file 17,922.
62. Ibid., files 25,529 and 57,696.
63. Ibid., file 44,301.
64. Ibid., file 19,536.
65. Ibid., file 57,054.
66. Ibid., file 25,466.
67. Ibid., files 6,580, 26,592, and 26,593.
68. Ibid., file 21,122.
69. Ibid., file 37,661.
70. Ibid., file 45,101.
71. Ibid., files 41,997 and 34,237.
72. Ibid., file 17,390.
73. Ibid., file 43,313.
74. Ibid., file 13,133.
75. Ibid., file 35,366.
76. Ibid., files 1,540 and 1,541.
77. Ibid., file 46,645.
78. Ibid., file 41,031.
79. Ibid., file 2,498.
80. Ibid., file 45,588.
81. Ibid., file 36,150.
82. Ibid., file 25,775.
83. Ibid., file 46,339.
84. Ibid., file 38,652.
85. Ibid., file 49,962.
86. Robinsohn, *Justiz als politische Verfolgung*, 77.
87. Ibid., and 139–140.
88. For example, in Bavaria a woman was sentenced to three years in a normal prison for repeating rumors about transports and gassing; see Kershaw, "Antisemitismus und Volksmeinung," 340.

373

89. See this chapter, "Characteristics of opponents, 1933–1944." For Robinsohn's data on sentencing and social classes, see *Justiz als politsche Verfolgung*, 71.

90. Ibid.; 28 percent of categories 5 and 6 were sent to a *Zuchthaus* for two or more years, versus 8 percent for categories 1–4.

91. Ibid., p. 72.

92. Ibid., pp. 22–24.

93. See chapter 6.

CHAPTER EIGHT

1. Aberhard Bethge, "Troubled Self-Interpretation and Uncertain Reception in the Church Struggle," in *The German Church Struggle and the Holocaust*, edited by Franklin Littell and Hubert Locke (Detroit: Wayne State University Press, 1974), 170, 176; Hermann Graml, ed., *The German Resistance to Hitler* (Berkeley: University of California Press, 1970), xii, xiii; John Conway, *The Nazi Persecution of the Churches, 1933–1945*, 261; Tennenbaum, *Race and Reich*, 77–78; Ernst Wolf, "Political and Moral Motives behind the Resistance," in *The German Resistance to Hitler*, edited by Hermann Graml, 203. For anti-Semitism in the Catholic church, see Lewy, *The Catholic Church*, 268–309, and passim; see also Bracher, *The German Dictatorship*, 389; Hans Peter Bleuel and Ernst Klinnert, *Deutsche Studenten auf dem Weg ins Dritte Reich: Ideologien, Programme, Aktionen 1918–1935* (Gütersloh: Mohn, 1967), 150; Klepper, *Unter dem Schatten*, 47, 682, 730; Fliedner, *Die Judenverfolgung*, 1:228; Meier, *Kirche und Judentum*, 12, 58, 60; Michael Müller-Claudius, *Der Antisemitismus und das deutsche Verhängnis*, 56. For anti-Semitism in the Protestant churches, see BA ZSg 101/2/24—1.11.33; Conway, *The Nazi Persecution*, 263, 377; Hans-Joachim Kraus, "Die evangelische Kirche," in *Entscheidungsjahr*, edited by Werner Mosse, 259; Tennenbaum, *Race and Reich*, 75; Tillich, "The Jewish Question, 256; Wolf, "Political and Moral," 211; Friedrich Zipfel, *Kirchenkampf in Deutschland 1932–1945: Religionsverfolgung und Selbstbehauptung der Kirchen in der nationalsozialistischen Zeit*, 119, 215–217; Kershaw, "Antisemitismus und Volksmeinung, 340; Franklin Littell, *The Crucifixion of the Jews: The Failure of Christians to Understand the Jewish Experience*; and Richard Gutteridge, *Open Thy Mouth for the Dumb!: The German Evangelical Church and the Jews, 1879-1950* (Oxford: Blackwell, 1976).

2. Allen, "Objective and Subjective Inhibitants in the German Resistance to Hitler," 121–123.

3. Quoted in Leuner, *When Compassion*, 138.

4. Quoted in Ger van Roon, *Neuordnung im Widerstand: Der Kreisauer Kreis innerhalb des deutschen Widerstandsbewegung*, 238; see also Michael Balfour and Julian Frisby, *Helmuth von Moltke: A Leader against Hitler* (New York: St. Martin's Press, 1972), 166; Conway, *The Nazi Persecution*, 223; Annedore Leber and Freya Moltke, *Für und Wider: Entscheidungen in Deutschland 1918–1945*, 70; Leon Poliakov, *Das Dritte Reich und die Juden: Dokumente und Aufsätze*

(Berlin: Arani, 1955), 432, 434; Steinert, *Hitlers Krieg*, 245; Weisenborn, *Der lautlose Aufstand*, 52–53.

5. Leber and Moltke, *Für und Wider*, 70.

6. Bernhard Stasiewski, comp., *Akten deutscher Bischöfe über die Lage der Kirche 1933–1945*, Kommission für Zeitgeschichte bei der Katholischen Akademie in Bayern, Veröffentlichungen, Reihe A, no. 5 (Mainz- Mathias-Grünewald-Verlag, 1968):42.

7. Ibid., 375.

8. Heinz Boberach, comp., *Berichte des SD und der Gestapo über Kirchen und Kirchenvolk in Deutschland 1934–1944*, 195–197.

9. Saul Friedländer, *Kurt Gerstein: The Ambiguity of Good* (New York: Knopf, 1960), 147; Steinert, *Hitlers Krieg*, 259.

10. Leber and Moltke, *Für und Wider*, 77; Leuner, *When Compassion*, 140.

11. Leber and Moltke, *Für und Wider*, 76; Leuner, *When Compassion*, 137.

12. Leber and Moltke, *Für und Wider*, 79.

13. Quoted in Leuner, *When Compassion*, 137.

14. Miles Ecclesiae, *Hitler gegen Christus: Eine katholische Klarstellung und Abwehr* (Paris: Societe d'Editions Européennes, 1936), 168, 181, 190.

15. Leber and Moltke, *Für und Wider*, 77.

16. Hans Müller, *Katholische Kirche und Nationalsozialismus: Dokumente 1930–1945* (Munich: Nymphenburger Verlagshandlung, 1963), 95.

17. Boberach, *Berichte des SD*, 7.

18. Tennenbaum, *Race and Reich*, 76; Leuner, *When Compassion*, 104.

19. Heinrich Portmann, *Dokumente um den Bischof von Münster*, 103.

20. Boberach, *Berichte des SD*, 21; Leber and Moltke, *Für und Wider*, 72; Leuner, *When Compassion*, 103–104; Pridham, *Hitler's Rise*, 152; Peterson, *The Limits*, 211; Stasiewski, *Akten*, 38, 54, 122–123; Tennenbaum, *Race and Reich*, 439, note 63.

21. Lewy, *The Catholic Church*, 289–291.

22. Meier, *Kirche und Judentum*, 9.

23. Pridham, *Hitler's Rise*, 161; Karl Thieme, "Deutsche Katholiken," 271–287.

24. HSD G 20/2/1049, p. 6—December 1934 (*Lagebericht des Regierungspräsidenten*); NA T-175, R 408, F 2932452 and F 2932453 (*Lagebericht. Reichsführer SS der Reichssicherheitsamt*, May/June 1934); SK Abt. 662.6/382—6.1.37 (*Flugblätter*, Biebernheim, Kreis St. Goar); Kuno Bludau, *Gestapo-geheim: Widerstand und Verfolgung in Duisburg, 1933–1945*, Forschungsinstitut der Friedrich-Ebert-Stiftung, Schriftenreihe (Bonn-Bad Godesberg: Verlag Neue Gesellschaft, 1973), 190; Boberach, *Berichte des SD*, 7–8; Klaus Gotto, *Die Wochenzeitung Junge Front/Michael: Eine Studie zum katholischen Selbstverständnis und zum Verhalten der junge Kirche gegenüber den Nationalsozialismus* (Mainz: Mathias-Grünewald-Verlag, 1970), 66–68; Stasiewski, *Akten*, 176–177.

25. Historisches Archiv der Stadt Köln, ed., *Ausstellung: Widerstand und Verfolgung in Köln* (Cologne: Historisches Archiv, 1974), 207–208, 225–236; Leber and Moltke, *Für und Wider*, 72, 75; Noakes and Pridham, *Documents*, 370–371;

Müller, *Katholische Kirche*, 106; Stasiewski, *Akten*, 88, 688, 703; Bernhard Vollmer, *Volksopposition*, 17, 21–22, 142. 276–277, 284–285; Kershaw, "Antisemitismus und Volksmeinung," 309–317.

26. Müller, *Katholische Kirche*, 87–89.
27. HSD G/90 Rep. 21 (*Staatsanwaltschaft* Köln), no. 37–23.4.33 (no case numbers).
28. Boberach, *Berichte des SD*, 77.
29. HSD G/21/5, 30655d—4.5.33 (*Lagebericht des Regierungspräsident*).
30. HSD G/90 Rep. 27 (*Staatsanwaltschaft beim Oberlandegericht Düsseldorf, Strafsachen*), no. 45—6Js 722/35 (1935).
31. Vollmer, *Volksopposition*, 259–260.
32. Ibid., 277.
33. Ibid., 290–291.
34. Ibid., 296; see also p. 21.
35. BA ZSg 110/1/167—19.12.35; ZSg 101/6/226—19.12.35.
36. SK Abt. 662.6/693—2.8.36 (*Bericht des Vertrauensmann*).
37. Ibid., 27.3.38.
38. *DB* IV/4 (April 1937):A-39–A-52.
39. *GR* III/9 (October 1937):A-6.
40. HSD G/90 Rep. 27 (*Staatsanwaltschaft beim Oberlandegericht Düsseldorf, Strafsachen*), no. 50—5.9.37 (18Js 1811/37).
41. NA T 81, R 225, F 5006310 (*Stimmungsbericht für den Monat*, November 1937, *Der Kreispropagandaleiter an der NSDAP Gauleitung Kurhessen*).
42. SD XXII J8 (report of emigrant Jew).
43. Stasiewski, *Akten*, 301.
44. Ibid., 300.
45. Steinert, *Hitlers Krieg*, 74; see also Kershaw, "Antisemitismus und Volksmeinung," 309–317.
46. Stokes, "The German People," 179, note 52.
47. NA T-175, R 259, F 2752165—12.8.40 (*Meldungen aus dem Reich*).
48. Steinert, *Hitlers Krieg*, 239, 248.
49. Conway, *The Nazi Persecution*, 266.
50. NA T-175, R 260, F 2753097–F 2753099—23.1.41 (*Meldungen aus dem Reich*).
51. Boberach, *Berichte des SD*, 768.
52. Historisches Archiv der Stadt Köln, *Ausstellung*, 209.
53. Portmann, *Dokumente*, 95–98.
54. Boberach, *Berichte des SD*, 643.
55. Ibid., 651.
56. Ibid., 684.
57. Ibid., 709.
58. Ibid., 783.
59. Ibid., 891.
60. Portmann, *Dokumente*, 74.

61. Boberach, *Berichte des SD*, 888.

62. Weisenborn, *Die lautlose Aufstand*, 47.

63. Behrend-Rosenfeld, *Ich stand*, 126, 160.

64. Leuner, *When Compassion*, 64.

65. HSD *Gestapoakten*, file 296.

66. Leuner, *When Compassion*, 108.

67. Helmut Baier, *Die Deutschen Christen Bayerns im Rahmen des bayerischen Kirchenkampfes* (Nuremberg: Verein für Bayerische Kirchengeschichte, 1968), 32, 67–69; Manfred Priepke, *Die evangelische Jugend im Dritten Reich 1933– 1936* (Hannover: Norddeutsche Verlagsanstalt, 1960), 41–43; Gerhard Schäfer, comp., *Landesbischof D. Wurm und der nationalsozialistische Staat 1940-1945: Eine Dokumentation* (Stuttgart: Calwer Verlag, 1968), 152; Peterson, *The Limits*, 267.

68. NA T 175, R 408, F 1932491 (SS *Lagebericht*, no date); T-580, R 112, Ordner 30—24.11.33 (*Gendarmerie in Wemling* to *Bezirksamt Donauwörth*); Joachim Beckmann, ed., *Kirchliches Jahrbuch für die evangelische Kirche in Deutschland 1933–1944* (Gütersloh: Bertelsmann Verlag, 1948), 275, 305, 327, 330, 348, 433; Hermelink, *Kirche im Kampf*, 52, 116–122; Leber and Moltke, *Für und Wider*, 63; Meier, *Kirche und Judentum*, 16–18; Snoek, *The Grey Book*, 38; Steinert, *Hitlers Krieg*, 73.

69. Quoted in Arthur Cochrane, "The Message of Barmen for Contemporary Church History," 201-202.

70. Wolf, "Political and Moral Motives," 211–212; see also Kraus, "Die evangelische Kirche," 267.

71. Leuner, *When Compassion*, 109.

72. Weisenborn, *Der lautlose Aufstand*, 46; Zipfel, *Kirchenkampf*, 215.

73. Meier, *Kirche und Judentum*, 37.

74. Ibid., 21–24; Leuner, *When Compassion*, 133.

75. Noakes and Pridham, *Documents*, 311; see also Hoffman, *Widerstand*, 273.

76. Friedländer, *Kurt Gerstein*, 40.

77. Leuner, *When Compassion*, pp. 114, 115.

78. Ibid., 196; Friedländer, *Kurt Gerstein*, 146; Leber and Moltke, *Für und Wider*, 67.

79. Ferdinand Friedensburg, "On Nazism and the Church Struggle," in *The German Church Struggle and the Holocaust*, eds. Franklin Littel and Hubert Locke, 254; see also Conway, *The Nazi Persecution*, 223; Klepper, *Unter dem Schatten*, 851, 859; Meier, *Kirche und Judentum*, 38.

80. Conway, *The Nazi Persecution*, 265; Friedländer, *Kurt Gerstein*, 145; Meier, *Kirche und Judentum*, 32, 33, 39; Snoek, *The Grey Book*, 88, 89; Schäfer, *Landesbischof*, 153–171.

81. *DB* IV/7 (July, 1936):A-100; Friedländer, *Kurt Gerstein*, 147; Roon, *Neuordnung*, 245; Weisenborn, *Der lautlose Aufstand*, 47.

82. Leber and Moltke, *Für und Wider*, 67-68; Leuner, *When Compassion*, 122; Roon, *Neuordnung*, 164; Weisenborn, *Der lautlose Aufstand*, 46.

83. Meier, *Kirche und Judentum*, 25–26; Weisenborn, *Der lautlose Aufstand*, 47.
84. *DB* II/11 (November 1935):A-39, A-40.
85. Terence Prittie, *Germans Against Hitler*, 106.
86. Snoek, *The Grey Book*, 39.
87. Leber and Moltke, *Für und Wider*, 65; Weisenborn, *Der lautlose Aufstand*, 67.
88. HSD G/21/5, 30655c—16.3.35 (*Lagebericht des Regierungspräsident*).
89. Quoted in Weisenborn, *Der lautlose Aufstand*, 67.
90. Bracher, *The German Dictatorship*, 385; Shirer, *The Rise and Fall*, 238; Snoek, *The Grey Book*, 40.
91. *DB* IV/6 (June 1937):A-39.
92. HSD, *Gestapoakten*, files 33,095 and 43,029.
93. Ibid., file 43,029.
94. HSD G/90 Rep. 27 (*Staatsanwaltschaft beim Oberlandegericht Düsseldorf, Strafsachen*), no. 50—18Js 1657/37 (December 1937).
95. Boberach, *Berichte des SD*, 921.
96. HSD G/90, Rep. 27 (*Staatsanwaltschaft beim Oberlandegericht Düsseldorf, Strafsachen*), box 56 (1938), 18Js 871/38—2AR 387/38.
97. Leuner, *When Compassion*, 119.
98. HSD, *Gestapoakten*, file 19,779.
99. Quoted in Leuner, *When Compassion*, 113–114.
100. Boberach, *Berichte des SD*, 323.
101. Ibid., 340, 376; see also NA T-175, R 258, F 2750361 (*Bericht zur Innenpolitische Lage* 1.12.39).
102. Boberach, *Berichte des SD*, 316; Conway, *The Nazi Persecution*, 375, 434, note 46; Wolf, "Political and Moral Motives," 211; Peterson, *The Limits*, 271.
103. Snoek, *The Grey Book*, 108.
104. NA T-175, R 258, F 2751198—8.4.40 (no document title).
105. Leuner, *When Compassion*, 119.
106. Kuno Bludau, *Gestapo-geheim: Widerstand und Verfolgung in Duisburg 1933–1944*, Schriftenreihe des Forschungsinstituts der Friedrich-Ebert-Stiftung, no. 98 (Bad Godesberg: Verlag Neue Gesellschaft, 1973), 208.
107. Snoek, *The Grey Book*, 106; see also Leuner, *When Compassion*, 130–133; *DB* IV/8 (August 1939):A-105.
108. Steinert, *Hitlers Krieg*, 172.
109. Prittie, *Germans Against Hitler*, 113.
110. Leuner, *When Compassion*, 122.
111. Leber and Moltke, *Für und Wider*, 68.
112. Quoted in ibid.; see also HSD, *Gestapoakten*, file 47,308.
113. Steinert, *Hitlers Krieg*, 147–148.
114. Conway, *The Nazi Persecution*, 263–264, 266–267; see also Weisenborn, *Der lautlose Aufstand*, 46; Zipfel, *Kirchenkampf*, 251–252.
115. SK Abt. 662.6/330—25.11.38 (*SD Unterabschnitte Koblenz* to *Aussenstelle Kochem*) and 532—20.12.37; *DB* III/6 (June 1936):A-98; *GR* VI/2 (February

1940):A-6; NA T-175, R 270, F 2766261—16.12.41 (*Meldungen aus dem Reich*); T-175, R 410, F 2934020—31.1.38 (*Lagebericht des SS*); T-175, R 271, F 2766984– F 2767027—5.6.42 (*Sonderbericht des SS*); BA ZSg 101/28/221–227—12.20.35; see also Boberach, *Berichte des SD*, 201–212, 278, 365, 383, 406, 597; Düwell, *Die Rheingebiete*, 236–246; Kraus, "Die evangelische Kirche," 267; Leuner, *When Compassion*, 100–114; Meier, *Kirche und Judentum*, 32–33; Portmann, *Dokumente*, 90–91; Vollmer, *Volksopposition*, 131; Zipfel, *Kirchenkampf*, 327– 328.

116. *Statistik des Deutschen Reiches*, vol. 552 (1939), no. 3:33–34.

117. See appendix B, table B.4 for the socioeconomic characteristics of Catholic and Protestant opponents in the Government District Düsseldorf.

118. See Kershaw, "Antisemitismus und Volksmeinung," 309–317, and chapter 6 above, passim; see also NA RG 260, 350/3–5, Rep. 49, pp. 8, 9.

119. Conway, "The Churches," 206.

CHAPTER NINE

1. See chapter 2.

2. This will be an exploratory rather than exhaustive study.

3. Müller-Claudius, *Der Antisemitismus*, 76–77, 175–176.

4. See chapter 2, "Anti-Semitism in the Early Nazi Party."

5. For NSDAP membership in 1933, see Schäfer, *Entwicklung*; for 1942 see Noakes and Pridham, *Documents*, 263.

6. *DB* II/8 (August 1935):A-40, A-42, B-2.

7. *DB* II/9 (September 1935):A-11, A-30, A-70; see also Linn, *Das Schicksal*, 34.

8. McKale, *The Nazi Party Courts*, 156-157.

9. SK Abt. 662.3/126, p. 101–19.1.37 (*Amtsleitung—Gau Koblenz-Trier, Amt für Kommunalpolitik to Gauleitung der NSDAP, Amtsleitung, Geschäftsmeister Koblenz*).

10. HSD G/90 Rep. 27 (*Staatsanwaltschaft beim Oberlandegericht Düsseldorf*), box 55, 4KL 33/38—2AR 357/38; box 59, 5Js 807/38—2AR 30/39; NA T-175 III, R 432, F 2962192 (SS *Gerichte. Information*), 1942 and F 2962206, 1943; see also T-175 III, R 257, F 2749060 (SS *Gerichte. Information*), 1941.

11. NA T-175 III, R 432, F 2962195 (letter dated 1943, SS-*Hauptscharführer*).

12. McKale, *The Nazi Party Courts*, 165, and his "A Case of 'Nazi Justice'— The Punishment of Party Members Involved in the *Kristallnacht*, 1938," 230.

13. Heyen, *Nationalsozialismus*, 125–163, cites a number of these instances.

14. NA T-175, R 432, F 2962185 (SS *Gerichte. Information*), 1942.

15. Ibid., F 2962135 and F 2962136, 1941.

16. Ibid., F 2962134, 1941.

17. HSD G/20/2, 1039, p. 13—28.5.35 (*Der Landrat der Reg. Bez. Aachen: Bericht über die politische Lage*).

18. SK Abt. 662.2/1—4.10.37 (*Gaugericht* Koblenz-Trier).

19. NA T-175, R 52, F 2565915, folder 554 (no title).
20. SK Abt. 662.7/5—23.8.35 (letter of the *Verhandlungsleiter* Koblenz-Trier); Abt. 662.2/2, 50/36—28.7.36 (*Gaugericht* Koblenz-Trier); Abt. 662.3/64, p. 216—3.3.38 (*Kreisgericht* Trier).
21. Müller-Claudius, *Der Antisemitismus*, 180–182; Fliedner, *Die Judenverfolgung* 1:368 (26.8.33); Peterson, *The Limits*, 348, 349, 393; for primary sources see NA T-175, R 239, F 2728222 (no title); SK Abt. 662.2/2, p. 53—25.5.36 (*Gaugericht* Koblenz); NA T 580, Ordner 30, R 112—30.11.37 (police report from Wallerstein); SK Abt. 662.3/64, p. 248—3.8.38 (*Kreisgericht* Trier).
22. SK Abt. 662.3/64—20.11.37 and 5.9.38 (*Kreisgericht* Trier); Abt. 662.3/130, p. 55–23.6.38 (*Bürgermeister* Osburg to *Amtsbürgermeister* Ruwer); Abt. 662.2/2, p. 40—22.7.36 and p. 41—2.11.36 (*Kreisgericht* Altenkirchen); Fliedner, *Die Judenverfolgung* 1:371 (30.10.36).
23. HSD G/21/5, 30655c—25.2.35 (*Reg. Präs. Lagebericht—Judentum*); SK Abt. 403/16914–31.1.34 (no title); Abt. 662.2/1—16.6.36 (*Kreisgericht* Neuwied), 15.7.37 (*Kreisgericht* Trier), 29.9.36, 2.10.36, 30.10.36 (*Gaugericht* Koblenz); Abt. 662.2/2—15.8.36 (*Kreisgericht* (no name given); 15.10.36, 26.10.36, 29.12.36, 22.1.37 (*Gaugericht* Koblenz-Trier); Abt. 662.3/64—2.11.35, 9.4.37, 1.9.37, 20.11.37, 24.9.38 (*Kreisgericht* Trier); Abt. 662.3/122—15.1.37 (letter from the *Amt für Kommunalpolitik* to the *Stützpunktleiter der NSDAP*), 14.8.38 (no title), 30.11.36 (*Der Landrat an den Beauftragten der NSDAP Trier*); Abt. 662.3/124— 1.10.37 (*Beschluss der Kreisgericht Trier*); Abt. 662.3/126—12.1.37 (*Amtsleitung. Ortsgruppenleiter Konz-Karthaus to Kreisleiter der NSDAP Trier*); Abt. 662.6/722 II/225—1/2—4.2.38 (RFSS: *Aussenstelle* Koblenz to *Unterabschnitt* Koblenz); DB III/1 (January 1936):A-21, A-33; DB III/8 (August 1936):A-75; GR IV/9 (August 1937):9; GR V/2 (March 1938):24; Herman Weinkauff, *Die deutsche Justiz und der Nationalsozialismus; Ein Überblick*, Veröffentlichung der Institut für Zeitgeschichte: Quellen und Darstellungen zur Zeitgeschichte, no. 16/1 (Stuttgart: Deutsche Verlagsanstalt, 1968), 16/1:326; Peterson, *The Limits*, 365; Genschel, *Die Verdrängung*, 87, 123.
24. McKale, *The Nazi Party Courts*, 63; see also Kershaw, ''Antisemitismus und Volksmeinung,'' 330.
25. GR V/12 (January 1939):A-19; GR V/11 (December 1938):A-29; see also Gilbert, *Nuremberg Diary*, 26–27, 261, 278, 293–294, 319–320 for criticisms.
26. GR V/11 (December 1938):A-27.
27. GR V/12 (January 1939):A-26.
28. Ibid., A-27.
29. GR V/11 (December 1939):A-17; GR V/12 (January 1939): A-18; DB VI/1 (January 1939):A-1, A-2, DB VI/8 (August 1939):A-99; GR V/12 (January 1939):A-27; see also SK Abt. 662.7/5—3.3.39 (*Kreisleitung Rheingau to Kreisgeschäftsführer Rheingau*); Grossman, *Die unbesungenen Helden*, 135 and passim; Peterson, *The Limits*, 267, 271.
30. DB V/12 (December 1938):A-49; GR V/11 (December 1938):A-27, A-28; DB VI/8 (August 1939):A-108.

NOTES TO CHAPTER NINE

31. Müller-Claudius, *Der Antisemitismus*, 76–77.

32. Melita Maschmann, *Account Rendered: A Dossier of My Former Self* (London: Abelard-Schuman, 1965), 41, 56–57; see also SD XXIIJ8, account of a member of the German Girls' League (no date).

33. Dawidowicz, *The War Against the Jews*, 3; see also Seydewitz, *Civil Life*, 95, 319.

34. Quoted in Hoehne, *The Order*, 432.

35. Toland, *Adolf Hitler*, 449–450.

36. Quoted in Friedlander, *Kurt Gerstein*, 142.

37. NA T-175, R 432, F 2962176 (*SS Gericht. Information*), 1942.

38. Ibid., F 2962191, 1942.

39. NA T-175, R 267, F 5486961, case 101.

40. HSD, *Gestapoakten*, file 34,795.

41. Schadt, *Verfolgung und Widerstand*, 298.

42. NA T-175, R 276, F 5486961, case 105.

43. *DB* VII/4 (April, 1940):A-46.

44. Boehm, *We Survived*, 119–130.

45. Peterson, *The Limits*, 274.

46. Friedländer, *Kurt Gerstein*, passim; see also see H. G. Adler, *Der Kampf gegen die "Endlösung der Judenfrage,"* Schriftenreihe der Bundeszentrale für Heimatdienst, no. 34 (Bonn: Bundeszentrale für Heimatdienst, 1958):58.

47. Görgen, *Düsseldorf und der Nationalsozialismus*, 222.

48. Hüttenberger, *Die Gauleiter*, 200.

49. Quoted in McKale, *The Nazi Party Courts*, 144–145.

50. Ibid., 145.

51. Adler, *Der Kampf*, 52.

52. NA T 175, R 59, F 2575261–F 2575271, July 1943 (*Der Kommandeur der Sicherheitspolizei Weissruthenien an den Reichsführer SS und Chef der Deutschen Polizei*).

53. See Gordon, "German Opposition," appendix I, table 63, p. 452, for the chronological development of opposition among Nazis in the district.

54. Ibid., appendix I, table 64, p. 452.

55. See appendix B, table B.5 for comparisons of Nazi opponents to the population and labor force of the Government District Düsseldorf.

56. See Gordon, "German Opposition," table 67, p. 456, for comparisons of Nazi opponents of persecution and early Nazi anti-Semites.

57. See chapter 7.

58. See Gordon, "German Opposition," appendix I, table 68, p. 459, for occupational comparisons of Nazi opponents of racial persecution and the NSDAP in 1935; see appendix I, table 69, p. 460, for occupational comparisons of Nazi opponents and Nazi party members from 1933–1945.

59. HSD, *Gestapoakten*, files 34,795 and 34,796.

60. Ibid., file 47,629.

61. Ibid., file 39,586.

62. Ibid., file 21,124.
63. Ibid., file 4,819.
64. Ibid., file 1,599.
65. Ibid., file 4,841.
66. Ibid., file 36,993.
67. Ibid., file 15,259.
68. Ibid., file 31,529.
69. Ibid., file 6,117.
70. Ibid., file 35,573.
71. Ibid., file 2,203.
72. Ibid., file 48,688.
73. Ibid., files 12,769 and 42,546.
74. Ibid., file 29,300.
75. Ibid., file 96,688.
76. Ibid., file 20,015.
77. Ibid., file 41,326.
78. Ibid., files 50,489 and 43,818.
79. Ibid., file 52,234.
80. Ibid., file 6,509.
81. Ibid., file 11,020.
82. Wolfgang Zapf, *Wandlungen der deutschen Elite: Zirkulationsmodell deutscher Führungsgruppen 1919–1961*, 162; for a good general account of resistance, see Bracher, *The German Dictatorship*, 370–399, 431–460; Roger Manvell, *The Conspirators: 20th July 1944* (New York: Ballantine Books, 1971), passim.
83. Moltke was a member of the former nobility, in which there was apparently considerable opposition to anti-Semitism; see Boehm, *We Survived*, 288; see Lochner, *The Goebbels Diaries*, 58, entry of January 25, 1942, for close associations of the German Crown Prince with Jews; *DB* III/10 (October 1936):A-10.
84. Balfour and Frisby, *Helmuth von Moltke*, 172.
85. Ibid., 173.
86. Ibid., 174.
87. Ibid., 175.
88. Ibid., 225; Boehm, *We Survived*, 178; Prittie, *Germans Against Hitler*, 223; see also Peter Hoffmann, *Widerstand, Staatsreich, Attentat: Der Kampf der Opposition gegen Hitler*, 159, 289, 346; Leber and Moltke, *Für und Wider*, 98; Roon, *Neuordnung*, 67.
89. Hoffmann, *Widerstand*, 288; Roon, *Neuordnung*, 67, 73, 114, 119, 164, 214, 238, 245, 283, 291, 326, 339, 587.
90. Bracher, *The German Dictatorship*, 394; Shirer, *The Rise and Fall*, 372; see also Hoffmann, *Widerstand*, 75.
91. Henry Cord Meyer, ed., *The Long Generation: Germany from Empire to Ruin, 1913–1945*, 304; see also Noakes and Pridham, *Documents*, 314.
92. Hoffmann, *Widerstand*, 159.
93. Ibid., 30; Peterson, *The Limits*, 66.

94. Hugh Gibson, ed., *The Ciano Diaries, 1934–1943* (New York: Doubleday, 1946), 26–27.

95. Genschel, *Die Verdrängung*, 107, 137.

96. HSD G/20/2, 1027, p. 49—5.4.35 (*Staatspolizeistelle für dem Reg. Bez. Aachen to Geheimen Staatspolizei Berlin—Geheim!*).

97. Genschel, *Die Verdrängung*, 116.

98. Schleunes, *The Twisted Road*, 153–155.

99. *GR* V/2 (March 1938):A-27.

100. Hoffmann, *Widerstand*, 104; Leber and Moltke, *Für und Wider*, 97, 110, 118.

101. See this section, above.

102. Robert O'Neill, *The German Army and the Nazi Party, 1933–1939* (London: Corgi Books, 1968), 61, 114.

103. *DB* II/8 (August 1935):B-16.

104. U.S. Department of State, *Foreign Relations* (1934) 2:400, The Ambassador in Germany (Wilson) to the Secretary of State, Berlin, November 16, 1938.

105. Manfred Messerschmidt, *Die Wehrmacht im NS-Staat: Zeit der Indoktrination*, 79,247; see also Klaus-Jürgen Müller, *Armee, Politik und Gesellschaft in Deutschland 1933–1945: Studien zum Verhältnis von Armee und NS-System* (Paderborn: Schöningh, 1979) on the weakening of traditional army values; Helmut Krausnick and Hans-Heinrich Wilhelm have written a very important book which I saw too late for appropriate references here; but for extensive army complicity, see their *Die Truppe des Weltanschauungskrieges: Die Einsatzgruppen der Sicherheitspolizei und des SD, 1938–1942.* Part I, *Die Einsatzgruppen vom Anschluss Österreichs bis zum Feldzug gegen die Sowjetunion: Entwicklung und Verhältnis zur Wehrmacht*; part 2, *Die Einsatzgruppe A der Sicherheitspolizei und des SD, 1941/42: Eine exemplarische Studie.* (Quellen und Darstellungen zur Zeitgeschichte, number 22. Stuttgart: Deutsche Verlagsanstalt, 1981).

106. Bracher, *The German Dictatorship*, 424, 431.

107. Steinert, *Hitlers Krieg*, 105.

108. Ibid., 250–251; Streit, *Keine Kameraden*, 50, 298–300, and passim.

109. Quoted in Steinert, *Hitlers Krieg*, 251.

110. Streit, *Keine Kameraden*, 54–59, 109–130; see also Krausnick and Wilhelm, *Die Truppe*, passim.

111. Ibid., 55.

112. Ibid., 299–300.

113. Ibid., 297–300; see also Hillgruber, "Die 'Endlösung' und das deutsche Ostimperium," 149.

114. Quoted in Hoehne, *The Order*, 342.

115. Quoted in ibid., 338.

116. Ibid., 428, 429.

117. Quoted in ibid., 430.

118. Steinert, *Hitlers Krieg*, 250, 252; for officers' disapproval of racial persecution, see Hoffmann, *Widerstand*, 204, 316–317; *GR* V/12 (January 1939):A-

21; Noakes and Pridham, *Documents*, 327; Steinert, *Hitlers Krieg*, 105–106; Stokes, "The German People," 178, note 48.

119. Hoehne, *The Order*, 405.

120. Ibid., 347.

121. Quoted in ibid., 348.

122. Quoted in ibid.

123. Helmuth Krausnick and Harold Deutsch eds., *Groscurth, Helmuth: Tagebuch eines Abwehroffiziers 1938-1940*, Institut für Zeitgeschichte, Quellen und Darstellungen zur Zeitgeschichte (Stuttgart: Deutsche Verlagsanstalt, 1970), 50, 91; Streit, *Keine Kameraden*, 119, 120.

124. Kren and Rappoport, *The Holocaust*, 91.

125. Ibid., and see Hoehne, *The Order*, 444.

126. Quoted in Foster, "Historical Antecedents, 16.

127. Ibid., 17.

128. Allen, "Objective and Subjective Inhibitants," 118–119, for his discussion of opposition in the military.

129. Maser, *Hitler*, 303.

130. Hans Mommsen, *Beamtentum im Dritten Reich*, 49; see also Adam, *Judenpolitik*, 39–41; Peterson, *The Limits*, 443–444.

131. Christopher Browning, "The Government Experts," 195; see also Goldhagen, "Weltanschauung" 396.

132. Browning, "The Government Experts," passim; see also Christopher Browning, *The Final Solution and the German Foreign Office: A Study of Referat B III of Abteilung Deutschland, 1940-1943* (New York: Holmes and Meier, 1978).

133. Browning, "The Government Experts," 195–196.

134. See table 9.2.

135. Browning, "The Government Experts," 193; see also U.S. Department of State, *Foreign Relations* (1938) 2:428, The Ambassador to Germany (Wilson) to the Secretary of State, Berlin, November 10, 1938.

136. Hubert Schorn, *Der Richter im Dritten Reich: Geschichte und Dokumente* (Frankfurt a.M.: Klosterman, 1959), 59, 147; see also U.S. Department of State, *Foreign Relations* (1934) 2:294, The Consul at Stuttgart (Moffitt) to the Secretary of State, May 25, 1934.

137. Schorn, *Der Richter*, 132–135.

138. HSD G/90 Rep. 27 (*Staatsanwaltschaft beim Oberlandegericht Düsseldorf, Strafsachen*), box 53, 16Js 272/38—2AR 224/38; box 54, 6KLs 3/38—2AR 231/38; box 55, 4KLs 2/38—2AR 244/38.

139. Hermann Weinkauff, *Die deutsche Justiz und der Nationalsozialismus: Ein Ueberblick*, Veröffentlichungen der Institut für Zeitgeschichte: Quellen und Darstellungen zur Zeitgeschichte, no. 16 (Stuttgart: Deutsche Verlagsanstalt, 1968) 1:132.

140. *DB* III/6 (June 1936):A-83.

141. Schorn, *Der Richter*, 161, 168; Düwell, *Die Rheingebiete*, 170.

142. Roon, *Neuordnung*, 197.

143. Weinkauff, *Die deutsche Justiz*, 122.

144. YIVO G-72, no. 67.

145. LBI AR 7183, box 13, folder 3, Kempen (20.11.42), no page number: *Der Landgerichtspräsident Kempen an Herrn Oberlandesgerichtspräsidenten Dr. Alfred Dürr.*

146. Schorn, *Der Richter*, 59, 113.

147. Rudolf Echterhölter, *Die deutsche Justiz und der Nationalsozialismus*, Veröffentlichungen der Institut für Zeitgeschichte: Quellen und Darstellungen zur Zeitgeschichte, no. 16 (Stuttgart: Deutsche Verlangsanstalt, 1970) 2:186–187; see also Werner Johe, *Die gleichgeschaltete Justiz: Organisation des Rechtswesens und Politisierung der Rechtssprechung 1933–1945, dargestellt am Beispiel des Oberlandesgerichtsbezirks Hamburg*, Veröffentlichungen der Forschungsstelle für die Geschichte des Nationalsozialismus in Hamburg, no. 5 (Frankfurt a.M.: Europäische Verlagsanstalt, 1967), passim.

148. Behrend-Rosenfeld, *Ich stand*, 67; Boehm, *We Survived*, 288 (comments of Leo Baeck); Fliedner, *Die Judenverfolgung* 1:377–378; Mommsen, *Beamtentum*, 48.

149. Echterhölter, *Die deutsche Justiz*, 203–204, 224–225; *DB* II/9 (September 1935):A-23.

150. Ilse Staff, ed., *Justiz im Dritten Reich: Eine Dokumentation* (Frankfurt a.M.: Fischer Bücherei, 1964), 156–159.

151. Carsten Nicolaisen, comp., *Dokumente zur Kirchenpolitik des Dritten Reiches: Das Jahr 1933*, 2 vols. (Munich: Chr. Kaiser Verlag, 1971), 1:130–131.

152. See chapter 4, "Functions of Anti-Semitism inside the Nazi Party." See also *DB* II/8 (August 1935):B-1–B-8, B-13.

153. *DB* III/6 (June 1936):A-84, A-85; Fliedner, *Die Verfolgung*, 2:377–379.

154. Ibid., A-85, A-86.

155. Adam, *die Judenpolitik*, 310.

156. McKale, *The Nazi Party Courts*, 135, 170; Noakes and Pridham, *Documents*, 471; Peterson, *The Limits*, 36, 41–42, 86.

157. Peterson, *The Limits*, 298.

158. *DB* II/9 (September 1935):A-37.

159. *DB* III/1 (January 1936):A-29.

160. Josef Wulf, *Presse und Funk im Dritten Reich: Eine Dokumentation*, 252.

161. Boehm, *We Survived*, 82.

162. LBI AR 7183, box 15, folder 2, p. 21; see also Ursula von Kardorff, *Berliner Aufzeichnungen: Aus den Jahren 1942-1945* (Munich: Biederstein, 1962), 33.

163. LBI AR 7183, box 3, folder 1, p. 173.

164. Ursel Hochmuth and Gertrud Meyer, *Streiflichter aus dem Hamburger Widerstand 1933–1945* (Frankfurt a.M.: Röderberg Verlag, 1972), 232–233.

165. Pätzold, *Faschismus*, 78. Also note that in World War II the German Communists demanded that Jewish Communists form their *own* resistance groups, which were captured and exterminated in 1942 (see Yehuda Bauer, *The Holocaust in Historical Perspective*, 76).

166. Mohrmann, *Antisemitismus*, 199.

167. Siegbert Kahn, *Dokumente des Kampfes der revolutionären deutschen Arbeiterbewegung gegen Antisemitismus und Judenverfolgung*, Beiträge zur Geschichte der deutschen Arbeiterbewegung, no. 3 (East Berlin: Dietz, 1960):555–557.

168. Quoted in ibid., 561.

169. Detler Peukert, *Ruhrarbeiter gegen den Faschismus: Dokumentation über den Widerstand im Ruhrgebiet 1933–1945* (Frankfurt a.M.: Röderberg, 1976), 197.

170. For specific papers opposing persecution, see Gerd Renken, "Die 'Deutsche Zukunft' und der Nationalsozialismus: Ein Beitrag zur Geschichte des geistigen Widerstandes in den Jahren 1933–1940" (Ph.D. dissertation, Free University of Berlin, 1970), 68–90, on *Die Deutsche Zukunft*; also see Leber and Moltke, *Für und Wider*, 82, for *Deutsche Rundschau, Die Frankfurter Zeitung*, and others.

171. Genschel, *Die Verdrängung*, 48.

172. BA ZSg 110/1/160—16.12.33.

173. BA ZSg 101/6/250—16.12.35.

174. *Deutsche Presse*, January 5, 1935, p. 5.

175. Ibid., January 19, 1935, p. 30.

176. BA ZSg 101/6/43—4.8.35.

177. BA ZSg 101/7/409—27.6.36.

178. BA ZSg 101/8/245—17.10.36.

179. BA ZSg 101/8/275—28.10.36.

180. BA ZSg 110/3/97—2.11.36.

181. BA ZSg 101/8/323—17.11.36.

182. BA ZSg 101/8/429—18.12.36.

183. BA ZSg 110/5/172—14.7.37.

184. BA ZSg 110/10/114--11.11.38.

185. BA ZSg 110/10/160—25.11.38.

186. BA ZSg 102/3/68 and ZSg 102/13/72—28.11.38.

187. Hardy, *Hitler's Secret Weapon*, 185.

188. Ibid., 186–195.

189. NA T 175, R 267, F 276259—15.3.42 and R 268, F 2764164—23.2.42 (*SD Sonderbericht, Hauptaussenstelle Erfurt*).

190. SD Abt. 662.7/5—4.5.43 (*Rundschreiben 34/43, Der Gaupropagandaleiter*).

191. Hagemann, *Die Presselenkung*, 36, 315; see also Balfour, *Propaganda in War*.

CHAPTER TEN

1. Kren and Rappoport, "Resistance to the Holocaust," 202.

2. For an excellent discussion of psychological theories of anti-Semitism, see Erich Cramer, *Ideologie und Handeln in Theorien über den Antisemitismus* (published Ph.D. dissertation, Hannover: Technische Universität Hannover, 1970);

see also Martin Kitchen, *Fascism* (London: Macmillan Press, 1976), 12–24; Reichmann, *Hostages*; Fred Weinstein, *The Dynamics of Nazism: Leadership, Ideology, and the Holocaust* (New York: Academic Press, 1980).

3. Kitchen, *Fascism*, 20–22.
4. Nolte, *Three Faces of Fascism*, passim; Kitchen, *Fascism*, 36–45.
5. Kitchen, *Fascism*, 71–82.
6. Quoted in Hoehne, *The Order*, 440.
7. Raul Hilberg, "The Nature of the Process," in *Survivors, Victims, and Perpetrators*, edited by Joel E. Dimsdale, M.D. (New York: Hemisphere Publishing Corp.), 435–456.
8. Ibid., 30–35.
9. John Steiner, "The SS Yesterday and Today: A Sociopsychological View," in *Survivors, Victims and Perpetrators*, edited by Joel E. Dimsdale, M.D., 435–456.
10. Quoted in Hoehne, *The Order*, 441.
11. Steiner, "The SS Yesterday and Today," 431.
12. Kren and Rappoport, *The Holocaust*, 130.

# Select Bibliography

For sources in addition to those listed in this bibliography, please see Sarah Gordon, "German Opposition to Nazi Anti-Semitic Measures between 1933 and 1945, with Particular Reference to the Rhine-Ruhr Area." Ph.D. dissertation, State University of New York at Buffalo, 1979, available on microfilm from University Microfilms, Ann Arbor, Michigan.

## MAJOR ARCHIVAL SOURCES

### Bundesarchiv (BA)

ZSg 101  Brammer *Sammlung*: press directives, 1933–1939
ZSg 102  Sänger *Sammlung*: press directives, 1933–1939
ZSg 110  Traub *Sammlung*: press directives, 1933–1939
ZSg 116  *Deutsches Nachrichtenbüro*: press directives, 1933–1939

### Hauptstaatsarchiv Düsseldorf (HSD)

#### DÜSSELDORF BRANCH

*Gestapoakten*: Cases of Germans arrested for *Judenfreundlichkeit* (friendliness to Jews) and Germans and Jews arrested for *Rassenschande* ("race defilement" or "interracial" sexual relations)

#### KALKUM BRANCH

G 20, G 21, G 90: Police and court records from the Government District Düsseldorf

### Hoover Institution, Stanford University (HA)

HM (Hoover Microfilms) 261, reels 1–3; OMGUS Surveys (Office of Military Government, U.S. consisting of postwar German opinion questionnaires)

389

SELECT BIBLIOGRAPHY

*Leo Baeck Institute, New York (LBI)*

AR 7183, Kreuzberger Collection: Miscellaneous records from other archives on German-Jewish affairs

*National Archives (NA)*

T 175: Records of the *Reichsführer* SS, *Reichssicherheitshauptamt* (Himmler and SS organizations)
RG 260, 350-3/5; OMGUS Reports (condensations of the OMGUS Surveys)

*Preussisches Geheimes Staatsarchiv (PGA)*

Rep. 77: Preussisches Ministerium des Innern
Rep. 90p: *Gestapo Lageberichte*

*Stadtsarchiv Düsseldorf (SD)*

SD XIII J8: Letters on Jewish affairs to and from the archive

*Staatsarchiv Koblenz (SK)*

Abt. 403, 441, 662.2, 662.3, 663.6, 662.7: Records of the *Sicherheitsdienst* (SD) and miscellaneous records for the district Koblenz-Trier

*YIVO Institute, New York (YIVO):*

G 96a: Miscellaneous propaganda notices

OTHER PRIMARY SOURCES

Baynes, Norman, H., ed. *The Speeches of Adolf Hitler: April, 1922-August, 1939.* New York: Howard Fertig, 1969.
Behrend-Rosenfeld, Else. *Ich stand nicht allein: Erlebnisse einer Jüdin in Deutschland.* Frankfurt a.M.: Europäische Verlagsanstalt, 1963.
Boberach, Heinz, comp. *Berichte des SD und der Gestapo über Kirchen und Kirchenvolk in Deutschland 1934–1944.* Mainz-Mathias-Grünewald Verlag, 1971.
————, ed. *Meldungen aus dem Reich: Reichssicherheitshauptamt; Auswahl aus den geheimen Lageberichten des Sicherheitsdienstes der SS 1939-1944.* Neuwied: Luchterhand Verlag, 1965.

Boehm, Eric. *We Survived: The Stories of Fourteen of the Hidden and Hunted of Nazi Germany.* Santa Barbara, California: Clio Press, 1966.

Boelcke, Willi, ed. *Kriegspropaganda 1939–1941: Geheime Ministerkonferenzen im Reichspropagandaministerium.* Stuttgart: Deutsche Verlagsanstalt, 1966.

————, ed. *The Secret Conferences of Dr. Goebbels: The Nazi Propaganda War.* New York: Dutton, 1970.

Broszat, Martin, et al., eds. *Bayern in der NS-Zeit: Soziale Lage und politisches Verhalten der Bevölkerung im Spiegel vertraulicher Berichte.* Munich: R. Oldenbourg Verlag, 1977.

Dodd, William E. *Ambassador Dodd's Diary, 1933-1938.* Ed. William Dodd, Jr. and Martha Dodd. New York: Harcourt, Brace and Co., 1941.

Domarus, Max, ed. *Hitler Reden und Proklamationen 1932–1945.* 2 vols. Munich: Süddeutscher Verlag, 1962, 1965.

Fliedner, Hans-Joachim. *Die Judenverfolgung in Mannheim 1933-1945.* 2 vols. Stuttgart: Kohlhammer, 1971.

Hassell, Ulrich von. *The Von Hassell Diaries, 1938-1944.* Garden City, N.Y.: Doubleday, 1947.

Hermelink, Heinrich, ed. *Kirche im Kampf: Dokumente des Widerstandes und des Aufbaus in der Evangelischen Kirche Deutschlands von 1933 bis 1945.* Tübingen: Wunderlich, 1950.

Heyen, Franz Josef, ed. *Nationalsozialismus im Alltag.* Veröffentlichungen der Landesarchivverwaltung Rheinland-Pfalz, no. 9. Boppard am Rhein: Bohldt, 1967.

Klepper, Jochen. *Unter dem Schatten deiner Flügel: Aus den Tagebüchern der Jahre 1932-1942.* Stuttgart: Deutsche Verlagsanstalt, 1956.

Lochner, Louis, ed. and trans. *The Goebbels Diaries.* New York: Doubleday, 1971.

Mommsen, Hans. *Beamtentum im Dritten Reich: Mit ausgewählten Quellen zur nationalsozialistischen Beamtenpolitik.* Stuttgart: Deutsche Verlagsanstalt, 1966.

Noakes, Jeremy, and Pridham, Geoffrey. *Documents on Nazism, 1919–1945.* London: Cape, 1974.

Portmann, Heinrich, ed. *Dokumente um den Bischof von Münster.* Münster: Verlag Aschendorff, 1948.

Sauer, Paul, comp. *Dokumente über die Verfolgung der jüdischen Bürger in Baden-Württemberg durch das nationalsozialistische Regime 1933-1945.* Stuttgart: Kohlhammer, 1966.

Schadt, Joerg. *Verfolgung und Widerstand unter dem Nationalsozialismus in Baden: Die Lageberichte der Gestapo und des Generalstaatsanwalts Karlsruhe 1933-1944.* Edited by Stadtarchiv Mannheim, Stuttgart: Kohlhammer, 1976.

Sozialdemokratische Partei Deutschlands. *Deutschland-Berichte.* Prague, Paris: SOPADE, 1935-1940.

—————. *Germany Reports.* English translation of the *Deutschland-Berichte.*

Thevoz, Robert, et al., eds. *Pommern 1934/35 im Spiegel von Gestapo-Lageberichten und Sachakten.* 2 vols. Veröffentlichungen aus den Archiven Preussischer Kulturbesitz, nos. 11, 12. Cologne: G. Grote, 1974.

Vollmer, Bernhard. *Volksopposition im Polizeistaat.* Stuttgart: Deutsche Verlagsanstalt, 1957.

SECONDARY SOURCES

Abel, Theodore. *Why Hitler Came to Power: An Answer Based on the Original Life Stories of Six Hundred of his Followers.* New York: Prentice-Hall, 1938.

Adam, Dietrich Uwe. *Die Judenpolitik im Dritten Reich.* Düsseldorf: Droste Verlag, 1972.

Adler-Rüdel, Salomon. *Ostjuden in Deutschland 1880-1940.* Leo Baeck Institute, Schriftenreihe wissenschaftlicher Abhandlungen, no. 1. Tübingen: Mohr, 1959.

Allen, William S. *The Nazi Seizure of Power: The Experience of a Single German Town, 1930-1935.* Chicago: Quadrangle, 1965.

—————. "Objective and Subjective Inhibitants in the German Resistance to Hitler." In *The German Church Struggle and the Holocaust*, edited by Franklin Littell and Hubert Locke. Detroit: Wayne State University Press, 1974.

Angress, Werner. "The German Jews, 1933–1939." In *The Holocaust*, 69–84. See Friedlander and Milton.

Ansbacher, Heinz. "Attitudes of German Prisoners of War: A Study of the Dynamics of National-Socialistic Followership." *Psychological Monographs*, General and Applied, 63/1, no. 288 of entire series: 1–32. Washington: American Psychological Association, 1948.

Bacharach, Walter Zwi. "Jews in Confrontation with Racist Antisemitism, 1879-1933." Leo Baeck Institute *Yearbook* 25 (1980):197–220.

Baker, Leonard. *Days of Sorrow and Pain: Leo Baeck and the Berlin Jews.* New York: Macmillan, 1978.

Balfour, Michael, and Frisby, Julian. *Helmuth von Moltke: A Leader against Hitler.* New York: St. Martin's Press, 1972.

Bauer, Yehuda. "Genocide: Was it the Nazis' Original Plan?" *Annals of the American Academy of Political and Social Science* 450 (July 1980):35–45.

———. *The Holocaust in Historical Perspective.* Seattle: University of Washington Press, 1978.

Bauer, Yehuda, and Rotenstreich, Nathan, eds. *The Holocaust as Historical Experience.* New York: Holmes and Meier, 1981.

Bennathan, Esra. "Die demographische und wirtschaftliche Struktur der Juden." In *Entscheidungsjahr 1932*, edited by Werner Mosse, 87–134. Tübingen: Mohr, 1966.

Beyerchen, Alan. "The Physical Sciences." In *The Holocaust*, 151–164. See Friedlander and Milton.

Bracher, Karl Dietrich. *The German Dictatorship: The Origins, Structure, and Effects of National Socialism.* New York: Praeger, 1972.

Bramsted, Ernst K. *Goebbels and National Socialist Propaganda, 1925-1945.* E. Lansing: Michigan State Univ. Press, 1965.

Broszat, Martin. "Hitler und die Genesis der 'Endlösung': Aus Anlass der Thesen von David Irving." *Vierteljahrshefte für Zeitgeschichte* 25/4 (October 1977):739–775.

———. "Soziale Motivation und Führer-Bindung des Nation-

393

alsozialismus." *Vierteljahrshefte für Zeitgeschichte* 18/4 (October 1970):392–409.

Browning, Christopher. "The Government Experts." In *The Holocaust,* 183–198. See Friedlander and Milton.

Buchheim, Hans, et al. *The Anatomy of the SS State.* London: Collins, 1968.

Bullock, Alan. "The Theory of Nazism: Hitler's Basic Ideas." In *Hitler and Nazi Germany,* edited by Robert Waite, 59–65. New York: Holt, Rinehart and Winston, 1969.

Cecil, Robert. *The Myth of the Master Race: Alfred Rosenberg and Nazi Ideology.* London: Batsford, 1972.

Childers, Thomas, "The Social Bases of the National Socialist Vote." *Journal of Contemporary History* 11 (1976):17–42.

Cohn, Norman. *Warrant for Genocide: The Myth of the Jewish World Conspiracy and the Protocols of the Elders of Zion.* London: Eyre and Spottiswood, 1967.

Conway, John. "The Churches." In *Holocaust,* 199–206. See Friedlander and Milton.

———. "The Holocaust and the Historians." *Annals of the American Academy of Political and Social Science* 450 (July 1980):153–164.

———. *The Nazi Persecution of the Churches, 1933-1945.* New York: Basic Books, 1968.

Davidson, Eugene. *The Making of Adolf Hitler.* New York: Macmillan, 1977.

Dawidowicz, Lucy. *The War Against the Jews, 1933-1945.* New York: Holt, Rinehart and Winston, 1975.

Dobroszycki, Lucjan. "Jewish Elites under German Rule." In *The Holocaust,* 221–230. See Friedlander and Milton.

Düwell, Kurt. *Die Rheingebiete in der Judenpolitik des Nationalsozialismus vor 1942.* Bonn: Röhrscheid, 1968.

Eyck, Erich. *A History of the Weimar Republic.* 2 vols. New York: Atheneum, 1970.

Feingold, Henry. "The Government Response." In *The Holocaust,* 245–260. See Friedlander and Milton.

Foster, Claude R., Jr. "Historical Antecedents: Why the Holocaust?'' *Annals of the American Academy of Political and Social Science* 450 (July 1980):1–19.

Friedlander, Henry, and Milton, Sybil, eds. *The Holocaust: Ideology, Bureaucracy, and Genocide*. Millwood, N.Y.: Kraus International Publications, 1980.

Friedländer, Saul. ''On the Possibility of the Holocaust: An Approach to a Historical Synthesis.'' In *The Holocaust as Historical Experience*. See Bauer and Rotenstreich.

Gellately, Robert. *The Politics of Economic Despair: Shopkeepers and German Politics, 1890-1914*. Beverly Hills, Calif.: Sage Studies, 1974.

Genschel, Helmut. *Die Verdrängung der Juden aus der Wirtschaft im Dritten Reich*. Göttingen: Musterschmidt, 1966.

Goldhagen, Erich. ''Weltanschauung und Endlösung: Zum Antisemitismus der nationalsozialistischen Führungsschicht.'' *Vierteljahrshefte für Zeitgeschichte* 24 (October 1976):379–405.

Gordon, Sarah. ''German Opposition to Nazi Anti-Semitic Measures between 1933 and 1945, with Particular Reference to the Rhine-Ruhr Area.'' Ph.D. diss., State University of New York at Buffalo, 1979.

Grossman, Kurt. *Die unbesungenen Helden: Menschen in Deutschlands dunklen Tagen*. Berlin: Arani Verlag, 1961.

Hackett, David Andrew. ''The Nazi Party in the Reichstag Election of 1930.'' Ph.D. dissertation, University of Wisconsin, 1971.

Haffner, Sebastian. *The Meaning of Hitler. Hitler's Use of Power: His Successes and Failures*. New York: Macmillan, 1979.

Hagemann, Jürgen. *Die Presselenkung im Dritten Reich*. Bonn: Bouvier, 1970.

Hamburger, Ernst. *Juden im öffentlichen Leben Deutschlands: Regierungsmitglieder, Beamte und Parlamentarier in der monarchistischen Zeit*. Leo Baeck Institute. Schriftenreihe wissenschaftlicher Abhandlungen, no. 19. Tübingen: Mohr, 1968.

Hamilton, Richard. *Who Voted for Hitler?* Princeton, N.J.: Princeton University Press, 1982.

Hilberg, Raul. "The Anatomy of the Holocaust." In *The Holocaust*, 85–94. See Friedlander and Milton.

―――. *The Destruction of the European Jews*. Chicago: Quadrangle Books, 1967.

―――. "The Significance of the Holocaust." In *The Holocaust*, 95–102. See Friedlander and Milton.

Hitler, Adolf. *Hitlers Zweites Buch*. Stuttgart: Deutsche Verlagsanstalt, 1961.

―――. *Mein Kampf*. Boston: Houghton Mifflin, 1971.

―――. *The Testament of Adolf Hitler: The Hitler-Bormann Documents, February-April, 1945*. London: Icon Books, 1962.

Hoehne, Heinz. *The Order of the Death's Head: The Story of Hitler's SS*. New York: Ballantine Books, 1971.

Hoffmann, Peter. *Widerstand, Staatsreich, Attentat: Der Kampf der Opposition gegen Hitler*. Munich: Piper, 1969.

Jaeckel, Eberhard. *Hitler's Weltanschauung: A Blueprint for Power*. Middletown, Conn.: Wesleyan University Press, 1972.

Kampmann, Wanda. *Deutsche und Juden: Studien zur Geschichte des deutschen Judentums*. Heidelberg: L. Schneider, 1963.

Kele, Max. *Nazis and Workers: National Socialist Appeal to German Labor, 1919–1933*. Chapel Hill: University of North Carolina Press, 1972.

Kershaw, Ian. "Alltägliches und Ausseralltägliches: Ihre Bedeutung für die Volksmeinung 1933–1939." In *Die Reihen fast geschlossen. Beiträge zur Geschichte des Alltags unterm Nationalsozialismus*, edited by Detler Peukert und Jürgen Reulecke. Wupperthal: Peter Hammer Verlag, 1981.

―――. "Antisemitismus und Volksmeinung: Reaktionen auf die Judenverfolgung." In *Bayern in der NS-Zeit II. Herrschaft und Gesellschaft in Konflikt*, edited by Martin Broszat and Elke Fröhlich, 281–347. Munich and Vienna: Oldenbourg Verlag, 1979.

―――. "The Persecution of the Jews and German Popular Opinion in the Third Reich." Leo Baeck Institute *Yearbook* 26 (1981):261–289.

―――. *Popular Opinion and Political Dissent in the Third Reich: Bavaria, 1933–1945*. N.Y.: Oxford University Press, 1983.

———. "Popular Opinion in the Third Reich." In *Government, Party and People in Nazi Germany*, edited by Jeremy Noakes. Exeter Studies in History, no. 2. Exeter: University of Exeter Print Unit, 1980.

Knütter, Hans-Helmuth. *Die Juden und die deutsche Linke in der Weimarer Republik*. Düsseldorf: Droste Verlag, 1971.

———. "Die Linksparteien." In *Entscheidungsjahr 1932*, 323–348. See Werner Mosse.

Krebs, Albert. *Tendenzen und Gestalten der NSDAP: Erinnerungen an die Frühzeit der Partei*. Stuttgart: Deutsche Verlagsanstalt, 1959.

Kren, George, and Rappoport, Leon. *The Holocaust and the Crisis of Human Behavior*. New York: Holmes and Meier, 1980.

———. "Resistance to the Holocaust: Reflections on the Idea and the Act." In *The Holocaust as Historical Experience*, 193–222. See Bauer and Rotenstreich.

Lamberti, Marjorie. "Liberals, Socialists and the Defence against Anti-semitism in the Wilhelminian Period." Leo Baeck Institute *Yearbook* 25 (1980):147–162.

Laquer, Walter. *The Terrible Secret: Suppression of the Truth about Hitler's "Final Solution."* Boston and Toronto: Little, Brown and Co., 1980.

Leber, Annedore, and Moltke, Freya. *Für und Wider: Entscheidungen in Deutschland 1918–1945*. Berlin: Mosaik Verlag, 1962.

Leuner, Heinz David. *When Compassion was a Crime: Germany's Silent Heroes, 1933–1945*. London: Wolff, 1966.

Leuschen-Seppel, Rosemarie. *Sozialdemokratie und Antisemitismus im Kaiserreich: Die Auseinandersetzungen der Partei mit den konservativen und völkischen Strömungen des Antisemitismus 1871–1914*. Forschungsinstitut der Friedrich-Ebert-Stiftung. Reihe: Politik und Gesellschaftsgeschichte. Bonn: Neue Gesellschaft, 1978.

Levin, Nora. *The Holocaust: The Destruction of European Jewry, 1933–1945*. New York: Schocken Books, 1978.

Levy, Richard. *The Downfall of the Anti-Semitic Political Parties of Imperial Germany.* New Haven, Conn.: Yale University Press, 1975.

Lewy, Guenter. *The Catholic Church and Nazi Germany.* New York: McGraw-Hill, 1965.

Lidtke, Vernon. "Social Class and Secularisation in Imperial Germany: The Working Classes." Leo Baeck Institute *Yearbook* 25 (1980):21–40.

Linn, Dorothee. *Das Schicksal der jüdischen Bevölkerung in Memmingen von 1933 bis 1945.* Stuttgart: Klett, 1968.

Lipset, Seymour Martin. *Political Man: The Social Bases of Politics.* Expanded and updated edition. Baltimore: Johns Hopkins Univ. Press, 1981.

Littell, Franklin. *The Crucifixion of the Jews: The Failure of Christians to Understand the Jewish Experience.* New York: Harper and Row, 1975.

———. "Fundamentals in Holocaust Studies." *The Annals of the American Academy of Political and Social Science* 450 (July 1980):213–217.

Littell, Franklin, and Locke, Hubert, eds. *The German Church Struggle and the Holocaust.* Detroit: Wayne State University Press, 1974.

Loewenstein, Kurt. "Die innerjüdische Reaktion auf die Krise der deutschen Demokratie." In *Entscheidungsjahr 1932.* See Werner Mosse.

McKale, Donald. "A Case of 'Nazi Justice'—The Punishment of Party Members Involved in the *Kristallnacht*, 1938." *Jewish Social Studies* 35 (July–October 1973):228–282.

———. *The Nazi Party Courts: Hitler's Management of Conflict in His Movement, 1921–1945.* Lawrence, Kansas: University Press of Kansas, 1974.

Maser, Werner. *Die Frühgeschichte der NSDAP: Hitlers Weg bis 1924.* Frankfurt a.M.: Athenäum Verlag, 1965.

———. *Hitler.* London: Penguin Books, 1973.

———. *Hitler's Mein Kampf: An Analysis.* London: Faber, 1970.

Massing, Paul. *Rehearsal for Destruction: A Study of Political Anti-Semitism in Imperial Germany.* New York: Harper and Row, 1949.

Meier, Kurt. *Kirche und Judentum: Die Haltung der evangelischen Kirche zur Judenpolitik des Dritten Reiches.* Göttingen: Vandenhoeck und Ruprecht, 1968.

Merkl, Peter. *Political Violence under the Swastika: 581 Early Nazis.* Princeton, N.J.: Princeton University Press, 1975.

Merritt, Anna, and Merritt, Richard. *Public Opinion in Occupied Germany: The OMGUS Surveys, 1945–1949.* Urbana: University of Illinois Press, 1970.

Messerschmidt, Manfred. *Die Wehrmacht im NS-Staat: Zeit der Indoktrination.* Hamburg: R. Decker, 1969.

Meyer, Henry Cord, ed. *The Long Generation: Germany from Empire to Ruin, 1913–1945.* New York: Walker and Co., 1973.

Mitchell, Allan "Polish, Dutch, and French Elites under the German Occupation." In *The Holocaust,* 231–244. See Friedlander and Milton.

Mohrmann, Walter. *Anti-Semitismus: Ideologie und Geschichte im Kaiserreich und in der Weimarer Republik.* Berlin: Deutscher Verlag der Wissenschaften, 1972.

Mommsen, Hans. "Der nationalsozialistische Polizeistaat und die Verfolgung vor 1938." *Vierteljahrshefte für Zeitgeschichte* 10, no. 1 (1962):68–87.

Morck, Gordon. "German Nationalism and Jewish Assimilation: The Bismarck Period." Leo Baeck Institute *Yearbook* 22 (1977):81–90.

Morley, John. *Vatican Diplomacy and the Jews during the Holocaust, 1939–1943.* New York: Ktau Publishing House, Inc., 1980.

Mosse, George. *The Crisis of German Ideology: The Intellectual Origins of the Third Reich.* New York: Grosset and Dunlap, 1971.

———. "Die deutsche Rechte und die Juden." In *Entscheidungsjahr 1932,* 183–248, See Werner Mosse.

———. *Germans and Jews: The Right, the Left, and the Search for a "Third Force" in Pre-Nazi Germany.* New York: Grosset and Dunlap, 1970.

———. "German Socialists and the Jewish Question in the Weimar Republic.'' Leo Baeck Institute *Yearbook* 16 (1971):123–151.

Mosse, Werner, ed. *Entscheidungsjahr 1932: Zur Judenfrage in der Endphase der Weimarer Republik.* Leo Baeck Institute. Schriftenreihe wissenschaftlicher Abhandlungen, no. 13. Tübingen: Mohr, 1965.

————. ''Der Niedergang der Weimarer Republik und die Juden.'' In *Entscheidungsjahr 1932*, 3–50. See Werner Mosse.

————. ed., and Paucker, Arnold, asst. *Deutsches Judentum in Krieg und Revolution 1916–1923.* Leo Baeck Institute. Schriftenreihe wissenschaftlicher Abhandlungen, no. 33. Tübingen: Mohr, 1976.

Müller-Claudius, Michael. *Der Antisemitismus und das deutsche Verhängnis.* Frankfurt a.M.: Knecht, 1948.

Needler, Martin. ''Hitler's Anti-Semitism: A Political Appraisal.'' *Public Opinion Quarterly* 24 (Winter 1960):665–669.

Neumann, Franz. *Behemoth: The Structure and Practice of National Socialism.* New York: Harper Torchbooks, 1966.

Nicholls, A. J., and Mathias, Erich, comps. *German Democracy and the Triumph of Hitler: Essays in Recent German History.* London: Allen and Unwin, 1971.

Niewyk, Donald. *The Jews in Weimar Germany.* Baton Rouge: Louisiana State University Press, 1980.

————. *Socialist, Anti-Semite, and Jew: German Social Democracy Confronts the Problem of Anti-Semitism, 1918–1933.* Baton Rouge: Louisiana State University Press, 1971.

Noakes, Jeremy. *The Nazi Party in Lower Saxony, 1921–1933.* London: Oxford University Press, 1971.

Nolte, Ernst. *Three Faces of Fascism: Action Française, Italian Fascism, National Socialism.* New York: Holt, Rinehart and Winston, 1966.

O'Lessker, Karl. ''The Author Replies.'' *American Journal of Sociology* 74, no. 6 (May 1969):735.

————. ''Who Voted for Hitler? A New Look at the Class Basis of Nazism.'' *American Journal of Sociology* 74, no. 8 (July 1968):63–69.

Orlow, Dietrich. *The History of the Nazi Party*. 2 vols. Pittsburgh: University of Pittsburgh Press, 1969, 1973.

Pätzold, Kurt. *Faschismus, Rassenwahn, Judenverfolgung: Eine Studie zur politischen Strategie und Taktik des faschistischen Imperialismus 1933–1945*. East Berlin: Deutsche Verlag der Wissenschaften, 1975.

Paucker, Arnold. "Der jüdische Abwehrkampf." In *Entscheidungsjahr 1932*, 405–502. See Werner Mosse.

————. *Der jüdische Abwehrkampf gegen Antisemitismus und Nationalsozialismus in den letzten Jahren der Weimarer Republik*. Hamburg: Leibnitz Verlag, 1969.

Payne, Robert. *The Life and Death of Adolf Hitler*. New York: Praeger, 1973.

Peterson, Edward. *The Limits of Hitler's Power*. Princeton, N.J.: Princeton University Press, 1969.

Pinson, Koppel. *Modern Germany: Its History and Civilization*. New York: Macmillan, 1959.

Poliakov, Leon, and Wulf, Joseph. *Das Dritte Reich und seine Diener*. Berlin: Arani, 1956.

Pratt, Samuel Alexander. "The Social Basis of Nazism and Communism in Urban Germany: A Correlational Study of the July 31, 1932 Reichstag Election in Germany." M.A. thesis, Michigan State College, 1948.

Pridham, Geoffrey. *Hitler's Rise to Power: The Nazi Movement in Bavaria, 1923–1933*. New York: Harper and Row, 1973.

Prittie, Terence. *Germans Against Hitler*. Boston: Little, Brown and Co., 1964.

Pulzer, Peter. *The Rise of Political Anti-Semitism in Germany and Austria*. New York: Wiley, 1964.

————. "Why Was There a Jewish Question in Imperial Germany?" Leo Baeck Institute *Yearbook* 25 (1980):133–146.

Rauschning, Hermann. *The Voice of Destruction*. New York: Putnam, 1940.

Reichmann, Eva. "Diskussionen über die Judenfrage 1930–1932." In *Entscheidungsjahr 1932*, 503–534. See Werner Mosse.

————. *Hostages of Civilization: The Social Sources of National Socialist Anti-Semitism*. Boston: Beacon Press, 1951.

401

Reitlinger, Gerhard. *The Final Solution: The Attempt to Exterminate the Jews of Europe, 1939–1945*. South Brunswick, N.J.: Yoseloff, 1968.

Rheins, Carl. "The Verband Nationaldeutscher Juden 1921–1933." Leo Baeck Institute *Yearbook* 25 (1980):243–268.

Ringer, Fritz. "The Perversion of Ideas in Weimar Universities." In *The Holocaust*. See Friedlander and Milton.

Robinsohn, Hans. *Justiz als politische Verfolgung: Die Rechtsprechung in "Rassenschandefällen" beim Landegericht Hamburg 1936-1943*. Schriftenreihe der Vierteljahrshefte für Zeitgeschichte, no. 35. Stuttgart: Deutsche Verlagsanstalt, 1977.

Roloff, Ernst-August. "Wer wählte Hitler? Thesen zur Sozial- und Wirtschaftsgeschichte der Weimarer Republik." *Politische Studien* 15 (May–June 1964):293–300.

Roon, Ger van. *Neuordnung im Widerstand: Der Kreisauer Kreis innerhalb des deutschen Widerstandsbewegung*. Munich: Oldenbourg, 1967.

Rothfels, Hans. *German Opposition to Hitler*. Chicago: Regnery, 1962.

Ruppin, Arthur. *The Jews in the Modern World*. New York: Arno Press, 1973.

Rürup, Reinhard. *Emancipation und Antisemitismus: Studien zur Judenfrage der bürgerlichen Gesellschaft*. Göttingen: Vandenhoeck, 1975.

Sauer, Wolfgang. "Comments on the Paper of Donald L. Niewyk." Leo Baeck Institute *Yearbook* 16 (1971):178–181.

————. "National Socialism: Totalitarianism or Fascism." *American Historical Review* 73 (December, 1967):404–424.

Schäfer, Wolfgang. *Entwicklung und Struktur der Staatspartei des Dritten Reiches*. Schriftenreihe des Instituts für wissenschaftliche Politik, no. 3. Hannover and Frankfurt: Norddeutsche Verlagsanstalt, 1957.

Scheffler, Wolfgang. *Judenverfolgung im Dritten Reich, 1933–1945*. Berlin: Colloquium Verlag, 1960.

Schleunes, Karl. *The Twisted Road to Auschwitz: Nazi Policy toward German Jews, 1933–1939.* Urbana: University of Illinois Press, 1970.

Schnaiberg, Allen. "A Critique of Karl O'Lessker's 'Who Voted for Hitler?' " *American Journal of Sociology* 44, no. 6 (May 1969):733–735.

Schoenbaum, David. *Hitler's Social Revolution: Class and Status in Nazi Germany, 1933–1939.* Garden City, N.Y.: Doubleday, 1967.

Schorn, Hubert. *Der Richter im Dritten Reich: Geschichte und Dokumente.* Frankfurt a.M.: Kostermann, 1959.

Schorsch, Ismar. *Jewish Reactions to German Anti-Semitism, 1870–1914.* New York: Columbia University Press, 1972.

Sellenthin, H. G. *Geschichte der Juden in Berlin und des Gebäudes Fasanenstrasse 79/80: Festschrift anlässlich der Einweihung des jüdischen Gemeindehauses.* Berlin: Lichtwitz, 1959.

Seydewitz, Max. *Civil Life in Wartime Germany: The Story of the Home Front.* New York: Viking Press, 1945.

Shirer, William. *The Rise and Fall of the Third Reich.* New York: Simon and Schuster, 1960.

Snoek, Johan. *The Grey Book; A Collection of Protests against Anti-Semitism and the Persecution of the Jews Issued by non-Roman Catholic Churches and Church Leaders during Hitler's Rule.* New York: Humanities Press, 1970.

Speer, Albert. *Inside the Third Reich.* New York: Avon Books, 1971.

Steinberg, Hans-Josef. *Widerstand und Verfolgung in Essen 1933–1945.* Schriftenreihe des Forschungsinstituts der Friedrich-Ebert-Stiftung. Hannover: Verlag für Literatur und Zeitgeschehen, 1969.

Steinert, Marlis. *Hitlers Krieg und die Deutschen: Stimmung und Haltung der deutschen Bevölkerung im zweiten Weltkrieg.* Düsseldorf: Econ Verlag, 1970.

Stokes, Lawrence. "The German People and the Destruction of the European Jews." *Central European History* 6/2 (1973):167–191.

Stone, Norman. *Hitler.* Boston: Little, Brown and Co., 1981.

Strauss, Herbert. "Jewish Emigration from Germany—Nazi Policies and Jewish Responses (I)." Leo Baeck Institute *Yearbook* 25 (1980):313–363.

Streit, Christian. *Keine Kameraden: Die Wehrmacht und die sowjet Kriegsgefangenen 1941–1945.* Institut für Zeitgeschichte. Studien zur Zeitgeschichte, no. 13. Stuttgart: DVA Verlag, 1978.

Tennenbaum, Frank. *Race and Reich: The Story of an Epoch.* New York: Twayne, 1956.

Thieme, Karl. "Deutsche Katholiken." In *Entscheidungsjahr 1932*, 271–288. See Werner Mosse.

Toland, John. *Adolf Hitler.* New York: Ballantine Books, 1976.

Toury, Jacob. *Die politischen Orientierungen der Juden in Deutschland von Jena bis Weimar.* Leo Baeck Institute. Schriftenreihe wissenschaftlicher Abhandlungen, no. 15. Tübingen: Mohr, 1966.

Turner, Henry, Jr., ed. *Nazism and the Third Reich.* New York: Quadrangle Books, 1972.

Waite, Robert. *The Psychopathic God: Adolf Hitler.* New York: Basic Books, 1977.

Wasserstein, Bernard. *Britain and the Jews of Europe, 1939–1945.* Oxford: Clarendon Press, 1979.

Weinreich, Max. *Hitler's Professors: The Part of Scholarship in Germany's Crimes against the Jewish People.* New York: Yivo Institute, 1946.

Weisenborn, Günther, ed. *Der lautlose Aufstand: Bericht über die Widerstandsbewegung des deutschen Volkes 1933–1945.* Hamburg: Rowohlt, 1962.

Whiteside, Andrew. "Comments on the Papers of William A. Jenks and Donald L. Niewyk." Leo Baeck Institute *Yearbook* 16 (1971):174–181.

―――. "The Nature and Origins of National Socialism." *Journal of Central European Affairs* 17, no. 1 (1957–1958):48–73.

Wiener, P. B. "Die Parteien der Mitte." In *Entscheidungsjahr 1932*, 289–322. See Werner Mosse.

Winkler, Heinrich. "Extremismus der Mitte? Sozialgeschicht-

liche Aspekte der nationalsozialistischen Machtergreifung."
*Vierteljahrshefte für Zeitgeschichte* 20, no. 2 (April 1972):175–
191.

————. *Mittelstand, Demokratie und Nationalsozialismus: Die
politische Entwicklung von Handwerk und Kleinhandel in
der Weimarer Republik.* Cologne: Kiepenheuer und Witsch,
1972.

Wolf, Ernst. "Political and Moral Motives behind the Resistance." In *The German Resistance to Hitler* edited by Hermann Graml. Berkeley: University of California Press, 1970.

Wolfson, Manfred. "The Subculture of Freedom: Some People
Will Not," 1–17. Unpublished paper delivered at the 1970
regional meeting of the Conference Group on German Politics.

Zelzer, Maria. *Weg und Schicksal der Stuttgarter Juden: Ein
Gedenkbuch.* Stuttgart: Klett, 1964.

Zipfel, Friedrich. *Kirchenkampf in Deutschland 1932–1945: Religionsverfolgung und Selbstbehauptung der Kirchen in der
nationalsozialistischen Zeit.* Berliner historische Kommission beim Friedrich-Meinecke-Institut der Freien Universität,
Veröffentlichungen, no. 9. Berlin: Walter de Gruyter, 1965.

Zmarlik, Hans-Günther. "Der Antisemitismus im Zweiten Reich."
*Geschichte in Wissenschaft und Unterricht* 14 (May 1963):273–
286.

# Index

LIBRARY OF CONGRESS CATALOGING IN PUBLICATION DATA

Gordon, Sarah Ann.
  Hitler, Germans, and the "Jewish question."

  Bibliography: p.
  Includes index.
  1. Antisemitism—Germany. 2. Jews—Germany—Politics
and government. 3. National socialism. 4. Hitler, Adolf, 1889-1945.
5. Holocaust, Jewish (1939-1945)—Causes. 6. Germany—Ethnic relations.
I. Title.
DS146.G4G57 1984        305.8'924'043        83-43073
ISBN 0-691-05412-6
ISBN 0-691-10162-0 (pbk.)

## Erratum

p. 77 The figures for white-collar employees reproduced in table 2.7 are taken from the wrong table in Childers's 1976 article. A correct reading of Childers's tables reveals that his distinction between the Nazi white-collar and Nazi civil-service relationship is valid. For clarification of his latest results, see his recently published *The Nazi Voter*, Chapel Hill, N.C.: University of North Carolina Press.